Rioja

Rioja

by John Radford

MITCHELL BEAZLEY

First published in Great Britain in 2004
by Mitchell Beazley, an imprint of
Octopus Publishing Group Limited,
2–4 Heron Quays, London E14 4JP.

A CIP catalogue record for this book is available from the British Library.

ISBN: 184000 940 3

The author and publishers will be grateful for any information which will assist them in keeping future editions up to date. Although all reasonable care has been taken in the preparation of this book, neither the publishers nor the author can accept any liability for any consequences arising from the use thereof, or the information contained therein.

Printed and bound in England by Mackays, Chatham

Contents

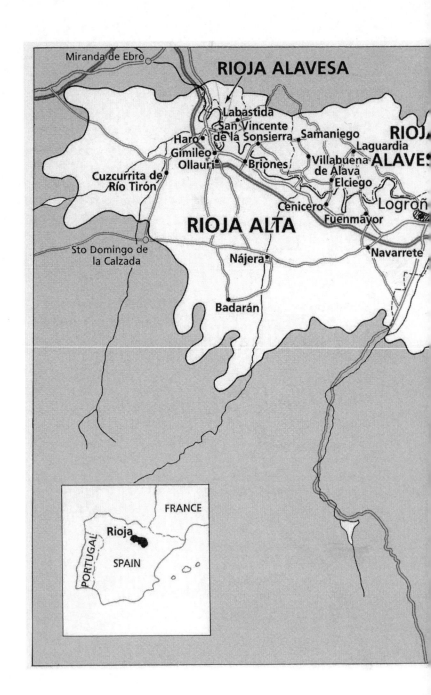

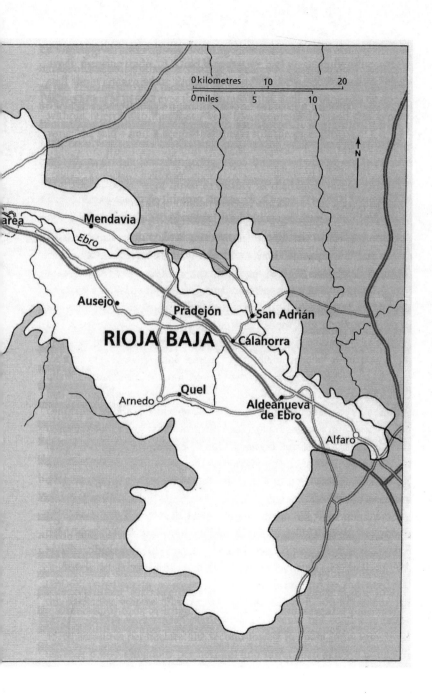

0 kilometres   10   20
0 miles   5   10

N

área

Mendavia

Ebro

Ausejo

Pradejón

San Adrián

RIOJA BAJA

Calahorra

Arnedo   **Quel**

Aldeanueva de Ebro

Alfaro

Acknowledgments

Many people helped in the research for this book, not least the bodegas themselves, who welcomed me and, in many cases, wined and dined me (no favours guys) but special thanks are due to several people who went out of their way to help. Firstly, Tom Perry from the Rioja Wine Exporters' Group and the outgoing CRDOCa who, between them, arranged visits and tastings for me on my various visits.

Tom was especially helpful in persuading people to meet me, advising on the bodegas, and arranging the itinerary (and changing it at short notice when I became bogged-down in over-long lunches), and Carmen Quemada from the *consejo* arranged a tasting, interviews, and, on one visit, accommodation and a hire car for me, all of which were an enormous help. María-Antonia Fernández Daza and the team at the biennial Los Grandes de la Rioja event arranged an excellent series of visits on top of the comprehensive tastings provided at the conference, and Reg Ward, export consultant based in Catalonia, got me visits to two of his most exclusive clients.

I'd also like to thank the Rioja Municipal Police force, who put a ticket on my car windscreen when Reg picked me up in his car and I left mine for a day and a half in a restricted-parking area. There was no fine to pay; the ticket said I had committed an offence and I really should get a penalty but they didn't want to do that, they just wanted me to know that my parking had inconvenienced other citizens and, very politely, would I please think in future, and help them to keep the traffic moving in Logroño? Civilized or what?

And finally the editorial team on the book, particularly Hilary Lumsden and Margaret Rand, who have exhibited the patience of Job in waiting for the final manuscript. I signed two contracts at roughly the same time, both with impossibly short deadlines, but, of course, there isn't a word for "No" in the freelance writer's vocabulary when work is on offer. I could not have wished for a more good-humoured, professional, and forgiving back-up team.

Preface

Rioja is probably one of the most written-about wine areas in Spain, but books dedicated to it in their entirety are few and far between, although all wine encyclopaedias devote at least a chapter to it (I know, as I wrote most of them). So I was delighted when Mitchell Beazley asked for this, the first comprehensive survey of what Rioja is and where it stands now, for nearly twenty years. I have covered the history of the region to put it into context, but the main thrust of the book is the present and the future: which are the leading bodegas, what kind of wine they are making, and what they think about the current state of regulation, vineyard management, winemaking, and – most important of all – the market.

It's the first protracted period I've spent in the region for quite some time (I always seem to be visiting Rioja on my way to somewhere else), and I was surprised by a number of things, not least the genuinely good, honest quality of even the most basic wines. Living in the UK, I had become accustomed to "everyday" Rioja being pleasant, well-made, and reasonable value for money – but not very exciting. The reverse is true in La Rioja itself. During one extended visit I had to file a piece for my occasional column in *OLN*, a UK drinks-trade paper. This is an extract from it, illustrating something which vexes the minds of Rioja producers greatly:

> *I realized with a shock that it's quite a while since I bought basic Rioja in England regularly and I wondered why, as the wines I'm tasting here are of generally excellent quality.*

My second bodega visit (and most subsequent ones) put the record straight – it's the price. Tempranillo grapes at the 2003 harvest averaged around one euro per kilo, which is one euro per bottle before you start.

Add to this the cost of actually turning those grapes into wine, storing it, ageing it, bottling it, and shipping it, and you can calculate the result. "The market is so competitive," grumbled my host, "that we find ourselves beaten down to price levels which are barely profitable." In his case, he had been offered 2.30 Euros a bottle ex-cellars by a major UK multiple which wanted to hit a particular price-point. What did he do? He presented samples which matched the price, and the buyer did the deal. Result? That particular chain's "bargain" own-brand Rioja was "made down" to meet that price. It has more press-wine, less freshness, less fruit than a similar wine from the same bodega sold in Spain. It's decent, acceptable wine, but it doesn't convey any of the real magic that is the nature of Rioja. And that particular chain is by no means alone – which is why, I realized in retrospect, I've stopped buying high-street Rioja.

Other things I discovered and rediscovered included the astonishing individuality of the bodegas – oh, and for the benefit of translators, the "anorak" awards in this book are a compliment, not a criticism. The region is full of individualists, many of whom disagree strongly over some or all aspects of winemaking and ageing: cultured or natural yeast, *maceración carbónica*; old or new wood, French, American or east European; fermentation in stainless steel or oak *tinas*… Or concrete tanks or the cask; historic, classic, modern, or new-wave vinification techniques. The range of different styles of wines is enormously encouraging, especially from a region that has historically grumbled about strait-jacket regulation.

Another change has been the marketing attitude of many of the bodegas. In the bad old days, there was little understanding of the techniques of marketing, and even export managers seldom tasted wines from other regions of Spain, let alone the rest of the world. The coming of New World wines to the English-speaking world also concentrated the minds of Rioja producers, who suddenly realized that their traditional export business was under threat. It took time, but the bodegas (or at least the majority of them) are now working more vigorously than ever to find out what the market wants, and sorting out how to provide it – not by turning out lookalike wines, but by addressing the styles of wine that are making the running, and interpreting Rioja in a different way. This is not without its critics, of course, and their voices are in this book, too.

Everything is not perfect in Rioja. Serious work is still needed, particularly in the regulatory department. It is true that the old CRDOCa was too hidebound and bureaucratic in its deliberations, but there are worries that the new OIPVR may veer in the opposite direction (*see* chapter seven). What Rioja does not need is another raft of anonymous Cabernet Sauvignon, Chardonnay, and Syrah, but all arguments are represented here.

There are criticisms in this book, but I hope that they will be taken in the spirit inherent in Brutus' speech in Shakespeare's *Julius Caesar*: "Not that he loved Caesar less, but that he loved Rome more." And a more modern cliché to finish with, borrowed from a former president of the United States: "There's nothing wrong with Rioja that cannot be cured by what's right with Rioja."

John Radford
Worthing, Sussex, England 2004

1

Introduction

WHY RIOJA?

Is it the gorgeous raspberry freshness of the Tempranillo grape, turned into *joven* wine in the mountains of Álava for drinking after Christmas, and made in a manner the Romans would still recognize? Perhaps it's the peppery spiciness of new American oak matched to the ripe fruit of a distant, long, golden autumn. Or is it the cigar-box subtlety and restrained but irresistible power of a *gran reserva* from one of the great years as it approaches its maturity?

For all of these reasons and many more, the world in general – northern Europe and America in particular – has grown to love the wines of Rioja. An unlikely miscegenation of centuries-old rural winemaking tradition and early "new technology" from Bordeaux; sufficient altitude to cool the vineyards; the right mix of clay, chalk, and iron in the soil; and a natural disaster at a conveniently situated border took Rioja wine from the relative obscurity of being merely the best red wine produced in Spain to being one of the world's greatest wines. This was achieved in the space of a century and a half – relatively quickly in wine terms in the days before the real "new technology" discovered that it could create vineyards from desert and have wine on the shelves in little over three years.

In many ways, it is the gentle evolution of Rioja that has underpinned its success. The style has been fashionable and unfashionable, and then fashionable again; indeed, it probably changed as much in the last quarter of the twentieth century as it did in the second half of the nineteenth, but we do the wine an injustice to think of it as a Victorian conjuring trick.

Wine from anywhere in the "Old World" is a product of what nature provides combined with the ingenuity of the local people and, perhaps most importantly of all, the available sources and nature of food available to those people. If we look at the history of this turbulent area (and we shall be doing that in a great deal more detail later on), we can pick out three major factors that govern the way a wine evolves.

The first is climatic. The reason that Bordeaux and Burgundy, at their finest, make wines which are unrivalled in the world is that they are on the northern limit of quality red wine viticulture. The vine's natural struggles, the microclimatic interstices of the Côte d'Or, and the well-drained, gravelly soils of the Gironde estuary are the foundations of the wine in those few great years when nature really does deliver perfect flowering, sufficient summer rains, a long, hot autumn, and ideal weather for the harvest. Add to this combination tried-and-tested grapes which have grown in the soils of their respective regions perhaps for centuries, plus up to a thousand vintages or more of trial and error in the vineyard and the winery, and you have a formula which can (and occasionally does) produce wines that positively sing with health, vitality, and the sheer joy of quality.

The Rioja wine lands are much further south, and might therefore be expected to form a more reliable source of red wine, year in and year out. Sheltered as they are to the north by the Cantabrian Mountains, the climate is more Continental, with hotter, drier summers and shorter, colder winters. Further south and east in Spain, indeed, the vineyards used to bake in the summer heat as the grapes dried and shrivelled on the vine, but Rioja has the benefit of altitude. Alfaro in the Rioja Baja is 301 metres (988 feet) above sea level: hot, with sandy soils and an ideal climate for the hardy Garnacha grape. Logroño, at the southern boundary of the Rioja Alta, is at 384 metres (1,260 feet); heading northwards from here the land climbs, the soil becomes more complex, and Tempranillo and Graciano start to take over the land from Garnacha and Mazuelo. Haro is only forty-four kilometres (twenty miles) from Logroño, but its altitude is 479 metres (1,572 feet). Across the river Ebro in the Rioja Alavesa, Laguardia is at 635 metres (2,083 feet); at this height, microclimates became all-important. A good example is the Granja Nuestra Señora de Remelluri at Labastida. Tucked right under the mountain range, its vineyards are on three levels just a few metres apart in terms of altitude, but the difference is such that the grapes on each level ripen almost exactly a week apart, so the harvest can be gathered at optimum ripeness with each section collected in turn. A typical Rioja house blend is able to source its grapes from these cool, highland vineyards, the hot, sandy south, and anywhere in between. This has also helped to give the wine consistency – a real benefit in export terms.

The second factor which governs the nature of a wine is the food that is available locally. In the days when all travel was on foot or horseback, people would forage for food as close to home as possible; it is no accident that vineyard areas on the estuaries of rivers – as in Galicia, the Loire Valley, and even the sherry country, for instance – tend to produce white wines. Fish and seafood were the easy options, and years of trial and error tended to favour wine that did not have tannin and other coagulants which might interfere with the fishy flavours – in other words, white. Rioja is land-locked and heavily forested, particularly in the north, and while the herdsman of the south kept cattle, sheep, and pigs, the woodsmen of the north found an abundance of game, both on the hoof (venison and wild boar) and on the wing (the red partridge is Spain's favourite game bird). These are meats with robust flavours, and they would have demanded a robust wine to go with them. Over the years, the tendency was towards strong, powerful red wines with plenty of character. As we have seen, nature was in a very good position to provide just that.

The third factor is the people. Seafaring people, hunter-gatherers, nomads, and herders, to take a few examples: all have different ways of doing things to suit their different ways of life, and the food and drink they consume reflects that. The valley of the river Ebro would have been attractive to settlers; its fertile soil and equable climate are excellent for farming, the river is a plentiful supply of water, and the woods and forests are a useful source of building materials. In addition, the northern part of the region is rich in iron ore, and the Romans found the local population making metal implements and vessels when they arrived there in the second century BC (which is why they called them the *Vascones* – "makers of vessels" – believed to be the origin of the name *Vasco* or *Basque*). So, once farming and a bit of industry was established, trade began with neighbouring settlements and the beginnings of civilization might have been discerned.

In due course, feudal lords became rich, and amused themselves by hunting in the forests to fill their baronial tables – which brings us back to those robustly flavoured flagons with which they accompanied it.

Wealth, indeed, was a decisive factor in Rioja's success after the Moors retreated from Logroño at the end of the first millennium. For many years, the region was the front line between Christian and Muslim Spain (witness the fortified towns north of the river) and naturally attracted frontline participants: kings, princes, generals, and knights, as well as their priests and bishops, professors and confessors. These were mainly rich, powerful people who lived well for their time, and could afford to pay for good wine. Even after 1561, when King Felipe II took himself and the royal entourage to Madrid, Castile was a fiercely political arena. La Rioja itself had Old Castile to the west, Navarra (or Navarre, as it was once known) to the north, and Aragón to the east, with the dog-ends of three former royal houses continually fighting over the regal leftovers, as well as Catalonia next-door-but-one to the east, with its own agenda for political machination. Life may have been challenging (and often short) for the spin-doctors and plotters, but it was very good indeed for the winemakers, who found a thriving market for their product.

These, then – climate, food availability, and the nature of the people – are the three main factors which established Rioja wine's quality and reputation in the years to the end of the seventeenth century. That's how it came into the modern era with such a flying start. That's why Rioja.

BUT WHY IS IT CALLED "RIOJA"?

There are a number of theories. Most people incline to the idea that it takes its name from the río (river) Oja, a stream which feeds the río Tirón, which runs through Haro to join the Ebro. Quite why this little trickle, rather than the mighty Ebro, should have given its name to an entire region is unclear, and there are alternative views. Santiago Ijalba, of the eponymous bodega, recently launched a "high-expression" wine called Ogga; he derived the name from documents of the Roman period, backed up by a manuscript of 1092, when the pilgrimage route known as the Camino de Santiago de Compostela was in its first "boom" period (see below for appropriate speculation). These seem to indicate that the name Ogga was used for the lands watered by the rivers Oja and Tirón, and when Spanish (rather than Latin) became the language of literature, this became, in archaic Latinate Castellano, Rivo Ogga, then Riogia, then Rioxa, and then (j, g, and x having been very interchangeable in early Spanish orthography) settling down as Rioja. Hubrecht Duijker, in his

1985 book on the region, offers a number of alternatives. The first goes back to medieval documents which recorded a tribe the invaders called *Ruccones*: an illuminated manuscript of AD 976 (now in El Escorial, Felipe II's palace and monastery complex near Madrid), copied at the monastery of San Martín de Abelda in Rioja, records this of Saint Isidoro (d. AD 626), who converted northern Spain to Christianity:

> *Astures et Ruccones in montibus reuellantes humiliabit et suis per omnia*
> *benibolus fuit. Hunc uni proprio morbo, alii inmoderato potionis austo*
> *asserunt interfectum sub imperatore Eraclio.* ("He subdued the Astures
> and Ruccones, rebels in the mountains, but he was very benevolent
> toward his people everywhere. Some people said that he died a
> natural death, but others believed that he was killed by a poisoned
> drink under Emperor Heraclius.")

In time, *Ruccones* became *Riugones* and, eventually in Spanish, *Riojanos*.

A further possibility is that the name derives from the Spanish *rojo* meaning "red", and is simply descriptive of the rusty, iron-rich soils of some of the region's best vineyards. Or, indeed, it could derive from the Basque construction *Ería-ogia* which translates into "bread country" (and has been variously recorded as *Erriotxa*, *Errioxa*, and *Errioja*. The earliest written reference to the region under the name Rioxa dates from a document of 1092 and as "Rioja" in a charter of 1099. Internationally it was recognized as a discrete part of Spain in 1177, when the kingdoms of Castile and Navarra both laid claim to it. Eventually the dispute was settled by arbitration from a neutral party, King Henry I of England, who ruled in favour of Castile, and formal treaties were signed. It was not, however, until 1978 that La Rioja the *autonomía*, or autonomous region, came into being as a result of the new Spanish democratic constitution.

Those are the theories, but I have another one – or at least a speculation. The fame of Rioja wine was further enhanced by pilgrims on the Camino de Santiago, which passes through the region from east to west via Logroño, Navarrete, Nájera, and Santo Domingo, at which last point the *camino* crosses the *río* Oja. How many millions of people have passed this way since the shrine was established in AD 816? And what was the experience like?

Imagine: it's a thousand years ago, you've been walking for sixteen hours, and your feet are killing you. Your whole body aches with hunger and fatigue, and as you stumble, almost automatically now, in the gathering gloom of the night, you take a sip of the bitter, brackish water which is all you have left in the bottom of your gourd. You lean heavily on your staff, wondering if you'll find shelter before darkness falls completely and the wolves come out of the forest in their own search for sustenance…

And then you see a light, and hear the distant tolling of a monastery bell. With each faltering step it becomes louder and the light becomes brighter. You catch the faintest sound of monastic voices united in plainsong and, though exhausted, your pace quickens, your heartbeat revives. Can that possibly be the smell of cooking, borne on the chilly night breeze? The track is a little smoother here, with flat stones laid side by side to assist the passage of ox-carts and donkeys. And then you see it: the monastery of Santo Domingo de la Calzada with its welcoming light and warming, open door. The monks relieve you of your pitiful burden and seat you at the refectory table, give you bread, soup, and wine, a bed, and the safety and warmth of the monastery until morning, when your pilgrimage will continue.

And though the bread may be coarse and dry, the soup of pulses and vegetables from the gardens of the monastery, and the wine made last autumn from grapes picked locally, trodden in the monastery's stone troughs, and stored in goatskins, yet the sounds and senses, tastes and smells and enjoyment of that meal mean more than supper with the king of Navarra. The food is better than the plumpest roast partridge and the wine as fine a vintage as ever graced the royal table. And the bed – a mattress stuffed with straw on a wooden trestle – is softer than a maiden's bosom.

And, when you've reached the end of your pilgrimage at the cathedral in Santiago de Compostela, and you want to write to the monks of Santo Domingo to thank them for their hospitality, what instructions do you give to the returning pilgrim who will deliver the letter for you? "To the brothers of the monastery of Santo Domingo de la Calzada, at the point where the Camino de Santiago crosses the *río* Oja…"

There are still pilgrims walking the route today (although the former monastery is now a splendidly restored *parador*: state-owned hotel) and the river Oja still runs through what is now the small town (population 5,000) of Santo Domingo de la Calzada. Then, as now, the journey entitles the pilgrim to free food and lodging at monasteries and hostels along the way. A thousand years ago, many would have had cause to bless the brothers of Santo Domingo for their modest supper, and, perhaps the monastery's position by the bridge over the river Oja provided La Rioja's first address. And its name, of course. You can imagine returned pilgrims asking about "the wine from the *río* Oja".

This would certainly explain why a wine land that is heavily dominated by the river Ebro and served by half a dozen main tributaries should take its name from what is little more than a winding stream which joins the river Tirón (itself little more than a brook) before the Tirón becomes a tributary of the Ebro at Haro. However, when the new constitution of Spain came into being after the death of Francisco Franco and the country was divided into autonomous communities, the wine and the region were sufficiently well known to give their name to the whole of what had been the province of Logroño, independent from Castille-León to the west and Navarra to the north and east.

Whatever the origins of its name, Rioja did rather well for itself in the second millennium. Spain's best-known red wine has been dominant throughout the country's vinous history, one of the basic commodities of trade throughout the country and the Mediterranean from ancient history up to medieval times. It was boosted as the forces of Castile won back the northern wine lands from the Moorish invaders and the conquering kings restored wine to its rightful place in gastronomy. It was bolstered by the sixteenth-century expansion of the Spanish Empire in the Americas and advanced again by the *método industrial* ("industrial method" of vinification) introduced by Luciano de Murrieta and his fellow pioneers in the 1850s and 1860s (*see* chapter seven). It was the great survivor of the bleak years of the mid-twentieth century, when almost all other Spanish wine was tarred with the brush of diluted, locally bottled "plonk" masquerading pathetically as "Spanish Burgundy" and "Spanish Claret". It was the great flagship of Spain's fight back as a serious wine-producing country from the 1970s onward and became a "find" for the aspiring middle classes in the boom-and-bust 1980s.

There are some of us who have known and loved it all our drinking lives. Others have only discovered it since so many new "boutique" wineries have sprung up to capitalize on the magnificent natural resources presented by the Tempranillo grape, the iron, clay, and chalk soils, and the heady river-valley climate. Many will discover it tomorrow – perhaps, even, as a result of reading this book.

And, in the third millennium, the bodegas are producing a wider range of better wines than at any time in Rioja's history. This is their story.

2

Ancient Times

THE EARLY IBERIANS

First, a potted history of Spain up to about AD 1200 to put things into context. No one knows for certain who first settled in the Iberian peninsula but it was probably the proto-Celtic tribes known as the Bell Beaker people (named after the characteristic pottery they left behind), who travelled north from Africa about 2500BC, along the inshore waters of what is now the west coast of western Europe, colonizing bits of it as they went. The most notable destinations were what we now call Galicia (plus Asturias, Cantabria, and the Basque Country), Brittany, Cornwall, Wales, Ireland, and Scotland, and as well as their pottery skills they were skilled metalworkers, which (much later) led the Romans to call them *Vascones*, which means "makers of vessels". This has (or so they say) come down to us as *Vasco* in Spanish, *Basque* in English and French, and *Euskal* in the Basque language.

The first written records date from about 1100 BC, when traders from Phoenicia (modern Syria) established a port at Gadir (now Cádiz in the sherry country) at what were then known as the "pillars of Hercules": what we now call the Straits of Gibraltar. Immigration from the eastern Mediterranean swelled the population, especially from 500BC during wars between Greece and its neighbours to the east, and then the Rome/Carthage conflict. Carthage conquered Spain in 218BC, but the Romans defeated the Carthaginians in 151BC and became the effective rulers of Spain, establishing their capital at Córdoba. The legions quickly spread northwards and found tribes which they dubbed the *Celtiberi* (i.e. the Celts who live in the valley of the river Iberus – today's Ebro) and the

Vascones making wine in a primitive way in the area that is now Rioja (as well as farther north in the Basque Country). To avoid expensive excursions back to Rome as the empire expanded, the Romans had a policy of making wine in the countries they conquered, and they introduced the "new technology" of the stone *lagar* ("trough"; *see* chapter six, page 41), probably universally by the first century AD.

From a technological point of view, winemaking changed very little for the next millennium and a half, but politically everything changed on a rolling basis. The Roman Empire (and thus Spain) was converted to Christianity, but the empire was in decline, and incursions by barbarian tribes began in AD409 with the Vandals; they were followed by the Swabians/Suevians and, once the collapse of the Roman Empire was complete in AD476, the Visigoths. It seems, however, that regardless of whether the country was being governed by a civilized or a barbaric power, the demand for wine remained constant.

MOORISH INFLUENCE

This even held true after AD711, in which year, after the battle of Guadalete, the Moors (Muslim peoples of mixed Arab and Berber descent from northwest Africa) conquered Spain and set about making it into an Islamic state. There's a popular view that this was disastrous for wine, but this is not entirely true. There were, indeed, two different Moorish administrations in (most of) Spain, and the first, from AD711–929 under the caliphate of Damascus, was very civilized indeed. These were people who had a great tradition of literature, art, architecture, and learning. They brought with them, for example, the art of distilling; they wanted the dry extract al kohl, which is the origin of our word "alcohol", for painting and cosmetics.

The Spaniards, however, quickly found a use for the liquid by-product, which had formerly only been used as a pharmaceutical to treat wounds and abrasions. They built the Alhambra palace in Granada, and before the end of the eighth century they had conquered all of Spain south of the Cantabrian Mountains. Indeed, the reason that the southernmost of the three Basque provinces is called "Araba" (Álava) is because that was the only Basque province which had been occupied by the "Arabs". Christian forces regrouped north of the Cantabrian Mountains in the Basque Country, Asturias, and Cantabria, and began to fight back. In the

early years of the ninth century, progress was slow, and many of the fortified towns we now admire in Álava and La Rioja are a testimony to those
times. The collapse of Moorish rule had begun in AD756; the increasing
insurgency by Castilian forces (in fact they were Castilian plus all sorts from
Catalonia, Navarra, León, and Asturias, but it is a convenient shorthand)
had led the ruling Moors to bring in extra forces from the fierce Berber war-
rior tribes of the Atlas Mountains in Morocco. The Berbers were skilled in
mountain warfare, but lacked the learning and the civilized, artistic
instincts of their masters, and quickly realized that, as the fighting force,
they could simply take over. There was a period of civil war and insurrec-
tions until AD929, when the Berbers ousted their Damascene predecessors
and established the caliphate of Córdoba under Abd-ar-Rahman I.

Meanwhile, the Castilian forces had exploited the disarray on the
Moorish side, and made progress southwards. The capital of Castilian
Spain switched between Navarra, Catalonia, and Castile at a time when
the various small kingdoms of northern Spain were beginning to unite.
León and Asturias had united in 931 under King Ramiro II, Castile and
Navarre (as it then was) united in 1067, and Aragón joined in 1134, so
that in 1150 Alfonso VII of Castile was styled "Emperor of Spain". But the
country was still very fragmented and far from united, with the Berbers in
control of much of the south. Northern Spain, however, was doing rather
well. Royal courts, universities, cathedrals, monasteries, and government
institutions had been established, and this meant that there were people of
rank, with money, prepared to pay for decent wine – and nothing estab-
lishes quality as fast as a ready market.

LA RIOJA

As mentioned in Chapter One, Rioja as a region was first recognized
(as Rioxa) in the year 1092, but its winemaking credentials had
been recorded rather earlier, more often than not in a monastic context. A
document of 863 records the cultivation of vines at the monastery of San
Mámes in Treviana in the Rioja Alta, and in 926 García Sánchez, king of
Navarra, deposited a will at the monastery of San Millán de la Cogolla
leaving his successor *Lucronio et Asa con omnibus terris, veneis, ortis, pamrii,
montibus*. This translates as "Logroño and Asa [a small town just north of
the Ebro between Lapuebla de Labarca and Elvillar] with all lands, vineyards, gardens, orchards, and mountains." In 934, Fernán González, the

conde de Castilla (count or earl of Castile), conducted a census of the county of Castile which recorded the extent of the vineyards, naming the main centres as Alesanco, Nájera, Cárdenas, Medrano, Clavijo, Enciso, and Arnedillo (most of which are in the Rioja Alta), as well as villages in the valleys of the rivers Iregua and Leza:

> *Omnes domus singulas metitas de vino in oblatione et singulos panes in offerta. Omnes villas de rivo de Alesanco et de rivo Cardimes, de vertice aqueusque ad Najeram.* ("All the individual houses [makers] of wine and bread. All the houses about the river Alesanco and the river Cardimes, which join [are tributaries of] the river Najera.")

More written references occur as the years pass and writing becomes, increasingly, a devotional activity, so we know that wine was a major part of the gastronomic and commercial landscape before the year 1000.

POETIC LICENCE
Probably the biggest single factor in the ancient history of Rioja wine was a mention by the poet Gonzalo de Berceo (born some time in the 1190s, died some time in the 1240s, or maybe later; authorities differ on the precise dates). He was a monk at the monastery of San Millán and he usually wrote poetry of a devotional nature. However, famously, he wrote the first-known [written] poem in the Spanish tongue, which includes the lines:

> *Quiero fer una prosa en román paladino en cual suele el pueblo fablar con su vezino ca non so tan letrado por fer otro latino bien baldrá, como creo, un vaso de bon vino.*

This translates into English as "I want to write a prose in the language in which the common people use to address their neighbours, as I am not learned enough to write in a different Latin. I trust it will still merit a glass of good wine." Rather inconveniently, de Berceo didn't record Rioja by name but, in those days, in the absence of refrigerated transport and decent containers, the only wine available in any area of Europe was wine made locally, so we may safely assume that Rioja is what he was enjoying.

PILGRIM'S PROGRESS
Another factor must have been the Camino de Santiago. Pilgrims had been walking from northern Europe to Santiago de Compostela since the

early ninth century, and wherever you begin (there are many starting points) all the trails unite at Logroño, coming in via the N-111 from Mendavia, crossing the stone bridge, up the Calle Ruavieja, crossing to the Calle de Barriocepo, through the gateway in the Murallas del Revellín (the old city walls), then left and right into the Calle del Marqués de Murrieta, then left and right through the Parque de San Miguel and westwards down the N-120 to Navarrete, Nájera, and Santo Domingo de la Calzada before crossing into the province of Burgos (*autonomía* of Castile-León) and points west.

In those days, food was never consumed without wine, and the monasteries were among the most enthusiastic growers of vines and makers of wine. Pilgrims would have been regaled with wine from Navarra, Rioja, Castile, León, and Galicia on their journey westward, and it may be significant that the wines from Rioja were the first to have their names known along the route. However, several royal edicts of Castile of the twelfth and thirteenth centuries prohibited the importation of wine from Navarra into Rioja. This may have helped to maintain the integrity of the local wine, but it also shows that already a difference was perceived in the quality of wines from Rioja and those from the surrounding area.

BRAVE NEW WORLD

A big leap forward came with the reunification of Spain and the discovery of America in 1492. Spain went forward into a golden age of prosperity, plundering the New World for its treasures, colonizing the Americas, and building export trade. Of course, the British and the French were busy plundering and colonizing, too, and this was the era of the freebooter, the buccaneer, the privateer, and the just plain pirate. But there was legitimate trade as well. The first (European) vines in America were reportedly planted in 1677 by French Huguenot immigrants on the Hudson River in what is now Ulster County, New York, so for more than the first century and a half of colonization there was massive opportunity for export trade.

Spain was not slow to respond. In 1580, for example, production in what is now the Rioja Alta alone was 318,330 *cántaras*, a *cántara* (literally "large flagon") being 16.16 litres in today's money, so representing 51,442 hectolitres: a remarkable amount for a region that still had few commercially sized producers. Prices were volatile, too, according to supply and demand. In 1513, a litre (juggling between *cántaras* and *arrobas*, another old unit of measure, becomes too complex at this point, so I have converted to modern measures) sold for 1.6 maravedis (coins originally equivalent to ten Roman denarii) rising to 6.8 in 1530, down to 5.6 by 1539, rising to 7.76 in 1548, and 12.1 in 1549. In July 1565, a litre had dropped to 3.2 maravedis, but by November the same year it was 6.4, and 5.75 in 1598. It's almost impossible to quantify these in modern terms, but there were thirty-four maravedis to the real, and a real was eventually to become five pesetas, and 166 pesetas eventually became a euro, so ten maravedis represents, perhaps, one centimo in modern money.

One of the next requirements for a burgeoning export trade was a suitable container. Barrels had been prohibitively expensive, but with the economy of scale provided by a large export market, they became affordable, and were pressed into service to ship wine to the Americas. Only sherry – then universally imitated and accepted as the world's finest wine – was more important than Rioja in Spanish wine terms, so it was natural that an industry started to grow, with wine shipped downriver to the Catalan coast or north to Bilbao. These barrels were of poor quality, however, and had to be lined with pitch or resin to prevent the wine from being spoiled or leaking out.

LEGISLATION

At home, the first steps in wine regulation (beyond the medieval bans on mixing Rioja with wines from outside the region) started to appear in the seventeenth century. The first formal act was a bye-law of 1635 in the city of Logroño which banned wagons and horses from roads adjacent to the crianza (maturation) cellars, in case the vibration disturbed the ageing wines, and there were various local regulations covering individual vineyards (still quite widely in monastic hands), the grapes they grew, and how much wine they made. The first real step towards quality control (or trade protection, or both) was the establishment in 1787 of the Real Sociedad Económica de Cosecheros de Rioja (Royal Economic Society of Rioja Wine-growers) which was the first to promote Rioja wine as a distinctive "appellation" – although no such term was used at the time – and to encourage its promotion as an industry. This was the era of Manuel Quintano y Quintano, who was to take the first step in industrializing Rioja wine production, even though the Napoleonic wars and local opposition would force a hiatus of more than half a century.

3

Rioja Up to Date

THE ORIGINS OF MODERN WINEMAKING

The next major development in Rioja's history came from Bordeaux. The French region was starting to assert itself as a major quality wine region in the late eighteenth century, a process that would culminate in it being perceived as "the world's finest wine", taking over that rather doubtful title from sherry around the time of the Great Exhibition of 1855. Prominent Riojanos started visiting Bordeaux from the third quarter of the eighteenth century to see what winemakers there were doing that might work in Rioja. There were many new ideas, including selection of grape varieties (and actually knowing the differences between them); better hygiene in the winery; more careful vine husbandry in the vineyard; de-stalking and multiple pressings, with the first-run juice separated for fermentation from the harder, later pressings; disinfecting barrels before they were filled, as well as filling, racking, pumping, and filtering.

The other big difference was the Bordelais' use of wood. Instead of fermenting in stone *lagares* or cement tanks, they had beautifully coopered vats made from oak, and they aged their wines in similarly well-made barrels of the same wood – barrels that were so meticulously coopered that they didn't need pitch or resin to line the inside to keep them watertight; instead, they were toasted with fire to seal the wood. They were, however, horrendously expensive for a wine region whose wines did not command Bordeaux prices.

Manuel Quintano y Quintano was a priest in Labastida who had carried on the monastic tradition of taking an interest in vines and wine. He visited Bordeaux from about 1780 and spent the 1786 vintage there, learning the techniques. He brought Bordeaux casks back with him, and began to experiment with fermenting and ageing wine in oak. His neighbours thought him a fool, but he proved his point in 1795 by exporting ten barrels and 1,050 bottles of wine to a customer in Cuba, who reported that not only had they survived the journey, but they were the best quality he had ever received from Rioja. However, the price of wine was strictly controlled by the Real Sociedad Económica (*see* chapter two), and Quintano's competitors, who didn't want to go to the expense of emulating his methods or the work of competing with his quality, lobbied the *sociedad* hard not to allow him to charge more for his wine than they charged for theirs – in spite of the fact that his cost of production was much higher. They won their case.

Meanwhile, the French revolution was under way, precluding any more cross-border visits. Once things had settled down after that, Napoléon began his process of trying to take over the entire continent, so wine took rather a back seat for quite a few years. In any case, in 1800 Quintano had been appointed the dean of Burgos Cathedral, and his interests moved from wine towards his new duties. However, his example was probably a major contribution to the shift in production away from white wines and towards the reds that were to become Rioja's trademark for the future. Indeed, there was to be an interregnum of half a century before the next step forward.

POLITICS AND THE NINETEENTH CENTURY

A bit more Spanish history: the early nineteenth century was a morass of political turmoil in the country after the death of King Fernando VII in 1833. His brother Carlos de Borbón (Bourbon) claimed the throne ahead of Fernando's small daughter Isabella, and there were six years of fighting before the Carlists admitted defeat. General Baldomero Espartero had been instrumental in the war, exacting a surrender from the Carlist forces in 1839, and in 1840 he was rewarded with the title of *Duque de la Victoria* ("Duke of the Victory"). He had entered parliament for the Progressive Party in 1837 and had become increasingly uncomfortable with the regency of Isabella's mother; Isabella would not be old enough to rule in her own right until she reached sixteen. In 1840, Espartero engineered a military coup, with himself as regent until such time as she should come of age. As a result, Isabella and her mother, the widowed queen María-Cristina, were driven into exile. Espartero proved to be a dictatorial regent, ruthlessly suppressing any opposition, and was himself eventually overthrown in 1843. He went into exile in London, taking with him his trusted aide-de-camp, Colonel Luciano Murrieta. Isabella returned in 1844, this time as queen regnant. As a result, Carlist opposition flared up again in 1847, led by Carlos's son Carlos Luís, but by 1849 this insurrection had also ended in defeat.

This is important in Rioja history for two reasons. In 1835, the prime minister, Juan Álvarez Mendizábal, believing that the religious orders favoured the Carlist cause, forced a law through the Cortes (Spain's legislative assembly) to curb the power and confiscate the property of the monasteries, much as Henry VIII had done in 1538 in England (though for very different reasons). Many wine estates were in monastic ownership, and these became available for the state to sell to fund the war. The second factor is that Murrieta and Riscal, the two legendary pioneers of what we are now calling "classic" Rioja, were both in exile: Murrieta in London and in a banking career with former General Espartero (now just calling himself the Duque de la Victoria), and Riscal in France simply to escape the turmoil that was political Spain at that time. Both men came back to Rioja via Bordeaux, but in different manners.

THE PIONEERS OF CLASSIC RIOJA

Luciano de Murrieta García Lemoine (later the Marqués de Murrieta) had been born in Peru, the son of the owners of a silver mine, and made a further fortune in, among other things, banking. While in London with the Duque de la Victoria, he enjoyed the good life in a perennial round of dinners, banquets, country-house weekends, and high living, but was dismayed by the low profile given to Rioja wine. The Duque happened to own a bodega in Rioja and recommended the wine business as a good investment for the future. Intrigued, Murrieta made his way to Bordeaux and studied winemaking there, before going to Rioja to make his first vintage in the Duque's bodega in 1852. He used Bordeaux wood and casks, and effectively became the first to produce "classic" Rioja. In 1872, he established an estate at Ygay, just south of Logroño, which is still one of the most beautiful and elegant in Rioja.

He was not alone. Camilo Hurtado de Amézaga (Marqués de Riscal de Alegre) had also been in exile in Bordeaux (although this time for supporting the losing side in the Carlist war) and had taken an interest in winemaking. He returned to Rioja with the same admiration for the

Bordeaux way of making wine as Luciano de Murrieta, brought Bordeaux vines with him as well as casks, and commissioned one of the leading architects of the day to build a Bordeaux-style *chai* (a building for maturing and storing wine) in the village of Elciego. His first experiments showed that Cabernet Sauvignon would flourish alongside Tempranillo in the vineyards, but the local winemaking technology simply hadn't been able to handle the grapes effectively. He founded the first purpose-built bodega for the making of the "new" style of Rioja in the town of Elciego between 1850 and 1860 and made his first vintage in 1860.

By now it had become obvious, at least to the local authorities, that Rioja's future lay in quality wines, and the regional government hired a French winemaker, rather appropriately named Jean Cadiche Pineau of Château Lanessan (later to become a *cru bourgeois*) in the Haut-Médoc, to advise growers and winemakers on Bordeaux methods. This was not an unqualified success; costs were much higher than with the traditional methods (especially the cost of oak casks), the business infrastructure of négociants and courtiers didn't exist, and – not least – proud Riojano *cosecheros* (grape-growers) and *bodegueros* (producers) didn't need this foreigner to teach them how to make wine their forefathers had made for generations. So Pineau generally got the cold shoulder from most of them, such that when his contract expired in 1868, it was not renewed. The feeling among rank-and-file *bodegueros* was that while the wines were very good, they were not Rioja.

Riscal stepped in and hired Pineau as his winemaker (although the term "winemaker" was not in use then and still has no direct equivalent in Castellano). There was no control over prices any more, so Murrieta, Riscal, and the other pioneers charged higher prices for their wines – and got them. There are few things which change people's attitudes as quickly as the prospect of a better deal, and the peseta finally dropped across most of the region. Another factor had been the establishment of quality cooperage in Rioja (still a major centre for barrels in Spain today) and the cheaper availability of oak from the Americas, which could be shipped over by the tree, dried, seasoned, and coopered in Rioja to make casks at much lower prices than, effectively, shipping expensive barrels of fresh air from Bordeaux.

OÏDIUM AND PHYLLOXERA

Meanwhile, developments in France were starting to force changes of their own. In 1852, just as Bordeaux was cresting the wave of world stardom at last, there was a widespread attack of oïdium (a fungal disease which had come across the Atlantic with plants from the USA as a result of increasing transatlantic trade), which devastated large tracts of the French vineyard for the entire vintage. French négociants came over the Pyrenees looking for wine to buy, and found something their fathers remembered as Bordeaux-style wine from the previous generation in full production. This was the first step in Rioja's international reputation, but oïdium reached Rioja in 1855 and decimated crops until 1862, when the solution – spraying the vines with a copper sulphate/calcium hydroxide solution ("Bordeaux mixture") – was eventually discovered.

A note about Bordeaux mixture. There are (at least) two stories about how this was invented. The first concerns attempts to deter children from pilfering grapes on their way to school in the Médoc by spraying roadside vines a ghastly, poisonous blue, using dissolved copper sulphate as the colouring agent (blue was the colour of poison in those days: witness the Victorian blue-glass poison bottles seen in many pharmacies). Growers noticed that the wines which had been sprayed survived oïdium much better than those that had not, and further research developed the mixture we know today: typically a 1:1:125 ratio of copper sulphate, calcium hydroxide (quicklime), and water. This discovery is credited to Professor P. Millardet of the University of Bordeaux.

The other theory, which goes back so far in my memory I cannot now remember the source, is that a grower somewhere in France noticed that the single vine outside his kitchen window had survived oïdium better than his vineyard vines. The only difference between it and them was that his wife would throw the washing-up water out of the window (and onto the vine) each day. The cooking pans were copper, of course, and the water came from lime-rich soils, and he made the connection. This may be apocryphal.

The vines struggled back to full production and had just about recovered when the inexorable southward march of the root-gobbling louse, *Phylloxera vastatrix*, (again from America) began to destroy vine roots right across the country. It hit France in 1867, and the Rioja export business boomed again, with French companies setting up in the region (an example is Bodegas Franco-Españolas), but the pest was not to be stopped by the Pyrenees. Phylloxera reached Rioja eventually, in 1899, but by then the process of grafting *Vitis vinifera* vines onto *Vitis labrusca* roots had been discovered, and the Rioja vineyards could be replanted with merciful speed – although it took more than a decade before the decline was halted.

A note about phylloxera: it's a louse that sucks the juice out of vine roots and thereby destroys the vine by lack of nutrients. American vines (*Vitis labrusca*) are much more vigorous and productive than the European variety and are immune to it for evolutionary reasons, but, sadly, their grapes are not suitable for quality wine production (although they do very well as table grapes). The phylloxera insect came from America in the roots of various fruit plants and was first spotted at Kew Gardens in London in experimental vines brought over from the USA. It then appeared in various parts of France (most notably Bordeaux and the Rhône), where experimental vineyards were being trialled with American vines; once the bug discovered this cornucopia of delicious roots, there was no stopping it.

Many, if not most, regions of Europe claim to have discovered the solution, most notably the cava country in the province of Barcelona where, in 1905, they erected a statue to viticulturist Marc Mir i Capella in Vilafranca del Penedès. The probable truth is that many growers in many regions planted American vines in desperation, in the hope that their grapes would be good enough for winemaking; then they noticed that, as the European vines around them failed, the American vines continued in vigorous good health. Since grafting in vine husbandry was already a well-established practice, it was only one step from that to the idea of grafting all European *vinifera* vines onto American labrusca roots. The universities of Bordeaux and Montpellier were heavily involved in the research, and the general feeling is that the solution was developed in 1887, by Professor Pierre-Marie-Alexis Millardet of the University of Bordeaux.

"MODERN" RIOJA AND THE TWENTIETH CENTURY

From an export point of view, this had been a boom time for Rioja, with the founding of some of what remain the region's greatest bodegas. Even as the French vineyards began to return to health, the export market seemed undimmed. A major factor was the completion of the railway line between Logroño and Bilbao in 1880, followed by a trade treaty with France in 1882 which cut import taxes between the two countries and boosted exports again. The period from 1870 to 1885 was the golden age of classic Rioja, with the foundation of new bodegas and a booming export market which, it seemed, would last for ever. A good deal of the wine found its way into export-market blends under fanciful French appellation names (particularly Bordeaux), and many of the so-called "Bordeaux" wines were much improved as a result. In contrast, the early 1900s were difficult for Rioja. Its main market, France, had had a massive vintage in 1893, which marked the start of a general decline in the country's need for imported wine, and the French government had tariffed strongly against imported wine to protect its own industry in 1892. In 1898, Spain lost its remaining colonies in Central and South America and the Philippines, and those markets effectively disappeared, too. In 1900, the main worry was phylloxera. Many bodegas sold up, closed, or merged, and many areas of vineyard were returned to general agriculture. Those vineyards that remained were replanted on grafted roots but, of course, vines need several years of growth before they can produce a viable crop, and it was 1913 before yields began to increase after a fourteen-year decline.

Trade did improve, however, and during World War I Rioja won export business to the USA, as France was unable to export. There was a ground swell of opinion that Rioja needed its own appellation system to guarantee the origin of the wine and prevent the use of the name by other regions of Spain – a practice that was becoming rife, as wines from almost anywhere could put any label they liked on their wines to capitalize on Rioja's reputation. The first regulatory council, known as a *consejo regulador* (CR), was constituted in 1926, and Rioja was the first wine region of Spain to be so regulated, although it was not then called a *denominación de origen* – a quality wine region.

REGULATING QUALITY

A note about regulation: contemporaneously, France was working towards the *appellation d'origine contrôlée*, or AOC system, which was instituted nationally in 1935, but a few regions of France, Spain, and Italy had their own fledgling systems in place before this. The French system was widely seen to be workable and well-organized, and when nationwide systems were rolled out in other countries, they tended to follow the French model; this has formed the basis for nearly all the quality-wine designation systems of Europe. In Spain, during the Second Republic (1931–6, which ended in the Spanish Civil War) there were attempts to "firm up" the system, and Cariñena got its own CR in 1932, with sherry, Montilla, and Tarragona getting theirs in 1932–3. During the Civil War,

Málaga received its CR in 1937, as a result of work done prior to the war, but apart from that, very little happened in the wine world, understandably, and it wasn't until afterwards that the term *denominación de origen*, or DO for short, began to be used as a direct translation of the French *appellation d'origine*. The abbreviation for *consejo regulador de la denominación de origen* is CRDO. The next one was to be Alella in 1953.

After World War II, and particularly as Spain opened up as a holiday destination in the late 1950s and early 1960s, large quantities of wine from Spain were exported, particularly to northern Europe where wine drinking was something of a novelty for all but the most well-off. Importers cheerfully labelled their wines "Spanish Claret", "Spanish Burgundy", and "Spanish Chablis". To be fair, it had been fashionable in the 1890s in Spain itself to use similar epithets to describe the wines but, in Europe at least, as export customers for Rioja joined the EU, one by one, they had to abide by community law that protects the names of wine regions in the market.

The UK, one of the biggest markets, joined in 1973, and customers who had been buying "Spanish Claret" *et al* were completely bewildered by something called *vino de mesa* (VdM): literally "table wine". Many importers responded by dreaming up fanciful names for their wines. In my early years in the trade it had been common practice in the UK to import red *vino de mesa* from Spain and label it as "Spanish Burgundy", etc., and *vin de table* from France and label it "Nuits-St-Georges", etc., with impunity. This had to stop, by law. One of our French suppliers tried to counter the problem by registering a red table wine under the brand name "Knights of St George", but this cut little ice with the customers. Fortunately for Rioja, it really had stuck to its guns in maintaining its name in the public eye, and in those days the only Spanish wines we sold under their own names were Rioja and Valdepeñas, the latter which has a history almost as long as that of Rioja. Indeed, in a survey conducted as long ago as 1989 among UK consumers, when asked for the name of a red wine region, Rioja came third after Burgundy and Beaujolais.

TECHNOLOGICAL INNOVATION

The other big change of the 1970s was new winemaking technology. Miguel Torres had installed the first temperature-controlled stainless-steel fermentation tanks in Pacs del Penedès in 1962, and the first Rioja bodega to be constructed from scratch using this equipment was Union

Vitivinícola in Cenicero, better known as Marqués de Cáceres. This was the brainchild of Enrique Forner, whose family had moved rather hurriedly to Bordeaux at the time of the Civil War (Forner *padre* had been a republican MP). There they went into the wine business, eventually owning two Bordeaux châteaux: Larose-Trintaudon and Camensac, both in the village of St-Laurent in the Médoc. Young Henri (as Enrique is known in France) learned the craft of winemaking under the eminent Professor Peynaud from the University of Bordeaux, and when he built his new, château-style bodega, it was with Peynaud's advice from the ground up. Forner believed that Rioja in the 1960s was much too oaky, and that the fruit component of the wine was being overshadowed. At that time, the *crianza* rules were much stricter than they are now, demanding very long periods in cask before bottling was permitted; they changed in the late 1970s, probably partly as a result of Forner's success. It is interesting to speculate what must have been on the minds of his neighbours when Forner installed his shiny new tanks; perhaps they shook their heads, as their great-grand-fathers had done at the time of Murrieta and Riscal, and expressed the feeling that while the wines were very good, they were not Rioja.

Needless to say, attitudes changed when Marqués de Cáceres made massive inroads into the export market as well as the home one, especially the *paradores* (state-owned hotels) which are very tourist-friendly and encourage people to buy the wines they've enjoyed on holiday after they get home. Most bodegas now routinely use stainless steel for fermentation (but *see* chapter six for some alternative recent developments). These are the "modern" wines of Rioja, fermented in stainless steel and given the absolute minimum of oak-ageing according to law. Many companies also use second- and third-year barrels to minimize the oak effect still further, although, interestingly, Cáceres now produces a *gran reserva* red and a *crianza* white, which Enrique Forner suggested he would never do, so the eternal circle is complete – or perhaps not.

On the regulatory front, there was another change to come before the end of the century. Italy introduced a new "super category" of quality wine (*denominazione de origine controllata e garantita*, or DOCG) in 1984, and Spain followed suit by establishing the *denominación de origen calificada* (DOCa: literally "qualified" – as in quality – denomination of origin) in 1988. Rioja was promoted to DOCa status on April 9, 1991, with a much tougher *reglamento* (set of rules) which demands, among other things, proof over a very long period that the winemaker can consistently maintain high quality, keep the base price of grapes at least 200 per cent of the average price for that grape throughout Spain, bottle at the bodega, and undergo very stringent tasting and testing regimes. There was a great deal of debate about whether the DOCa should have been awarded on a district basis (as with *grand cru* in Champagne and *classico* in Italian wines), or only to wines of *reserva* status and above, or only in exceptional years, or on an ad hoc basis according to the results of the tastings. In the end, however, it was awarded to everybody willy-nilly, regardless of the quality of the wines they produced. If they could hack the Rioja back label, they were *calificada*, regardless. For this reason, no other DO in Spain seemed keen to apply for promotion to the new category for quite a long time. The second was Priorato in 2003, although because the people there speak Catalan, it's *denominació d'origen qualificada* or DOQ.

Sadly, Mother Nature failed to deliver a quality vintage of a sufficient quality to allow the new DOCa Rioja to strut its stuff in 1991, and 1992 and 1993 were dismal, on account of drought. In 1994, she finally came up trumps with an excellent but small vintage, topping that in 1995 with an excellent and decent-sized vintage; *gran reserva* wines from the latter are likely to be drinking well towards 2010.

A word about vintages: the CRDOCa classifies the quality each year in the spring after the vintage, when *crianza* wines have gone into cask. The system is sledgehammer-subtle, with five grades. They used to be: *Deficiente* (Deficient); *Regular* (Regular); *Buena* (Good); *Muy Buena* (Very Good) and *Excelente* (Excellent); but the lower two grades mysteriously mutated during the 1990s; so it now looks like this:

Mediana (Average *) And not deficient, honest, guv.
Normal (Standard **) In other words "average".
Buena (Good ***) In this writer's view, the minimum level at which the wine should be allowed to use the name Rioja. Good *jóvenes* and *crianzas*.
Muy Buena (Very Good ****) Expect good *reservas* from the better houses in these years.
Excelente (Excellent *****) Expect very good, long-lived *reservas* and *gran reservas* from the best houses.

Statistically, in the fifty years between 1951 and 2000, there were seven *****, eleven ****, nineteen ***, nine **, and four *, although modern vineyard and winemaking techniques make it unlikely that a * vintage will ever happen again, unless there are earthquakes, tornadoes, or forest fires. It also shows that, even given the fairly primitive winemaking conditions of the 1950s and 1960s, still seventy-four per cent of the vintages were at least buena in quality. Naturally, in practice, some bodegas make fabulous wines in the most dismal years (1997 and 2000 were cases in point), and some bodegas will make dismal wine in the most fabulous years. These are annotated where possible in the listing of main bodegas (*see* chapter eight).

RIOJA: THE NEXT GENERATION

And what of the future? Well, the 1990s brought its own new generation of "maverick" winemakers looking for even more from their soil, vines, microclimate, grapes, and vinification. They fall into two groups. In the first are those who are growing "experimental" grapes such as Cabernet Sauvignon, Merlot, and Syrah, and using super-modern vineyard tecniques to maximize ripeness, making wines deeply expressive of their terroir; Hacienda de Susar (or whatever they're calling it this week) in Alfaro is a prime example.

The other group is working with the classic Rioja grapes but harvesting on an ad hoc basis according to ripeness, sorting them before pressing, and prolonging maceration and extraction to push the grape as far as it will go. Exponents include Allende, Roda, Benjamín Romeo, Miguel Merino, and Sierra Cantabria, and, indeed, many of what we might think of as "classic" bodegas are starting to produce a top-of-the-range wine in this category.

These are the wines I have called "post-modern" Rioja (*see* chapter six for details), and these are the wines about which so many people, within and without Rioja, are shaking their heads and saying that while the wines are very good, they're not Rioja.

But this is where we came in.

4

On the Ground

GEOGRAPHY, GEOLOGY, AND CLIMATE

There's Rioja and there's La Rioja. The first is the wine, the second is the *autonomía* which represents about two-thirds of the vineyard area. Because Rioja wine long predates the modern constitution of Spain, it is made not only in the *autonomía* of La Rioja, but also north of the river in the Basque Country province of Araba (Álava) to the north, and the *autonomía* of Navarra to the northeast, although administration for all the wines is centralized in Logroño, the capital of La Rioja.

The non-La Rioja bits are generally north of the river Ebro, with the exception of a "tongue" of La Rioja, which juts north of the Ebro around the main wine town of San Vicente de la Sonsierra up towards the Sierra de Toloño (part of the Cantabrian mountain range), encompassing the wine towns of Rivas de Tereso, Peciña, and Ábalos. Other than that, the river marks the northern boundary of La Rioja for all of its course, and the wine-producing area is just over half of the area of the *autonomía* of La Rioja; the southern part (which may make wine but not under the DOCa Rioja) is known as "La Sierra". The river Ebro is the most important waterway in the region and roughly follows the northern boundary of La Rioja for about 120 kilometres (seventy-four miles).

The Rioja wine-producing zone is cupped between the Cantabrian Mountains in the north and a number of mountain ranges in the south: from east to west, the Montes de Alayo, Yuso, and Suso; the Sierra del Moncalvillo (Rioja Alta) and Las Peñas de la Hez; and the Sierra de Achena and Sierra de Yerga in the Rioja Baja. This provides a unique range of microclimates for growing vines.

Rioja Alta

Rioja is divided into three sub-zones. The Rioja Alta is that part of La Rioja west of (and including) Logroño to the western boundary with the province of Burgos (*autonomía* of Castile-León), although there are some vineyards (but no bodegas) in Miranda de Ebro, which is an enclave of La Rioja within the province of Burgos.

The southern boundary of the Rioja Alta wine land is a diagonal line running southeast to northwest through the towns of Matute, San Millán de la Cogolla, Villarejo, (just short of) Santo Domingo de la Calzada, and Tormantos. The eastern boundary is the river Iregua, with a tongue of land following the river as far as vineyards around Varea. The main tributaries of the river Ebro are the Tirón, the (perhaps eponymous; *see* chapter two) Oja, and the Najerilla, all of which flow from the southern mountain range of the Sierra de la Demanda.

This is Tempranillo country, and also Mazuela and Graciano in the warmer microclimatic areas. There are approximately 25,000 hectares of vines in the Rioja Alta.

Rioja Alavesa

The Rioja Alavesa is the area within the province of Álava (Basque Country) north of the Ebro up to the foothills of the Cantabrian Mountains, and including the wine towns of Labastida, Samaniego, Villabuena, Eciego, Laguardia, and Oyon. This is the smallest of the three sub-regions (some 12,000 hectares of vines), but many of the producers are *cosecheros* who own small parcels of land, belong to cooperatives, or sell their grapes to the major bodegas. This is Tempranillo heaven, where many of the very best grapes are harvested from the coolest vineyards.

Rioja Baja

The Rioja Baja is east of Logroño, mainly in La Rioja encompassing the wine towns of Villamediana, Agoncillo, Pradejon, Ausejo, Arnedo, Calahorra, Quel, Aldeanueva de Ebro, and Alfaro. It also extends north of the river into Navarra, with the most notable wine towns being Mendavia, Andosilla, San Adrián, and Azagra. In La Rioja, the Ebro tributaries (once again from the south) are the Iregua, Leza, Cidacos (which is also home to the Moscatel-based *vino de la tierra del Valle de Sadacia*), and Alhama. In Navarra, the tributaries flow from the northern

Cantabrian Mountains and include the Ega, which joins the Ebro at San Adrián, and the Aragón, which joins at Alfaro.

The popular view of the Rioja Baja is of a hot, dry, lowland area which grows mainly spicy Garnacha for blending with cool, austere upland Tempranillo from the Alta and Alavesa, but this is increasingly erroneous. Alfaro, arguably the "capital" of the Rioja Baja, is low indeed, at 301 metres (987 feet) compared with Laguardia at 635 metres (2,083 feet), but the town of Quel is at 490 metres (1,607 feet), and elsewhere the Baja is striking back with the promise of high-quality, new-wave wines from such producers as Álvaro Palacios (Palacios Remondo) and Amador Escudero (Valsacro). It was Amador who warned me in 2004 to "look out for the Rioja Baja: we are on the warpath". There are around 21,000 hectares of vines in the Rioja Baja.

La Rioja statistics

Area   503,400 ha
Vineyard area   62,147 ha
Population (1996 census)   268,206
Average DOCa wine production per year 300,000 hl
Average wine production per year (including *vino de mesa*) 1,000,000 hl

Influence of the Ebro

The geology of the region revolves around the river Ebro and its tributaries. Along the course of the rivers the local soil tends to be alluvial, which means that it's fertile and gives the vines a relatively easy life. The mountain sources of the rivers, however, are largely on limestone bedrock, which means that even the alluvial plains have a good deal of calcium carbonate in the soil which is excellent for vine-growing. Better yet are the clay soils of the upper slopes, especially in the Rioja Alta and Alavesa, where there are areas of chalk-rich and iron-rich soil which offer a "tiger-stripe" picture of red and white topsoils on a map of the region.

North of the Ebro in the west, the vineyards tend to be tucked in towards the mountain foothills, and the soils are high in chalk. South of the river in the Rioja Alta, as well as chalk there's a good deal of iron in the soil, which provides individual plots with rich trace elements to feed the vines and grapes. In the Rioja Baja, the higher areas have iron-rich clay, and the lower vineyards are clay and alluvial. Altogether the range of soils and microclimates has provided winemakers with a wide variety of "ingredients" from which to make their own style of Rioja. In recent times there has been a major trend towards sub-regional and single-estate wines rather than the region-wide blends that have been the hallmark of Rioja for so many years, and this is likely to continue as vineyard ownership is consolidated into fewer and larger hands.

CLIMATIC DIFFERENCES

Although the Cantabrian Mountains shelter Rioja from the excesses of climate provided by the Atlantic Ocean to the west and the bay of Biscay to the north, the highlands of the Rioja Alavesa and Alta are high enough and northerly enough still to be subject to Atlantic influences. Many vineyards are right in the lee of the foothills of the mountain ranges, and susceptible to early morning mists and cooling effects. The vineyards of Remelluri, for example, are tightly tucked into the foot of the mountains, and mist, fog, and cooling showers are a fact of life. This is a largely positive effect, as at these altitudes even a single-degree reduction in temperature can make a significant difference to the acidity and ripeness of the grapes at harvest time. Generally in the highlands, early spring sunshine leads into long, hot summers and mild autumns with cool breezes at night. Winters can be very cold, with frost and snow in places, and this, too, is advantageous in that it depletes insect populations, with a beneficial reduction in pests (and pesticides) in the vineyard.

The Rioja Baja has, by contrast, a much more Mediterranean type of climate, although it's as well to remember that there also are sporadic, cooler highlands here.

In the lowlands it is hotter and drier. Statistically the average temperature varies from 12.8°C (55°F) in the west (at Haro, with an altitude of 479 metres/1,571 feet) to 13.9°C (57°F) in the east (at Alfaro, with an altitude of 301 metres/987 feet), with a top temperature of 40°C in summer and a winter low of −4°C (104°F and 25°F). Average rainfall is 450 millimetres (eighteen inches) in Haro, 397 millimetres (sixteen inches) in Logroño, and 360 millimetres (fourteen inches) in Alfaro, although in the highlands it can be anything up to 1,000 millimetres (thirty-nine inches; *see* the table opposite for comparisons) and average sunshine is 2,800 hours per year.

The reticulate nature of Rioja's mountainous microclimatic niches makes it something of a winemaker's self-service buffet, and the range of different wines being produced is testimony to that diversity.

Average rainfall comparison	Millimetres
Haro	45
Logroño	397
Alfaro	360
Berlin	580
Dublin	740
Edinburgh	1,100
London	900
Madrid	450
New York	1,200
Paris	612
Rome	800
San Francisco	500

5
Green Shoots

GRAPES, VITICULTURE, AND VINEYARD MANAGEMENT

There has been an increasing awareness in Rioja, or, indeed, a return to the awareness that good wine starts in the vineyard, and that vineyard management is the key to quality as much as winemaking equipment and skills. Wine, as everywhere, starts with the choice of a grape.

The debate continues about permitting new varieties to be grown in Rioja (*see* chapter eight) but, as yet, there are three groups of grapes likely to be found in the region. The largest of them is, of course, made up of the recommended/authorized/permitted varieties. Next come "experimental" grapes, and finally "reclaimed" varieties: the ancient grapes grown in Rioja over the past thousand years or so, some of which are in experimental nursery vineyards even now.

Recommended varieties

TEMPRANILLO

Tempranillo is the most important, not just here in Rioja, but all over Spain, where it may variously be known as Cencibel (Castile-La Mancha), Tinto Fino, Tinto del País, Tinto de Toro (Castile-León), Ull de Llebre (Catalonia). In most of northern Spain, and especially in the Rioja Alta and Alavesa it is the principal quality red variety. Its origins are obscure, although there have been rumours over the years that it may have a common ancestor with the Pinot Noir of Burgundy. There have even been suggestions that it was originally brought to Spain by Burgundian monks on the Camino de Santiago – though no one has ever explained how you transport living vines for several weeks on the back of a donkey. In the absence of genetic fingerprinting (although that may well be on its way), general opinion seems to be that it is a native Castilian variety which occurred naturally in the vineyards and, by trial and error, was spotted as a good investment by early winemakers.

Tempranillo is a thick-skinned, glossy black grape which gets its name (*temprano* means "early") because it ripens in mid- to late September, about two weeks earlier than the Garnacha. The grape and its wine are robust in character, and single-variety examples naturally reach about thirteen per cent alcohol by volume (abv) and are resistant to oxidation, which makes them a good choice for principal grape. In addition, it likes calcareous soils and can ripen well even in the cool highlands of the Rioja Alavesa. However, by itself the Tempranillo makes early maturing wine that wouldn't be able to age for the length of time and in the graceful manner for which Rioja is renowned. In the Basque Country, of course, they love it young, fresh, and glistering with fruit, but in the rest of Rioja, where wines are made to be matured, it's usually blended with other varieties for the final *cuvée*.

The ultra-modern, high-expression wines tend to be at least ninety to ninety-five per cent Tempranillo from low-yielding vineyards, usually with the rest made up by Graciano. Tempranillo makes up eighty-one per cent of the red vineyard and seventy-four per cent of the Riojano entire vineyard (*see* table on page 37).

GARNACHA

Garnacha is the northern-Spanish original of the grape the French call Grenache. It is believed to have originated in Aragón and Navarra in the days when they were independent kingdoms and covered areas that now include southern France – hence the grape's cross-border identity. Until relatively recently, Garnacha was regarded as little more than a workhorse grape for making bulk *rosados* (rosés) and uncomplicated, hot-climate reds, but winemakers in Priorato (Catalonia) and latterly Zaragoza discovered that those neglected, low-yielding, old-vine plantations could be turned into wine at unheard-of quality (and price) levels. It is grown widely elsewhere in Spain, most notably for high-quality wines in the north – Aragón, Navarra, and Catalonia – and for everyday-quality wines in the south, principally La Mancha and the Levant, where it may be known as the Tinto Aragonés or Lladoner. You may also see wines labelled *Garnacho* in the masculine, and this is an adjectival form of the name; *la uva Garnacha* (Garnacha the grape) is feminine, *el vino Garnacho* (Garnacho the wine) is masculine. It's probably not grammatically correct, but we know what they mean (the same thing happens with Mazuelo).

The Rioja variant is known in full as Garnacha Tinta or Garnacha Riojana, is the main red grape of the Rioja Baja, and plays some part in nearly all Rioja wines. It grows well on hilly, rocky ground, even when it's relatively windy, but needs long, hot autumns to give of its best in terms of ripeness. In the Rioja Baja, it's a vigorous grape, resistant to many fungal diseases of the vine, and can produce wines of up to sixteen per cent abv. Its main use in the Rioja *cuvée* is to add strength and warmth to the wine, and its main growing area is the Rioja Baja. There was a trend to replant with Tempranillo some years ago, but a new generation of winemakers in Alfaro and surrounding parts is teasing out much more complexity and character than was ever imagined, and indeed, Bodegas Conde de Valdemar (formerly Bodegas Martínez Bujanda) produced an Alavesa varietal Garnacha to *gran reserva* level as long ago as 1994, and it was (and is) splendid. Garnacha makes up fourteen per cent of the red vineyard and thirteen per cent of the total.

MAZUELO

Mazuelo is also a grape of Aragonés origin, grown elsewhere in Spain under the name Cariñena, and in southern France as Carignan. This is another grape that has come back from the brink of obscurity, thanks mainly to work done with old plantation vines in Priorato and Zaragoza (although interestingly it is hardly planted at all in the DO Cariñena, which is from whence, presumably, it takes its name). The grape can achieve 13.5 per cent abv in hot years, and its tannin and high acidity help to give the final *cuvée* the kind of longevity that good Rioja demands, even when it is only present in fairly small amounts; this is just as well, given that it represents only 3.4 per cent of the red vineyard and three per cent of the total. A very few bodegas (notably La Marquesa) make a varietal Mazuelo but, after years of decline, it is at last increasing in the vineyard.

GRACIANO

Graciano is a small, black, tough-skinned variety which produces high-quality wines as well as being resistant to vineyard diseases, with the exception of botrytis. This is the grape that gives great Rioja wines the edge; even in very small quantities, most new-wave wines and many of the great classic *gran reservas* will contain three to five per cent Graciano to provide them with structure and tannins into their old age. Half a dozen bodegas make a varietal Graciano (the first were probably La Marquesa and Contino in 1993), but it is in such demand by the major producers to add to their blends that it's almost an act of conspicuous bragging to put one on the market. The wine is very tannic when young, but matures well and elegantly under the *crianza* system, especially given the new trend for new French oak. It still represents only about one per cent of the vineyard.

VIURA

Viura is the major white variety of Rioja, known as Macabeo in northeastern Spain, and Macabeu in France. It came into its own particularly with the introduction of the "new-style" cold-fermented whites in the 1970s (pioneered by Marqués de Cáceres). However, traditionally it used to be added in small quantities to the red wines of Rioja to add a certain fire and brilliance to the colour, and it is still added to some Alavesa wines to help the acid balance. Time has moved on, however, and experiments with Viura have thrown up some greater complexity and character, although wines for traditional *crianza* ageing do tend to need the admixture of some Malvasía (*see* below). Barrel-fermentation seems to extract a lot more complexity from this variety, and some excellent examples are currently on the market. Fundamentally, though, except in the hands of a very careful winemaker, this variety turns out clean, rather neutral, and uninspiring wines on its own. It has ninety-six per cent of the white wine vineyard, 8.3 per cent of the total.

MALVASÍA

Malvasía Riojana or Subirat-Parent (as it's known in Penedès), is Viura's partner in white Rioja. The grape adds a certain musky weight to the blend and marries well with the vanillin from oak barrels during *crianza*. Indeed, the very greatest and long-lived classic white Rioja wines (for example, those from López-Heredia and Marqués de Murrieta) will have anything up to ten per cent of this variety, and sometimes more. When ripe, the grapes are tinted red (hence its German name of Früher Roter Malvasier), and although the vine is susceptible to fungal diseases in the vineyard, in good years it produces vigorous wines high in tartaric acid, which give the counterpoint to the sometimes "squeaky-clean" style of the Viura. I have yet to encounter a wine made entirely of this grape – at least in Rioja. It occupies just 1.3 per cent of the white-wine vineyard, and one-tenth of one percent of the total.

GARNACHA BLANCA

Garnacha Blanca is the white counterpart of the red and has started to be appreciated as a quality variety since old-vine examples from Priorato have shown particularly well. It produces good quantities of reasonable-quality wine, if a little lacking in acidity. It is often used as a "buffer" variety to smooth out a blend in underripe years. Its great advantage is that it's a very robust vine, resistant to disease, and bodegas which own old plantations guard it jealously, as, with the Viura and the Malvasía Riojana, it adds body and weight to wines for long ageing in the barrel.

Experimental varieties

Every wine region in the world has experimental grape varieties growing alongside the indigenous vines to see what, if anything, can be done with them to improve the *cuvée*, and Rioja is no exception. Some of these may make it into the "recommended" category under the new Organización Interprofesional del Vino de Rioja (OIPVR; Interprofessional Organization of the Wines of Rioja). The usual suspects are to be found at large.

CABERNET SAUVIGNON

Cabernet Sauvignon was one of the first varieties to be planted in the 1850s in Rioja at the time of changeover from "traditional" *joven* wines to the "classic" Rioja we know today, perhaps most famously by the Marqués de Riscal in Elciego. He was not alone, however, and there are small plantations of Cabernet, used in many cases to replace scarce and expensive Graciano in the final *cuvée*.

MERLOT

Merlot is a relative newcomer, used by some bodegas as above because it has a less obvious organoleptic style than Cabernet Sauvignon, and it does surprisingly well in hot, dry years.

SYRAH

Also a newcomer, mainly represented at Hacienda de Susar in the Rioja Baja, where its hot, dry legacy performs very well in arid years, However, the distinctive "peppery" style is a bit alien to the nature of Rioja and it may become little more than a curiosity unless, of course, there are big changes at the OIPVR (*see* chapter eight).

CHARDONNAY

In La Rioja, Chardonnay has been around for rather longer than many people think. In July, 1993, I was entertained to lunch by a much-loved (and now retired) *bodeguero* of a very traditional bodega who produced a bottle of "Rioja Chardonnay" with the tapas. I asked him if it was legal and he replied "Yes – as long as we don't take it outside the bodega gate." They had planted one hectare to try it out and, for all I know, it is there still and may soon become legal (once again, *see* chapter eight). It was well-made and pleasant enough – not particularly redolent of the craggy and misty landscapes of Rioja, but you never know…

Reclaimed varieties

Over the centuries, Rioja has grown many oddball local varieties, often misnamed, misunderstood, and misrepresented, but in the last ten years of the old Consejo Regulador de la Denominación de Origen Calificada (CRDOCa), a lot of effort went into looking for forgotten varieties that might offer an alternative to the "usual suspects" listed above under experimental varieties. One man who has devoted a good part of his life to researching these varieties is Juan Carlos Sancha González, who manages to combine his duties as a director of Bodegas Viña Ijalba with those of associate professor of viticulture at the University of Rioja. In the latter role he co-wrote a book called *Variedades Minoritarias en la DOCa Rioja: Proyecto de Recuperación* ("Minority Varieties of the DOCa Rioja: Reclaim Project") that seeks to identify and rediscover some of the old varieties from the region which might be coaxed back to life to add to the diversity of modern Rioja wine. In 1912, forty-four varieties of vine were grown in Rioja. By 1942, this had fallen to eleven, and today there are just seven recommended in the *reglamento*. The Estación Enológica (Oenology Station) in Haro had, however, been taking samples of plant material and seeds since 1904, and this bank of germoplasm, genes, and DNA was transferred to the university in 1988. It is with these that Juan Carlos has been working, on the basis that "It's better to reclaim historical varieties [which have evolved with the soil and climate of Rioja] than to import foreign ones."

MATURANA

The most high-profile reclaimed variety of the moment, of which Juan Carlos has two hectares of red and two hectares of white and produces varietals from both of them. The red has been identified by genetic fingerprinting to be the Merenzao of Galicia, where it is also known as María Ardoña and Bastardo. The quality of the wines is excellent, yet the vines are very low-cropping and unlikely to appeal to the accountant-driven modern bodega.

TEMPRANILLO VARIANTS

There are also "sports" (biological deviations) of the Tempranillo such as Tempranillo Blanco (a vine mutation) and Tempranillo Peludo ("hairy" Tempranillo because of the vine tendrils), which produces smaller, more compact bunches with higher concentration, albeit at lower yields, and is being trialled by, among others, Sierra Cantabria.

MONASTEL DE RIOJA

Another old variety in the nursery but not yet planted commercially is the Monastel de Rioja (no relation to the Monastrell/Mourvèdre of southern Spain/Rhône or the Moristel of Somontano), and others are in the pipeline.

OTHER VARIETIES

As an academic exercise you may like to look out for the following, although breath-holding is not recommended: Blanca Alargada, Blanca Falsa, Blancaza, Calagraño, Calagraño Francés, Colgadera, Cojón de Gato, Garnacha Roya, Garnacha Tardía, Garnacha Tintorera (widely planted in the Levant), Graciano de Alfaro, Granadina, Granegro Tintorera, Grano Alargado, Miguel de Arco, Morato, Moscatel de Grano Gordo, Moscatel de la Tierra, Navarra, Regiruelo, Ribadavia, Sabor a Menta, Tempranillo del Barón, Tempranillo Royo, Tempranillo Temprano, Teta de Vaca, Tintoreras, and Turruntés. The following are mentioned in historical documents but had died out before 1904 and there is now no known source of plant material: Royales, Morisca, Yjaurel, Granadina, Mollar, Morate, San Jerónimo, Anaves, Cirujal, and others.

I rather like the idea of Cojón de Gato, which translates literally as "cat's bollock". In the English-speaking world, we are canine and plural in this respect, but the general tone suggests consummate excellence. Perhaps it will be a variety worth waiting for.

Statistics

Here is a snapshot of the vineyard situation in hectares in 2004.

Variety	La Rioja	Álava	Navarra	Total ha	% Red	% Vineyard
Tempranillo	30,340	11,131	4,601	46,073	81.17	74.13
Garnacha	7,053	160	667	7,880	13.88	12.68
Mazuelo	1,331	106	470	1,906	3.36	3.07
Graciano	402	120	113	635	1.12	1.02
Other red	76	<1	19	96	0.17	0.15
Experimental	90	47	33	170	0.30	0.27
Total red*	**39,291**	**11,565**	**5,904**	**56,760**		

Variety	La Rioja	Álava	Navarra	Total ha	% White	% Vineyard
Viura	3,743	1,130	310	5,184	96.23	8.34
Malvasía	46	21	3	70	1.30	0.11
Garnacha blanca	21	<1	<1	22	0.40	0.03
Other white	86	7	2	95	1.76	0.15
Experimental	13	3	0	16	0.30	0.03
Total white*	**3,909**	**1,162**	**316**	**5,387**		

	La Rioja	Álava	Navarra	Total ha	% Red	% White
TOTAL VINEYARD				**62,147**	**91.33**	**8.67**

Totals have been rounded up.

Viticulture

Here, as everywhere in the wine world, debate continues about vine density. Do you plant them wide and free and give every vine the maximum amount of space for nutrient and rainfall, or do you plant them close together to encourage the survival of the fittest, and green-harvest the underachievers in early August? The *reglamento* permits planting at a minimum of 2,850 vines per hectare and a maximum of 4,000, and a typical plantation might have vines in a rectangular pattern with a metre (3.28 feet) between vines and 2.8 metres (just over nine feet) between rows, which would give approximately 3,600 vines per hectare. However, older vineyards may have vines fairly randomly planted, and grapes destined for "high-expression" winemaking may be very old, low-yielding, and spaced in many different ways.

The important regulation is probably the maximum number of *yemas* (buds) per hectare, as it's the buds that will become the bunches. Where vines are trained *en vaso* (free-standing bush: what the French call *gobelet*; in both languages it means "wine glass") they may have a maximum of twelve buds per vine. Vines are pruned to three *brazos* (arms) with two renewal spurs, known as *sarmientos*, each bearing two bunches of grapes, so each vine will produce twelve bunches per vintage. Where they are trained on wires (*en cordón* or *espladera*), the same rules apply – unless they are pruned *vara y pulgar*, when only ten buds are allowed.

To explain *vara y pulgar*: clench your fist, then make a "thumbs-up" sign. Now extend your forefinger while keeping the other fingers clenched. Your thumb is now the *pulgar* (literally "thumb" in Spanish) and your forefinger is the *vara* ("stick"). The "thumb" is the shoot that will become next year's "stick". The "stick" has the five buds that will produce the five bunches of grapes. After the vintage, last year's "stick" will be cut off and the "thumb" tied down to become next year's "stick", with its earliest bud (*i.e.* the one nearest the main vine stem) next year's "thumb". Only Garnacha is excepted from this rule; regardless of how it is trained it may have fourteen buds (and subsequently fourteen bunches of grapes) per vine.

The maximum number of buds per hectare is 36,000, unless the vineyard is entirely Garnacha, in which case it's 42,000. Yields are maximized at 6,500 kilograms per hectare for red wines and 9,000 kilograms per hectare for whites (plus or minus twenty-five per cent, according to the quality of the year), and the *rendimiento* (the amount of must which may be pressed per kilo of grapes) is set at seventy to seventy-two per cent (variable according to the quality of the vintage). To explain what this means, we need to remind ourselves that a kilo of grapes can, if pressed hard enough, produce a litre of juice. If done so it would, of course, be thin stuff with lots of hard tannins from the pips and stalks. For this reason, every CRDO (*see* chapter four) sets a rendimiento level, which may be between sixty-five and seventy-five per cent. To calculate the final yield, multiply kilograms per hectare by the rendimiento and, in this case, that gives us 46.8 hectolitres per hectare for reds and 64.8

hectolitres per hectare for whites. The idea, of course, is that growers will weed out the poorer bunches in a green harvest to pick only the ripest, healthiest bunches at vintage time. That's the theory, anyway.

Rootstocks and vineyard problems are boring but important. Spain was one of the last countries to be affected by phylloxera in the nineteenth century, with Rioja falling victim in the 1890s (Jumilla didn't get it until the 1980s, thanks to surrounding sandy soils). Today, nearly all vines are grafted onto American roots, the most popular (according to soil type) being Rupestris de Lot, Richter-110, Richter-99, Millardet-41B, and Selection Oppenheim 4. Fungal diseases such as mildew and oïdium are a problem in wetter areas such as the Rioja Alta and Alavesa, with botrytis a problem, particularly, for Graciano; red spider mite is the main insect pest (its larvae suck the sap out of the vine leaves), and highland vineyards may suffer from frost and high winds in the winter and spring. This is a conversation-stopper at dinner parties.

6
The Wines

VINICULTURE AND THE CRIANZA SYSTEM

Many different styles of wine have been made in Rioja over the past centuries, and I have divided them into four sections: historic, classic, modern, and post-modern. The different styles and their histories (for more details, *see* chapters three and four) are described below. **NB** Every bodega in Rioja makes its wine in a slightly different way. What follows is a generalized view.

Historic Rioja

During the research for this book, I spent two extended periods in Logroño, during which I adopted a local cyber-café (the Cafetería Yimar in the Calle Chile, for the record; he's a bit glum but she is gorgeous) to keep in touch with the world outside. Being something of a victim of tortilla and *jamón serrano*, I ordered a *ración* of both and, taking the plunge, a glass of the house red, which cost sixty pence. When it arrived, it was bright purple, lip-smackingly fresh, exploding with fruit, and so gulpingly delicious that I bought a bottle (at over-the-bar prices) to smuggle back to my lodgings. It also took me back to a day, perhaps twenty years previously, when I'd done the same in a bar in Laguardia, in the Basque Country, during a trip in which we'd been treated royally and fêted with fine food and *reservas*. The freshness and fruit, the price (about ten pence in today's money) and the simple yet complete enjoyment was exactly the same. The following week, I made a detour to visit the tiny bodega of Perez Irazu (*see* chapter ten) where the *gerente* (manager), Samuel Rodolfo, told me proudly that he was carrying on the great tradition of young, fresh Tempranillo wines of the Basque Country. These are the "historic" wines of Rioja. I like to think that a reincarnated

Roman visiting the region might recognize them as similar to the wines which became so popular in Rome in the first century AD that Emperor Domitian (AD 81–96) ordered the destruction of the Spanish (and other) vineyards in AD 92 to protect the Italian wine industry. Fortunately, his instructions were ignored.

It is said that the Romans, who invaded in the second century BC, found the local inhabitants in what is now Rioja making wine in a primitive way, and introduced "new technology" in the form of properly excavated *lagares*: cisterns in which grapes could be trodden and fermented on the skins prior to running the wine out through a suitable plug-hole into clay amphorae or other appropriate containers (animal skins were very popular, as the local people ate the animals and then used their skins for the wine). One such cistern, a 75,000-litre example, survives at Funes, which is in what is now the province of Navarra, and has been dated from this period. The "technology" was very simple, and was what we now call the *semi-maceración carbonica* (carbonic maceration) or the "Beaujolais method". The fermenting grapes formed a cloud of carbon dioxide over the pulp, preventing oxidation. When the cloud cleared, the wine was run off, and presumably completed its malolactic fermentation in the skins/amphorae. It was almost certainly drunk straight away. This style of winemaking is still in use in parts of the Spanish countryside, where it is known as the *método rural*, or rural method. Although barrels have been around since about 350 BC, they were very expensive for what was considered an everyday wine as well as one that was rather unreliable. Certainly the price would have been beyond the reach of the Celtiberi tribes which inhabited northern Spain at that time.

The modern version is rather more high-tech. There are *maceración carbonica* (MC) wines made from whole bunches of grapes and de-stemmed versions made from individual berries, but they are now routinely fermented in stainless steel or fibreglass at low temperatures. The grapes go directly to the tank, which is sealed for MC and left open for de-stemmed grapes. MC wines ferment in the same tank, and are run off once alcoholic fermentation is complete. De-stemmed wine is run off as juice and fermented in a separate tank. In both cases, the grape pulp goes to the press, where the press-wine is extracted and run off into further tanks for fermentation. The press-wine is then added back in judicious quantities to balance the tannins in the free-run wine before bottling. The wines may be on the market before Christmas, but certainly by Easter of the following year.

Most *cosecheros* (grape-growers) make at least some wine for themselves, if only for domestic use. Those who are members of the Consejo Regulador de la Denominación de Origen Calificada or the Organización Interprofesional del Vino de Rioja (CRDOCa/OIPVR) may also sell it with a Rioja *contraetiqueta* (back label). Those who are not members but are registered with a major bodega or cooperative (which will be a member of the CRDOCa/OIPVR) may only sell their own wine as *vino de mesa* with a *cosechero* back label. It is not classified as DOCa Rioja, but it is very popular, very cheap, and very cheerful. Indeed, some *cosechero* wines go to *crianza* and *reserva* level, although, strictly speaking, the terms should not be used on *vino de mesa*. One big change came in 1989, when the criteria for becoming a bodega *de crianza* were relaxed. Previously a producer had to have at least 500 casks and a production of 2,250 hectolitres before it could use the terms *crianza*, *reserva*, and *gran reserva*. This was repealed in 1989, giving many small firms (especially in the Basque Country) the opportunity to switch from selling grapes to making wine.

Classic Rioja

These are the wines most of the world thinks of when you say the name "Rioja". Classic, ripe Tempranillo fruit; toasty oak; structured and ready to drink relatively young, but the best of them able to keep for many years. American oak (brought in cheaply from the Spanish colonies) was the key to early developments, even though the first of the new generation of barrels came from Bordeaux.

As described in chapter three (*see* pages 14–15), one early pioneer in 1780 was Manuel Quintano y Quintano, a priest from Labastida with an interest in wine. He visited Bordeaux and saw what was then, by Riojano standards, high-technology winemaking, and he replicated it with his brother in the family bodega. He imported good, well-coopered French barrels which did not need pitch or some other interior coating to make them watertight. He proved his point by shipping a large consignment to a customer in Cuba which arrived in, if anything, better condition than when it had departed. His neighbours, however, were horrified by the thought of having to buy fabulously expensive barrels, and the regulatory body at the time wouldn't allow him to charge more for his wine than his neighbours were charging for theirs, so the project foundered on infrastructure costs.

It was to be more than fifty years before the next step forward. Luciano de Murrieta y García Lemoine was born in Peru and was not at all intimidated by the local regulatory authorities. He worked in banking in London, where he struck up an acquaintance with the Duque de Vitoria (they were both in political exile). He quit banking and went to study winemaking in Bordeaux, eventually returning to Logroño around 1850. His friend the duke offered Murrieta the use of a bodega he owned in the region, and the first vintage of what we may call "classic" Rioja was made by the latter in 1852 in 1,000-litre Bordeaux oak casks. Later that same decade, the Marqués de Riscal created the first purpose-built bodega for the "new-style" wines and, although there were quite a few molehills still to come along the way, classic Rioja was born.

The 1,000-litre barrels evolved into large oak vats, which evolved into concrete tanks lined with epoxy resin, which evolved into fibreglass tanks with cold-water cooling, which evolved into stainless-steel with "water jackets": double-skinned walls through which cold water could be passed to keep fermentation temperatures down to a manageable level.

The new-style wines were dubbed *método industrial* in comparison with the *método rural* wines described above (*see* "Historic Rioja"), because they could be made in large quantities in much more controlled conditions and, indeed, fetched a higher price: something that tends to concentrate the minds of competitors very effectively. A typical modern "classic" bodega will make its red wines something like the following.

Bodegas which buy in large quantities of grapes take trailer-loads into the *tolvas* (hoppers) at vintage, which are sorted by sugar content assessed by a sampler on the weighbridge. Other bodegas, especially those which own their own vineyards, may harvest into small plastic trays holding fourteen to eighteen kilograms (thirty-one to forty pounds) of grapes, which will then go to a sorting table. This is a white, well-lit, moving belt where bunches are examined and accepted or rejected according to the quality of the grapes. This has been used in other parts of the world, but was pioneered in Rioja in 1995 by Marqués de Riscal, which instructed the sorters to select "only bunches which you would be happy to eat". In some cases the rejected bunches are made into wine which is sold off; in others, they are vinified separately and used judiciously in the final blend.

In either case, the grapes go straight to the tanks, which are likely to be of stainless steel, although many bodegas still maintain the oak vats (notably Muga and Remelluri); concrete tanks are even making a modest comeback. Stainless steel, however, affords the winemaker pin-sharp control over temperature (and thereby speed) of fermentation, and the most forward-looking bodegas are likely to have *autoevacuaciones* (self-emptiers): steel tanks shaped like flying saucers with a lid on the top and bottom. The grapes pass by gravity from the de-stalker into the top of the tank, ferment inside it, and, once fermentation is complete and the new wine is run off through a valve into a holding tank, the "flying saucer" is hoisted by a mobile crane over the press, and the lower "lid" is opened to allow the pulp to fall into the press. In this way the wine doesn't ever have to be pumped from tank to tank, which avoids bruising the grapes. The pulp is then pressed and fermented as normal to provide the press-wine. The winemaker then selects the *cuvée*, blending free-run and press-wine to get the mix of fruit and tannins s/he wants, depending on whether the wine is destined to become *joven, corta-crianza, crianza, reserva* or *gran reserva* (*see* "The crianza system", pages 46–8).

For white wines, the grapes go directly to the press (which is likely to be pneumatic) and may spend some time in maceration, especially if the winemaker wants to use the natural yeasts that are present on the grape skins, and to extract some of the primary grape flavours. After pressing, the must is run off into tanks for fermentation.

Rosado (rosé) wines may be made from a blend of red and white wines after fermentation, or (more usually) from red grapes macerated for several hours on the skins before being run off and fermented in the same way as white wines.

Modern Rioja

This is made essentially in the same way as classic Rioja, but was a reaction against the heavily oaky styles which had evolved since Murrieta and Riscal launched "Bordeaux-style" wines in the 1850s. The leading proponent was Enrique Forner of Marqués de Cáceres, whose family heritage included ownership of Bordeaux châteaux. He returned to his native Rioja and established a new "château-style" bodega in the village of Cenicero, including the region's first full-scale stainless-steel fermenting hall, where he vowed to make Rioja with minimal oak and maximum fruit. Many producers have since followed suit, but the difference tends to be in the ageing methods (*see* pages 46–8) rather than the vinification. The "squeaky-clean" school of white Rioja made from pure Viura at low temperatures in stainless steel was one of the first manifestations of this style.

Post-modern Rioja

This is a made-up term to describe the "new-wave" wines which are currently being made in the region. I use the term "post-modern" because so many of the techniques, in vineyard and winery, are actually reinventions of traditional techniques. The following are some of them.

VINEYARD MANAGEMENT

Hands-on, vine-by-vine husbandry; canopy management to prune away overhanging leaves in the last stages of the ripening period; green harvesting; hand-selection of bunches; driving down of yields.

TABLE-SORTING

Rigorous selection of grapes (which have already been selected in the vineyard), with ruthless rejection of anything substandard. Some producers (*e.g.* Remírez de Ganuza) even cut the bunches in half because the top half has higher ripeness levels than the pointy bit at the bottom. Others (*e.g.* Benjamín Romeo) actually perform a *Beerenauslese* and select the individual ripest grapes from the bunches.

MACERATION

Winemakers tend to want high extraction and may leave the fermenting wine of super-ripe grapes on the skins for anything up to thirty days to get enormous structure and tannins.

BARREL-FERMENTATION

For white wines and red, and sometimes for red wines undergoing malolactic fermentation. There are many fewer white wines in this category than red, but old plantations of Garnacha Blanca come into their own with these methods.

The result of these methods is red wines of tremendous extraction, structure, and, usually, alcoholic strength (up to fifteen per cent alcohol by volume). Not everyone is happy with this style of winemaking. I recall in 2000 visiting Bodegas Roda in Haro with a group of journalists attending the biennial tasting of Los Grandes de la Rioja. Among the party was an old friend and colleague and someone who knows Rioja much better than I, Jeremy Watson. He tasted the wines and shook his head. "These are magnificent wines," he said, "but they're not Rioja." I wonder if that's what they said to Manuel Quintano in 1795 and Luciano de Murrieta in 1852.

Many winemakers of classic styles also view the new-wave *alta expresión* (high-expression) wines with suspicion. They are occasionally denounced as "obvious", "over-extracted", and, the ultimate insult, apparently: "catwalk wines". Their makers defend them as the ultimate expression of terroir, microclimate, and winemaking. Indeed, most of the classic bodegas now produce a *tête-de-cuvée* wine, perhaps made from their best old plots and typically aged in new French oak, which comes perilously close to the new-wave style. One slight worry is that some bodegas may be making a new, high-expression wine from their small stock of old-vine grapes, which would formerly have gone into the mainstream wines, thereby improving quality across the board.

My own view, however, is that I'm delighted to see such a range of different, diverse, and fascinating styles emanating from a single region without recourse to the endless, anonymous "international varieties" which now, sadly, dominate so many Spanish DO regions. It will be fascinating to see how these wines develop as they approach maturity. The oldest of them were made only around 1997, so it remains to be seen whether they will age with the grace and elegance of the classic wines of 1982, 1964, and 1958.

The crianza system

To simplify the examples below, I have taken an imaginary 2000 vintage base-wine, because it was one year old in 2001, two years old in 2002, etc. The word *crianza* translates literally as "breeding" or "upbringing", and is used as a generic term to describe Spain's ageing regulations as well as specifically to describe *crianza* wines (*see* below). Spain's national wine laws changed slightly in 2003, but the CRDOCa announced no changes to the *reglamento* in Rioja. Every bottle carries a *contraetiqueta* to certify its origins, and this will say *cosecha*, *crianza*, *reserva*, or *gran reserva*. The terms are explained below, and *cosecha* can be particularly ambiguous. Legal terms are preceded by *; the rest are unofficial. The ageing year in Rioja is always calculated from October 1 in the year of the vintage, and it's worth bearing in mind that quality *reservas* and *gran reservas* are very likely to exceed the minimum ageing requirements laid down by the law.

JOVEN

The word simply means "young" and this covers a multitude of styles. By law, wine called *crianza* must spend a minimum of twelve months in oak casks (overwhelmingly *barricas* of 225 litres), so if a winemaker feels that his wine has had enough oak after, say, eight months, and decides to bottle it, he cannot use the term *crianza*. All "historic" Rioja is *joven*, and most "classic" bodegas will make one as well, often with no oak at all. Our 2000 vintage could have been on sale by Christmas 2000, but is usually released in the spring of the year following the vintage – in this case 2001. *Contraetiqueta:* Cosecha 2000.

CORTA-CRIANZA

This is not an official term and may not appear on labels, but it is used by some bodegas to indicate that the wine has spent at least some time in oak, but less than the minimum required for *crianza* (*i.e.* twelve months). One of the pioneers of the style was Bodegas Palacio, which released Cosme Palacio with about three months in oak for the whites and six or seven for reds in the 1990s. *Contraetiqueta:* Cosecha 2000.

GENERICO

Another unofficial term that is not permitted on labels and is likely to be found on wines of two types. Modern Rioja winemakers use it because they feel that the traditional epithets (*crianza*, etc.) make their wine sound old-fashioned. They want the wines to stand on their own merits rather than be associated with ancient oaky styles. In addition, "new-wave" wines use it almost exclusively, even if they have been in oak for thirty months and could genuinely claim to be *gran reserva*. *Contraetiqueta:* Cosecha 2000.

*CRIANZA

Red wines must spend a minimum of twelve months in oak casks and a further twelve in the bodega, typically in bottle, although some may spend a "resting" period in the tank before bottling. They may be released after two calendar years: *i.e.* on October 1, 2002. *Contraetiqueta:* Crianza 2000.

White and *rosado* wines must spend a minimum of six months in oak and six in bottle, and may be released after one calendar year: *i.e.* on October 1, 2001.

*RESERVA

Red wines must spend a minimum of three calendar years in the bodega, of which twelve months must be in oak casks. So our theoretical 2000 vintage may be released on October 1, 2003. *Contraetiqueta:* Reserva 2000.

White and rosado wines must spend at least two calendar years in the bodega, with at least six months in oak, and our vintage 2000 may be released on the October, 1, 2002. *Contraetiqueta:* Cosecha 2000.

RESERVA ESPECIAL

An unofficial term permitted on labels which denotes wines made from selected grapes or individual plots to a higher quality level than the mainstream *reserva*. They tend to be wines which are made from grapes on the cusp of *reserva/gran reserva* quality, made by bodegas which would rather produce a top-end *reserva* than a borderline *gran reserva*. *Contraetiqueta:* Reserva 2000.

*GRAN RESERVA

The greatest of the "classic" wines of Rioja, and they must send a minimum of twenty-four months in the cask and thirty-six months in the bottle, which means they can be released after five years: *i.e.* on October 1, 2005. In practice, wine good enough for gran reserva is likely to spend much longer than this in the bodega before release. *Contraetiqueta:* Gran Reserva 2000.

White and *rosado* wines must spend at least four years in the bodega, of which at least six months must be in cask, so our putative 2000 vintage could be released on October 1, 2004.

White *gran reservas* are not commonplace, but a few bodegas (most notably López-Heredia Viña Tondonia and Marqués de Murrieta) turn out some very fine examples. *Rosado gran reservas* are even rarer; I have only ever once encountered one: a *rosado* from Berberana which was found, bottled but unlabelled, bricked up in a forgotten cellar, and rediscovered in about 1980, when I was still in the wine trade. No one knew what the vintage was, but the building work had been carried out in the mid-1960s and the oldest labels they still had in stock were 1966, so they labelled it 1966 *gran reserva* and we sold the lot at a bargain price. I doubt whether anybody is making wines like that today.

7
The Way Ahead

REGULATION

Rioja appointed Spain's first Consejo Regulador de la Denominación de Origen (CRDO) in 1926, and it changed its name to CRDOCa when Rioja became a DO *calificada* (DOCa) in 1991. For all of that period it fulfilled what has become the role of all other CRDOs, which is to enforce the *reglamento* (code of regulations), decide on matters of policy relating to everything from grape varieties grown to yields at harvest time, and to promote the wines nationally and internationally. Inevitably this brought the CRDOCa into confrontation with some growers and producers from time to time, when producers wanted to experiment with different styles of wine, vines, methods, and even pruning and training. As a result, and in the light of changes to the national Spanish wine law made in June 2003, the regional government passed a law on March 26, 2004, paving the way for the creation of a new supervisory body to be called the Organización Interprofesional del Vino de Rioja (OIPVR: the Interprofessional Organization of the Wines of Rioja). This was the first of its kind in Spain, and the CRDOCa became the subdivision of the OIPVR just five days later on April 1, 2004.

To understand the momentous changes of the spring of 2004 in Rioja, we need to understand the way agricultural law is made in Spain. The constitution of 1978, which created the constitutional monarchy that is Spain today, recreated some of the original administrative diversity of the country before Franco, with seventeen autonomous communities (*comunidades autónomas* or simply *autonomías*) roughly matching the cultures and peoples who made up the original Spain, some going all the way back to 1492. Each of the *autonomías* has total responsibility for local legislation on local matters, and that includes agriculture – which, in turn, includes wine and the regulation of wine.

Rioja is one of only seven *autonomías* that consist of a single province, and it has a population of about 270,000 people, half of whom live in the regional capital, Logroño. This means that the Gobierno de la Rioja (regional parliament) is very much closer to its voters than those of the larger regions, and that political pressure on members of the government can be much more focused when interested parties want to get changes made. On the face of it, the new OIPVR is much more democratic and even-handed than the old CRDOCa, giving 100 votes to the *cosecheros* (growers) and 100 to the bodegas. The voting system is, however, a kind of "electoral college" based on hectares of vines for growers and litres of production for bodegas. This is how it works:

GROWERS
Nine syndicates, sixteen members, 100 votes. The biggest growers' syndicate is the Federación de Cooperativas Agrarias de la Rioja (Federation of Cooperatives of Rioja) or FeCoAR, which represents the co-ops and has thirty-seven votes and five members on the committee of the OIPVR.

BODEGAS
Six syndicates, sixteen members, 100 votes. The biggest bodega syndicate is the Asociación de Empresas Vinícolas de la Zona de Rioja or AEVZR (better known as the Rioja Wine Exporters' Group), which represents many of the major bodegas and has fifty-nine votes and eight members of the committee of the OIPVR, including its inaugural (two-year-term) president, Victor Pascual Artacho, who is vice-president of Bodegas AGE, which belongs to Spain's biggest wine group, Bodegas y Bebidas, since 2001 a fiefdom of multinational Allied Domecq.

There are, in addition, independent bodegas which belong to none of the syndicates and prefer to plough their own furrow in their own way within the *reglamento*. They have no vote within the OIPVR unless, at some future time, they decide to join one of the existing syndicates, or join with other bodegas to create one of their own. Changes in policy must achieve a seventy-five per cent majority vote with a minimum fifty per cent from either side (*i.e.* growers and bodegas).

What's the difference? Well, as you can see, the two biggest syndicates have so many votes (ninety-six out of 200) that between them they can now probably influence changes in a way that would have been impossible under the old regime of the CRDOCa. But what has changed on the ground? The biggest alteration is that, while the CRDOCa will still be the "police force" of Rioja, it will no longer make policy about future developments. This will be the remit of the OIPVR – and here is where the perceived danger lies.

The way it was

The CRDOCa believed (quite correctly) that Rioja is the leading region of Spain for the production of quality wine, with forty per cent of the domestic market; the only wines bigger in export terms are cava and sherry – completely different markets. Nationally, it felt that "everyone in Spain returns to Rioja" at some point. The export market, however, is an entirely different matter and the "New World" is a real challenge, but Rioja's great strength is its perceived quality, value, and, above all, consistency, which make it a reliable buy for the consumer.

Outgoing president Ángel Jaime believed that the discipline of the DOCa was a positive factor in maintaining quality, and that consumers know what they're getting when they buy Rioja, which is not necessarily the case with other DOs. The regulation "keeps the faith" and also keeps things on a commercial footing. The CRDOCa made changes to the *reglamento* on an "evolutionary" basis, believing that constant changes only cause confusion in the long run. It did, however, approve the "new-wave" bodegas and "high-expression" wines, but also believed that the market for "classic" wines (*i.e.* wines made from grapes sourced from right across the region) was still the most important in commercial terms. Fashion is fickle, and while new developments must be investigated, it's important to retain what has been tried and tested in the past. Rioja, while it is now in a permanent state of change – as any wine region has to be to survive – must not forget its roots. The region has a large proportion of old-vine plantations (the average age of the vineyard is approximately twenty years), and it's important that Rioja fills all the corners: accessible and affordable everyday wines, the great classics, and the new single-vineyard and high-expression wines all form part of the matrix.

There was no change to the *reglamento* as a result of the new Spanish wine laws of 2003, and future changes, if any, will now be the remit of the OIPVR. There has been talk for many years of creating a *vino de la tierra*,

Alto Ebro, to encompass Aragón, La Rioja, and Navarra, but there has been little enthusiasm outside of Aragón, and the general feeling has been that it would only cause confusion and dilute the image of Rioja wines, which has been hard-won and is heavily maintained. "Quality, originality, and communication," said Jaime, are the watchwords of the *consejo regulador*, with the heaviest accent on communication: "Maintain the quality, insist on the originality, then, above all, communicate those things to the outside world."

Styles of wine

What about the different styles of Rioja? The *consejo* was very happy with the diversity of styles that is modern Rioja. Traditional Rioja is, of course, a mix of grapes, perhaps Tempranillo from the cool Alavesa, Graciano and Mazuelo from the Rioja Alta, and hot, spicy Garnacha from the Rioja Baja. For the better part of two centuries the region has hedged its bets with the regional mix, burnished in oak casks and only released when it's ready to drink, and this has been its unique sales point throughout. But, of course, Rioja has always changed: Manuel Quintano in the 1780s, Napoléon in the 1800s, Murrieta and Riscal in the 1850s, phylloxera in the 1890s, the *consejo regulador* in the 1920s, Enrique Forner in the 1970s, and a whole generation of "young Turk" winemakers from the 1990s onwards have all led the region in new directions. Its strength has been that Rioja can still be the original, fruit-bursting, lip-smacking wine that might be recognized by a ghostly returning Roman, and the ancient, dreaming, strawberry-and-vanilla-scented wine of the ex-Bordeaux pioneers, as well as wine from single estates such as Remelluri and Valpiedra, and single-vineyard wines such as Contino's Viña del Olivo and Murrieta's Capellanía. Then there are the high-expression, blockbusting "new-wave" wines from such as Allende, Roda, Sierra Cantabria, Viña Izadi, *et al.*, as well as everything in between. Rioja in the twenty-first century can be classic (from all over the region), sub-zonal (*i.e.* Rioja Alavesa, Rioja Alta), *finca* (single-estate), or *pago* (single-vineyard). If and when any new DO *pagos* are created, they will be welcomed by the *consejo regulador*. As long as quality is the watchword, Rioja is big enough to recognize good new ideas and welcome them…

Except in some respects. One "no-go" area for the CRDOCa was what are delicately referred to as "new varieties", for which read "old varieties".

Both Murrieta and Riscal planted Bordeaux varieties in Rioja in the 1850s, at a time when the Tempranillo barely had a name to call its own. In time, they both discovered that the Tempranillo had simply been the victim of primitive winemaking and that it had good qualities if handled properly (an almost-epitaph now for many varieties that were formerly despised, although too many to list here). Murrieta passed through a number of owners before the Cebrian family bought it in 1982, by which time Tempranillo was in the ascendant. Riscal, however, is still in the hands of the founding family and still has plantations of old Cabernet Sauvignon.

Perhaps this is the moment for a little author archaeology. In 1989, I was part of a group of journalists invited to Haro for a large-scale tasting of *reservas* and *gran reservas*, plus bodega visits in the interim. One of these was a visit to Riscal, where we were hosted by José-María Muguiro Aznar, a member of the extended family that owns the bodega. One of the other visitors was the late and lamented-by-many Tony Lord, founder and then editor of *Decanter* magazine. José-María announced that they had a plantation of old-vine Cabernet Sauvignon and that they were planning to make a Cabernet-heavy premium wine for launch in the early 1990s. "Lordy" was contemptuous: "They'll never let you do it!" he insisted. José-María shrugged, and pointed out that their plantation of Cabernet Sauvignon dates back to 1856, while the *consejo regulador* only dates back to 1926 – some seventy years later. The resultant wine was Barón de Chirél, which has done good business at the box office ever since, even at about £30 a bottle at UK prices.

The get-out clause for all of this, of course, is the awarding of "experimental" status. You have to have some sympathy for the *consejo regulador*, which doesn't want Rioja to "do a Navarra" and become an anonymous region making wines from every imaginable grape with little or no public image.

History: for decades Navarra was seen as "sub-Rioja", making similar wines but at lower prices, as well as *rosados* which did well on the local market but not much elsewhere. The CRDO Navarra fought back by experimenting with other varieties, rootstocks, winemaking, and ageing methods, and, in one sense, succeeded brilliantly. Today's Navarra wines are diverse, with maximum flexibility for bodegas and the opportunity to express the individuality of the bodega through every different aspect of variety, viticulture, and winemaking. There are wines made from the same grapes as are grown in Rioja, but also everything from Pinot Noir to Gewürztraminer, and there are some wonderful examples of creative modern winemaking. The downside seems to be this: people go into a shop and if they see a bottle of Rioja they think "strawberry and vanilla" (Tempranillo and oak); if they see a bottle of Navarra they think at best "What's that?", at worst "Chardonnay? Oh no, this bottle next to it is the same wine from Hungary and it's half the price. I'll buy that." In other words, Rioja has a perceived nature and identity, whereas Navarra does not.

So, back to "experimental" status. There are a number of vineyards with this licence and they're likely to be growing the ubiquitous Cabernet Sauvignon, Merlot, and possibly Syrah, but not Chardonnay, which is absolutely forbidden. Which means that the odd hectares of Chardonnay that are being grown (and I've seen them) do not exist. And, indeed, I would and will side wholeheartedly with the *consejo regulador* to banish this grape from Rioja. In Burgundy, it makes wines of the most exact expression on mineral soils close to the northern margin of cultivation (for still wines). In Chile and California, it makes decent, characterful wines at high altitudes, and even in Australia there are individual wines which, while lacking much in the way of individuality, have a certain bullish charm. In Spain, there are good Chardonnay wines, but for every Miguel Torres and Enate there are a dozen bland, overblown, stateless, "prairie wine" Chardonnays which have little or no national or regional character.

Cabernet Sauvignon is a slightly different matter, as it has been planted in Rioja (and other parts of Spain) for more than 150 years. The *consejo regulador* considers that the benefits it brings to the blend are duplicated by the Graciano, which is a local variety and can (and does) do the job as well or better; indeed, many of Rioja's high-expression wines have an admixture of Graciano precisely because it adds weight, structure, and aromatics to the blend. The problem seems to be that Graciano is a low-cropping variety, very susceptible to botrytis, which needs maturity in the vine to give of its best, while the Cabernet Sauvignon crops younger, and more heavily when mature. That said, most of the winemakers to whom I spoke did seem to share the view that, except in cases where the grape is planted historically (such as Riscal) or in classified experimental vineyards (such as Dominio de Susar), it should not be introduced as a generally permitted variety. In the words of one winemaker: "A region such as Rioja does not need to become the producer of just another Cabernet Sauvignon. We can do better than that."

There is some small amount of Merlot and Syrah in Rioja, and one or two (particularly younger) winemakers expressed an interest in Merlot, as a "top-up" variety for wines made almost entirely from Tempranillo from the higher vineyards, to add some weight and longevity without the flavour-shift which Cabernet, even in relatively small quantities, can give. Once again the *consejo regulador* would direct them to the Graciano, which has all the same qualities as well as long-time adaptation to the soil and climate of Rioja... *if* they can find it.

A footnote on Graciano: one of the new-wave houses held a tasting in London in 2002, and the winemaker described Graciano as "a virtual grape". In other words, it hardly exists outside a few scattered plantations that are jealously guarded by the people who own them, and is rationed out to the highest bidder at harvest time. I found this difficult to understand, since several bodegas produce (albeit modest quantities of) varietal Gracianos, and the high-expression wines, particularly in the Alavesa, seem to manage to find five to ten per cent to add to their finest Tempranillos. Perhaps what he really meant was that he wanted to make wine only from his own vineyards and had not been able to buy any plots of Graciano.

Other grapes the *consejo regulador* wants to encourage might also be described loosely as "virtual": Maturana, Tempranillo Peludo, Maturana Blanco, Tempranillo Blanco, and Garnacha Blanca. The Maturana is an historic variety that is still grown in very small quantities and, indeed, at least one bodega (Viña Ijalba) has produced a varietal from it which shows well enough and does have an unmistakable Riojano character. Tempranillo Peludo ("hairy Tempranillo") is a sport of the mainstream vine (it's the leaves that are hairy, of course – not the grape, which would otherwise look like a gooseberry), with smaller berries and a higher ratio of concentration: more skin per gram of pulp and smaller bunches (typically 750 grams – just over one and a half pounds – rather than the normal one kilogram or 2.2 pounds). Again, growing this grape sacrifices quantity for quality, which is a hard decision to take for many producers.

Maturana Blanca and Tempranillo Blanco are both mutations of the black original and, outside of the nursery, are seldom seen. Garnacha Blanca is doing excellent work in old plantations, particularly in Priorato, but there is very little in Rioja, and it would seem likely that there will need to be a lot of development work before any practicable vineyard clones can be widely planted successfully. Meanwhile, of course, the French varieties are here now, tried and tested, with their characteristics mapped out over many vintages. It is hardly surprising that some winemakers look hungrily at them – or that the *consejo regulador* has been determined to keep them out.

The future for white wines

No one attempts to deny that white wines are secondary in importance to Rioja's main business, which is turning out Spain's flagship red wine; indeed, white grapes and wines command a commensurately lower price on the market. Even so, there are some die-hard enthusiasts and there is some very interesting work being done with white wines, particularly those made from Garnacha Blanca and Malvasía Riojana. Production is, however, declining, and there are those who say that Spanish white wines should be left to those areas that specialize in them. It is perhaps not a coincidence that one of Rioja's premier bodegas, Marqués de Riscal, chose to make its white wine in Rueda. On the other hand, the top white wine in one of the many tastings which preceded this book was Viña Tondonia 1987: a *reserva* wine from one of Rioja's most traditional bodegas, López Heredia. Recent highlights have included "terroir-friendly" wines such as Organza from Sierra Cantabria and Fernández de Piérola, as well as high-expression Viura wines from producers such as Muga and Cosmé Palacio, in addition to the old classics like Murrieta – so white Rioja is still very much alive and kicking, even if its profile is not as high as it might be.

Perhaps this is the moment for a little more author-archaeology. In 1972, when I was first in the wine trade working for a single-outlet independent shipper and merchant in Nottingham, we had a bottle of Marqués de Murrieta Blanco Reserva returned by a restaurant customer because, thanks to the attentions of an inept sommelier (for which read "moonlighting, impoverished university student"), the cork had snapped in two. There was nothing wrong with the wine, of course, but we couldn't sell it, so I took it upon myself to institute a staff training session and tasted the wine. It was so good that I sent the cellar-boy across the road to the chip shop for two deep-fried haddock and we consumed fish and wine in a style of which Jesus and his disciples would have been proud.

When the boss returned from his three-hour lunch (yes, it was *that* long ago in the wine trade…), I told him that we had successfully educated the staff about *crianza* white Rioja. Far from being pleased, he was adamant that not one of us was ever to recommend that style of wine to a customer without referring to him first. "Very few people understand that type of wine," he said – and it seems that this is still the case. Pity.

Yields

The 2000 vintage went down in history as the biggest-ever (3,108,000 hectolitres: just over 820 million bottles) and one of the least interesting for most producers (though not those who green-harvested in July and August), with vast quantities of indifferent *joven* wine and massive declassification by the CRDOCa which, after the event, still left a large quantity of thin, pink/red gruel on the market at rock-bottom prices and quality. One very well-respected company in particular used one of its anonymous *sous-marque* brand names to put a *joven* red on the UK market at £2.99 retail (which represents about fifty pence ex-cellars), and I bought a case out of curiosity. I returned ten bottles to the retailer for a refund (I only opened the second bottle in disbelief at the poverty of quality in the first), and the branch manager agreed with me that he, too, had thought it the worst travesty of Rioja he had ever encountered. Unfortunately, however, the wine writer of a national broadsheet had liked the wine and recommended it wholeheartedly, and the stuff was flying out in pallet-loads as a result. In desperation, I rang the producer (traced through the bottling serial-number on the label) and asked what they thought they were doing by putting a wine at this quality level on the market. They rang back to say that they had tasted it in the office and felt that it "was all right for the price". Well, that's all very well, but what did it do for the reputation of Rioja wine generally? How many people bought it because of the price and then vowed never to buy Rioja again?

Ángel de Jaime defended the levels permitted, as well as the CRDOCa's power to raise or lower them according to the needs of the particular vintage. For red wines, the limit is 6,500 kilograms per hectare, which, at a *rendimiento* (yield) of seventy per cent, represents 45.5 hectolitres per hectare: the second-lowest in Spain (only Priorato is lower at 6,000 kilograms per hectare) and lower than generic Bordeaux and Burgundy. They are able to vary the yield according to the nature of the year by plus or minus twenty-five per cent; for example, the 2003 vintage was set at 118 per cent of base yield, although it must be understood that this is purely in terms of production (*i.e.* kilograms per hectare) and not *rendimiento*, which is the amount of juice that may be extracted per kilo of grapes.

Fraud

Everybody, inside and outside the trade, has heard the stories: truckloads of Tempranillo grapes/must/wine travel by night from obscure areas of Spain to Rioja where they are clandestinely unloaded at unnamed bodegas and then mysteriously become Rioja. Indeed, these types of stories surface on a regular basis about every major wine region.

A little historical context: in my early days in the wine trade in the 1970s there was a received wisdom that the biggest vineyard in Burgundy was Beaune railway station, where, it was said, tankers of anonymous wine would arrive by night, etc. etc. No one had actually seen or been involved in these nefarious activities, but people knew someone who knew someone who had. This story was emphatically trumped by that of a 100,000-tonne tanker containing wine from Rioja (presumably loaded at the seagoing port of Logroño) which docked in Bordeaux harbour in 1972 and exchanged its documentation at the customs office for *acquits verts* (literally "green permits"), reclassifying the wine as appellation Bordeaux, after which the ship sailed for America to unload generic Bordeaux at quintuple the original price. The man who told me this swore it was true. A friend of a friend of his had seen it with his own eyes.

In a Rioja context, Ángel de Jaime brushed off the accusation that non-Rioja grape is routinely made into wine with the *contraetiqueta* Rioja. "Every year," he says, "some grower in, say, La Mancha, will go to the bar in the evening and tell everyone who will listen that he has just sold a vast consignment of grapes or must or wine to a big company in La Rioja. He is probably telling the truth. The business infrastructure in this region is heavily geared towards wine, and there are dozens of bodegas bottling *vino de mesa* for the mass market – some 100 million litres per year in total – which happen to be in the province of La Rioja. They are perfectly entitled to buy grapes, must or wine anywhere in Spain and process and sell it as VdM, under their own or customers' own labels."

How can we be sure? According to Ángel de Jaime, "Vineyards are inspected, vines counted, and yields calculated and predicted on a rolling basis. At vintage time, inspectors from the CRDOCa visit bodegas and, in the case of larger producers, sit in the weighbridge offices with the bodega's own staff, noting down the quantity of grapes which has come in, the growers who have delivered, varieties, ripeness levels, and any other data which are available on the day. We also have historical data from the bodegas showing the levels of production which have been achieved in the past, and we check these against current production. We do not claim to be infallible, but we do believe that we are credible in our validation."

Theoretically, it could be very profitable to buy La Mancha or Madrid or Méntrida Tempranillo at, say, twenty-five pence per kilo and pass it off as Rioja, but if a bodega is committed to the purchase or production of a certain amount of grapes at Rioja prices, what benefit is there in padding it out with cheaper grapes? What do you then do with the genuine article for which you've paid full price? If you make more wine, then you'll have to prove to the CRDOCa where it came from, or it won't get the *contraetiquetas*.

The way it is

It's much too early to pronounce on the effect that the OIPVR will have on the future of Rioja regulation, but the big break with the past will be this policy business. Critics of the CRDOCa had always complained that it was too strait-laced and inflexible in matters of the development of the region, and that it was staffed by "jobs-worth" civil servants who had little point of contact with the market, nationally and internationally, and a slavish devotion to the letter of the *reglamento*. Be this as it may, the CRDOCa did maintain the integrity of Rioja's reputation for seventy-eight years, and very effectively, too. The OIPVR is undoubtedly commercially oriented, but it remains to be seen whether this will be for the long-term benefit of the wine.

On the morning of the last-ever meeting of the CRDOCa in its original format (March 31, 2004), I was at Bodegas Domecq in Elciego interviewing its director, Javier Elizalde. He had to leave early to get to the meeting and I asked him what was likely to be on the agenda when the OIPVR met for the first time. His opinion was that one of the most prominent items would be extending the range of grape varieties for white Rioja, with such as Verdejo a possibility for addition to the current canon. And? You guessed it: Sauvignon Blanc, Chardonnay...What next?

The Cabernet–Merlot–Syrah lobby would obviously like to pursue these options, and there is a case to be made for one or more of them to be used as "top-up" varieties in areas where it's difficult or impossible to ripen Graciano. The danger is that some winemakers might be drawn into the temptation to give the world yet another Cabernet Sauvignon or Merlot, which is very thin ice for a traditional region such as this. During the 2004 Grandes de la Rioja event, I was interviewed by the regional newspaper, *Diario de Rioja*, and I expressed these fears. They printed the interview practically word for word, under the heading "There are millions of Cabernet Sauvignons, but there is only one Rioja". Rioja has worked extremely hard to establish itself as a world-class wine with individuality, diversity, and quality. It is Spain's biggest export red DO wine; on the home market it has thirty-two per cent of the off-trade and forty-five per cent of the on-trade. That is, presumably, because people like it, can afford it, and buy it repeatedly. They tinker with Rioja at their peril.

The OIPVR may, indeed, be more democratic than the old CRDOCa, but I leave this subject with a comment from the director of a small, high-quality bodega who was musing on the fact that the number of votes depends on the area of vineyard for growers, and the amount of production for bodegas. "It's democracy," he said, "but it's democracy by the litre."

8

Opinion

WHAT THE BODEGAS THINK

In order to avoid asking every bodega the same twenty questions about their installations, I sent round a questionnaire, and many (though not all) of them filled it in. While I was at it, I thought it would be a good idea to get another "snapshot" of modern Rioja: what the bodegas think about the current state of the wine market at home and abroad, the prospects, the threats from the New World or other European producing countries, and the way they think that the industry should be conducting itself in the future. The following is a digest of the replies I received. It is by no means a scientific survey or an opinion poll, just rumblings from people actively involved at the sharp end of wine production, promotion, and sale in Rioja.

What has been the biggest threat to the success of Rioja wine over the past twenty years?

Several issues were raised here, but the top three were bureaucracy and inflexibility under the old Consejo Regulador Denominación de Origen Calificada (CRDOCa), the fluctuation in grape (and therefore wine) prices in recent years, and industrial bodegas turning out bog-standard *joven* wines at rock-bottom prices for the supermarket trade which do nothing for the reputation of Rioja.

ON BUREAUCRACY:

"Bureaucracy and regulation: not only from the CRDOCa but local and national government which, all too often, make decisions to keep themselves in power politically rather than for the benefit of Rioja."

"Rigidity of direction, failure to preserve quality levels and failure to promote."
"Failure to investigate wines coming in from outside the region, lack of innovation in winemaking."
"The increase in production per hectare and failure to authorize new varieties of grapes."

ON COMPLACENCY:
"Many [threats], from the monopoly of the large wine cellars and hotel groups, to the belief that Rioja was the navel of the world, protected by a private God."
"Rioja is its own worst enemy. Lack of control in the vineyards and lack of self-criticism in the wines."
"Failure of internal organization, disparity of criteria within the DO, and overconfidence."

ON WINE QUALITY:
"Mass production of commercial wines... Disappointing wines that are made by (theoretically) established houses, in terms of quality and image... Therefore lowering the quality perception of Rioja by the consumer."

ON PRICE:
"Excessive price rises in short periods of time."
"Poor price stability."
"Excessive consequences of price fluctuation."
"Commercially, in the export market the sale of low-price vino joven has made selling high-quality wines much more difficult. In some countries, consumers only associate Rioja with 'cheap and cheerful'."

ON COMPETITION:
"High-quality wines from other DOs."
"Wines from emergent countries, technical developments in new DOs, and unnecessary restrictions within the DOCa Rioja."

What is the biggest challenge facing you as a Rioja bodega in the immediate future?

This question addressed individual challenges in the twenty-first-century market, and the prime concern seemed to be making – and selling – quality wines, particularly from smaller bodegas in the face of competition from the "industrialists". The answers show that there is no lack of aspiration.

WE WANT...

"To be a brand in home and export markets which reflects a Rioja that is value for money."

"To make wines that suit the taste of export markets."

"To find enough quality grapes to make quality wine."

"To open up new markets, consolidate quality, maintain prices, and grow."

"To raise the range with single-vineyard and old-vines wines."

"To make the world aware of the vinos de autor (signature wines) and other wines made by the small bodegas, and get them into their proper place in the market."

"To show that a small bodega without publicity can have great quality."

OTHER COMMENTS

"It's tough for smaller bodegas, no matter how good their wines, to get noticed among the big boys."

"The challenge is the same every year: to make wine as good as or better than last year."

How important is the concept of terroir in your wines?

There was much more consensus here, and terroir would seem to be the flavour of the age. The word "fundamental" was prominent. Some bodegas said that it's only one of a number of factors which affect quality in their wine, but everyone agreed that it's what makes Rioja Rioja.

QUOTES

"Our major treasure and best selling-point."

"It's only one of three parameters: vintage, terroir, and 'savoir faire'. We prefer the concept of vino de autor."

"Very high importance. We make our wines with the idea that they should taste of the Rioja Alta/Alavesa [two different bodegas]."

"Very important, but only one element in the finished wine."

And my favourite: "Transcendental. Implicit in the calificada." If only.

What do you think about using internationl varieties in Rioja? What role do they have to play in the future of Rioja?

This was a rather more heavily argued question. As we have seen elsewhere in this book, there are those who will make a case for using "international" varieties to replace the difficult and scarce Graciano and only-good-from-old-vines

Garnacha with reliable clones of Cabernet, Merlot, *et al*. A minority of wine-makers want to make varietals, but the majority are cautiously willing to try them out up to, say, twenty to thirty per cent – as long as they don't destroy the signature Tempranillo style of Rioja. There was a certain consensus about new varieties for white Rioja wines. Those bodegas with access to wonderful old plantations of Garnacha Blanca are greatly privileged, but Viura makes crisp and fresh rather than great and complex wine, and the classic old, oaky white Rioja with lots of Malvasía Riojana has become very much a niche market. There was less enthusiasm for red varieties but, interestingly, those in favour were quite measured in their responses. Those against were more trenchant.

IN FAVOUR:

"There's no reason why the quality of the wine should fall if we plant other varieties. Those that rely mostly on the fact that they come from Rioja as their main selling point will struggle if Rioja allows 'foreign' vines to be planted. We could certainly experiment and do some interesting research that quite probably would allow us to make very good wines."

"Not for reds, but we need something more than the Viura for whites."

"They could bring our wines closer to the taste of the international market, which is also a growing taste in Spain, but only in a proportion that doesn't lose the character of our wines: say a maximum of twenty to thirty per cent."

"We shouldn't close the door totally on new varieties, but we mustn't allow them to wipe out the personality of Rioja."

"We should consider the use of the varieties. We need to protect ourselves, but without being exclusionist."

"Very positive. We could have up to twenty per cent of our land planted with new varieties and use them to boost quality."

"They could give us new frontiers. There is terroir still to be discovered that could be very appropriate for them, with proper information for the consumer, and respect for the method of production."

"They could live alongside our own varieties, without losing the typicality of those already authorized."

NOT SURE:

"They could improve our wines and make us more flexible and competitive, but could also lead to our losing the typicality that has made Rioja world-famous."

AGAINST:

"An error of historic proportions."

"They might raise the average quality of the wine, but their introduction would risk losing Rioja's identity: the price of becoming 'average'."

"We should maintain our identity with our autochthonous varieties."

"There's no need. We have varieties with more than 100 years' acclimatization to our climate and soils."

"We'd rather work with Graciano and Mazuelo."

"Not particularly necessary, except perhaps for white wines."

"We have a world-class variety with Tempranillo, which gives our wine its prime characteristic."

"Totally unnecessary."

"We have yet to exploit the full potential of our native varieties."

Is there a future for white and *rosado* wines in Rioja, or would it be better to concentrate on the reds?

Most respondents believe that there is a future for whites and *rosados*, but there is a strong ground swell of opinion that new varieties really are needed to revitalize the white wine sector, and that real quality *rosado* is available but, given its market representation, you couldn't get the price to make really good wines a reality.

QUOTES:

"There's not much scope with the current varieties for white wine. Rosado could be better quality, but at a price the market would probably not like."

"We could make better whites if we could plant other varieties."

"There could be a great future, but not with the grapes we have at the moment. We need new white varieties."

"If you can make good red, you can make good white and rosado."

What more could be done to promote Rioja wine both in Spain and abroad?

The general view here was that the CRDOCa had failed to promote effectively, and that while some of the Rioja organizations had mounted effective campaigns on their own account, it would be better if all the various campaigns pooled their resources and mounted a generic campaign concentrating on the Rioja name. However, there were dissenters who suggested that wide variability of quality in the wines of the region would simply cloud the issue. The other general view was that promotion is too closely focused on the trade (which is very price-sensitive) when there are opportunities to create enthusiasts and ambassadors using Rioja's natural resources.

QUOTES:
"Improve the general quality of the wine and use the money spent in generic campaigns more wisely."
"Pull all the strategies together and concentrate the various economic forces in just one direction to optimize limited resources."
"Put more money behind it [a popular view], and get a more realistic view of the market."
"Offer more quality at good prices. Remind people that most Rioja is not cheap supermarket joven or 'guru' wines at astronomical prices."
"Persuade export buyers not to insist on prices that squeeze out quality for them and profit for producers."
"Educate the public. Anyone who has seen and tasted the wines will become a customer."
"In Spain: business and corporate – the 'yuppie' market. Abroad: a generic marketing campaign focusing on the wine's value for money."
"Hybrid marketing of the wine, food, tourism, and the region as a whole."
"Develop awareness of the uniqueness and diversity of Rioja's terroirs, rather than the 'generic' image that Rioja has at the moment. The success of the 'new-wave' wines in export markets proves that singularity sells."

What do you think of the permitted levels of production in Rioja: 6,500 kg/ha for red wines and 9,000 kg/ha for whites?

There was considerable debate about this, with a number of bodegas feeling that a blanket limit really didn't square with the range of wine being produced at the moment. Several producers echoed this comment: "If you want higher quality, you can always produce less."

Too high	7%
About right	91%
Too low	2%

QUOTES:
"These levels were set when the average age of vineyard was much older. You

can get more quality red grapes now: up to 9,000 kg/ha. But if you up it to
7,500, would they then produce 12,000?"
"We don't believe you can set parameters right across the DO. Every vineyard
is its own world."
"Production should be fixed by winemakers, not bureaucrats."
"For high-quality wines, it's irrelevant."
"It should be fixed each year before the harvest."
"Other training and pruning systems should be tried to see if they can increase
production without lowering quality."

What do you think about the regulations for ageing in oak for *crianza*, *reserva*, and *gran reserva* wines?

This was another hotly debated category, possibly the most contentious
of the survey. Although most respondents were happy to go along with
the current limits, a large minority wanted a *corta-crianza* (or semi-*crianza*)
to be able to make wine with some oak (and tell the customer about it)
without going the full twelve months. But there were quite a number of
dissenters to the whole system.

Too much time in oak	33%
About right	66%
We need a category with less than twelve months	36%

QUOTES:
"You can't base a system on time – only quality."
"Consumers don't understand them and they constrain winemakers."
"We believe that time in oak should be a function of the age of the barrel and the
structure of each wine. There must be more flexibility."
"Production should be fixed by winemakers, not bureaucrats."
"Reduce time in oak, increase time in bottle."
"Gran reserva needs to change. Of much more importance is whether the
barrels are new or old."
"We should be talking about the quality, not the ageing process."
"There should be a differentiation between joven and generico" [currently both
carry the contraetiqueta "cosecha"].
"Reserva should be two years; gran reserva: four."

"It's over-regulated: time in oak, time in bottle. Consumer taste has changed, production methods have changed, but our reglamento has not."

"Gran reserva barrel-ageing requirements might result in wines too lacking in fruit for modern tastes. However, traditional Spanish consumers (the majority) feel more comfortable with these classifications. Bottom line: there's no obligation to follow any of these classifications other than the basic cosecha if you want to make your very own wine."

"Crianza should be shortened and we need to be able to state the number of months [in cask] for jóvenes."

"Gran reserva is a difficult concept to understand outside Spain."

"Corta crianza is needed for more modern wine, adaptable to foreign markets."

"The terms are known and understood in Spain, so we can't do without them, but there could be more differentiation for different quality levels."

"Too much time and too much old oak; the concept is becoming obsolete. We should have three levels: vino joven, vino classico (crianza, reserva, etc.), and vino de autor."

"It's an obsolete concept that more time equals better, and it also encourages inappropriate pricing levels."

"We need more flexible nomenclature with the new wines coming from Rioja."

"The names are so well-known in Spain that it would be difficult to change them, but time in oak should be decided annually according to the vintage."

What is your opinion of using irrigation in Rioja?

There was a small minority who wanted it banned altogether, but most were happy with its use in extreme circumstances. All were against its use simply to increase yields.

QUOTES:

"If it's simply to replace missing rain in dry years, it's good. If it's to increase yields, then it's bad."

"All other things equal, and given adequate rainfall, irrigation is probably worse than having the real thing. This is certainly the case if the focus of irrigation is on high yields. However, we don't always, everywhere, have much rain at the right times; irrigation can save a harvest."

"It shouldn't be banned; 2003 was a hot year in which it was needed. We should have a map showing the high-risk areas of Rioja and take it from there."

"Regulating this is impossible."

If you could change some aspect of the *reglamento*, what would it be?

This is a bit of a pre-emptive question, as under the new OIPVR the *reglamento* is already under review. Yet what do the *bodegueros* want? One producer gave a cry from the heart: "Implement the new national law." This law has reduced *crianza*-in-oak regulations nationally, but the *reglamento* in Rioja has not changed.

QUOTES:

"More flexibility, more professionalism."
"Prohibit irrigation and pesticide treatment for thirty days before the harvest."
"Less intervention in quality measures, lighter regulation. That will increase quality."
"Allow more information on the label" [a popular request].
"Many things, but most of all getting some leadership from the CRDOCa"
"We need two new levels: Rioja genérico (larger yields, vinos jóvenes); Rioja superior (lower production, single vineyards)."

OPPOSITION:

"Abolish restrictions on planting 'foreign' varieties."
"New varieties, more liberty in vines per hectare, training and pruning but not for increased yields. Vary crianza times according to the year."

There have been calls for a *vino de la tierra* Alto Ebro, including Aragón, Navarra, and Rioja, allowing more flexibility to winemakers in their choice of vine varieties and winemaking methods. Is this a good idea?

This generally got the bum's rush, but those who were in favour gave a number of interesting reasons for supporting it.

Yes	**28%**
No	**63%**
Maybe	**9%**

QUOTES:

"Better to have a VdlT España [actually on the cards] to compete with the New World."

"If it makes good wines, then yes. If it's going to be another fiasco, then no." (So what was the last fiasco? Intriguing.)

"Much better to restructure the DO, reserving DOCa for low-yield, single-vineyard vines, etc." (A popular choice, with several very different suggestions as to how to modify the gradings.)

"It would only tell people 'these are inferior wines'. Better to concentrate on improving quality."

"The danger is that Rioja DOCa becomes the traditional producer that does not evolve versus the more modern next-door neighbour. This should be avoided in any case."

"Yes! and put all the sub-standard wines in it!"

This was my favourite: "Perfect as long as it's not associated with Rioja. You can't ring the mission bell and hear the mass at the same time; we cannot distribute the gold if we are touched by the lottery, and wring out the bulge if it is the afternoon tea of lions." Er, yes. Couldn't have put it better myself.

How important is it for your business to be a member of the DOCa Rioja?

The most important thing for my business	6%
Very important	62%
Important	30%
Not very important	2%

How strongly is the *reglamento* enforced?

Very strongly	52%
Strongly	42%
Not very strongly	0%
Weakly	2%
Strongly for some but not for others	4%

One bodega voted, "between strongly and very strongly, depending on who's dealing with whom", which might explain the four per cent of bodegas that voted for "Strongly for some but not for others". Perhaps this, too, will change under the OIPVR. Or perhaps not.

What is the biggest benefit you get from being a member of the DOCa Rioja?

Most bodegas admitted that the Rioja name does make a difference in the world outside, although not everybody was happy with the image presented by some of their fellow bodegas.

QUOTES:

"The credibility provided by the name, built up over the years, the volume of business, and the ability to respond to a crisis with good results."

"The image of Rioja."

"The DO has helped develop an environment which, in most cases, is conducive towards the production of very good wine on a relatively large scale."

"Rioja is known by every consumer in Spain, and well known internationally."

"We shelter under the umbrella of the CRDOCa."

"Participating in the shared inheritance, recognized by consumers as a guarantee of quality."

"Help in setting up the business and getting it going."

And a positive: *"Rioja sells!"*

And a negative (but only one): *"If I leave the CRDOCa I can't put a vintage date, grape variety, or region on the label."*

Any other comments?

IN FAVOUR:

"Rioja is a great DO with the ability to mould itself to the actual market. It can react and rejuvenate itself without losing its identity and prestige."

AGAINST:

"We need to replace the CRDOCa (there have been no elections for three years) and introduce a system of, say, grandes pagos de Rioja with a maximum of 5,000 kg/ha; DOCa Rioja with a maximum of 6,500 kg/ha, and DO Rioja 10,000 kg/ha, perhaps with vino de la tierra at the bottom."

"Change the way the reglamento is applied. Focus it on improving quality and service to members."

It rather looks as if those against have got their way with the sidelining of the DOCa as a department of the OIPVR.

But only time will tell.

A Directory of Rioja

PROFILES OF THE BODEGAS

This chapter lists the most prominent bodegas (and some more obscure and up-and-coming ones) and information has been supplied by the bodegas themselves and from other sources, including my own visits and tastings. It is extraordinarily difficult to get some bodegas in Spain (not just in Rioja) to reply to questions or even answer their emails, and in the event (and after a bit of nagging) about half of those contacted did actually send in a completed questionnaire, in some cases three months after the deadline had passed. I do appreciate that there are always more urgent, more pressing demands on a bodega's time than being pestered by writers, but the sad truth is that if they don't provide the information, it isn't going to be included. To quote Ángel Jaime, outgoing president of the CRDOCa: "Maintain the quality, insist on the originality, then, above all, communicate those things to the outside world." Quite. It doesn't matter how good the wines are if they don't tell anybody about them.

For this reason, the amount of detail in the profiles which follow varies according to whether the bodega in question returned the questionnaire and/or how well I know it from personal visiting. Aspects of vineyard practice and winemaking are only mentioned in detail if they differ significantly from the normal, accepted methods. In each case contact and website details (where available) are given for further information, although some of the websites were still very much *en obras* and unavailable at the time of publication.

It is accepted that the main grape in most red wines (unless otherwise specified) is Tempranillo and in most whites is Viura. If ageing epithets (*crianza, reserva*, etc.) are used, they refer to red wines unless specified otherwise. Tasting notes vary from the general to the more detailed according to whether I tasted the wine at a formal tasting or on the hoof, in the bodega, at a wine show, or somewhere where there was only the opportunity to give a general note and a mark for the wine.

The list is alphabetized using the most common name for the bodega, with the "official" name beneath. Some bodegas are better known by the name of their wines than by their real name (the most prominent is probably Marqués de Cáceres which is actually called Unión Vitivinícola) and others are known by shortened versions of their real name (e.g. Marqués de Riscal, which in full is Vinos de los Herederos de Marqués de Riscal). I have chosen what I perceive to be the most widely accepted name for these bodegas (I agonized for hours over Fernando Remírez de Ganuza but finally listed him under "R" and not "F", even though Benjamín Romeo is under "B" and not "R". Miguel Merino was easier), but if you can't find the one you're looking for please use the index at the end of the book. Names beginning with "El" are listed under "E" and "La" under "L". Names are read without spaces, so that "La Marquesa" comes after "Lagunilla".

"Group" denotes whether the bodega is a member of a group of wine businesses, either in Rioja or elsewhere; "unrelated" means that it is a member of a non-wine-related group. Date of foundation can be confusing, as some companies quote the date of incorporation, others the date of planting, others the date of last change of ownership, name, or address, so please be aware that different sources may list different dates. In disputed areas I have gone with the bodega's own date.

Ratings

In order to keep things relatively simple I have used a five-star system to categorize the quality of the wines produced by the bodegas. I have only marked wines I have actually tasted in the twelve months prior to publication of this book. Please remember that these are only personal assessments and others may wish to disagree.

***** Excellent
**** Very good
*** Good
** Decent, reliable
* Run-of-the-mill, but acceptable
0 Sub-standard

Wines that show potential when young but need time for opening up, or wines that vary between lesser and greater years may be marked **>***

or ***>****. The first is how they rate as young wines, the second their potential for development, or the first how they rate in lesser years, the second how they rate in the best years.

MAIN BODEGAS

AGE

Bodegas AGE, Barrio de la Estación, s/n, 26360 Fuenmayor, La Rioja.
Tel: 941 293 500. Fax: 941 293 501. Website: www.byb.es. Email:
bodegasage@byb.es. Contact: Eva María Matute Sáez. ByB Group contact: Isabel
Adrián. Winemaker: Elena Adell San Pedro. Established: 1967. Type: SA. Own
vineyards (ha): 500. Buy in: Yes. Group: Bodegas y Bebidas (Allied Domecq).
Barrels: 35,000; Sales national: 74%; export: 26%. Top export markets: EU,
Japan, Switzerland. Visits: contact bodega. Principal wines: Azpilicueta Crianza;
Reserva; Siglo Saco; Marqués del Romeral Gran Reserva

The foundation date of 1967 is a little misleading, as AGE has its origins in 1881, when Félix Azpilicueta y Martínez established a company called Bodegas Romeral near this site, because it was close to the newly completed railway to Bilbao via Logroño, with all the export possibilities thus presented. Indeed, the bodega had its own branded railway tankers for bulk wines well into the 1980s. Azpilicueta was something of an innovator, bearing in mind that this was a time when exports to France were burgeoning, and any new techniques or equipment were of tremendous interest to the big buyers. He was one of the first to install glass-lined tanks for extra hygiene during fermentation, for example, and to mechanize the transfer of wine between tanks and casks.

The second partner in what was to become a joint company was Bodegas Las Veras, founded in 1926 by one Cruz García Lafuente, also in Fuenmayor. In the intervening years the Rioja wine business had crashed into recession and then started to bounce back, and competition was fierce. The two companies eventually agreed to work together, at least in the export department, in 1964 (after only forty-two years of nose-to-nose confrontation) and eventually merged in 1967, along with a third bodega from Navarrete, about three kilometres (1.9 miles) south of Fuenmayor, named after its founder Melquíades Entrena (who went on to take over Berberana; *see* page 91). The building of a new bodega was begun in Fuenmayor to consolidate the strength of the new enterprise. The joint venture took the initials of the three shareholders – AGE, for Azpilicueta, García, and Entrena – so presumably it could have been called GAE, EGA or GEA, depending on how boardroom discussions were going at any one point in the negotiations.

The company built a solid reputation for reliability and the new state-of-the-art bodega was able to produce the sort of quality wines the export market was demanding. The sale of forty-nine per cent of the company's stock to an American distributor in 1971 ensured a healthy market in the USA, which was very significant in AGE's development. The firm built on this foundation throughout the 1970s and 1980s and created a range of brand names that were to endure, perhaps most notably the Siglo ("century") range; to give it an enduring individuality, Siglo Saco was bottled and then wrapped in jute sacking before labelling.

In 1995, AGE was bought out by Bodegas y Bebidas, then as now the largest wine group in Spain, and further investment allowed it to develop the bodega, equipment, and marketing. In 2001, Bodegas y Bebidas was bought out by Allied Domecq (*see* page 81), one of the biggest multi-national drinks groups, and the massive investment available has been ploughed back into new installations. Today, the original AGE bodega has been extended and improved, and the Azpilicueta wines have been included in the "Iverus" project (*see* Bodegas y Bebidas, page 96). The winemaker at AGE is Elena Adell, a young woman who qualified as an agricultural engineer at the University of Navarrea in Pamplona, and studied winemaking in Montpellier, qualifying in 1998. She worked at Château Canon-La Gaffelière in St-Émilion, Brown Brothers in Australia, Clos du Val in California, and Concha y Toro in Chile before joining Bodegas y Bebidas. She now oversees winemaking at a number of the group's bodegas, with a special interest in the wines at AGE, and drives the low-key, silver-grey Mercedes-Benz that seems to have become the trademark of the rising generation in Rioja.

The Azpilicueta wines (***), especially the Reservas (****), are the most important here, and the Marqués del Romeral Gran Reserva (****) is generally excellent. The Siglo range (**) is reliable and represents value for money without being particularly exciting; indeed the whole operation gives the impression of dependability, investment, and permanence.

ALAVESAS

Bodegas Alavesas, Ctra de Elciego s/n, 01300 Laguardia, Álava. Tel: 902 227 700. Fax: 902 277 701. Website: www.cofradiasamaniego.com. Email: bodega@cofradiasamaniego.com. Contact: Rodrigo Fajardo Barreras. Chief executive: Miguel Ángel Alonso Borrás. Winemaker: Alberto Serrano Espinosa. Established: 1970. Type: SA. Own vineyards (ha): 100. Contract (ha): None. Own production: 40%. Buy in: Yes. Number of staff: 30. Group: yes – Bodegas Durón and unrelated. Barrels: American and French. Annual production (hl): 10,500. Sales national: 80%; export: 20%. Top export markets: UK, USA, Japan. Visits: by appointment; groups and individuals. Open weekdays: 10am–1pm; 4pm–8pm.

Principal wines: Solar de Samaniego Joven; Crianza; Reserva; Gran Reserva

Pharmaceuticals and the wine business have a long relationship in Spain (perhaps because of the unparalleled profitability of the former and the investment potential of the latter; nobody ever lost money on buildings and land). One of the most recent examples is Bodegas Roda (*see* page 88) and one of the biggest is Abadía Retuerta in Castile-León, but the first in the modern era was this, founded by one Miguel-Ángel Alonso Samaniego who had made his fortune with Laboratorios Alter (established in the 1940s). He pulled together interested landowners and growers to form a limited company which was registered in 1972, with a new bodega completed in time for the 1973 vintage. The bodega built a steady reputation over the next two decades, but it also built something else: the Cofradía de Solar de Samaniego.

A slight digression here to explain the name. "Samaniego" was, of course, the maternal name of the founder, and quite probably comes from the village of the same name in the eastern highlands of the Rioja country (Alavesa). "Solar" in this context does not mean "solar" from *sol* meaning "sun", but "plot" – as in individual plot of land from "solo": "on its own". So the name means "Samaniego's plot of land", being, in this case, Laguardia, and specifically the bodega's own vineyards. In his 1985 book, Hubrecht Duijker draws a parallel with the eighteenth-century poet Félix-María de Samaniego (1745–1801), whose fables are as famous in Spain as those of Aesop are in the English-speaking (and presumably Greek-speaking) world. The website www.perfildemujer.com/samaniego.htm has the most popular of them. The connection seems to have been that in the past, the company's *crianza* wines were labelled "Solar de Iriarte", after another eighteenth-century poet and fabulist, Tomás de Iriarte (1750–91), but this brand name has since been dropped.

Back to the Cofradía de Solar de Samaniego, the "Fraternity of Samaniego's Plot of Land". This is a wine club for private individuals, organizations, and corporate bodies to buy or reserve wine directly from the bodega at advantageous prices. This is, according to the company, good news for the customer, who pays less, and for the bodega, which gets a better margin overall. Certainly it has become very successful, and the *cofradía* has 35,000 active members in Spain who buy eighty per cent of the bodega's wine. They can, if they wish, store the wine at the bodega and hire a dining room for family celebrations, parties, weddings, and corporate events secure in the knowledge that the wine has never left the cellar in which it was made and should be in perfect condition. The cellars themselves are immaculately kept, atmospheric and extensive, and well worth a visit.

The basic range (**) of red wine is branded Bodegas Alavesas and Solar, all the rest, white, *rosado*, and red, are branded Solar de Samaniego for the outside market, and Cofradía de Solar de Samaniego for members. *Crianza* and *reserva* (***) wines are very reliable, and the Gran Reserva and Selección Vendimia (****) are excellent. There is also a varietal Graciano (****) at the same level of quality.

ALCANADRE

Vinícola Riojana de Alcanadre, San Isidro, 46–48, 26599 Alcanadre, La Rioja.
Tel: 941 165 036. Fax: 941 165 289. Website: www.riojanadealcanadre.com.
Email: vinicola@riojanadealcanadre.com. Chief executive: Carmen Rodríguez Martínez. Winemaker: María Martínez, Olga Martínez. Established: 1957.
Type: S Co-op. Members: 300. Own vineyards (ha): 700. Barrels: 300. Visits: bodega shop open weekdays: 11am–1pm. Principal wines: Aradón Joven (Tinto, Blanco, Rosado); Barzagoso Joven Blanco; Crianza, Reserva Tinto; Silval Tinto Crianza, reserva; Viña Romita Joven (Tinto, Blanco, Rosado)

The Aradón Joven Tinto (***) is a lovely example of the fresh, crisp, gluggable Tempranillo/Garnacha style, but also carries some weight and offers excellent value for money. Barzagoso Reserva (***) has good length and a nice balance of fruit and tannins.

ALEJOS

Bodegas Alejos, Pol. El Sequero – Parcela 27, 26509 Agoncillo, La Rioja.
Tel: 941 437 051. Fax: 941 437 077. Email: b.a.alabanza@teleline.es.
Chief executive: José-María Ruíz-Alejos Herrero. Winemaker: Susana Fernández.

Established: 1988. Type: SA. Own vineyards (ha): 25. Barrels: 500. Visits: Bodega shop. Open weekdays 11am–1pm and 3pm–5pm. Principal wines: Alabanza Crianza, Reserva, Selección; Tornasol

Smart, modern bodega with the latest technology and an ambition to produce "high-expression" wines from *joven* to *reserva*. Tornasol is from organic vineyards. The Alabanza Selección (****) has very good, tightly packed fruit, concentration, and excellent length.

ALICIA ROJAS

(Offices): Virgen del Pilar 1, 26004 Logroño, La Rioja. Bodega: Ctra N-232 Km 376, Ausejo, La Rioja. Tel: 941 430 010. Fax: 941 430 286. Website: www.bodegasaliciarojas.com. Email: info@bodegasaliciarojas.com. Contact/Chief executive/Winemaker: Alicia Rojas Gil. Established: 1965. Type: SA. Own vineyards (ha): 125. Own production: 100%. Buy in: No. Number of staff: 13. Group: No. Barrels: 700. Type: American and French. Annual production (hl): 700. Sales national: 85%; export: 15%. Top export markets: EU, UK, Germany. Visits: by appointment; groups and individuals. Open weekdays: 9.30am–5.30pm. Principal wines: Solarce (Tinto, Crianza, Reserva, Blanco, Rosado); Collado de la Estrella (Tinto, Crianza, Reserva, Blanco, Rosado); Finca Alicia Rojas (Crianza, Reserva)

Alicia Rojas is the third generation of the family to run the bodega, and came into the business when women were not supposed to do such things. Even today, in Spain, it's customary to find women working in public relations and export management, but not actually running bodegas or making wine, and in many bodegas it's still only the senior female staff who speak any foreign language. Alicia Rojas would have none of this, and persuaded her father to let her go to high school in Bilbao. For a youngest child (and a girl at that) to go to university was considered unnecessarily expensive, especially as she wanted to study engineering, but the seventeen-year-old Alicia did persuade her family to let her go to England, and eventually paid her own way through a law degree, shuttling between England, France, and Switzerland, and learning languages on the hoof. After a spell with the airline Iberia, she returned home in 1980 to nurse her ailing father and found the family business in a ruinous state. She went back to college part time to study agriculture, and gradually and painstakingly replanted the vineyards, rebuilt the bodega, and eventually became one of the first growers in Rioja to apply for organic status.

Her daughter Nerea Ortíz de Piñedo, an industrial engineer, and son-in-law Luís Alcalde, an agricultural engineer, joined the business in 1998, becoming the fourth generation to work the vineyards.

Wines Alicia Rojas likes to make her wines tightly concentrated with plenty of tannin and the ability to keep for many years. The Finca Alicia Rojas Crianza (***) fits this description perfectly and needs time to develop; the Reserva (***>****) has more weight and warmth but is still packed with tannins and "locked-in" fruit; these are wines to keep. The white Malvasía (**>***) is a light, fresh, dry white with some subtle fruit.

ALLENDE

Finca Allende, Plaza Ibarra, 1, 26330 Briones, La Rioja. Tel: 941 322 301. Fax: 941 322 302. Website: www.finca-allende.com. Email: sales@finca-allende.com. Contact/Chief executive/Winemaker: Miguel-Ángel de Gregorio. Established: 1995. Type: SL. Own vineyards (ha): 42. Own production (%): 100%. Buy in: No. Barrels: 1,760. Type: French. Sales national: 25%; export: 75%. Top export markets: EU, Germany, UK. Visits: by appointment. Open weekdays: 11am–1pm and 4pm–6pm Principal wines: Allende Blanco, Tinto; Aurus; Calvario.

This is a spanking-new winery in a big, plain, tin shed behind a gorgeous, crumbling mansion in this most beguiling of eighteenth-century Rioja towns. Miguel-Ángel and his sister Mercedes plan to do up the mansion at some point in the future, but the work on the wine comes first; in the meantime, it continues to crumble imperceptibly, but there are bits of wooden boarding here and there so you don't step into any holes. *Allende* means "out in front" and is descriptive of the ambitions the bodega has set itself and, indeed, given the prices the wine commands, is achieving. Miguel is often described as one of the *enfants terribles* of the new wave in Rioja winemaking, but in reality he and Mercedes are easygoing, pleasant-natured, and laid-back workaholic fanatics who will let nothing stand in the way of their quest for excellence.

Way back when Miguel-Ángel was a six-month-old baby, his father, Nicolás de Gregorio, moved from La Mancha to Rioja to work for Bodegas Marqués de Murrieta at Ygay. As a result, Miguel grew up with wine in the blood, metaphorically speaking. He qualified as an agricultural engineer, and at the age of twenty-five was making wine at Bodegas Bretón (*see* page 99) and spearheaded the success of, particularly, their flagship single-vineyard wine, Dominio de Conte.

But Miguel and Mercedes had ambitions to go it alone, and from about 1986 they started buying up small plots of old vines around Briones, which is almost unique in the Rioja Alta for its soils that are largely chalky clay but above the alluvial level of the Ebro Valley. In the far-off, low-yielding, long-maceration days of his formative years, and in good vintages, Rioja generally and Murrieta in particular were turning out wines of great concentration and complexity, rather like the high expession wines of the twenty-first century, although usually with a need for a great deal of cellarage before they were ready to drink. This was a significant factor in Miguel-Ángel's winemaking development: he wanted to recreate that level of depth, complexity, and expression, but in wines which didn't need to be kept for twenty years before they were ready to drink. This tells us a lot about his winemaking style once he became his own boss.

The first vintage under the Allende name, a 100 per cent Tempranillo, was put on the market in 1995 and achieved instant acclaim. There's a white wine, too, made from barrel-fermented Viura and Malvasía Riojana picked from fifty-year-old-plus vines, but Miguel's main interest is in the reds. In 1996, Allende launched Aurus, a wine made from selected, small, sixty-year-old-plus vine plots including some Graciano, often picked dangerously late as they waited for the right levels of ripeness, and aged in Tronçais oak. Costs were high, and the wine had to sell at a silly price, but they sold the lot. And then came Calvario. Miguel had spotted this tiny (3.5ha) single vineyard four years before he was able to persuade the owner to sell it. It has rough, stony soil and a southeastern aspect: perfect for ripening old-vine grapes, which produce approximately one kilogram (2.2 pounds) per vine. The vines (Tempranillo ninety per cent, Garnacha eight per cent, Graciano two per cent) were all planted in 1945, the grapes are hand-selected, and the wine ages for about fourteen months in new Alliers oak

Miguel is also a very nice man. I was walking across a zebra-crossing in Logroño one morning in the spring of 2004 when a car screeched to a halt (and, yes, it was a low-key, silver-grey Mercedes-Benz) and he jumped out. He was on his way to a doctor's appointment but demanded that I join him for lunch if I had the time. Although I had sixty bodega appointments to cover in the next few weeks, I managed to meet him eventually, in the magnificent crumbling mansion, for a tapas lunch after a tasting, sitting on plastic folding chairs at hired tables and eating

Briones *jamón* and Briones *chorizo* (Briones has its own gastronomic sub-culture within Rioja). It was splendid, and one day the mansion will be a palace again... After the next vintage, or the one after that.

The Allende attitude manifests itself in the company's brochure. Where most brochures have half-tone pictures of the moustachioed founder, piles of barrels, elegant frontage of the new bodega, sunset vineyard shots, and a picture of the present boss with a paragraph about how wonderful s/he is, Allende's brochure is a comprehensive survey of the vineyards, with soil analysis, bioclimatic data, lithology, and bedrock-structure diagrams. Miguel-Ángel de Gregorio has identified no fewer than ninety-two different terroirs on his land, and he loves and lives in his vineyards, cosseting every vine to its final maturity. Indeed, he almost got the "Rioja vineyard anorak" award in this book. But that was before I met Benjamín Romeo (*see* page 89).

Allende Blanco (****) is barrel-fermented in new French oak and is possibly one of the highest-expression white wines of Rioja, though nothing like the traditional *crianza*; Allende Tinto (****>*****) has a big, spicy, Tempranillo warmth with a hint of austere French oak, while young. Aurus (*****) is a wine of enormous power, concentration, complexity, and length, and has all the hallmarks of longevity. Calvario (*****) is softer, warmer, riper, and more approachable when young. If I had to choose between the last two, I would have to choose them both, but only if someone else were paying.

ALLIED DOMECQ
See AGE, Bodegas y Bebidas, Domecq, Juan Alcorta, Ysios.

ALTANZA
Bodegas Altanza, Ctra N232 Km 419.5, 26360 Fuenmayor, La Rioja. Tel: 941 450 860; Fax: 941 450 804. Website: www.bodegasaltanza.com. Email: altanza@bodegasaltanza.com. Contact: Ervigio Adán Ruíz, Export manager. Chief executive/Winemaker: Óscar Martínez Hueda. Established: 1998. Type: SA. Own vineyards (ha): 100. Contract (ha): 50. Own production: 50%. Buy in: Yes. Number of staff: 19. Group: unrelated. Barrels: 8,000. Type: French, American, Russian. Annual production (hl): 8,000. Sales national: 83%; export: 17%. Top export markets: Mexico, UK, Switzerland. Visits: groups and individuals. Open weekdays: 8am–1pm; 3pm–6pm. Principal wines: Altanza Reserva Especial; Lealtanza Gran Reserva; Reserva; Crianza; Club Lealtanza

This is a beautiful new bodega set about with gardens and an avowed intention to go back to the roots of the land, of the vines, of Rioja. The initial investment came from local property, tourism, and development company Bemo Servicios, and represents another brick in the wall of wine-as-tourism, which seems to be informing most of the new and upgrading bodegas in Rioja.

The bodega is certainly impressive, equipped to the highest standard with stainless steel for alcoholic fermentation and oak *tinas* (vats) for malolactic fermentation to increase micro-oxygentation. Everything is spotlessly clean and elegantly laid out. I was particularly taken with the large area of glass floor in reception which allows visitors to look down on the (air-conditioned, natch) barrel-cellar beneath.

The first vintage was made in 1998 but the bodega's ambition was to make only *reserva* and *gran reserva* wines, so the first wine to come to the market was the 1998 Reserva in March, 2002. Since then, the decision was taken in 2000 to include a *crianza* wine, due to the variable quality of grape available in that vintage. Whether they will continue to make *crianza* in better years has not yet been decided.

The wines are all good quality and all Tempranillo. Lealtanza Crianza (***) has classic Tempranillo fruit with an oaky bite and silky palate; the Reserva (****) is also classic in style, with good crisp, soft fruit and good length. The Gran Reserva (*****) is a textbook example of the genre: strawberry-and-cream nose, oak and fruit in perfect harmony on the palate. Club Lealtanza (****>*****) is a *reserva* made from selected grapes from the oldest vines, with tight, dark fruit, complexity, warmth, and spice. Altanza (*****) is a *reserva* made from hand-selected grapes with malolactic fermentation in cask rather than *tina*, and in the more modern style: extracted, hefty fruit, depth, length, and power. These are impressive wines for such a new venture.

AMÉZOLA DE LA MORA

Bodegas Amézola de la Mora, Paraje Viña Vieja, s/n. 26359 Toremontalbo, La Rioja. Tel: 941 454 532. Fax: 941 454 537. Website: www.bodegasamezola.com. Email: bodegasamezola@fer.es. Contact: Pedro Usatorre, Commercial director. Chief executive: María-Cristina Downes de Amézola. Winemaker: Javier García Castellanos. Established: 1986. Type: SA. Own vineyards (ha): 60. Barrels: 2,700. Sales national: 60%; export: 40%. Top export markets: UK, Switzerland, EU.

Visits: by appointment. Open weekdays: 9am–1.30pm. Principal wines: Solar de Amézola Gran Reserva; Señorío Amézola Reserva; Viña Amézola Crianza; Íñigo Amézola Joven

The Amézola de la Mora family has lived in this part of Rioja since time immemorial, and the bodega is ancient, although it stopped making wine at the time of the phylloxera disaster, when the head of the family, the Conde de Hervías, grubbed up the dying vines and replanted with cereals. In 1970, his great-grandchildren Javier, who was running the family estate, and Íñigo, a successful Madrid lawyer, decided to return the old bodega to production and replant with vines, and they helped finance the project by leasing some thirty hectares of land to Bodegas y Bedidas for Campo Viejo (*see* Juan Alcorta, page 132). They sold off the grapes from the first few vintages while they were restoring and re-equipping the bodega, and made their first vintage in 1986. The wines gained a good reputation early on and generally follow the classic tradition of Rioja.

Sadly, both brothers have died; Íñigo was killed in a particularly nasty car accident in Madrid in 1999 and his Argentine-born widow, María-Cristina Downes, took over the business, determined to keep it going and make it ever-more successful as a suitable memorial to her husband and brother-in-law. The company is now jointly owned by María-Cristina and her two daughters: María (born 1981) and Cristina (born 1982), who have been groomed to take over the business as their mother gradually "takes a back seat" over the next few years. The daughters were five and six when the first vintage was produced, and have quite literally grown up with the business. They are currently the youngest joint-proprietors of any Rioja bodega.

The wines are in the classic mode and only made from the bodega's own vineyards, which are mainly Tempranillo with some Graciano and Mazuelo. The Crianza (***) is very reliable and has the fruit and oak in perfect balance. The Gran Reserva (****) has a majestic structure and length. Interestingly, the Joven (****) commands a rather higher price than your average young wine for its complexity and surprising maturity.

ANTIGUA USANZA

Bodegas Antigua Usanza, Camino Garugele, 26338 San Vicente de la Sonsierra, La Rioja. Tel: 941 334 156. Fax: 941 334 156. Email: usanza@prorioja.es. Contact: Estíbaliz Arrieta. Chief executive: Miguel-Ángel Rodríguez Ruíz.

Winemaker: José-Ramón Martínez González. Established: 1989. Type: SA. Own vineyards (ha): 7. Buy in: Yes. Barrels: 2,100. Sales national: 90%; export: 10%. Top export markets: Germany, Denmark, Switzerland. Visits: by appointment. Open weekdays: 10am–1pm; 4pm–6pm. Principal wines: Antigua Usanza Crianza; Viña Azai Joven

This is a family run company in an area which offers some of the best terroir in Rioja. Although this bodega has modernized greatly in the fermenting hall, its barrel-cellars are traditional, labyrinthine, consistent-temperature tunnels excavated in the bedrock to a length of 1.2 km (0.7 miles). In winemaking they use a good deal of Garnacha, and pride themselves on handling it rather more creatively than many other bodegas.

Antigua Usanza Crianza (***) is a nicely structured wine with good tannins, full fruit, and a spicy length. Reserva (****) has more weight and a big-fruit structure; I wrote "'classic fruit and oak in harmony". Gran Reserva (****>*****) has that mature pot-pourri nose so classic of *grandes reservas*, with gentle, long-lived maturity – ten to fifteen years from good vintages.

ARCO-BODEGAS UNIDAS

See Berberana, Lagunilla, Marqués de Griñón, Marqués de la Concordia
Note This company makes some excellent wines but has an absurdly complex company structure which seems to change its name and those of its wines on a weekly basis, so this list should help you find what you're looking for (unless it has changed again while you were reading this):

Berberana is no longer a bodega but a brand name for wines made at Bodegas Lagunilla in Cenicero (formerly Bodegas Berberana).

Lagunilla is now the name of the Cenicero bodega as well as brand name for wines made there.

Marqués de Griñón is the name of a subsidiary company and a brand based and produced at the Cenicero bodega (but it's also a separate operation run by the Marqués de Griñón – *see* the entry on page 144).

Marqués de La Concordia is a bodega and a brand, produced at Hacienda de Súsar in Alfaro.

ARTADI

Cosecheros Alaveses/Bodegas Artadi, Ctra de Logroño, s/n, 01300 Laguardia, Álava. Tel: 945 600 119. Fax: 945 600 850. Website: www.artadi.com. Email: info@artadi.com. Chief executive: Juan-Carlos López de la Calle.

Winemaker: Jean-François Gadeau. Established: 1985. Type: SA. Own vineyards (ha): 70. Own production: 100%. Sales national: 40%; export: 60%. Visits: contact bodega. Principal wines: Artadi Joven; Viñas de Gaín Crianza; Pagos Viejos; Grandes Añadas; Viña El Pisón

This is a great bodega that seems to have happened almost by accident. The founder, Juan-Carlos Lopez de la Calle, persuaded some of his fellow *cosecheros* that their grapes were too good to sell to the big bodegas, and pooled their joint seventy hectares of vineyards in an attempt to mount a joint marketing venture as a small cooperative. In the first instance they made simple *joven* wines, but even then, the quality, particularly of the red wines, shone through. Gradually they refined their winemaking processes and the business became a limited company in 1992. Today they are recognized as one of the leading quality producers of the Rioja Alavesa, seldom out of the medal-winning tables in international competitions. The main wines are made from single-vineyard or individually selected old-vine grapes, of which the shareholders seem to have a generous supply. The main bodega is a modern but rather mundane building south of the city of Laguardia, but in the narrow streets of the old town they have a beautiful old bodega and tasting room that is only open to groups by prior appointment.

It's difficult to fault or, indeed, classify these wines. They have the nose and complexity of classic Rioja but, at the top end, the power and extraction of the new wave. The basic Artadi (***) *jóvenes* have real weight, bite, and power. Viñas de Gaín (****) reeks of ripe Tempranillo fruit and toasty oak; Pagos Viejos (*****) is subtle, complex, spicy, oaky, and delicious; and Grandes Añadas (*****) and Viña El Pisón (*****) are enormously concentrated and give the impression that they will live for ever. Which should be just about long enough to pay off the mortgage you took out to buy them.

AZABACHE

Viñedos de Aldeanueva, Avda Juan Carlos I, 100, 26559 Aldeanueva de Ebro, La Rioja. Tel: 941 163 039. Fax: 941 163 585. Website: www.adeanueva.com. Email: va@aldeanueva.com. Contact: Javier Martínez. Chief executive: Abel Torres. Winemaker: Martín Sáenz. Established: 1956. Type: S Co-op. Own vineyards (ha): 2,572. Own production: 100%. Barrels: 12,000. Sales national: 35%; export: 65%. Top export markets: EU, Other Europe, Japan.

Visits: by appointment. Open weekdays from 11am, Saturdays by arrangement.
Principal wines: Azabache Joven (Tinto, Blanco, Rosado) to Gran Reserva,
varietal Tempranillo; Bodegas de Ábalos Joven (Tinto, Blanco, Rosado) to Reserva;
Torre Aldea Joven (Tinto, Blanco, Rosado) to Reserva. Some of the wines are
organic (ecológico)

A member of the "Rioja Baja Strikes Back" tendency, this is a co-op but
with a very commercial outlook, possibly helped by the fact that the
wines for the infant Viña Herminia (below) were made here until 2001,
and Azabache was probably the dominant wine of the area until Álvaro
Palacios came home (*see* Palacios Remondo, page 172). The wide range of
terroirs and microclimates provided by such a large area of vines
allows production of a wide range of different styles and qualities, but
all characterized by their value for money.

Azabache Tempranillo Joven (***) is an excellent example of young,
fresh Tempranillo of the sort that is commonplace in the Alavesa but
relatively rare here in the Baja. The Azabache Ecológico (****) is
astonishingly good for the price, with brilliant fruit, savoury notes, and
some complexity of structure. Azabache Crianza (***) is a more classic
style with a good Tempranillo/oak balance, and Azabache Tradición
Reserva (***) follows that style with good structure and some power.

BAGORDI

Bodegas Bagordi, Ctra Estella Km 33, 31261 Andosilla, Navarra. Tel: 948 674
860. Fax: 948 674 238. Website: www.bagordi.com. Email: info@bagordi.com.
Winemaker: Guillermo de la Vega. Established: 1996. Type: SL. Own vineyards
(ha): 58. Contract: 26. Barrels: 1,000. Sales national: 40%; export: 60%.
Top export markets: Canada, EU, Japan. Visits: contact bodega. Principal wines:
Bagordi Joven (*blanco, rosado, tinto*); Crianza, Reserva; Garnacha; Eco (organic);
Graciano Eco

The name derives from the Basque word *Bagoa* which means the beech
tree or a grove of beech trees, and these flourish in this area of the Rioja
Baja. The bodega is strikingly modern, spotlessly clean, and has state-of-
the-art equipment. The vineyards are carefully divided into plots with
different terroirs, mainly Tempranillo but with Garnacha Graciano and
Merlot for reds, and Viura for whites, and some may be irrigated in
drier years. They also run El Club de la Barrica ("The Cask Club") for
customers who want to buy their *reservas en primero* (*en primeur*).

Bagordi Crianza (***) is an elegant wine in the classic style but with more than a touch of individuality about it. The Reserva (***>****) has more weight, depth, and fruit, and has good ageing potential.

BARÓN DE LEY

Barón de Ley, Ctra de Mendavia-Lodosa Km 5, 31587 Mendavía, Navarra.
Tel: 948 694 303. Fax: 948 694 304. Website: www.barondeley.com.
Email: info@barondeley.com. Chief executive: Eduardo Santos-Ruiz. Winemaker:
Gonzalo Rodríguez. Established: 1985. Type: SA. Own vineyards (ha): 160. Group:
El Coto de la Rioja (*see* page 119). Barrels: 13,800. Sales national: 50; export: 50.
Top export markets: Germany, UK, Scandinavia. Visits: contact bodegas; groups only.
Principal wines: Barón de Ley Joven (*blanco, rosado*); Crianza; Reserva; Finca
Monasterio

No, in case you were wondering, there isn't a Barón de Ley in the Spanish aristocracy. The name was chosen as it also means "Lord of the Law" in Spanish – a kind of guarantee that it would be textbook Rioja made to the most exacting standards. So don't mention the Cabernet Sauvignon. The monastery whose estate houses the very smart, modern bodega goes back to 1548, when it was built as a fortification at a riverside location known as Imas, between Castile and Navarra, after the forced incorporation of Navarra into the merged kingdoms of Castile to the west and Aragón to the east. The Navarros were not happy, and not averse to the odd armed incursion across the river Ebro.

It was subsequently taken over by Bénédictine monks who made wine (and the famous liqueur) there until the expropriation of Mendizábal (*see* chapter three) which took monastic properties into public ownership. The monks left in 1836, and the Imas estate passed through several hands until it was given to General Martín Zurbano after the first Carlist war. Zurbano was arrested and shot in 1845, but not before he had lost the entire estate in a game of cards to a French count. The count didn't want land in Spain, where political turbulence was rife at that time, and had it valued. In the event, the estate manager, Cayo Muro, came up with the cash, paid the debt, and became owner of the estate. Once again it passed from hand to hand, family to family, until the founders of Barón de Ley bought it from the Sanz-Pastor family in the early 1980s.

The idea behind Barón de Ley was that the regional government of Navarra wanted the crumbling monastery to be restored and formed a partnership with this new private company to plant an initial ninety hectares of vines and begin restoring the monastery with a grant from public funds. The formal company foundation was in 1985, and work started immediately. One of the founding shareholders was Eduardo Santos-Ruíz, who was later to be instrumental in the takeover of El Coto (*see* page 119).

Early results were patchy. The new bodega was coming on apace, the monastery restoration was going according to plan, but the wines were very variable and in some cases decidedly dodgy; dirty barrel aromas, unfinished fermentation, and volatile acidity were not uncommon in the late 1980s. Once the building work was completed, however, the wine-makers got into their stride. By the early 1990s, Barón de Ley was carving itself a reputation for increasingly reliable quality. In 1979, the UK group Bass put the El Coto estate on the market. Realistically, Barón de Ley was too small to buy a giant concern such as El Coto, but the company's reputation and financial record was such that a venture capital group put up the extra money for the purchase, and the two became a group in 1979, with Santos-Ruíz as chief executive. He and his colleagues continued to plough ahead, the company's wines continued to make a name for themselves in the outside world, and in 1997 the group went public, bought out the venture capitalists, and became independent.

By now, winemaking was pin-sharp in its focus and quality (indeed, the bodega won its ISO 9002 quality certification in that year) and the monastery was magnificently restored, with the monks' old cells and refectories turned into bedrooms and dining rooms for visiting buyers and dignitaries, with a level of luxury their former inhabitants would probably have regarded as sinful.

Today Barón de Ley is yet another "Rioja Baja Strikes Back" bodega turning out wines of exemplary quality, and at reasonable prices, too.

The Barón de Ley range encompasses white and *rosado jóvenes*, but reds start with Reserva (***>****) and go up to Gran Reserva (****>*****). These are big, classic, structured wines with tremendous ageing potential. The flagship wine is Finca Monasterio (*****) from a single vineyard in the old monastery garden, with sixty per cent Tempranillo and forty per cent, er, "others" (don't mention the Cabernet Sauvignon). It's a wine of great complexity, structure, fruit, and aromatics. These wines are fantastic value for money.

BENJAMÍN ROMEO

Vinos de Benjamín Romeo, Amorebieta 6 Baja, 26338 San Vicente de la Sonsierra, La Rioja. Tel: 941 334 228. Chief executive: Benjamín Romeo. Established: 1996. Type: private company. Own vineyards: 7ha. Own production: 100%.

Visits: No. Principal wines: Gallocanto; La Viña de Andrés; Cueva del Contador; Contador.

Benjamín Romeo was the winemaker at Artadi (*see* page 84) between 1985 and 2000, when it was building its worldwide reputation. His attention to detail in the bodega and (especially) the vineyard border on the obsessive, and that paid off for Artadi in a very big way. Meanwhile, his father, Andrés, was a *cosechero* in San Vicente de la Sonsierra, growing grapes and selling them to the co-op in the traditional manner. When Andrés started to think about retirement, Benjamín turned his attention to the family vineyards, and decided that he could "do an Artadi" with the family business.

In 1995, he began a complete analysis of the family's vineyards, selling some and buying others, especially those on the higher slopes with more chalk in the soil, and away from the alluvial river valleys – in any case, with vines no younger than twenty years old. The centre of San Vicente rises to 1,105 metres (3,624 feet) and Romeo's vineyards are all between 400 and 600 metres (1,312 and 1,968 feet): above the alluvial layers but not so high as to impede ripening or risk frost and wind damage. He also bought some underground cellars dating back to the twelfth and sixteenth centuries, particularly one in the foundations of the church, under the bell tower which is known as "Cueva del Contador". It gets its name from the days when the cool cellars of the church were used to store bags of flour, dried vegetables, cereals, and other crops, as well as goatskins of wine, which needed to be kept at a constant temperature and away from damp during the winter – in other words, perfect for wine storage. The *contador* (literally "counter") was the bookkeeper who checked all the goods in and out in a large ledger to make sure that everything was accounted for.

If Romeo is passionate in the bodega, he is obsessive in the vineyard. Of his seven hectares, 3.5 provide grapes for the single-vineyard La Viña de Andrés, named after his father. The other 3.5 are divided into twenty-two separate plots (that's an average of about forty metres [131 feet] square per plot scattered around the town, some with just a few dozen vines, many aged up to 100 years old. He knows not only every square metre of every vineyard, but every vine. On a spring visit with him to one of the plots – just about big enough to park half a dozen cars on – he fell upon the vines individually, examining the growth, removing a half-formed leaf growing in the wrong direction, scooping out handfuls of the chalky clay soil around a vine to allow recent rainfall easier access to the roots. During the ripening season, he visits the vineyards every single day and, allegedly, examines every grape on every vine, green harvests a bunch here and a bunch there if he thinks it's necessary, and cuts away leaves if they're obscuring the sun. Most of the plots are surrounded by wild flowers and herbs such as thyme, wild fennel, and sage, and Romeo is convinced that elements of the aromatics of these plants provide the microflora that inform the flavours of the grape. I am no botanist, but I suspect that he may be right.

And it doesn't stop there. At harvest time, all the grapes are hand-selected, and only bunches with which Romeo is satisfied get to the small oak *tinas* for alcoholic fermentation. Temperature control is by *placas* (devices lowered into fermentation vats to cool the wine), and once the primary fermentation is complete, the wine undergoes malolactic fermentation in new French oak *barricas*, renewed every year. Any wine that doesn't meet Romeo's standards is sold off to other bodegas (I think there's a queue most years), and that which passes his exacting palate will, typically, stay in the casks for about eighteen months or until he decides it's ready to be bottled. It is racked only at the time of the waning moon.

Meanwhile, Romeo commissioned a unique bottle for which he pays Euro 1.20, and he travels to Extremadura to select the individual trees from which he wants his corks made – in the case of Contador, the same as those bought by Château Pétrus in Pomerol – and he's happy to pay Euro 1.00 per cork to ensure quality, even to the extent of deciding which end of each cork will be the one to come into contact with the wine. All wines are bottled unfiltered.

The first vintage was in 1997, but it was very much an experimental one, as were the next three. In 2000, Romeo was satisfied that he had got the wine on the road to where he wanted it, and left Artadi to concentrate on the family business. The first "real" vintage was in 2001, and it was then that the various styles and brand names were finalized. Production, as you will have gathered, is minuscule. We were having lunch in the

Restaurante Las Duelas in Haro (highly recommended, by the way) and I popped outside to reschedule an appointment (always a necessity when having lunch in Spain). I mentioned that I was having lunch with Benjamín Romeo and my conversant expressed surprise: "You've tracked him down? You're having lunch? Be careful you don't drink his entire year's production!" I did venture the comment that, while he was arguably making a wine that was three times as good as most of the others, he was doing ten times the work to achieve it. I don't think he was amused.

One anecdote (unconfirmed by the man himself) concerns his wine's rating by the Great Wine Pundit, Robert M. Parker Jr., in the USA. The GWP gave Contador 2000 a score of 98+. When he was given the news, Romeo railed in disbelief. "Is that *all*?" he is reported to have demanded. And, by the way, no low-key, silver-grey Mercedes-Benz here: only a battered, white four-wheel-drive pick-up truck can access the steepest of those vineyard slopes. If there were a "vineyard anorak" award in this book, it would go to Benjamín Romeo.

Gallocanto ("Cock Crow" – ****) is a white wine which is made from approximately equal proportions of Viura, Garnacha Blanca, and Malvasía Riojana, fermented in the cask with no malolactic fermentation, and powerful, with honeyed and oaky hints. La Viña de Andrés (****>*****) is all Tempranillo with big, tight fruit and powerful tannins. All the wines, in common with all top-level Rioja producers, are made from hand-selected bunches of grapes, but Contador (*****) is also Tempranillo, made from individually hand-selected berries from the ripest bunches (the rest go into Cueva del Contador, which may be considered the "second wine" of the bodega). This *Beerenauslese* process creates a wine of tremendous aromatic, dark-fruit aromas, with concentrated fruit and tannins, endless length, and a structured austerity that promises much for the future. These wines are already legendary.

BERBERANA

Bodegas Lagunilla, Ctra Elciego, s/n, 26350 Cenicero, La Rioja. Tel: 941 453 100.
Fax: 941 453 114. Website: www.berberana.com. Email: info@berberana.com

The company formally changed its name from Berberana to Lagunilla in 2004, but Berberana remains the main brand. Lagunilla wines (*see* page 135) are also made in this bodega. The Berberana bodega in Fuenmayor retains the name for its bodega and brand, but the wines are *vinos de mesa*.

The vast, modern building that is the main Berberana bodega started off as a small family business in 1877, belonging to the Martínez Berberana family in Ollauri, whose cellars were near to the old Paternina (*see* page 175) bodega. They ran it successfully for ninety years until 1967, when they sold it to Melquíades Entrena, who had just sold his own family bodega to the group which had become Bodegas AGE (*see* page 74). Perhaps he was already nostalgic for the wine business. In any case, the business soon outgrew the small bodega in Ollauri, and Entrena decided to create a purpose-built installation close to the railway and the main road between Haro and Logroño, and this made its first vintage in 1975.

The Ollauri cellars still belong to the parent company, and provided the putative address for the wines branded Marqués de Griñón (*see* page 144), as part of the joint venture agreed in 1994, until 2000; the address was then changed to that of Dominio de Súsar but then changed again to the address of Bodegas Lagunilla – *see* the entry on Marqués de Griñón for further ramifications). In 1981, Melquíades Entrena died and the company was bought by the RuMaSA group, which was then buying up anything in the Spanish wine business that wasn't nailed down. This ended in tears in 1983, when RuMaSA tried to take over the Banco de España, was investigated by the Spanish government, forcibly taken into public ownership, and split up into its former component parts. The Berberana group was bought by a number of shareholders, including five local co-ops, and floated on the stock exchange in 1990.

One of the main shareholders was financier Víctor Redondo Sierra, and he masterminded the growth of Berberana into what has now become one of Spain's biggest groups, with holdings in Penedès and right along the river Duero, including a venture in the Douro region of Portugal and in Argentina. He it was who, in 1994, engineered the joint venture with the Marqués de Griñón to market a range of high-quality wines under the Griñón brand name, and arranged the acquisition of Lagunilla (*see* page 135) in that same year. In 1999, the group was consolidated under the name Arco-Bodegas Unidas, and in 2001 the international division, United Wineries International, moved its headquarters to London. In 2002, the group acquired the Dominio de Súsar estate in the Rioja Baja (*see* Marqués de la Concordia, page 145), and is also creating a chain of hotel/bodegas under the name "Haciendas de España". An associated company, Berberana Vinícola, has a large bodega making *vino de mesa* on the N-232 at Fuenmayor; you will no doubt have seen the Berberana Dragon Tempranillo.

Throughout all this, Berberana continued on its way making wines in the time-honoured manner. In the last years of the Entrena ownership things had been a little chaotic. I remember in the early 1980s coming across a parcel of *rosado* wine which had somehow become "lost" in the system for so many years that there was no record of it in the company's books. It was, however, unquestionably at least twenty years old, and the CRDO (as it was then) did happen to have some *contraetiquetas* from the 1966 vintage left in its stationery cupboard, so the company was allowed to sell the wine as 1966 Gran Reserva Rosado: the only one I've ever tasted (they don't make 'em like that any more). After the brief RuMaSA ownership things were tightened up and Berberana maintained its reputation for turning out reliable, decent, well-made wines at reasonable prices, a reputation that continues today.

D'Avalos Tempranillo (***) has six months in oak and is made from grapes from the co-op shareholders. It has nice, bright fruit and a decent length. Viña Alarde Reserva (***>****) has twenty per cent Garnacha and is classic Rioja, with the right balance between fruit and oak (my note reads "good, solid Rioja"). Carta de Oro Gran Reserva (****) also has twenty per cent Garnacha with thirty-six months in oak and is equally classic: round, mellow, and rich with a soft, oaky ripeness.

BERCEO
See Gurpegui (page 127)

BERONIA

Bodegas Beronia, Ctra Ollauri-Nájera Km 1.8, 26220 Ollauri, La Rioja. Tel: 941 338 000. Fax: 941 338 266. Website: www.beronia.com. Email: beronia@beronia.com. Contact: Cristina Zubizarreta. Winemaker: María-Jesús Sáez. Established: 1973. Type: SA. Own vineyards (ha): 10. Buy in: Yes. Group: González-Byass. Barrels: 16,000. Sales national: 65%; export: 35%. Top export markets: Germany, Holland, UK. Visits: contact bodega. Principal wines: Beronia Blanco Viura; Blanco Fermentado en Barrica; Crianza; Reserva; Gran Reserva; Mazuelo; Tempranillo Fermentado en Barrica

The origins of this bodega go back to a group of eighteen friends who were members of a *chiquiteo* – a peculiarly Basque wine and food society – from San Sebastián who wanted their own bodega. This was accomplished and the first vintage made in 1973. It takes its name from the Berones, an ancient tribe which occupied a good deal of the Ebro Valley in about 850 BC, about the time the first wines were being made in what was to become Jerez, in the southwest. Whether they made wine themselves is not recorded, but the bodega named after them proved to be a little under-capitalized, and within less than a decade (in 1982) a majority stake was sold to sherry giant González-Byass, which had been looking for a suitable property in Rioja for a number of years.

G-B brought with it investment, a massive network of world markets, and a salesforce and public relations machine the original investors could only have dreamed about. Today the bodega is very modern indeed, and with all the admin, sales, and marketing done in Jerez, the staff are free to concentrate on wine and winemaking. Seven of the original eighteen friends still own twenty-five per cent of the business between them, and G-B is very keen to buy up their shares, but with such a powerhouse of a company in charge, the minority shareholders are understandably reluctant to give them up. Grapes are bought on contract from growers within a radius of about ten kilometres (six miles) of the bodega, but particularly from the immediate surrounding area. Those in the immediate vicinity belong to the bodega itself and the policy is to keep the grapes as "local" as possible.

Wines Beronia Blanco (**) is a fresh, uncomplicated Viura with some skin contact before pressing to maximize the herby character of the grape; Blanco Fermentado en Barrica (**>***) has four to five months on the lees, giving it an oaky nose and more complexity. Tempranillo Fermentado en Barrica (***) is a real departure; barrel-fermented red wines are hardly known anywhere, and certainly not in Rioja. Hand-selected whole bunches are put into the tank and macerated to get the level of extract and colour required by the winemaker. Once this has been achieved, it passes by gravity into the cask (new, medium-high-toast American oak) and is allowed to ferment without cooling at temperatures which would make a "modernist" Rioja winemaker wince: up to 30°C (86°F), after which it undergoes malolactic fermentation, again in the cask. The whole process is very slow: anything up to five months in the barrel, with a total of anything up to eight to ten months on the lees. The result is remarkable: big extraction, dark purple colour, heavy, dark fruit, and oaky hints but low tannins – very drinkable when young, almost like a cross between *maceración carbonica* and post-modern high-extraction winemaking. Crianza (**>***) has characteristic light oak, fruit, and decent structure. Reserva (***) has fifteen per cent Graciano, which shows on the structure and tannins. Reserva Mazuelo (***>****) is the only varietal Mazuelo in Rioja at *reserva* level, and is rather unusual with richness, power, and a clean, tight-fruit finish. Gran Reservas (***>****) have a great deal of warmth and ripeness but these, too, tend to drink early and need to be drunk up within about eight years, even from great years. A new departure, unnamed at the time I tasted it, is a "high-expression" wine with eighty-eight per cent Tempranillo, the rest Mazuelo and Graciano, with twelve months in new French, American, and Bulgarian oak. It's in that typical powerful, concentrated, dark-fruit, high-extract style (****>*****).

BILBAÍNAS

Bodegas Bilbaínas, Estación 3, 26200 Haro, La Rioja. Tel: 941 310 147. Fax: 941 310 706. Website: www.codorniugroup.com. Email: b.haro@codorniu.es. Contact: Mabel Oyono. Chief executive/Winemaker: José Hidalgo Togores. Established: 1901. Type: SA. Own vineyards (ha): 256. Contract (ha): 200. Own production: 66%; Buy in: Yes. Number of staff: 50. Group: Codorníu. Barrels: 25,000. Type: American and French. Annual production (hl): 20,000. Sales national: 80%; export: 20%. Top export markets: Switzerland, USA, UK. Visits: by appointment; groups and individuals. Open: October–March, tours Tue–Fri 10am, 12 noon, 4.30pm; Saturdays 10am, 12 noon; Sundays 11am. April–September, Tue–Sun at 10am and 12 noon. Principal wines: Viña Pomal Gran Reserva; Reserva; Crianza; La Vicalanda Gran Reserva; Reserva

During the interregnum between the Rioja boom of the 1870s and early '80s, and the next (and rather short-lived) Rioja boom of the 1920s, French companies which had invested in the region were anxious to get out, and bodegas were available at relatively modest prices. Meanwhile, a Bilbao wine merchant, Santiago de Ugarte y Aurrecoechea, was tapping into the industrial boom of the port city, and wanted to ensure that he had ready supplies of good wine from Rioja. In 1901, he did a deal with Sauvignon Frères y Cía in Haro and bought their bodega, changing its name to Bodegas Bilbaínas in the process. His ceramic-tiled pediment is over the old main door, still advertising *Champan Lumen* and *Coñac Faro*; today the company's sparkling wine is called Royal Carlton and is made under the *denominación* cava, and the brandy seems to have disappeared altogether.

Ugarte took over a splendid winery in the typical honey-gold stone of the region, and with its own railway siding; the tracks (no longer connected to the main line) may still be seen alongside the old loading bay. The business expanded through various contacts, and Ugarte realized that the export market was vital to the company's future. Indeed, from 1925 to 1966, it had a dedicated office in London to service the UK market. Santiago de Ugarte retired in 1929 and handed the business over to his two sons, who continued in his expansionist style. In the 1970s, the next generation took over in the form of the founder's grandson-in-law Gonzalo Díez de Corral, and grandson, another Santiago Ugarte. They continued to expand the bodega and also increased the area of vineyards to become one of the largest vineyard landowners in Rioja.

Fast-forward to 1997, and the bodega had become a shadow of its former self, neglected as the Ugarte family had fragmented, and once again up for sale. The shining armour on this occasion belonged to cava giant Codorníu, and investment and refurbishment were immediate. Today, the elegant formal gardens and the old bodega are elegantly caparisoned, the entrance hall has been restored to its original magnificence, and Bilbaínas still has the largest area of privately owned vineyards in Rioja. In addition, the wines destined to become *reserva* and *gran reserva* are sourced from the company's own vineyards, the names of which are, perhaps, even better known that that of the bodega: Viña Pomal, Viña Zaco, Viña Paceta, and the very small La Vicalanda.

Viña Pomal Crianza (***) is absolutely reliable, all Tempranillo with twelve months in American oak. Reserva (****) is also Tempranillo, very traditional but twelve months in French oak. Viña Paceta (****) Tempranillo Crianza is made from grapes of high-altitude vineyards and has big, chewy, weighty fruit. La Vicalanda Reserva (****) is a single vineyard of 9.5 hectares within Viña Pomal and is also Tempranillo but with twelve months in new French oak. Gran Reserva (****>*****) has two years in new French oak.

BODEGAS Y BEBIDAS

See AGE, Domecq, Juan Alcorta, Ysios.

This group has been part of the Allied Domecq multinational group since 2001, and is Spain's largest wine company, with bodegas all over the country. It's also running what used to be called the Iverus Ars Vinum project, in which some bodegas are making wines more expressive of the terroir of their individual vineyards. Their labels used to carry the epithet *Ars Vinum* ("the art of wine"), but PR gurus in the UK pointed out that this could give rise to schoolboy sniggering (always a feature of British or, at least, English life), and it has latterly been removed and replaced with just the trademark "Iverus", which features the logo of a duck in flight. The group owns or controls 3,560 hectares of vineyards within the DOCa Rioja, in all three sub-zones, of which 875 hectares are in Quel, the highest village in the Rioja Baja at 490 metres (1,607 feet).

BORDÓN

Bodegas Franco Españolas, Cabo Noval, 2, 26006 Logroño, La Rioja.
Tel: 941 251 300 Fax: 941 262 948. Website: www.francoespanolas.com.
Email: comercial@francoespanolas.com. Contact: Juan-Carlos Llopart.
Chief executive: Marcos Eguizábal Ramírez. Winemaker: Carlos Estecha.
Established: 1890. Type: SA. Own vineyards (ha): 50. Buy in: Yes. Group:
Paternina. Barrels: 15,000. Sales national: 60; export: 40. Top export markets:
South America, Scandinavia. Visits: contact bodega. Principal wines: (White):
Diamante; Diamante Semidulce; Rinsol; Viña Soledad; Viña Soledad Tête de
Cuvée; Rioja Bordón Blanco. (Rosado): Rioja Bordón Rosado. (Red): Rioja Bordón
Crianza; Reserva; Gran Reserva; Royal Reserva; Excelso Gran Reserva; Barón de
Anglade Reserva

This bodega, as its name implies, dates from the time when phylloxera devastated the French vineyards and Rioja was the first port of call to buy wines. It was founded by a Frenchman, Frédéric Anglade Saurat, who bought and planted vineyards in 1890, although the bodega proper was not a business entity until 1901, around which time the present bodega, in the classic Rioja style, was built. After the "bust" of the early twentieth century (*see* chapter three) and the renaissance of Bordeaux, the French shareholding lost interest, and by 1922 it was entirely in Spanish hands.

The wines won an early following, as they had been originally formulated to suit the discerning French market, and Franco-Españolas became a reliable and respected name for wines which were, if not in the front rank, then certainly of a reliable and consistent quality, right through the Spanish Civil War, World War II, and beyond. The next big change came in 1973, when the company was bought out by RuMaSA, which was then buying up bodegas and vineyards as if there were no tomorrow.

When it turned out that there actually *was* no tomorrow, it came on the market again.

A side-note here about RuMaSA: the name is an acronym of Ruíz-Mateos SA. This was started by one José-María Ruíz Mateos y Jiménez de Tejada in 1961. He was a native of the province of Cádiz, a nobleman, businessman, and politician, and enjoyed early success in the entrepreneurial world of business, particularly in the wine business (Don Zoilo Sherry, which he established, is still one of the most reliable names in Jerez). In 1981, after many acquisitions, his company "overstretched" itself and was investigated by the Spanish government, then a hard-line PSOE (socialist) administration led by Felipe González Márquez. The investigators found what, in order to avoid any accusations of libel, we shall refer to as "accounting irregularities" and the company was taken into public ownership, its assets disposed of willy-nilly. Ruíz-Mateos saw this as a socialist plot against the richest man in Spain, and has continued to fight his case through the courts; elements of it are still *sub judice* even as you read this, so we will say no more.

In the event, Bodegas Franco-Españolas came on the market in 1985, which is when Marcos Eguizábal Ramírez comes into the story. He is a Riojano, born in El Villar de Arnedo, near Pradejón in the Rioja Baja. He moved to Logroño and thence Madrid, and made a fortune in the construction business. Wanting to return to his roots, he bought Franco-Españolas in 1985, along with Bodegas Paternina (*see* page 175). Although he is now in his eighties, he still visits the bodega on a weekly basis.

The bodega is remarkably unspoiled despite the suburban sprawl from the centre of Rioja (a friend of mine who lives in an apartment by the *circunvalación*, right on the southern edge of the city, had a telephone call from an estate agent wondering if she would like to sell, as there was great demand for housing in the "city centre" – presumably for Olympic race-walkers) and it retains much of its turn-of-the-century charm. Winemaking kit is modern and the style is classic, for the most part. The wines are largely old-fashioned but, perhaps, none the worse for that.

Bordón is the main brand. Bordón Blanco (**) is a *joven* Viura, pleasant, fresh, delicious. Rosado (*) is eighty-five per cent Garnacha and fifteen per cent Viura, an old-fashioned blend, giving a pleasant, if rather neutral style. Tinto Crianza (**) is well-made, with twelve months in American oak. Reserva (***) is very nice: twenty-four months in

American oak, with fruit and a good, spicy length. Gran Reserva (***>****) does have the perfumed, elegant, silky oak and is usually ready for immediate drinking. Baron d'Anglade (****) is named after the company represented by the founder, a *reserva* made from hand-selected grapes and aged in Alliers oak; delicious ripe fruit, spicy with some austere oak on the finish. An unusual departure is Diamante Semidulce (**), made from mainly overripe Malvasía and with a delicate, floral sweetness.

BRETÓN

Bodegas Bretón Criadores, Ctra Fuenmayor Km 1.5, 26370 Navarrete, La Rioja.
Tel: 941 440 840. Fax: 941 440 812. Website: www.bodegasbreton.com.
Email: info@bodegasbreton.com. Contact: Eladio Fernández. Chief executive: José Luís Benítez. Winemaker: Javier Ortega. Established: 1985. Type: SL.
Own vineyards (ha): 106. Contract (ha): 150. Own production: 40%. Buy in: Yes.
Number of staff: 18. Group: No. Barrels: 7,000. Type: American and French.
Sales national: 70%; export: 30%. Top export markets: EU, Germany, UK. Visits:
by appointment; groups and individuals. Open weekdays: 8am–1pm;
2.30pm–5.30pm. Principal wines: Loriñón Blanco barrel-fermented; Crianza;
Reserva; Gran Reserva; Dominio de Conte Reserva de Finca; Alba de Bretón
Reserva Viñas Viejas; Pagos del Camino Garnacha de Finca Viñas Viejas.

The origins of Bretón go back to 1983, when Pedro Bretón, with backing from local business people in Logroño, built a bodega in the city, with a first vintage in 1985 that came on the market in 1988. The winemaker was Miguel-Ángel de Gregorio, who set the standards by which the bodega's wines are still judged. The first brand was Loriñón, after the forty-hectare vineyard of the same name, and in 1989 a wine was made from the twenty-two-hectare vineyard of Dominio de Conte. In 1995, the flagship Alba de Bretón was created, and then Pagos del Camino, made from eighty-year-old Garnacha vines in a tiny 1.3-hectare vineyard in Navarrete beside the Camino de Santiago. This was Miguel-Ángel de Gregorio's last year at Bretón, as he left to establish his own bodega, Allende (*see* page 79).

The company's reputation was maintained and later enhanced by the building of a brand-new bodega in Navarrete, which made its first part-vintage in 2001, and the first almost-full one in 2002. Some wine was still made in the old bodega in Logroño, but the new bodega made the whole vintage from 2005. Winemaking kit is state-of-the-art and, interestingly, this is one of the bodegas that has installed modern, computer-controlled basket presses rather than pneumatic or other types. The grapes are fermented whole in the tank, then passed to the presses, which have three pressure settings to produce three levels of must. All of these are fermented separately and then the winemaker decides how they will be blended for the final *cuvée*. The new bodega also has what I can only describe as a "side-chapel" for Alba de Bretón in which the wine matures in reverent silence in thirty-five new French oak casks, while worshippers visit in suitable awe. Pedro Bretón's daughter María-Victoria Bretón Sáenz is now the managing director.

Wines Loriñón is the largest vineyard element of Bretón, and the white Loriñón Fermentado en Barrica (**>***) is made from Viura with three months on the lees in new American oak: crisp, rich, savoury, and delicious. The Crianza (***) is mainly Tempranillo with fifteen per cent in equal parts of Graciano, Mazuelo, and Garnacha, and fourteen months in American oak: good structure, tannins, and locked-in fruit. The Reserva (***>****) has sixteen to twenty months in American oak and shows the classic fruit/oak relationship with a very nice length. The Gran Reserva (****) develops a mature, slightly "gamey" ripeness and spicy fruit. All these wines need three to five years after release to show at their best. Dominio de Conte (*****) is a 90/10 Tempranillo/Graciano mix with fourteen to eighteen months in new American oak and shows impressive ageing potential, concentration, and complexity. Pagos del Camino (*****) is made from the tiny plantation of ancient Garnacha and is fermented on the skins for twenty-two days before pressing, then aged in new French oak for malolactic fermentation. It offers a very spicy, dark, and yet still fresh and almost "sweet" fruit with wonderful concentration. Alba de Bretón (*****) is made entirely from old-vine Tempranillo and offers tremendous extraction, fruit, power, spice, and yet a freshness of fruit which is quite amazing.

CAMPILLO

Bodegas Campillo, Finca Villa Lucía, 01300 Laguardia, Álava.

Tel: 945 600 826. Fax: 945 600 837. Website: www.bodegascampillo.es.

Email: info@bodegascampillo.es. Winemaker: Miguel-Ángel López-Davalillo.

Established: 1990. Type: SL. Own vineyards (ha): 50. Buy in: Yes. Group: Faustino Martínez, Marqués de Vitoria, Valcarlos, Condesa de Leganza, Victorianas. Barrels:

12,000; Sales national: 75%; export: 25%. Top export markets: Canada, EU, Switzerland. Visits: contact the bodega. Principal wines: Campillo Blanco; Rosado; Crianza; Reserva; Gran Reserva; Reserva Especial; Campillo Reserva Pago Cuesta Claro Raro

One of the most beautiful bodegas in Rioja, purpose-designed and built, and inaugurated in 1990, although the first vintage was actually made here from the surrounding vineyards in 1988, and wines under the brand name "Campillo" had actually been around for very much longer than that. The parent company has been buying grapes and wines, and blending and ageing them since the first bodega in 1861. The wine wasn't bottled until 1930, and the first brand name to be used was Campillo. As things developed, the Campillo brand became Faustino's "Bordeaux-style" wine, and the main bodega produced the "Burgundy-style" wine; this was how the market was in the mid-to-late twentieth century.

The idea for a dedicated bodega came from the head of the family, Julio Faustino Martínez, who took over the group in 1957. He wanted to recreate the style and feel of a Bordeaux château sitting among its own vineyards, and building started in 1988. The bodega was named after the Faustino family's first brand name, and was formally opened in 1990. It's surrounded by seven vineyards in some of the best chalk-rich clay of the Rioja Alavesa, growing mainly Tempranillo.

A bit more author-archaeology: in 1989, I was a member of a party of journalists invited to the Estación de Enología (Oenology Station) in Haro for a tasting of *reservas* and *gran reservas*, and one of them was a Campillo Reserva. I was impressed and asked whether we could visit the bodega and the response was, er, well, no, because they don't have one. They buy where they can, they make where they can, the end result comes out of Bodegas Faustino. Fast-forward to 1992, and after a near-fatal road accident I found myself in hospital in Kettering, Northamptonshire, England. After three or four days of semi-consciousness I awoke to find a case of six bottles from Jeremy Watson and my chums at Wines from Spain in London waiting for me (in adversity, you do find out who your real friends are). One of the bottles was the 1982 Campillo Reserva, and one of the senior nurses (dash'd attractive, as I remember) assured me that even people with head and pelvic injuries such as mine were encouraged to enjoy a glass or two of wine with their meal. Hospital food tends to be less than exciting, but the pork roast they brought seemed just right, and the wine, once opened, perfumed the ward with raspberry, cherry, vanilla, and spice – a bit cruel for the chap in the opposite bed who was on nil-by-mouth for a double hip operation later that day, but I hadn't eaten or tasted anything but water for nearly a week. As I was about to partake, a porter appeared with a trolley and asked "Radford?" I nodded. "X-ray," he replied as I was hoisted on to the trolley and wheeled away, the wine, untasted, languishing on my overbed table. By the time I returned the only food left was cold cod casserole which is, perhaps, not really appropriate with 1982 *reserva* Rioja. But I drank the bugger anyway, and enjoyed every drop. So this is a declaration of interest.

The wines are mainly Tempranillo. Campillo Crianza (***>****) is very reliable and reaches great heights in good years, in the classic style. Reserva (****) has a little Cabernet Sauvignon to "lift" the nose and play down the twenty-four months in oak. Gran Reserva (****>*****) is selected Tempranillo and can be astonishingly good in otherwise unspectacular years; Reserva Especial (****>*****) has, typically, about twenty-five per cent Cabernet Sauvignon and fifteen per cent Graciano and is made from old, low-yielding vines. It's only made when the right grapes are available and in great years can be truly outstanding, and offers the prospect of very long ageing. Reserva Pago Cuesta Claro Raro (*****) is an experimental wine first made in 1998 from a small single-vineyard plantation of Tempranillo Peludo vines. It was bottled only in magnums and jeroboams, launched in October 2003, and sold out in December, 2003. It's as big as a house and as austere as monk's cell, but may start to open out at about ten years old. They are looking at the prospect of doing the same with the 2001.

CARLOS SERRES

Bodegas Carlos Serres, Avda Sto. Domingo, 40, 26200 Haro, La Rioja.
Tel: 941 310 279. Fax: 941 310 418. Website: www.carlosserres.com.
Email: info@carlosserres.com. Established: 1896. Type: SA.
Principal wines: Serres Joven Tempranillo; Viura Lágrima; Garnacha Rosado;
Blanco Fermentado en Barrica; Carlos Serres (Crianza, Reserva, Gran Reserva);
Onomástica Reserva Especial

The foundation date above predates the present company in name and address. The business was a wine merchant run by a Frenchman, Alphonse Vigier, who had moved to Rioja during the boom years. Along with many others he elected to return to France when it became apparent that the recession was here to stay, and he went in 1896, leaving the business to his partners Charles Serres (also a Frenchman, from Orléans) and Cipriano Roig. They decided that, as there wasn't much money in buying and selling wine, they could do better if they started making the wine and selling, thereby culling both maker's and wholesaler's share of the profit. They bought an existing bodega in the Calle de las Cuevas in Haro (just down the hill from Berceo) and called it Bodegas Cipriano Roig. The venture was successful, and in 1904 its name was changed to Bodegas Roig y Serres. The son of Charles Serres, also Charles but now Hispanicized as Carlos Serres, took over in 1932 and changed the name again to Bodegas Carlos Serres Hijo, although the "Hijo" ("son") was dropped before very long. The company moved to its present address in a newly built bodega in 1966, and became a limited company in 1975 under the third generation of the Serres family.

Onomástica Reserva Especial (****) is the bodega's flagship wine, made from Tempranillo and Graciano from thirty-year-old vines with, typically, twenty-four months in French oak: made in the classic, long-lived Rioja style, but not too oaky, with good tannic grip and fruit balance even at ten years old. It represents excellent value for money. The name means "Saint's Day" or "Fiesta", with the implication that this is a wine to enjoy on special occasions.

CASTILLO DE CUZCURRITA

Castillo de Cuzcurrita, SA, Del Puente, 26214 Cuzcurrita de Río Tirón, La Rioja.
Tel: 941 301 620. Fax: 944 151 071. Website: www.cuzcurrita.com.
Email: castillodecuzcurrita@cuzcurrita.com. Winemaker: Ana Martín Onzain.
Established: 1999. Type: SA. Own vineyards (ha): 7. Buy in: Yes. Group:
unrelated. Barrels: 135. Type: French. Annual production (hl): 750. Visits:
contact bodega. Principal wines: Señorío de Cuzcurrita; Castillo de Cuzcurrita
This must be one of Rioja's prettiest bodegas, within the walls of a medieval castle surrounded by elegantly manicured gardens, and also including a private canal: the mill-race of an old hydroelectric generation plant that once supplied what at the time was the tiny settlement of Cuzcurrita de Río Tirón. The Tirón, of course, is a tributary of the Ebro, and the village (which still has fewer than 500 inhabitants) is almost impossibly picturesque. The reason for the castle's original existence was

that this is right on the western edge of Rioja, just a few kilometres from the province of Burgos in Castile-León and, as recorded elsewhere in this book, relationships between La Rioja and its much bigger western neighbour were once less than cordial.

The castle had been a bodega for many years but didn't have the economy of scale to make a decent profit. The altitude didn't help; at 519 metres (1,702 feet) it's hard to make the grapes ripen, and the winemaking kit was, by all accounts, rather primitive, so the wine wouldn't have commanded a particularly good price. The bodega was abandoned in 1989, although the owners continued to work the vineyards and sell the grapes each harvest time.

In 1999, the castle and its vineyards were bought by Lexus, the motor group, as an investment property and a working bodega, and they called in one of Spain's leading flying winemakers, Ana Martín, to get it up and running again. "I think they were a bit taken aback," she says with a giggle, "when I told them how much it was going to cost to bring the equipment up to date!" But, by all accounts, they swallowed hard and paid up. The first vintage was in 2000, and Ana was still working with the old cement tanks and press. The wine, in her words, was "acceptable", but she decided it wasn't good enough to put on the market under the new name, and it is reserved for tasting by visitors to demonstrate how the bodega has evolved since then. The new kit was finally all in place for the 2001 vintage, which was the first to come on the market in any quantity. The main wine is Señorío de Cuzcurrita, but she has earmarked certain plots to make a flagship wine called Castillo de Cuzcurrita in the very best years.

One good thing the previous owners left behind, however, was the vineyard: all twenty- to thirty-five-year-old vines, with five hectares within the castle's own grounds and two outside. While ripening and colour are still a challenge at this altitude, by lowering yields (to 5,000 kilograms per hectare against the permitted maximum of 6,500) and being judicious in terms of picking, Ana can get the fruit she needs. The company is also actively buying more vineyards in the area.

The Señorío de Cuzcurrita (***>****) has good, ripe, spicy fruit and a lot of tannin which should ensure good keeping qualities. The wine is all Tempranillo with, typically, twelve to fourteen months in French oak no older than second-year.

CONTINO

Viñedos del Contino, Finca San Rafael, Laserna, Laguardia, 01321 Álava.
Tel: 945 600 201. Fax: 945 621 114. Website: www.cvne.com. Email:
laserna@contino-sa.com. Contact: María Urrutia. Chief executive: Víctor Urrutia.
Winemaker: Jesús Madrazo; email: jesus.madrazo@contino-sa.com. Established:
1973. Type: SA. Own vineyards (ha): 62. Own production: 100%. Buy in: No.
Group: CVNE/Contino/Viña Real. Barrels: 2,000. Type: American and French.
Annual production (hl): 3,000. Sales national: 80%; export: 20%. Top export
markets: UK, Switzerland, Mexico. Visits: by appointment; groups and individuals.
Open weekdays: 10am–2pm; 4pm–7pm. Other languages: English and French.
Principal wines: Contino Crianza; Reserva; Gran Reserva; Graciano; Viña Del Olivo

The history of this joint venture goes back a long way before the date
above. The Contino estate is on the Álava bank of a bend in the river Ebro,
and since it became a singular entity has only ever made wine from its
own sixty-two hectares of vineyards. It is dominated by a magnificent old
mansion house which dates from the fifteenth century and now houses
bottle cellars and accommodation for visiting guests. It was heavily renovated
in 1974 and again in the late 1980s, after a chemical infection from an
injudiciously used wood preservative had spread through the cellars. The
interior accommodation was also totally refurbished in the late 1990s,
but the outside of the building retains its ancient charm and looks much
as it has done for centuries.

In the 1940s the individual *cosecheros* who owned the land had started
selling their grapes to CVNE (*see* page 109) in Haro, which had had a
reputation for high-quality wines since the nineteenth century. A company
called Sociedad Vinícola Laserna was formed in 1974 in which some of
the *cosecheros* were bought out and the remainder became shareholders,
with CVNE. One of those vineyard owners was the Sánchez family, and
Eduardo Sánchez, who is now the millionaire publisher of ¡Hola! magazine
in the Spanish-speaking world and Hello! magazine in the English-
speaking world. He took an interest in the joint venture, realizing its
potential to make one of Rioja's great wines.

In 1987–8, the cellars became infected with TCA, the chemical
compound that causes wines to become "corky", and every scrap of
wood had to be ripped out and replaced. The company took this as an
opportunity to do a major restoration of the building, which involved
serious investment. Several of the smaller shareholders got cold feet at

this, and Sánchez stepped in to buy their shares, resulting in a roughly 50/50 split with CVNE, plus a very few remaining small shareholders. It was at this time that they decided to change the name to Viñedos del Contino and become a limited company.

Contino was a non-hereditary title of rank which has long died out, but was given to Pedro de Samaniego, who lived in the house during the reign of the Catholic monarchs (1452–1504). He was a member of the royal bodyguard appointed to watch over the family *continuamente* (continually), from which the title is derived; indeed, in the fifteenth century the estate included, quite literally, "the vineyards of the *contino*".

Jesús Madrazo Real de Asúa is a member of the family which owns CVNE, and he was the winemaker at Contino until 1998, during which period he was the first to experiment with French oak. Rigorous in his selection of grapes, in 1993 he rejected the lot and they were all sold off. He was also meticulous in his selection of finished wines. For these reasons, as well as the natural advantages of the site, the wine earned itself an impressive reputation for quality and reliability.

José retired in 1998 and his son, Jesús Madrazo, took over. He had been working alongside his father for many years and was well-versed in the nature of Contino wine. He has turned out to be no less innovative than his father, particularly in experiments with individual plots of vineyard, most notably the Viña del Olivo (old vines around an ancient olive tree) and a varietal Graciano. He is no less perfectionist, as well; I remember being there at vintage time one year when it started to rain, about 10.30 in the morning. He immediately stopped the harvest, brought in the grapes that had already been picked, and sent the harvesters home rather than risk picking in the wet or – almost as bad – waiting for the rain to stop and harvesting grapes with water still on them.

Contino originally only made *reservas*, but there are now five wines in the range, all but the Graciano mainly Tempranillo with five to fifteen per cent of Garnacha, Mazuelo, and/or Graciano. Contino Crianza (***>****) is very reliable, a good cut above your average *crianza*, with eighteen months in oak. Reserva (****>*****) is perhaps the bodega's strongest suit, as it has been the mainstay of production for so long: twenty-four months in oak. In outstanding years, these are arguably the best *reservas* in Rioja (*pace* Remelluri; *see* page 184). Gran Reserva (*****) is only made when Jesús is happy that the finest grapes have been harvested and is never less than outstanding. Contino is fortunate in having a decent-sized plantation of Graciano (and the microclimate to ripen it fully) and releases a Graciano varietal (*****) with fourteen months in oak. Viñedo del Olivo (*****) is a selection of the best grapes from vines around a 1,000-year-old olive tree on the oldest part of the estate. Its concentration, power, and fragrance are astonishing.

CORRAL

Bodegas Corral, Ctra de Logroño Km 10, 26370 Navarrete, La Rioja. Tel: 941 440 193. Fax: 941 440 195. Website: www.donjacobo.es. Email: info@donjacobo.es. Contact: Cristina Martínez De Luís. Chief Executive: Federico Javier Martínez Blanco. Winemaker: Pedro Tofé Salaverri. Established: 1898.

Type: SA. Own vineyards (ha): 40. Contract (ha): 120-140. Own production: 100%. Number of staff: 14. Group: No. Barrels: 4,800–5,100. Type: American and French. Annual production (hl): 10,000. Sales national: 40%; export: 60%. Top export markets: UK, Scandinavia, USA. Visits: by appointment. Groups only. Open weekdays: 10am–2pm; 5pm–8pm. Principal wines: Don Jacobo Blanco, Rosado; Crianza; Reserva; Gran Reserva; Altos de Corral Reserva

This is very much a family affair and has been since its foundation. It was established by Saturnino Daroca, a returning veteran of the Carlist wars. Understandably looking for a quieter life, he planted vines on land he owned near Navarrete, and bought a house and wine cellar from the local monastery. He was succeeded by his daughter and son-in-law Martín Corral, and they carried on the family business. It was their children, however, who were to make the biggest leap forward for the bodega. Brothers Gregorio and Florencio Corral Daroca decided to take their wines outside the local area and sell in wider Spain and even abroad, and built export markets in much of Europe, Scandinavia, the USA, and Canada.

The family found that they needed more capacity and decided to build a modern winery in Navarrete; this was completed in time for the 1974 vintage. The bodega actually backs on to the Camino de Santiago (hence the brand name of the wines), which is a rough track at this point, though well polished by the feet of pilgrims or the hooves of their donkeys (or, as I saw on a recent visit to the bodega, the tyres of their mopeds) over the past 1,000 years. Next door to the bodega, alongside the *camino*, are the ruins of the chapel of Santa María, once part of the hospital of the order of San Juan, which, from 1185, ministered to and lodged pilgrims for many centuries. In spite of the fact that so little is left, it really does still have an air of peace and tranquillity, even on a rainy and overcast Saturday morning.

In 1978, the brothers Corral, now aged seventy-one and seventy, decided that they needed to hand on the day-to-day running of the bodega to someone whom they could trust and who had the energy to succeed, and lit upon the twenty-six-year-old Javier Martínez Blanco, son of *cosecheros* in Cenicero and someone with whom they had had dealings for several years. He had a reputation for being a bit of a showman (always good when dealing with customers) and joined the company as general manager in that year. His sister Valvanera later joined in the export department, and Javier's daughter Cristina now looks after marketing and public relations. Gregorio Corral died in 1980, and his brother Florencio in 1990. Javier became the chief executive and bought a minority shareholding in the company; the majority still belongs to the Corral family.

One of Javier's first projects was the development in the 1990s of the single estate Altos de Corral, on a ten-hectare site above the town of Navarrete at an altitude of 549 metres (1,800 feet) with red, iron-rich soils littered with large stones and planted in twenty-five-year-old Tempranillo, cropping at 4,500 kilograms per hectare: about two-thirds of the permitted maximum. It also has magnificent views across the Ebro Valley and is a little exposed, but Javier Martínez plans to make a flagship wine from this vineyard in only the very best years. The first was made in the magnificent vintage of 1995, but even in that year, only twenty-five per cent of the grapes were used for Altos de Corral. As the vines age, he hopes to increase the proportion incrementally. The second vintage was made in 1998.

A footnote on Javier and his daughter: they agreed to meet me on a Saturday, knowing that weekends are a "dead zone" for visiting bodegas. As I was leaving, they had a whispered conversation and Javier said to me, "I spend four months of the year away from home, travelling all over the world to sell my wine, and I know what it is to spend the weekends alone in a hotel: room with no one to see. Would you like to come and have dinner with us at home tonight?" I was quite taken aback at their generosity. As it happened, I knew that the weekend was going to be empty and had already planned dinner with a friend in Logroño that night and a day of feverish writing-up of notes in my lodgings for the Sunday, so I was unable to accept. But I thought it was a wonderful gesture: not just giving up a chunk of the sacred family weekend to meet an old hack, but offering to extend it into the evening and invite him into the privacy of the home. Corral is still very much a family affair.

Corral red wines tend to be eighty to 100 per cent Tempranillo with the rest mostly Garnacha and Mazuelo; there is a little Graciano, plus Viura for the white wines. Don Jacobo Blanco (**>***) is in a very pleasant, fresh, herby style, walking the tightrope between the Viura's fruit and acidity. Rosado (**>***) is 50/50 Tempranillo and Garnacha with seven hours' maceration, and Javier describes it as a "a *rosado* for red-wine drinkers": musky, fresh, savoury, and with some weight. I made a side note that these were two of the most pleasant, subtle wines I'd tasted that week. In the reds, Don Jacobo Crianza (***) is described as an "anytime wine": good, spicy, fruit; decent length; delicious. The Reserva (***>****) is weightier, richer, and more complex, with an excellent finish. Gran Reserva (****) is described by Javier as a "classic" wine aimed at the traditional Rioja-lover (*i.e.* it really needs food to show at its best); it has a powerful balance and that hint of oxidation that characterizes wines with a long time in cask – typically twenty-eight months. I tasted the first two vintages of Altos de Corral to see how the wine develops. The 1998 (****>*****), with fourteen to eighteen months in American oak, has high-end aromatics and a sweet fruit which I described in my notes as "knockout", but it does have good balance and doesn't take your breath away as do some of the modern, high-expression wines. The 1995 (*****) has tamed that power, and emerges with a beautiful structure and complexity and a delicious, elegant length. Javier is of the opinion that it's too heavy to drink throughout a meal, but I suspect few will agree with him.

CVNE

CVNE, Barrio de la Estación s/n, 26200 Haro, La Rioja. Tel: 941 304 800. Fax: 941 304 815. Website: www.cvne.com. Email: haro@cvne.com. Contact: María Urrutia. Chief executive: Víctor Urrutia. Winemakers: Basilio Izquierdo and María Larrea. Established: 1879. Type: SA. Own vineyards (ha): 150. Contract (ha): 450. Own production: 50%. Buy in: Yes, but only in Rioja Alta. Number of staff: 156. Group: includes Viña Real and Contino. Barrels: 42,000. Type: American and French. Annual production (hl): 40,000. Sales national: 80%; export: 20%. Top export markets: UK, Switzerland, Mexico. Visits: by appointment;

groups and individuals. Open weekdays: 10am–2pm; 4pm–7pm. Principal wines:
Cune Crianza; Reserva; Blanco Joven; Rosado Joven; Imperial Reserva; Gran
Reserva; Real de Asúa; Monopole Blanco Joven

The initials stand for Compañía Vinícola del Norte de España, and the
acronym is usually pronounced "COO-nay". As it was so widespread the
company eventually gave up and adopted it as a brand name: Cune. The
firm was founded in the boom years of Rioja, and almost by accident.
Eusebio and Raimundo Real de Asúa served in the second Carlist war and
were involved in the lifting of the siege of Bilbao, where they settled once
the war was over. Eusebio, however, was taken ill. He had always been
asthmatic, and a cold winter in the trenches fighting in the war had made
his condition worse. His doctor recommended a drier climate, and in
1877 he moved to Haro, where he bought an apartment. His children
were at school in Bilbao, so they and his wife only visited during the
school holidays. It was a time when Rioja and wine were synonymous.
Export to France, still in the grip of the phylloxera epidemic, was increasing
exponentially. Eusebio had been educated in Bordeaux and developed a
taste for the wines of Bordeaux, and he quickly got to know the French
and Riojano movers and shakers in the wine business. He summoned his
brother from Bilbao, a new friend from Rioja, Isidro Corcuera, who was a
vineyard expert, and he contacted friends with contacts in the trade in
Spain and France; between them they set up the company in 1879. The
railway line from Bilbao to Logroño had already arrived in Haro (Logroño
was connected the following year), so it seemed to make sense to be as
close as possible to the railway station. The name of the company at that
time was Corcuera, Real Asúa y Compañia SCM (Sociedad Colectiva
Mercantil), reflecting the names of the two major shareholders.

At this time, the company did not make any wine. It was an
almacenista: buying and blending young wines, ageing them, and then
selling them into the market. In 1882, they decided to build a bodega on
the site, but to do this they had to transform into a limited company. In
the process they decided to change the name to CVNE and so it has
stayed. The wines continued to be appreciated for their quality, and for a
brief period in the early 1900s the bodega produced a Rioja Espumoso,
although no examples of it remain.The buildings were rebuilt and
improved, new equipment was brought in (mainly from France in the
early twentieth century), and the company continued to prosper.

Fast-forward to 1974, and the establishment of what is now Contino (*see* page 105). The winemaker of CVNE, José Madrazo Real de Asúa, took on responsibility for winemaking at the new bodega in Laserna and retained overall control at CVNE as well. In 1989, he oversaw the installation of what was then arguably the most modern winery in Spain, if not the world. This was the first automated system in Rioja, and has to be seen to be believed. The grapes are received into *autoevacuaciones* (self-emptying tanks, sometimes known as flying saucers, with lids on top and underneath) on a carousel. When the winemaker thinks that enough grapes are in the tank, the carousel moves on and the next tank is filled. Meanwhile, the previous tank is hoisted by an overhead crane over one of eighty-two fixed tanks, and its contents fall by gravity and start to undergo fermentation in that tank. In this way, the winemaker can ferment in as many as eighty-two batches, selected by vineyard, variety, ripeness, or whatever he chooses. The wine is then run off, again by gravity, to the floor below for malolactic fermentation. The fixed tank is on stilts, raising it high enough for another "flying saucer" to be wheeled underneath by a forklift truck after fermentation and run-off, so that the pulp can fall, again by gravity, into a fresh tank to be hauled by yet another mobile crane above the press such that the pulp can fall into it. This was ground-breaking in its day, but is almost commonplace now.

In those days, CVNE made its mainstream wines plus the flagship Imperial and Viña Real in this winery in Haro. The difference between them was that Imperial was (mostly) Rioja Alta grapes (bottled in a "Bordeaux" bottle) and Viña Real was (mostly) Rioja Alavesa grapes (bottled in a "Burgundy" bottle). Even though the Haro bodega is barely five kilometres (three miles) from the border with Álava, there were worries that the time taken to bring the grapes to the winery was too long to ensure optimum quality. In addition, even with eighty-two tanks to play with, the winemaker was running out of space in Haro. For this reason, the company decided to invest in a dedicated new bodega in the Laguardia area, and since the 2001 vintage, Viña Real (*see* page 209) has been a stand-alone operation with wines made there from 100 per cent Alavesa grapes. Similarly, Imperial is now 100 per cent Alta grapes. Since the retirement of José Madrazo in 1998 (although I understand that he drops in now and then to irritate his successors), each of the wineries in the group – CVNE, Contino, and Viña Real – has its own dedicated winemaker.

The wines are all Rioja classics. I have fond memories of the late 1980s and early '90s when I used to lodge with friends in south London. It would have been rude to offer them money, so I always paused at a wine merchant on the walk down from the tube station. The merchant seemed to have an inexhaustible supply of Imperial Gran Reserva 1973 for about £32 a magnum, which we inevitably demolished over dinner the same night. Of course, 1973 wasn't a particularly brilliant year (*Buena* *** according to the CRDOCa) but this did not restrict our enjoyment one jot, even given that the wine was fifteen-plus years old at the time. I remember it as perfumed, aromatic, complex, delicate, and delicious. The Cune *jóvenes* (**) are all good quality, the Crianza and Monopole white (***) better, and the Reserva (***>****) is a good, mainstream wine. Imperial (****>*****) is a legend in its own lunchtime, and Real de Asúa (*****) is a flagship wine made from forty-plus-year-old vines from the village of Villalba, hand-selected in only the best vintages, and fermented in small oak *tinas* rather than the big winery. The first vintage was the 1994, and it is, perhaps, a fitting tribute to the memory of the founding father of the bodega, Eusebio Real de Asúa.

DARIEN

Bodegas Darien, Avda Mendavia 29, 26006 Logroño, La Rioja. Tel: 941 258 130. Fax: 941 270 352. Website: www.darien.es. Email: info@darien.es.
Contact: María Vicente. Chief executive: Juan-Luís González Najarro. Winemaker: Tomás Iturriaga de Pablo. Established: 1999. Type: SL. Own vineyards (ha): 66. Contract (ha): 40. Own production: 65%. Buy in: Yes. Number of staff: 13. Group: No. Barrels: 1,727. Type: American and French. Annual production (hl): 3,800. Sales national: 60%; export: 40%. Top export markets: USA, UK, Switzerland. Visits: contact bodega. Principal wines: Darien Tempranillo; Crianza; Reserva; Selección; Delius

This is a project founded by construction millionaire Luís Ilarraza, with ambitious plans that include a brand-new, state-of-the-art, purpose-built bodega on the Zaragoza road out of Logroño, just east of the Ygay estate of Marqués de Murrieta. The company already owns extensive vineyards in this area. The bodega and the wine are named after Georges Darien (1862–1921), the radical French writer, and the *alta expresión* wine is named after the English composer Frederick Delius (1862–1935). Future additions to the range will follow this artistic theme.

The bodega started out in 1999 as Viñedos y Bodegas XXI, but, as with so many producers in Rioja and beyond, changed its name to that of its main wine, Darien, in 2004, ready for the move to the new bodega in 2005. The company's first home was the old Palacios Remondo (*see* page 172) bodega in Logroño when that company decided to consolidate its activities near its main vineyards in Alfaro. The Logroño bodega is a reasonably smart, modern affair with plenty of stainless steel and a generously proportioned underground barrel cellar. Winemaker Tomás Iturriaga de Pablo knows it very well indeed, as he worked here for Palacios Remondo before the relocation. Tomás is of the modern school of winemaking, refusing to describe himself as a winemaker. "The wine makes itself," he says. "I just help it along." This is an attitude becoming very prevalent in Rioja, and much to be desired. External affairs are handled by the dynamic (and fabulously attractive) export director, María Vicente. Bodegas Darien has all the hallmarks of becoming a touchstone bodega of the new Rioja, and it may be rather a trivial point, but I was somehow reassured by the company trademark which is a kind of "smiley'" cut-out in the top right-hand corner of the labels, business cards, and the company brochure. Silly, perhaps, but you remember the label and, through it, the wine. Top brands have been built on less.

Wines Darien Tempranillo (***) is a fresh, easy-drinking young wine that is quite simply delicious. Crianza (****) is mainly Tempranillo but has an unusual twenty to thirty per cent of Garnacha, as well as Mazuelo and Graciano, with good, ripe, warm fruit and a crisp, complex finish. Reserva (****) is also mainly Tempranillo but is more austere, structured, and layered on the palate, with a hint of cacao. Selección (****>*****) is made from a selection of the year's best grapes, and varies in content year by year, depending on which varieties have fared well, but always mainly Tempranillo. The style is concentrated, tannic, and austere, but packed with slow-release fruit. These are wines to keep. Delius (*****) is the *alta expresión* wine, made only in the best years from the most rigorous selection of grapes, and typically about seventy-five per cent Tempranillo and twenty-five per cent Graciano with eighteen to twenty-four months in new, mainly French, oak. It's very concentrated, hot, and spicy, with massive fruit, power, depth, and length, with every indication that it will live for a very long time.

DINASTÍA VIVANCO

Dinastía Vivanco, Ctra N-232 Km 197.3, 26330 Briones, La Rioja.
Tel: 941 322 332. Fax: 941 322 316. Website: www.dinastiavivanco.es. Email:
infobodega@dinastiavivanco.es. Chief executives: Rafael Vivanco Sáenz, Santiago
Vivanco Sáenz. Established: 1915. Type: SA. Own vineyards (ha): 300. Barrels:
15,000. Visits: (shop, restaurant, and museum) every day; (bodega) by appointment
Principal wines: Dinastía Vivanco Crianza; Reserva

The foundation date above bears little relationship to the modern bodega, a palatial complex on the N-232 as you enter Briones from the Logroño end. It all started with Pedro Vivanco González, who started making wine in 1915 on a domestic scale; in those days, every family had its patch of vines and made wine for home consumption, and, if there happened to be a surplus, might sell it to neighbours whose patch of vines was a little smaller. There was a gentle evolution from domestic to business until the next generation took over. Santiago Vivanco and his wife, Felisa, developed the business side of things and built up something of a reputation for their wines in neighbouring provinces. Their son Pedro Vivanco Paracuellos qualified as a winemaker and viticulturalist at the end of the 1960s, and became something of an expert in the terroirs, microclimates, and viticulture of the whole region. In the 1970s, he bought and sold wine, vineyard land, and property, and became a multimillionaire as a result. During this time, he amassed a collection of old vineyard implements and equipment, and had a burning desire to create a foundation and a museum to communicate his own love of the vine and wine.

Pedro's two sons – Santiago, a lawyer, and Rafael, an agricultural engineer – shared their father's passion for wine memorabilia, and collected books, maps, art, and crafts associated with wine. Eventually the various strands of these enthusiasms came together at a new site, among the family's vineyards in Briones, and the company was renamed Dinastía Vivanco ("Vivanco Dynasty") in honour of the grandfather and especially the great-grandfather who had started it all off in 1915.

The palatial new bodega incorporates not only the usual winery equipment but a conference centre, library, and museum of wine culture, as well as a shop and restaurant with the most spectacular, uninterrupted view of the Cantabrian Mountains. The building is a palace, set about with ponds, fountains, and vineyards, stuffed with antiques, paintings, tapestries, and pottery, and, for the record, the wine museum is without doubt the best I have ever visited: not just the usual collection of old implements, tools, and vehicles, but video displays demonstrating every aspect of viticulture, winemaking, cooperage, and even glass-blowing (the bodega has its own, distinctive bottle). Tens of millions of euros have been invested here: if you find yourself within an hour's drive of Briones, this is a must-visit.

The wines – ah, yes. Well, this is the difficult bit. I was treated royally at the bodega, given an excellent luncheon, and had plenty of time to visit the museum, et al., and to taste the wines. I had tasted them before at a wine symposium in Logroño, and a second tasting at the bodega only confirmed my first thoughts. In desperation I asked for back-up samples of both wines and tasted them a third time in the privacy of my own office, but the results were the same. Both *crianza* and *reserva* have a kind of overpowering wood-bitterness that sucks the fruit out of the wines, almost as if the barrels have been over-toasted or the grapes simply didn't have enough ripeness to cope with the oak-ageing. On the third occasion I tasted at 11am, when the wines were first opened, then again two hours later, then again four hours later, and then again with food, and yet again the following morning after they had been open for twenty-four hours. Dinastía Vivanco Crianza (*) had "decent fruit over-shadowed by wood", but what fruit it did have disappeared into the rather frightening acidity throughout the day. Reserva (0) showed the same characteristic wood-bitterness right at the start and it, too, descended into sharp, tart acidity during the day.

I don't think the wine was faulty (*i.e.* it wasn't corky, volatile, sulphurous, or with any of the regular wine faults). Had I bought either of these wines in a restaurant, I wouldn't have sent them back, but I would have ordered something else to drink on the night and taken them home for the kitchen. I should perhaps record that the actual vintages were 2001 for the Crianza and 1998 for the Reserva. Other vintages may be different, but I am tempted to wish that rather more of the tens of millions of euros invested in this magnificent endeavour had been spent on the winemaking, rather than the antiques.

DAVID MORENO

David Moreno Peña, Ctra de Villar de Torres s/n, Badarán, La Rioja.
Tel: 941 367 338. Fax: 941 418 685. Website: www.davidmoreno.es.

Email: davidmoreno@davidmoreno.es. Contact/Chief executive/Winemaker: David Moreno. Established: 1981. Type: private company. Own vineyards (ha): 8. Contract (ha): 110. Own production: 8%. Buy in: Yes. Number of staff: 10. Group: No. Barrels: 2,000. Type: American and French. Annual production (hl): 6,500. Sales national: 85%; export: 15%. Top export markets: UK, Switzerland, Germany. Visits: groups and indviduals. Open weekdays: 9:30am–1.30pm; 4pm–8pm. Principal wines: David Moreno Blanco/Rosado; Tinto Joven; Crianza; Reserva; Monasterio de Yuso Gran Reserva; Vobiscum (these are the brand names in Spain; some wines are all labelled Monasterio de Yuso and others all labelled David Moreno in export markets)

It is impossible not to like and respect David Moreno, the cheerful, chubby chappie from the tiny village of Badarán who proved the doubters wrong and created a major business from something that was barely there at all. Indeed, his bodega in this obscure small town (pop. 771) gets 12,000 visitors a year: the most in Rioja, says Moreno. In addition, he sells twelve per cent of his production in the bodega shop.

The ultimate origins of the business lie with his grandfather, Ponciano Moreno, who established a family bodega in 1912, but this, again, was in the days when every family had a patch of vines and made wine for itself, selling any surplus to neighbours, friends, and relatives. The reality of today's bodegas, however, rests with Moreno himself. When he was a young man, there was little work available in the village apart from unremitting toil in the fields and vineyards, and in 1963, Moreno and his family, in common with many others, moved to the big cities in search of work. Moreno qualified in engineering and got a job in Barcelona with SEAT (then an offshoot of FIAT in Italy, now a subsidiary of VW-Audi in Germany). Restructuring during the recession of 1979–80 saw him made redundant, and he returned to Badarán with no job but a large cheque.

The young Moreno had always been fascinated by his grandfather's wine business and bought a book on winemaking by Professor Émile Peynaud (of the University of Bordeaux). He read it through and announced that he was going into the wine business. His grandfather told him he was mad and that there was no chance he would get his money back, but Moreno went ahead anyway. Following the instructions in the book, he bought grapes and made his first vintage in 1981, at the age of thirty-three. It didn't seem too bad and he made a modest profit, so he did it again the following year, and the next...

Since then, he has learned – and, indeed, invented – a few new tricks, including one of adding the press-wine to the free-run wine after alcoholic fermentation has completed, and then performing a further ten days of *remontaje* ("pumping over": the process of circulating fermenting red wine to cover the cap of floating grape skins) to improve the structure of the finished wine. Moreno also maintains a wine club, in which members can buy their own cask or bottles, store them at the bodega, come and sample, bring friends for lunch or celebrations; and there is a special club area within the bodegas for members only.

I first met Moreno in the late 1990s, at which time he was expanding what had become a modern, industrial-style bodega. I seem to remember that he had had a section of the roof removed to allow the installation of some more stainless-steel tanks and was waiting for the crane to arrive. Today the bodega is hardly recognizable, and Moreno presides over a splendid bodega with magnificent barrel cellars with visitor facilities and a dining room in one corner, and a production of getting on for a million bottles a year. It couldn't have happened to a nicer man.

Moreno built his reputation on solid, dependable, everyday-quality wines rather than blockbusting award-winners, and his bread and butter is still in that sector. David Moreno Blanco Joven (**) is a pleasant, fresh, gluggable Viura. Tinto Joven (**) is Tempranillo/Garnacha with a delicious, lip-smacking fruit. Crianza (***) is mainly Tempranillo with up to fifteen months in oak, and has more than its share of structure and complexity. Reserva (***>****) is smooth, spicy, warm, and mature. Gran Reserva (****) has a lovely, elegant, perfumed maturity. Vobiscum (****>*****) is a limited-edition, high-expression wine made from a selection of the best grapes: big fruit, very long, aged in new Alliers oak, and made only in the best years. The first vintage was 2001.

DOMECQ

Bodegas Domecq, Ctra de Villabuena, 901340 Elciego, Álava. Tel: 945 606 001. Fax: 945 606 235. Website: www.domecq.es. Email: rioja@domecq.es.
Contact/Chief executive: Javier Elizalde Martínez. Winemaker: Gerardo Ruíz de Vergara. Established: 1973. Type: SL. Own vineyards (ha): 300. Contract (ha): 350. Own production: 40%. Buy in: grapes and wines. Number of staff: 23.

Group: Allied Domecq. Barrels: 21,500. Type: American 90%, French 10%. Annual production (hl): 35,000. Sales national: 70%; export: 30%. Top export markets: Switzerland, EU, UK. Visits: by appointment; groups and individuals. Open: tours weekdays at 11am. Principal wines: Viña Eguía; Marqués de Arienzo Crianza; Reserva; Gran Reserva; Reserva Especial

Domecq, then an independent company, was one of the first of the sherry companies to recognize that diversity in their products was going to be the future for the business, as the bulk sherry market was unstable (and, indeed, proved to be substantially unstable after 1979). After casting about for bodegas for sale, the company bought Bodegas Palacio (*see* page 170) in Laguardia in 1972, and formed a joint-venture partnership with the Canadian Seagram Group, selling fifty per cent of the equity. It quickly became apparent that the ways of the Canadians were not the ways of the Jerezanos, and Domecq sold its half to Seagram and went back on the acquisition trail, eventually deciding on a new-build option and, after soil analyses, buying a plot of land in Elciego and building a brand-new bodega in 1973, featuring what was then the latest stainless-steel technology and what is still today an effective, modern winery. The company bought vineyards from smaller growers, replanted some and retrained others on wires (which was technically illegal at that time, although it is perfectly normal now). Indeed, Domecq was one of the first to train vines in this way and spearheaded changes in the *reglamento* for the whole region.

The driving forces behind the project were José-Ignacio Domecq, then head of the family and known to all as "the nose" for his uncanny tasting ability, and the ubiquitous Professor Émile Peynaud from the University of Bordeaux, who advised on vineyard and winery practices.

Domecq was taken over by Allied Lyons in 1984 (to become Allied Domecq, *see* page 81) and benefited immediately from the worldwide distribution network thus provided. Since then, the bodega has gone on to build itself a reputation for solid, dependable quality at reasonable prices. In recent years the range has been rationalized: Viña Eguia is the basic brand in Spain, and in export markets Marqués de Arienzo goes across the range.

The Marqués de Arienzo Crianza (**) is mainly Tempranillo with twelve months in oak and is a textbook *crianza*; Reserva (***) has twenty-four months in cask and a good balance of fruit, oak, and tannins.

Gran Reserva (***>****) really does benefit from ageing and is a likely candidate for ten-years-plus in good years. Reserva Especial (****), made only in the best years, tends to have more fruit and less oak, with a lovely warm, ripe finish and very good ageing potential.

EL COTO

El Coto de Rioja, Camino Viejo de Logroño 26, Oyón, Álava. Tel: 945 622 600. Fax: 945 601 575. Website: www.elcoto.com. Email: jubera@elcoto.com. Contact: Víctor Charcán. Chief executive: Julio Noain. Winemaker: Javier Escobar. Established: 1970. Type: SA. Own vineyards (ha): 400. Contract (ha): 2000. Own production: 18%. Buy in: Yes. Number of staff: 93. Group: Barón de Ley. Barrels: 70,000. Type: American, French. Annual production (hl): 150,000. Sales national: 65%; export: 35%. Top export markets: Sweden, Switzerland, UK. Visits: by appointment; groups and individuals. Open weekdays: 8am–1pm; 3pm–8.30pm. Principal wines: El Coto Blanco/Rosado; Crianza; Coto de Imaz Reserva; Gran Reserva; Coto Real

Although the bodega – which is larger than some Rioja villages, with its own one-way system and signposting – is in the *municipio* of Oyón (Oion in Basque), its magnificent tasting room has a panoramic window looking out across the river and over the city of Logroño, just a couple of kilometres away. The Spanish language has a bewildering number of different words for "single estate", each with its own subtle subtext. *Propriedad* (private property), *finca* (private estate), *pago* (vineyard land), *estancia* (country estate), *herencia* (inherited family estate), *dehesa* (pasture land), and *granja* (farmland) are some examples, but Coto has traditional associations with a private estate for hunting, as witness the roadside signs seen all over Spain – *Coto Privada de Caza*: "private hunting estate", accompanied by a black-and-white rectangle divided diagonally. This is because Spanish national law enshrines the right of citizens to hunt small game (typically rabbits, hares, and red partridge) over any countryside unless it is specifically forbidden by the owner. The hunting connection is with El Coto de Imaz, a hunting lodge in Mendavia, twenty kilometres (12.4 miles) east of Logroño and north of the river, in the province of Navarra. It now belongs to the parent Barón de Ley (*see* page 87) estate, which is why the *reserva* and *gran reserva* wines are named after it.

The company was subsequently sold to the Banco Unión, later taken over by the Banco Urquijo, which was itself taken over by the giant Banco

Hispano Americano. In 1986, the Bank sold it to UK company Bass, which then also included Alexis Lichine, Pasquier-Desvignes, Château Lascombes, Cognac Otard, and others. Bass sold it to the much smaller Barón de Ley (which had a little help from a venture capital company called Mercapital) in 1979, and Eduardo Santos-Ruíz became chief executive of the group. In 1997, the group went public and bought back the Mercapital share of the business, with Santos-Ruíz retaining his own thirty-per-cent share. He remains the group's chief executive, while Julio Noain, the managing director of El Coto, looks after the daily running of the business.

There is little hint of hunting country at the bodega, however; it's industrial in scale, spotlessly clean, with completely modern equipment and massive capacity. Interestingly, its main parts were designed by Jesús Martínez Bujanda who went on to re-establish his own family bodega in Oyón (*see* Valdemar, page 200) in 1984.

Wines El Coto Blanco Viura (**) and Rosado Tempranillo/Garnacha are pleasant, fresh, and fruity with a hint of herb and spice respectively. All the reds are Tempranillo. Crianza (**>***) has fourteen months' oak, and a soft, chewy-fruit style. Coto de Imaz Reserva (***) has full fruit and a classic style. Gran Reserva (****) is a true classic, with all the lovely elegant fruit and oak of yore, and real ageing capability. Coto Real (****) is in a more concentrated, extracted style, probably to drink sooner than the Gran Reserva, with tighter, duskier fruit.

FAUSTINO

Bodegas Faustino, Ctra Logroño s/n, 01320 Oyón, Álava. Tel: 945 622 500. Fax: 945 622 106. Website: www.bodegasfaustino.es. Email: info@bodegasfaustino.es. Contact: Ricardo Aguiriano. Chief Executive: José-Luís Fernández de Jubera. Winemaker: Rafael Martínez Palacios. Established: 1861. Type: SL. Own vineyards (ha): 758. Contract (ha): 1,100. Own production: 40%. Buy in: Yes. Number of staff: 110. Group: Campillo, Marqués de Vitoria, Valcarlos, Condesa de Leganza, Victorianas. Barrels: 41,000. Type: American and French. Annual production (hl): 90,000. Sales national: 60%; export: 40%. Top export markets: UK, Switzerland, Denmark. Visits: by appointment; groups and individuals. Open weekdays: 9am–6pm. Principal wines: Faustino VII Joven; Faustino V Blanco; Barrel-fermented; Rosado; Faustino Crianza; Faustino de Autor Reserva Especial; Faustino V Reserva; Faustino I Gran Reserva

This the biggest family-owned landowner in Rioja and one of the best-known worldwide. Its wine goes in the Burgundy bottles, some of which are tinted or frost and most of which have "old master" reproductions on the label, which makes them some of the most recognizable in Rioja. I did once ask Faustino who the paintings were, and I seem to remember that someone told me anecdotally that they were paintings that used to hang in the boardroom; the chief executive, Julio Faustino, quite liked them and decided to put them on the labels, but the official response is that it's so long ago that no one knows. The images include those of Rembrandt and Gluck. One of the more recent innovations, Faustino de Crianza, does carry a picture of the founder on the label.

That founder of the bodega was Eleuterio Martínez Arzok, who bought a house and vineyard in Oyón in 1861 and started to make wine and sell it in bulk, as was the custom of the time. In 1904, his son Faustino Martínez Pérez de Albéniz was born and, sadly, this was also the year in which phylloxera struck the vineyards. Don Eleuterio died in 1920 without seeing his business fully back to health. Faustino Martínez did manage to get things back together in due course, and even started bottling the wine (something of a radical departure) from 1930 onwards; the brand names were Campillo, Parrita, Famar, and Santana.

Faustino's son Julio Faustino Martínez took over in 1957 and launched the first Faustino brand (named in honour of his father) in 1960. The firm was in expansionist mode at this time, buying and planting vineyards and making its first export sales. Both the Faustino and Campillo brands were becoming well known, and the business continued to expand with the creation of a dedicated bodega for Campillo (*see* page 100) in 1990 and by buying neighbouring Marqués de Vitoria (*see* page 155) in 1995. Today Faustino describes itself as making the "traditional" style of wine, while Marqués de Vitoria makes "modern"-style wines. The group also owns properties in La Mancha and Navarra, and a new bodega in Ribera del Duero incorporating a forty-room hotel, designed by the British architect Sir Norman Foster.

On a technical level, the winemaking manages to be thoroughly modern and the fermenting halls are spotlessly clean. The winemaker supervises every aspect of production personally, even to the extent of going to the USA every year to choose the oak for the bodega's casks. In addition, while not being formally organic, the company proudly boasts that throughout the group's vineyards it uses more than 2,500 tonnes of manure each year

The ranges (I, V, and VII) overlap a bit, so to avoid confusion we'll do this by colour. White wines comprise the basic Faustino VII Blanco Joven (**) which is a light, fresh Viura. Faustino I (**>***) is a *blanco joven* Viura but from older vineyards, with longer skin contact and a bit more character. Faustino V (***) is a Blanco Fermentado en Barrica with four months on the lees and has very pleasant structure without too much oak. There are two *rosados*: Faustino VII (**) is a light, fresh Tempranillo/Garnacha *joven*: drinkable and very pleasant. Faustino V (***) is all Tempranillo, from older vines and with twelve hours' skin contact – indeed, one of the most delicious *rosados* I've tasted. The red wine range is the widest. Faustino VII (**) is from young vines with about five per cent Mazuelo with ten months in oak. Faustino V Reserva (***>****) is all Tempranillo from vines more than twenty years old with sixteen months in new American oak. Faustino I Gran Reserva (****) has five per cent Mazuelo and ten per cent Graciano from vines more than thirty years old, and typically spends eighteen months in American and twelve in French oak; my most recent tasting note (from the 1995 vintage) has it as a "benchmark" *gran reserva* in the classic style: perfumed fruit and vanilla, warm, mellow, ripe, long on the palate. Faustino de Crianza (***>****) is a relatively recent addition to the range, all Tempranillo and aged in new American and (non-new) French oak and being a kind of halfway house between the classic style of Faustino VII and the new-wave *crianzas*. Top of the range is Faustino de Autór (****>*****), a *reserva especial* made only in the best years from very low-yielding vines from the company's three oldest vineyards (all planted in 1968), aged in new Tronçais and Alliers oak. The wine has twelve per cent Graciano and three per cent Cabernet Sauvignon and enormous structure, fruit, and power. Faustino also makes a sparkling wine under the cava *denominación*.

FERNÁNDEZ DE MANZANOS

Bodegas y Viñedos Fernández de Manzanos, Ctra San Adrián-Azagra Km 47, 31560 Azagra, Navarra. Tel: 948 692 500. Fax: 948 692 500. Website: www.bodegasfernandezdemanzanos.com. Email: info@bodegasfernandezdemanzanos.com. Contact: Guillermina Roldán. Chief executive: Víctor Fernández de Manzanos. Winemaker: Víctor Fernández de

Manzanos. Established: 1890. Type: SL. Own vineyards (ha): 150. Own production: 100%. Buy in: No. Number of staff: 8. Group: No. Barrels: 1,000. Type: American and French. Annual production (hl): 7,000. Sales national: 95%; export: 5%. Top export market: Germany. Visits: by appointment; groups and individuals. Principal wines: Berri Tinto Joven; Rosado; Blanco; Marichalar Tinto/Rosado/Blanco Joven; Semicrianza; Crianza; Reserva; Mágnum Reserva; Fernández de Manzanos Crianza; Reserva

This is not one bodega but three: a small installation in Aldeanueva de Ebro, which is mainly concerned with local sales; the old family bodega in Azagra where the wine was made until the 2004 vintage; and a brand-new bodega on a hilltop on the main road to San Adrián incorporating a fourteen-room hotel: and restaurant.

It's a family concern: Lorenzo Fernández de Manzanos established the company in 1890 with an ambition to grow grapes and make and sell his own wine, which was a bold move at a time when smaller growers were content to sell to the larger bodegas. The old cellars in Azagra still feature the underground tanks and storage areas with which Lorenzo worked in those days, although the wine has been made across the road in a much more modern bodega for several decades.

The family today is represented by Víctor Fernández de Manzanos and his wife, Guillermina Roldán Ruiz, a charming and hardworking young couple who have transformed the business from an artisanal bodega to something much more modern. Víctor worked with his father in the vineyards from his schooldays, studied chemical engineering in Barcelona, and subsequently viticulture and œnology at the University of Madrid. Guillermina had no interest in wine in her early life, trained as a lawyer, and became a civil servant with the local government in La Rioja. Her career moved from one department to another and eventually became involved with wine administration. It was in the course of this phase of her life that she met and subsequently married Víctor; they have two children currently at school and college.

In 1998, Víctor wanted to expand the business and realized he couldn't do it alone. He persuaded Guillermina (eventually; she had always been a dyed-in-the-wool career woman) to leave her job and take over the management of the company to allow him to concentrate on the vineyards and their ambitious plans for the new bodega. Today, they're a strong double act with a sound company and, by the looks of it, a great future.

Back to the new bodega: reflecting modern practice, it's built into a hillside to allow grape transfer by gravity only, with reception on the top floor (which is level with the road), fermentation takes place one floor down and the basement (which is at ground level at the bottom of the hill) houses new concrete tanks and the barrel cellars. I had remarked on the renaissance of concrete tanks, with several bodegas restoring old ones, but these were the first I had seen constructed from new. They are only used for storage and blending, and Víctor explained that he'd decided on concrete simply because it offered better temperature stability than any other material. In the heat of a long autumn, the thick concrete walls provided protection for the wine, and if cooling were needed, it was much simpler (and cheaper) to use *placas* within the tanks, rather than thousands of litres of cold water to chill stainless steel. He was also concerned about vibration; there has been some research into wines stored for long periods in stainless-steel tanks which suggests that even the minuscule vibration caused by traffic rumbling by a bodega and forklift trucks running in and out can have an effect on the micro-oxygenation of the wine.

Another aspect of modern practice is the tourist element. Most new bodegas are now being built with some tourist potential, and many older ones are adding it. The hotel and restaurant are scheduled for opening in 2006, and the hotel terrace has fabulous panoramic views over the Ebro Valley towards Calahorra.

There are three wine ranges. Viña Berri (**) are *jóvenes* made from younger vines in all three colours and with a very pleasant, everyday quality. Viña Marichalar is a thirty-hectare single estate at 400 metres (1,312 feet) in San Adrián, named after the family that once owned the estate. The Tinto Joven (**>***) is very fresh and Tempranillo-fruity, but with a bit of weight and even some complexity. Crianza (***) has warmth, spice, fruit, and classic structure (a "textbook" *crianza* according to my notes) with twelve months in American and French oak. Reserva (****) is similarly classic in style with eighteen months in oak; I wrote "wonderful balance, delicious". Top of the range is V. Fernández de Manzanos, made from a selection of the best grapes of the year (and not at all in less good years). The Crianza (****>*****) has eighteen months' oak and a very richly fruity, weighty style with an excellent, very long finish.

FERNÁNDEZ DE PIÉROLA

Bodegas Fernández de Piérola, Ctra Logroño s/n, 01322 Moreda, Álava.
Tel: 945 622 480; Fax: 945 622 489. Website: www.pierola.com. Email:
bodegas@pierola.com. Contact/Chief executive: Carlos Bujanda Fernández de
Piérola. Established: 1996. Type: SL. Own vineyards (ha): 35. Contract (ha): 80.
Own production: 50%. Buy in: Yes. Number of staff: 6. Group: No. Barrels: 1,500.
Type: American and French. Annual production (hl): 3,500. Sales national: 90%;
export: 10%. Top export markets: Switzerland, Germany, Netherlands. Visits: by
appointment; groups and individuals. Principal wines: Vitium Reserva Especial;
Fernández de Piérola Crianza; Reserva; Blanco Fernández de Piérola Fermentado
en Barrica; Vino de Labraz Joven

Carlos Bujanda Fernández de Piérola comes of a long line of *cosecheros*
stretching back 100 years or more, but in his childhood the family vineyards
were merely to grow grapes for selling, and a young man's duty was
to carve a professional career for himself in the city. And, indeed, he did,
doing a degree in business management at Zaragoza and getting a
job with the Álava regional council. After two years, he switched to the
private sector, and joined the marketing department of Marqués de
Cáceres (*see* page 141). He later moved for promotion to Bodegas Campillo
(*see* page 100) as general manager but, having worked with wine for several
years, began to get the feeling that he wanted his own bodega. Eventually,
like so many of his generation, Carlos decided to quit his safe, well-paid,
and pensionable job and turn the family vineyard into a family bodega.

He started building and went on an œnology course at the same time,
finally completing both in 1996, in time for the harvest. Such is the
nature of Alavesa village life that his friends and neighbours rallied round
and sold their grapes to him rather than the big bodegas with whom they
had historically done business, and the first vintage was released in 2000.

The bodega is a very handsome building with a round, two-storey
frontage and, as you'd expect, the most modern kit. The company now
owns and/or controls a total of 115 hectares of vineyard in and around the
village of Moreda, Carlos making the wine and his elder brother looking
after the vineyards, but he doesn't describe himself as a winemaker. Once
again, in common with many of the new generation, he describes himself
as a "wine helper". "Let the grape make the wine," he says, "and don't
interfere unless it's absolutely necessary." As a result, he fines only with
bentonite, doesn't fine-filter at all, and professes to want to make wine "as

natural as we can". Just to add the finishing touch, all the wines come in a distinctive bottle with a flanged top and no capsule, the cork topped with a seal.

Wines All wines are branded Fernández de Piérola. Blanco Fermentado en Barrica (***) is made from Viura from twenty- to thirty-year-old vines and fermented with natural yeast: the grapes are de-stemmed and put in a tank at 5°C (41°F) for three days' skin contact, and then the must is run off into new barrels for fermentation, followed by three months on the lees with regular *batonaje* (stirring), then coarse filtration and bottling in the spring after the vintage to keep the wood in perspective. The barrels are then used for ageing red wine of the same vintage. Crianza (***>****) is made from Tempranillo from twenty-five- to thirty-year-old vines with eighteen months in new oak, and my most recent note describes "long, savoury, wild fruit" and good tannin balance. Reserva (****) offers considerable warmth and ripeness with big, soft, savoury fruit. Top of the range is Vitium (*****), all Tempranillo from two small vineyards with vines between eighty and 100 years old. Yield is about 2,500 kilograms per hectare (the legal maximum is 6,500). It gets thirty days' maceration and fifteen to sixteen months in mainly French new oak ("looking for a little less wood"). It's a wine of huge, explosive fruit, spice, length, and perfume: astonishing.

FINCA VALPIEDRA

Finca Valpiedra, Termino Montecillo s/n, 26360 Fuenmayor, La Rioja.
Tel: 941 450 876. Fax: 941 450 875. Website: www.bujanda.com. Email: info@fincavalpiedra.com. Contact: Ana Martínez Bujanda. Chief executive: Jesús Martínez Bujanda. Winemaker: Gonzalo Ortiz. Established: 1999. Type: SL. Own vineyards (ha): 80. Own production: 100%. Group: Valdemar (*see* page 200). Barrels: 4,000. Sales national: 50%; export: 50%. Top export markets: Canada, EU, UK. Visits: contact bodega. Sole wine: Finca Valpiedra

This is a venture by Bodegas Valdemar (known until 2003 as Bodegas Martínez Bujanda), which actually bought this eighty-hectare estate from Bodegas Montecillo (*see* page 158) in 1973 at the time when that business was bought by the sherry giant Osborne. Since then, painstaking work in the vineyards (including replanting) and massive investment in the bodega have turned this into one of Rioja's finest single estates. No expense has been spared in any aspect, and the results are unequivocally impressive. The company's mission statement is "to produce a wine from a single vineyard, to get the highest expression of the vineyard, every year". It's the second-biggest single-vineyard estate in Rioja, at an altitude of 406 to 427 metres (1,332 to 1,401 feet) on a bend in the river Ebro (a bit like a reverse Contino, *see* page 105, geographically, with the river to the north), with alluvial soils, sandy with large stones and a good level of carbonate.

In the early days, the grapes were used at the parent bodega, and went into the mainstream Conde de Valdemar wines, but the target was always to produce a single-estate wine; the first vintage was in 1994, although Valpiedra didn't become a separate company until 1999. Today, the vines are a minimum of twenty-five years old, ninety per cent Tempranillo, six per cent Cabernet Sauvignon, and four per cent Graciano and Mazuelo. The winery is a marble palace with every modern contrivance, and the wines are among the most reliable in Rioja for quality and consistency. All wines are aged in new oak, which is 50/50 French and American, and typical ageing is eighteen months. The wines are generally sold as *reservas*, but this varies according to year; in difficult years it may be a *crianza*, in great years perhaps a *gran reserva*. The final decision is down to the winemaker and the family.

The Finca Valpiedra (****>*****) is a real traditional Rioja with a perfect balance of crisp fruit, tannin, and oak. This is a wine with the potential for great longevity.

GURPEGUI

Bodegas Luís Gurpegui Muga, Avda Celso Muerza 8, 31570 San Adrián, Navarra. Tel: 948 670 050. Fax: 948 670 259. Incorporating BERCEO. Bodegas Berceo, Cuevas, 32, 26200 Haro, La Rioja. Tel: 941 310 744. Fax: 941 304 313. Website: www.gurpegui.es. Email: export@gurpegui.es. Contact: Leila Guerra. Winemaker: Jacques Humeau. Established: 1872. Type: SA. Own vineyards (ha): 118. Contract (ha): 1,500. Own production: 7%. Buy in: Yes. Number of staff: 50. Group: Gurpegui (also in Navarra), Berceo. Barrels: 14,000. Type: French. Annual production (hl): 90,000. Sales national: 75%; export: 25%. Top export markets: Germany, UK, Italy. Visits: by appointment; groups and individuals. Open weekdays: 9am–1pm; 3pm–6pm. Principal wines: [Gurpegui] Viñadrián Joven Tinto, Blanco, Rosado; Primi "Semicrianza"; [Berceo] Viña Berceo Crianza; Gonzalo de Berceo Reserva; Gran Reserva; Los Dominios de Berceo Prefiloxérico

The foundation date above is that of Bodgas Berceo, the oldest bodega in Haro, and one that has one or two features which might have been considered eye-openingly modern at that time. The first is that the bodega is built into a hillside on five levels; the grapes are received at the top, pass to giant Limousin oak *tinas* on the fourth and third levels, then, after fermentation, to storage tanks on level two. Wines for ageing in wood then go on to the barrel cellar at level one, but the point is that all transfers are accomplished by gravity, with no need for pumping. The other is the press carousel, which has three press baskets on three trucks revolving on a metal rail. While one is being filled, the second is being pressed, and the third is being emptied, providing an early "continuous" method of processing the grapes.

Bodegas Luís Gurpegui was founded in 1921 in San Adrián, in a bodega that had also been built in 1872; initially, it made wines for sale in bulk. The founder was Primitivo Gurpegui Muro, who was an itinerant cooper, travelling from bodega to bodega and making barrels on an ad hoc basis. In Haro, he met and later married a girl called Bibiana Muga, whose own family was to go on to establish its own Rioja company (*see* Muga, page 160) in 1932. Because in Spain children take the names of both their father and mother, their son was Luís Gurpegui Muga, and it is his name that was given to the company when it became a formal business entity rather than simply a private family company. An interesting sidelight: the Muga company of Haro went on to become rather more famous internationally, and challenged the right of Gurpegui to use the name "Muga" in its title. This was only resolved in 2003, when Gurpegui pointed out that they had been using the name for eleven years before Muga was even founded.

Luís himself, who is now the company president and semi-retired, took over a rather old-fashioned business from his founding father and introduced a good deal of modernization, including bottling lines for the first time in the 1970s, and bought Bodegas Berceo around 1980. His eldest son, Primitivo, is now responsible for the day-to-day business management of the company. A recent addition has been a spanking-new bodega on an industrial estate on the edge of San Adrián with the very latest mechanical handling and bottling equipment.

Gurpegui has a policy of making the wine in the area where the grapes were grown, but much of the "post-production" work is done at the new bodega. The company owns vineyards in the Rioja Alta for Berceo wines and Baja for Gurpegui wines, and the most recent acquisition has been two small plots of vines, including two hectares in Baños de Ebro, on a bend in the river, which were planted in 1870 and never suffered from phylloxera as a result of their sandy soil. From the low production of these vines, winemaker Jacques Humeau makes the company's flagship wines – but not at flagship prices. If you do visit, ask to see Luís' collection of classic cars.

Primi (***) is a new-style wine majoring in fruit and freshness, mainly Tempranillo with a little Merlot and five to six months in oak: delicious, with soft fruit and spice and excellent value for money. Berceo Blanco (**) is a barrel-fermented Viura with four to five months on the lees: pleasant, fresh fruit, and a hint of oak. Berceo Crianza (***) is also a new-style *crianza* with less emphasis on the oak and more on the fruit, but good soft tannins and a decent structure. Berceo Reserva (***>****) has a very small proportion of Cabernet Sauvignon and is described by Jacques Humeau as a "halfway" style between classic and post-modern Rioja: lovely aromatic nose but heavyweight fruit buried in a crisp, tannic structure. Dominios de Berceo (****) is the wine made from pre-phylloxera vines in that sandy corner of the Ebro: very subtle, dark fruit, gentle tannins, good length. Dominios de Berceo 36 (****) is made from the vines planted in 1936 and has lovely, silky, mouth-filling fruit but still with an integrated structure.

HEREDAD UGARTE

Heredad Ugarte, Crtra Logroño Vitoria Km 69, 01300 Laguardia, Álava.
Tel: 945 282 844. Fax: 945 271 319. Website: www.heredadugarte.com. Email: info@heredadugarte.com. Contact: Maier Rico, export manager. Chief executive: Asunción Eguren Cendoya. Winemaker: Esther García. Established: 1989. Type: SA. Group: Eguren. Own vineyards (ha): 115. Barrels: 3,300. Sales national: 65%; export: 35%. Top export markets: Germany, Japan, EU. Visits: daily at 10am; other times by arrangement. Principal wines: Martín Cendoya; Cédula Real; Dominio de Ugarte; Heredad Ugarte; Ugarte

Although the present bodega and company date from 1989, the Ugarte family has been involved in the wine business since 1870, when Amancio Ugarte began to make wine from his own vineyards in San Vicente de la Sonsierra. There was, however, no formal company structure until his grandson, Victorino Eguren Ugarte, created the modern company and bodega. He is still very active in the bodega, although his daughter Asunción is in charge of the day-to-day running of the business. The bodega is a fascinating building, set into a hillside such that the entrance is at road level but the cellars are burrowed back into the rock, on several levels. An abiding memory is of the outside loo in the car park, which also burrows into the mountainside and looks like something that would have been familiar to the Flintstones.

Inside, there's a tasting area for visitors and also private bins where customers can reserve their own wines. In addition, the bodega runs a *club de barricas* where individuals can buy a whole cask of a particular wine (generally from the smaller, older vineyards) as their own private reserve. They may perhaps enjoy this with guests in the Martín Cendoya dining room, named after the company's flagship wine which is, in turn, named after Victorino's late brother-in-law, who worked alongside him for many years as the company's viticulturist. *Cédula real* in Spanish means "Royal Despatch", named after an official letter from or to the king, and the wine so labelled always carries an appropriate wax seal. The company also produces olive oil and *orujo*, and owns a *vino de mesa* bodega in Castile-La Mancha called Bodegas Eguren.

The red wines are mainly Tempranillo. Ugarte (**>***) has twenty per cent Garnacha and six months in oak, and has good, tight, fresh, delicious fruit. Heredad Ugarte (**>***) Crianza has eight per cent Garnacha and fifteen months in oak, which keeps the freshness and gives it a bit of structure. Dominio de Ugarte Reserva (***>****) has five per cent Graciano with good, dark, tight fruit, a crisp, oaky structure, and a lovely perfume. Cédula Real Gran Reserva (****) has big spice and structured tannins but still with freshness: a twenty-year wine. Martín Cendoya (****>*****) is a *reserva especial* with fifteen per cent Graciano and five per cent Mazuelo, and all grapes are from eighty- to 100-year-old vines, harvested at 3,000 kilograms per hectare (the legal maximum is 6,500), with malolactic fermentation and twenty-four months in oak casks with American staves and French ends. It has a lovely, elegant, understated fruit-perfume nose and a rich, round, balanced structure on the palate: delicious.

IZADI
Viña Villabuena, Herrería, Travesía 2, nº 5, 01307 Villabuena, Álava. Tel: 945 609

086. Fax: 945 609 261. Website: www.izadi.com. Email: izadi@izadi.com. Contact: Lalo Antón. Chief executive: Gonzalo Antón. Winemaker: Ángel Ortega. Established: 1987. Type: SA. Own vineyards (ha): 66. Contract (ha): 120. Visits: contact bodega. Principal wines: Viña Izadi Crianza; Reserva; Selección; Expresión

This is a beautiful, not to say elegant, bodega spread out over five floors on the steeply rising road between Elciego and Samaniego, sandwiched between Bodegas Luís Cañas up the hill and across the road, and Bodegas Valserrano down the hill and round to the left. Villabuena is a wine village probably unique in Rioja; it has 350 inhabitants and thirty-six wineries, most small *cosecheros*, of course – every family has a vineyard. Most make some wine, many sell their grapes, but it is interesting that three of Álava's best bodegas should be here, within a stone's throw of each other, in a such a tiny settlement.

This is another case in which the name of the wine is infinitely better known than the name of the bodega. The business was founded by the present chief executive, Gonzálo Antón, in 1987. He runs the restaurant Zaldiarán in Vitoria (one star and three *couverts* in the Michelin guide) and wanted wines for himself and his cheffy chums, who include the guru Basque kitcheneer Juan-Mari Arzak in San Sebastián (three stars and four *couverts*) and other luminary names in northern Spanish cooking.

Today, the bodega is very modern and geared up for gastronomic events and tourist visits as well as having the latest winemaking kit. The main tasting room is equipped with comfortable sofas, tapestries, bookshelves, and a grand piano, as well as individual tasting tables (and a fascinating view down the valley). There's a bit of football memorabilia here and there, too, reminding us that Gonzalo is also the president of the Football Club of Álava, which probably explains why his son (also Gonzalo but, to avoid confusion, known by the familiar name of Lalo) is usually to be found looking after the bodega.

In terms of the wine, Gonzalo rocked the establishment, not just in Álava but in Rioja, by calling in Mariano García as a consultant for his Izadi Expresión. García is well known as the winemaker at Vega Sicilia for thirty years, as well as other projects, but all of them, so far, in neighbouring Castile-León. Lalo explains that he was called in, not particularly for his winemaking skills, prodigious though they be, but for his skill in grape selection, tasting, and, especially, his expertise in the use of oak. Izadi spends approximately Euro 1 million per year on oak barrels, so they need to get it right. The results were impressive – such that Expresión took the top marks at one of the (many) tastings I undertook in the research for this book. You may be interested to know that it had been misclassified, and that none of the tasters knew that it was Rioja until the covers were removed afterwards.

The three ranges of wine – Crianza/Reserva, Selección, and Expresión – tend to be sourced from the company's individual plots. Expresión grapes come from four hectares of old vines yielding about 3,000 to 3,500 kilograms per hectare; Selección from ten hectares yielding about 4,000 kg/hl; and the mainstream wines from other areas, but not exceeding 5,000 kilograms per hectare production (remember the legal maximum is 6,500). The grapes are fermented individually by plot in small tanks, and then tasted blind and graded after alcoholic and before malolactic fermentation. In some years (2002 was a good example), none of the wine is considered good enough for Expresión, so they don't make any. The wines are aged in largely new and mainly French oak (although they are experimenting with east-European oak, in common with many other bodegas) for as long as winemaker Ángel Ortega sees fit, and then bottled. The results in every case are impressive, and the best wines of this bodega are among the best in all Rioja.

Tempranillo is in the majority throughout. Crianza (****) has thirteen to fourteen months in one- to two-year-old American barrels and has the trademark big fruit. Reserva (****) goes through the selection tables and will typically have fifteen per cent Graciano and twelve per cent Garnacha with twenty to twenty-four months in one-year-old French barrels. Selección (****>*****) has fifteen to twenty per cent Graciano with eighteen to twenty months in new French oak; Expresión (*****) tends to be 100 per cent Tempranillo from the oldest plots, with eighteen to nineteen months in new French oak. I gave the 2001 vintage 19.5 out of twenty.

JUAN ALCORTA

Bodegas Juan Alcorta, Camino de Lapuebla 50, 26006 Logroño, La Rioja. Tel: 941 279 900. Fax: 941 279 901. Website: www.byb.es. Email: info@byb.es. Contact: Isabel Adrián. Chief executive: Guillermo Oraá. Winemaker: Elena Adell San Pedro. Established: 2001. Type: SA. Own vineyards (ha) 400. Contract (ha): 1,500. Buy in: Yes. Number of staff: 70. Group: Allied Domecq. Barrels: 70,000.

Type: 70% American, 30% French. Annual production (hl): 300,000. Sales national: 60%; export: 40%. Top export markets: UK, USA, Scandinavia. Visits: by appointment; groups and individuals. Tours weekdays at 11am, 1pm, and 4pm. Principal wines: Marqués de Villamagna Gran Reserva; Viña Alcorta Crianza; Reserva; Campo Viejo Crianza; Reserva; Gran Reserva; La Finca Crianza; Reserva

We need to begin with another bit of author-archaeology here. I joined the wine trade in the UK in 1972, and the company for which I worked was one of a very few at that time to have Spanish wines that weren't labelled "Spanish Burgundy" or "Spanish Graves". Our mainstay Rioja was Campo Viejo Crianza 1968, which came in a beautiful two-litre *botellone* and sold for a retail price of £1 9s 11d for a 75cl bottle. That became 56p, which in today's money represents £4.75 UK tax and duty paid – not markedly different from the price today. It was the time of the "bistro boom", and every street corner in every major UK city had a little restaurant with red-and-white checked tablecloths and an empty Chianti *fiasco* with a candle in the middle. We sold the wine into these restaurants with gusto, and although I sometimes thought that they really wanted the bottle to replace the *fiasco* with the candle in it, the wine was good, and good value, too.

A great deal has changed, but Campo Viejo is still with us. The original company was founded in 1963 by SAVIN, a *vino de mesa* company with ten bodegas throughout Spain, which had started the dangerously modern practice of actually bottling its wine in the 1950s. The company quickly outgrew the original bodega in Aldeanueva de Ebro, and it moved to a purpose-built bodega on a major industrial estate in Logroño in 1965. This was a good example of the less aesthetic style of 1960s architecture, and continual additions and "improvements" left the building with a rather ugly hotch-potch effect on the outside, and a rapidly ageing set of bodega equipment inside.

Rather than try to modernize the existing bodega, the company decided to build a brand-new, purpose-built facility with massive room to expand on a site just outside the city. In common with current practice this would incorporate a visitor centre, tasting rooms, and a dining room, as well as the very latest technology. I first visited it in February 2002, at which time it was a vast building site, with a biting wind blowing south from the Cantabrian Mountains, muddy underfoot, and loud with construction machinery, although this discomfort was ameliorated by the company of the delightful and professional Isabel Adrián, ByB's communications director, who was showing me round. My next visit was eighteen months later, in the autumn of 2003, by which time the bodega was almost complete and resplendent with new winemaking technology. Can you remember when bodegas bragged that they had a computer looking after their fermentation tanks? Well, this one has a computer on *every* tank to maintain pin-sharp accuracy during fermentation; they buy 9,000 new barrels every year, and the whole thing covers four hectares, plus, of course, the surrounding vineyards.

Winemaker Elena Adell (who works right across the ByB group) has *carte blanche* to source grapes from any of the company's properties throughout Rioja, although she says that they are trying to crank up the quality now that the bodega is fully up and running. She is opposed to irrigation unless it's absolutely necessary (for example, in arid years), although even in the heatwave of 2003 they managed without it, thanks to the stony soils in most of the vineyards. The opportunity is here, however, should it be needed. In the meantime, the wines of what is now known as Juan Alcorta (named after the company president) seem to have undergone a change up in quality. The old bodega has been recycled as offices.

Wines La Finca de Campo Viejo Crianza (***) is sourced from Rioja Baja grapes, mainly in the Alfaro region, and has lovely ripe fruit, balanced oak, and a decent length. Reserva (***>****) has that classic strawberries-and-cream flavour, with the vanilla from the oak. Viña Alcorta (***) Crianza is made from local Tempranillo and has warm, ripe fruit and a hint of oak (but not overpowering). Reserva (***>****), with eighteen months in oak, has a ripe, silky palate and a good length. Elena Adell explains that the *finca* wines are hotter, more robust, and aimed at the off-trade, while the Alcorta range is softer and more classic, although with fruit prominent, and aimed at the restaurant trade. Campo Viejo wines need food, as well. Crianza (***) is made from grapes from all over the region, mainly American oak, and is spicy, crisp, and smooth, but still fresh. Reserva (***>****) has prominent oak (eighteen months) and spice, with a gamey hint on the nose and good, powerful structure on the palate. Gran Reserva (****) has twenty-four months in oak and is in the big, smoky, aromatic, old *gran reserva* style.

LA EMPERATRIZ

Bodegas La Emperatriz, Finca Viña La Emperatriz, 26241 Baños de Rioja, La Rioja. Tel: 941 300 105. Fax: 941 300 231. Website:

www.bodegaslaemperatriz.com. Email: correo@bodegaslaemperatriz.com.
Chief executive: Eduardo Hernaiz López. Winemaker: José-María Pangua.
Established: 1999. Own vineyards (ha): 125. Barrels: 1,500. Visits: contact
bodega. Principal wines: Viña Acedo Blanco Joven/Rosado Joven; Crianza Tinto;
Reserva Tinto

The empress of the title is Maria Eugénia Ignacia Augustina Palafox de
Guzmán Portocarrero y Kirkpatrick, ninth countess de Teba, known for
short as Eugénia de Montijo (1826–1920), who was the last empress of
France (1853–71) while married to Charles Louis Napoléon Bonaparte,
known for short as Napoléon III. She had been born to a noble family
(half Scottish, half Spanish) in Granada, and owned extensive lands all
over Spain, including Rioja, although at that time her estate produced
wine for distilling, and the resultant brandy was shipped to the French
court in Paris and called *coñac* just to add to the confusion. The bodega
owns part of this historic vineyard, the Finca la Emperatriz, which
inspired the name.

The bodega is spankingly modern, beautifully designed, and elegantly
purpose-built in the midst of the estate, but made only three wines in its
early years as time, and the vineyards, progressed. The first oak-aged
wines were the Crianza and Reserva 2000 vintage, released in 2003 and
2004, respectively.

Viña Acedo Crianza (***) has four per cent Mazuelo and shows
powerful tannins when young, rather pushing the fruit into the
background, but develops well. Reserva (****) shows the way forward,
with the same grape mix but twenty-two months in new oak and a further
twenty in bottle, which brings out the elegance and structure of the wine:
solid fruit, complexity, and development.

LAGUNILLA

Bodegas Lagunilla-Berberana, Ctra Elciego s/n, 26350 Cenicero, La Rioja.
Tel: 941 453 100. Fax: 941 453 114. Website: www.lagunilla.com. Email:
info@lagunilla.com. Contact: Carlos Núñez Rodríguez. Chief Executive: Víctor
Fernández Aldana. Winemaker: Carmelo Angulo Bernedo. Established: 1885.
Type: SA. Own vineyards (ha): No. Controlled vineyards: 5,000ha. Buy in: Yes,
grapes and wines from 4 co-ops. Number of staff: 220. Group: Arco-Bodegas
Unidas. Barrels: 52,500. Type: American and French. Annual production (hl):
120,000. Sales national: 50%; export: 50%. Top export markets: UK, Holland,

Scandinavia. Visits: No. Principal wines: Lagunilla Crianza; Reserva; Gran Reserva; Casa del Comendador

This bodega was founded by Felipe Lagunilla San Martín, who is credited with some of the early work that contributed to the solution to the phylloxera crisis and was created a *comendador* ("commander of the order") by the king as a result, which explains the name of the flagship wine. It built itself a reputation for reliable, quality wines for nearly 100 years and then was taken over by Croft (part of UDV, latterly Diageo) in 1973. In due course Lagunilla became little more than a brand name within the group, the bodega becoming an *almacenista*, buying in ready-made wines and ageing and blending them, but also improving and extending the bodega. The expanding Arco-Bodegas Unidas group bought the business in 1995 with a view to return it, eventually, to winemaking, and in 2004 the name changed to Bodegas Lagunilla-Berberana. Today, the grapes are supplied by four cooperatives which are also minority shareholders in the business.

Lagunilla Casa del Comendador (****) has twenty per cent Garnacha and twenty-four months in American oak which has a good fruit/oak balance, tannins in proportion, clean, fresh, and good.

LAN

Bodegas LAN, Paraje de Buicio s/n, 26360 Fuenmayor, La Rioja.
Tel: 941 450 950. Fax: 941 450 567. Website: www.bodegaslan.com.
Email: bodegaslan@fer.es. Contact: Trinidad Villegas. Chief executive: Enrique Abiega. Winemaker: Buenaventura Lasanta. Established: 1974. Type: SA. Own vineyards (ha): 70; Contract (ha): 150. Own production: 20%. Buy in: Yes. Number of staff: 40. Group: Bodegas Señorío de Ulia, Santiago Ruíz. Barrels: 25,000. Type: French. Annual production (hl): 10,000–15,000. Sales national: 60%; export: 40%. Top export markets: Switzerland, Germany, USA. Visits: yes. Open weekdays: 9am–12.30pm; 3pm–5.30pm. Principal wines: LAN; LAN Crianza; Reserva; Gran Reserva; Viña Lanciano Reserva; Edición Especial Reserva; Culmen de Lan Reserva; LAN Hecho a Mano

There seems to be some debate over the precise date of this bodega's foundation. The bodega itself says 1974 on the questionnaire but 1972 on its website; the official Rioja handbook and Julian Jeffs (*see* Bibliography) say 1973, and Hubrecht Duijker (*see* bibliography) says it's actually 1970, the date when the Elorriaga and Valdés families first signed the joint-venture deal to establish a bodega. Whenever it was, it takes its name from the initial letters of the three provinces that produce Rioja wine: Logroño, Álava, and Navarra (so maybe its orthography should actually be "LÁN"). Originally, the company did business in rented space, but ambitious expansion plans and the need for a permanent base saw the establishment of a limited company in 1973, followed by the building of a new bodega in Fuenmayor, which made its first vintage in 1974. It was extended in 1975 and again in 1980, and progressively modernized, such that today it has the among the most modern equipment and is one of the smartest bodegas along the N-232. The barrel cellar is not only cathedral-like (as are most of them in Rioja) but spotlessly clean and equipped with an ingenious metal device that supports three casks end-to-end – not, you understand, the standard cradle but a minimalist piece of equipment designed especially for LAN. They call them "skis" and they were designed to work with the bodega's (also unique) two-crane lifting system. So there is no wood (apart from the casks themselves) to harbour unpleasant arthropody or mycology in the barrel halls.

This is a very reliable bodega, but it doesn't follow the usual rules. LAN Crianza up to 2000 (***>****) had Garnacha and Mazuelo with twelve months in oak in classic style. From 2001, LAN (not necessarily but possibly *crianza*) has some Graciano as well and rates (****). Reserva (****) is selected from better grapes and has eighteen months' oak; another burnished, classic style. Gran Reserva (****>*****) has twenty-four months' oak and, in good years, is magnificent. Culmen de LAN (*****) also has Graciano with eighteen months in barrel, from the single-vineyard El Rincón ("the corner"), and is one of the bodega's flagship wines. As is Viña Lanciano Edición Limitada (****>*****), which also has Graciano and eighteen months in cask. There are no second-rate wines at LAN.

LA MARQUESA
Bodegas de La Marquesa – *see* Valserrano, page 204.

LA RIOJA ALTA
La Rioja Alta, Avda de Vizcaya s/n, 26200 Haro, La Rioja. Tel: 941 310 346. Fax: 941 312 854. Website: www.riojalta.com. Email: riojalta@riojalta.com. Contact: Gabriela Rezola, PR. Chief executive: Guillermo de Aranzábal. Winemaker: José Gallego. Established: 1890. Type: SA. Own vineyards (ha): 425. Own production: 50%. Buy in: only grapes. Group: Barón de Oña (*see* below), Lagar de Cervera, Áster.

Barrels: 46,000. Type: American. Annual production (hl): 22,500. Sales national: 75%; export: 25%. Top export markets: UK, Mexico, Germany. Visits: by appointment. Open weekdays: mornings only. Principal wines: Gran Reserva 890; Gran Reserva 904; Viña Ardanza Reserva; Viña Arana Reserva; Viña Alberdi Crianza; Marqués de Haro Gran Reserva

This is unquestionably one of the benchmark bodegas of Rioja: traditional in style but not afraid to experiment, innovate, and reinvest, and largely family-owned from its foundation in 1890. This is how it was: in the boom years of Rioja, a French wine merchant called Albert Viguier built the cellars near the newly opened railway station in Haro, but like so many of the French investors, decided to go home when the boom came to an end. He sold it to a consortium of local families in 1890: Daniel-Alfredo Ardanza, Saturnina García Cid, Dionisio del Prado, Felipe Puig de la Bellacasa, and Mariano Lacorte were the first investors. Some provided cash, others land and vineyards, perhaps most notably Daniel-Alfredo, whose name is commemorated in the company's *reserva* Viña Ardanza, which literally means "Ardanza's vineyard". An early recruit to the board was the Alberdi family, and their name, too, is commemorated in the Viña Alberdi Crianza. Originally modestly named the Sociedad de Cosecheros de Vino de La Rioja Alta, it became a limited company under the present name in 1904, and in 1944 transferred its offices from Bilbao to Haro.

The company's trademark, representing the river Oja framed by four oak trees, was registered in 1902 and has never changed. Indeed, it's as agreeably old-fashioned as the wines. Despite having no French share-holding, the cellar was run by a Frenchman from the Médoc, Charles Gaillat, and his meticulous and detailed notes on the day-to-day running of the business have been preserved as a testament to the way in which the company built its reputation. Today, La Rioja Alta is a publicly quoted company, but although the shareholding is much wider than it was, descendants of the founding families still have a controlling interest and the place still feels like a family enterprise. Indeed, Guillermo de Aranzábal Agudo, the current boss, is the fifth generation in the winery, great-grandson of one of the founding families.

In spite of its tradition credibility, one of the bodega's strengths is that it has never been afraid to innovate if innovation would produce a better-quality wine. It switched from fermenting in oak to stainless steel in a gradual process during the 1980s, for example, and one illustrative example of the approach is on the bodega tour, when visitors see, in one room, barrels being racked, cleaned, and sterilized by hand in the traditional way, and in the next the same process being carried out automatically by the latest high-tech equipment.

In 1988, the company expanded with Lagar de Fornelos in the DO Rías Baixas. Interestingly, Rioja Alta used to make an excellent white *reserva* under the Viña Ardanza label, but this was phased out once Lagar de Fornelos came into full production, which I thought was a great pity. Yet you do have to understand how difficult it is to sell austere, complex, oaked white Rioja – and how much easier it is to sell bright, peachy-fruit Rías Baixas. In 1987, the company bought an estate in Ribera del Duero, planted a vineyard, and built a bodega called Áster. The first commercial vintage (also called Áster) came to the market in 2004. Then, in 1995, Torre de Oña (*see* page 119) in Laguardia came on the market, and that also joined the group.

Wines These are some of the best and certainly among the most reliable Rioja has to offer. Viña Ardanza Reserva (****) is the mainstream wine, mainly Tempranillo with some Garnacha and anything up to thirty-six months in oak, depending on the year: classic Rioja structure and with the ability to age very elegantly. Viña Alberdi Reserva (***>****) has Mazuelo in place of the Garnacha, with twenty-four months in wood, and has a softer, less-structured style. Viña Arana (***>****) has some Graciano and thirty-six months in oak, and in style falls between the Alberdi and the Ardanza. The flagship wines are both named after the two most important events in the bodega's history: Gran Reserva 904 (****>*****) was originally called "1904" to commemorate the year in which the company was incorporated, but the "1" was dropped to avoid confusion with the vintage date. The wine has typically ten per cent Graciano, the rest Tempranillo, and forty-eight months in oak with thirty-six in the bottle before release. Gran Reserva 890 (*****) has a similar pedigree (originally "1890": the foundation year) and has a similar varietal recipe, but with eighty-four months in oak and a further sixty in bottle before release. Obviously only the very finest grapes from the oldest, low-yielding vines will cope that that level of ageing, and the wine has enormous, power, structure, and longevity. The 904 gets the grapes which almost, but didn't quite, get into the 890, and is more approachable and sooner, but still a very fine wine indeed. And then there's the Marqués de Haro, but they only bring that out for special occasions. I'm looking forward to my invitation…

LUIS CAÑAS

Bodegas Luís Cañas, Ctra Samaniego 10, Villabuena, Álava. Tel: 945 223 373 /623 386. Fax: 945 609 289. Website: www.luíscanas.com. Email: bodegas@luíscanas.com. Contact: María Sánez. Chief executive: Juan Luís Cañas Herrera. Winemaker: Fidel Fernández Gómez. Established: 1928. Type: SA. Own vineyards (ha): 90. Contract (ha): 200. Own production: 30%. Buy in: Yes. Number of staff: 27. Group: No. Barrels: 4,300. Type: American and French. Annual production (hl): 12,600. Sales national: 80%; export: 20%. Top export markets: UK, Germany, Switzerland. Visits: by appointment; groups only. Open weekdays: 10.30am–1.30pm; 4pm–6pm. Principal wines: Luís Cañas Tinto Joven; Reserva de la Familia; Blanco Joven; Blanco Fermentado en Barrica; Reserva; Gran Reserva; Rosado; Crianza; Amaren Reserva; Amaren Graciano; Tempranillo; Hiru Tres Racimos

This is an elegant, smart, modern bodega towards the top of the hill on the Samaniego road out of Villabuena, just across the road from Izadi (*see* page 130). The family history is very long, with vineyard ownership stretching back for more than 200 years. In 1928, the family started making its own wine and selling it in bulk, but bottling only began in 1970, when Luís Cañas turned his family business into a limited company. Luís retired in 1989, and his son Juan Luís Cañas took over at the age of thirty-three, with a burning zeal to take the bodega forward into new areas. He certainly seems to have succeeded; the company's flagship wine Hiru Tres Racimos won the Rioja regional trophy at the inaugural *Decanter* World Wine Awards in 2003.

The basic Luís Cañas range is made every year and covers the full gamut of Rioja from *joven blanco* to *gran reserva*. In the better years, Amaren wines are made with a particular selection of grapes, and in the very best years Hiru Tres Racimos is made from the very finest grapes. The name of this last means "three bunches of grape'" (*hiru* is the Basque word for "three"), although the technical director, Fidel Fernández, is quick to point out that this is a figurative name implying that the vines from which the grapes have come are very low-yielding, although most of the vines really do only produce a maximum of three bunches (full-yield vines may produce ten bunches of 150 grams each). Luís Cañas Crianza (***) is a soft, warm, Tempranillo wine with good length. Reserva Selección de la Familia (****) is a "best-of-year" selection of grapes, with fifteen per cent Cabernet Sauvignon, twelve months in new French, and twenty-four months second-year American oak. The Cabernet perfume is prominent, but the palate has lovely fresh, spicy fruit: a wine to keep. Amaren Reserva (****) is made from Tempranillo from sixty-year-old vines, and has twelve months in new Alliers oak. This is classic *reserva* writ large: big fruit, spice, and complexity – wonderful. From here on up, the wines are all *generico* – in other words, not classified as *crianza*, *reserva*, etc. This is seen as giving the wine an old-fashioned image which is fine for classic wines but not in keeping with the upfront winemaking style of the new-wave range. Amaren Graciano (****>*****) has grapes from vines eighty-three to ninety-six years old in the village of Leza and at least twelve months in new French oak from a variety of forests. It has enormous, almost explosive power and fruit and needs a long time in the bottle to come to maturity. Hiru Tres Racimos (*****) is made from hand-selected Tempranillo from sixty-year-old vines, with eight months in assorted French oak. If the Amaren Graciano is "almost explosive", then this is nuclear: a powerful nose, almost reminiscent of curry spices, gives on to a wine with blockbusting fruit – restrained with powerful tannins. This is very much one of the new-wave, high-expression styles that are causing so much controversy. To those who don't like this style of wine, I say send your unwanted bottles to me, care of this publisher.

MARQUÉS DE CÁCERES

Unión Viti-Vinícola, Ctra Logroño, 26350 Cenicero, La Rioja. Tel: 941 454 000. Fax: 941 454 400. Email: marquesdecaceres@fer.es. Contact: Cristina Forner, Anne Vallejo. Chief executive: Felipe Aizpún. Winemaker: Fernando Gómez; Ramón Veiga, José-María Cervera, Fernando Costa. Established: 1970. Type: SA. Own vineyards (ha): 2. Contract (ha): 2,000 with 90 growers. Own production: 100%. Number of staff: 70. Barrels: 40,000. Type: 50/50 French/American. Annual production (hl): 70,000. Sales national: 50%; export: 50%. Top export markets: USA, UK, Norway. Visits: by appointment. Open weekdays: 8.30am–1.30pm, 3pm–6pm. Principal wines: Marqués de Cáceres Blanco Joven; Rosado Joven; Satinela; Antea Joven; Crianza Vendimia Seleccionada; Reserva; Gran Reserva; MC de Marqués de Cáceres; Gaudium

This is the bodega that started the big changes in Rioja in the 1970s, and the history of the Forner family's flight to France and eventual return is told in chapter three of this book. Founder Enrique Forner had been advised in his Bordeaux properties by Professor Émile Peynaud of the University of Bordeaux, and when his ambitions turned to his home turf, he turned once again to the great man for advice. He wanted to build a château-style bodega and to make a "village wine" using grapes from older, better vineyards owned by the local growers. The family was originally from Valencia, and Enrique's father had been in the wine business there in the 1930s. His French connections attracted him to the region of Rioja (still the first-choice foreign wine of France), and he surveyed the region to find what he (and the prof) could identify as having the best soil, vines, and grapes for the sort of wine he wanted to make. They found them in the village of Cenicero. A side-note here: the name of the town means "ashtray" in modern Castellano, and it is so called because it's the site of an old Roman crematorium, and there are strata of bones and bone-ash deep in the soil. I am no geologist, but could it be that those long-dead Romans are still fertilizing the vines of Cenicero?

The new winery was built to Forner's specifications and ready in time for the 1970 vintage, while he did deals with local growers for the supply of grapes; some 170 are still shareholders. It is an exceptionally handsome building, very much in the château style, with imposing iron gates and a magnificent boardroom with an internal window overlooking the barrel cellars. The name of the wine is that of the Marqués de Cáceres, a family friend from the Valencia days who allows his name to be used in return for a royalty payment to a charity of his choosing.

The technical equipment has evolved from what was the state of the art in 1970, and this is one of Rioja's most modern wineries. In spite of Enrique's belief that Rioja wine was too oaky and that the white shouldn't have any oak, he did eventually decide to make a *gran reserva* (although not until the criteria had been amended by the CRDOCa) and even a white Rioja with six months in the cask. The first wines reached the market in 1975, and it's true to say that Cáceres has developed an enviable reputation for quality, reliability, and consistency. In an article some years ago I was asked to describe the bodega in one line, and I wrote: "Not a single bad bottle in thirty years", which is probably an exaggeration, but doesn't seem very far from the truth.

Today Enrique takes something of a back seat while his impossibly glamorous daughter Cristina heads the company. Public affairs are in the hands of the feisty and elegant Anne Vallejo, who, despite spending the past quarter of a century in Rioja (with more than two decades at Cáceres), has a Glaswegian accent that is as strong as ever.

Wines Marqués de Cáceres Blanco (***) is the trademark, fresh Viura with no oak, but it does have the advantage of being rather less "squeaky-clean" than some of its rivals: clean, fresh, crisp, and delicious. Rosado (***) is also a *joven* with twenty per cent Garnacha, delicately perfumed and also delicious. Blanco Crianza (***>****) is 100 per cent Viura with, usually, the legal minimum six months in oak to give a crisp oaky shell but allowing the herby fruit of the grape to show through. Antea Fermentado en Barrica (***>****) also has a small percentage of Malvasía Rioja and is fermented in new French oak, and left on the lees until the winemaker decides that it's had enough, which varies from vintage to vintage. The style is subtly rather than overtly oaky, with a delicious hint of toast. The reds all have about fifteen per cent Garnacha and Graciano. Crianza (****) in its early days was ground-breaking in its minimal use of oak (the legal twelve months) and emphasis on bottle-ageing, but so much has changed in Rioja that it's now almost a mainstream classic; it has warm, ripe, slightly "warm rubber" tones on the nose, and good length. Reserva (****) has twenty-four to twenty-six months in oak, great maturity of style, and a very long finish. Gran Reserva (****>*****) has twenty-six to twenty-eight months in French oak, plus anything up to 120 in bottle before release. This is a long-lived wine which keeps its fruit and structure right through to the end.

Two relatively recent additions rather break the mould of the main range: Gaudium (***** the Latin word for "joy"; no serious bodega these days seems to be complete unless it has a top-of-the-range wine with a Latin name) is made from grapes from old-plot vines, hand-selected, and only in the greatest vintages; the first was 1994. The grape mix is similar to that of the main range, but the wine gets eighteen months in new French oak followed by a minimum of twenty-four in bottle, and is released when the winemaker thinks it's ready. Typically, this is a big wine with tight, dark fruit, structure, complexity, and length, and prominent tannins but in proportion to the "locked-in" fruit. MC (*****) is the latest addition: a high-expression wine made from selected old-vines

Tempranillo given a short time in new French oak; it's known colloquially at the bodega as "baby Gaudium". The first vintage was 2002 and this was my tasting note: "very tight, big fruit; warm, ripe, vanilla notes; powerful, structured tannin/fruit balance; excellent". I gave it nineteen out of twenty.

MARQUÉS DE GRIÑÓN

Ctra Elciego s/n, 26350 Cenicero, La Rioja. Tel: 941 453 100. Fax: 941 453 114. Established: 1994. Type: SA. Other information: *see* Berberana (page 91) Principal wines: Marqués de Griñón Alea Crianza; Colección Personal Ä16; Tempranillo

This is a complex story. Carlos Falcó, Marqués de Griñón, made his name by confounding the critics and making world-class, high-value wines on his mainly fruit-growing estate at Malpica de Tajo, in the province of Toledo (Castile-La Mancha). He branched out into other areas of Spain, and in 1994 signed a joint-venture deal with Arco-Bodegas Unidas (*see* page 84) to market a Rioja under the Marqués de Griñón name, with which came an exchange of shares that does not concern us here. Falcó does not make the wine, but has a role in the selection of the final *cuvées*, and his name as one who has approved the wines carries tremendous clout. The wines are made by Berberana (*see* page 91), originally at the old winery in Ollauri, but since 2001 at the Dominio de Súsar in Alfaro, and that's the address listed above. The idea was that Berberana, known best for well-made if unexceptional wines, could produce a premium range under the Griñón name. In the late 1990s, I asked what they had done with the grapes that go into the Griñón wines before the joint venture, and they told me that they didn't do anything with them; they didn't even have them until they were selected or bought in specifically for the new range.

In the meantime, the new Spanish wine law of 2003 had come into being, and Carlos Falcó's original estate in Malpica had become the first DO *de pago* in Spain, a category reserved for private estates of international reputation and quality. This caused him to rethink his plans for the future, and this is reflected in the new deal. These are the main points:

1. Lagunilla-Berberana will make and market Marqués de Griñón Alea Crianza and Marqués de Griñón Tempranillo for the foreseeable future, and Marqués de Griñón Reserva until the end of 2006, using a wholly owned subsidiary called Bodegas de Crianza Marqués de Griñón SA. Wines will be made in the Cenicero bodega, now Bodegas Lagunilla.

2. Carlos Falcó creates an entirely new, family-owned company called Pagos de Familia Marqués de Griñón SA, with a brief to develop in other areas of Spain "including Rioja".

3. The various cross-over shareholdings are bought back.

4. Arco-Bodegas Unidas will make a separate range of wines under the Marqués de la Concordia (*see* below) label at the Hacienda de Súsar; indeed, winemaker Carmelo Angulo claims that he will have a varietal Merlot on the market within a few years with a Rioja back label, and, given the uncertainty over policy-making under the new OIPVR (*see* chapter seven), he may very well be right.

So, in the future, we shall see wines from both companies under the Griñón banner. It is even possible that Carlos Falcó will be the first to create a *pago* DO within Rioja. Eventually, it seems that Lagunilla-Berberana will continue to make the "everyday" Griñón Rioja while Falcó's family company will make *reservas*, *gran reservas*, and estate wines. What this will do to the internal politics of La Rioja will be interesting to see.

Marqués de Griñón Tempranillo (***) has six months in barrel and is good, fresh Tempranillo with fruit and just the right amount of oak. Alea Crianza (***>****) has fifteen months in barrel and offers a more structured palate, with oak prominent but not dominant. Colección Personal Reserva (****) is blended from selected wines with an average of twenty-four months in barrel, and is excellent in good years.

MARQUÉS DE LA CONCORDIA

Bodegas Marques de la Concordia, Hacienda de Súsar, Avda del Ebro s/n, 26540 Alfaro, La Rioja. Tel: 941 453 100. Fax: 941 453 114. Website: www.haciendas-espana.com. Email: adelgado@haciendas-espana.com. Winemaker: Carmelo Angulo. Own vineyards (ha): 15. Barrels: 1,000. Visits: contact bodega. Principal wines: Marqués de la Concordia Hacienda de Súsar Signa/Crianza/ Reserva/Varietals

This is the current name (I forget whether it's the third or fourth now) for wines made at the Hacienda de Súsar, a private estate bought by Arco in the late 1990s because it had experimental status and was planted with Cabernet Sauvignon, Merlot, and Syrah, as well as Tempranillo. They spent two or three years retraining the vines on the Smart-Dyson model and produced the first vintage in 2001 under the name "Enartis".

Subsequent vintages became Marqués de Griñón Enartis, Marqués de Griñón Hacienda de Súsar – no, wait a minute; was it "Dominio de Súsar"? Or it might have been Haciendas Enartis... Well, whatever it was, it's now Marqués de la Concordia, Hacienda de Súsar, and it is here that group winemaker Carmelo Angulo proposes to break the mould of Rioja by making an historic Rioja Merlot and/or Syrah. We shall see.

Marqués de la Concordia (***>****) is all Tempranillo with six months in new oak with medium-plus toast, delicious fruit, and good oak/fruit balance. Crianza (***>****) is all Tempranillo with eighteen months in oak with a rich, oaky, classic style. Reserva (****) is another classic style: rich, with excellent fruit and a delicious finish. Syrah (**** – experimental) has the peppery spice, warmth, big tannins, big fruit, big everything... But is it Rioja? Merlot (*** – experimental) spiky-spicy aromatics with soft fruit and a lot of tannin, but good. But is it?

MARQUÉS DEL PUERTO

Marqués del Puerto, Ctra Logroño s/n, 26360 Fuenmayor, La Rioja.
Tel: 941 450 001. Fax: 941 450 051. Email: bmp@mbrizard.com. Contact/Chief executive/Winemaker: José-María Nieves Nuin. Established: 1972. Type: SA. Own vineyards (ha): 0.5. Contract (ha): 200–250. Buy in: Yes. Number of staff: 10. Group: Marie Brizard. Barrels: 6,500. Type: American and French. Annual production (hl): 10,000. Sales national: 85%; export: 15%. Top export markets: Switzerland, USA, France. Visits: by appointment; groups and individuals. Open weekdays: 9am–3pm. Principal wines: Marqués del Puerto Blanco/Rosado Joven; Blanco Fermentado en Barrica; Crianza; Reserva; Gran Reserva; MM Reserva; Román Paladino Gran Reserva.

This is another example of *cosecheros* coming together to create a bodega and make their own wine. The story begins in 1968 with the formation of a company called López Agós y Compañía, after primary shareholder and general manager Federico López Agós. The founders built a new bodega on the main Haro-Logroño road (the N-232) in time for the 1972 vintage, which has not gone down in the annals of Rioja as a quality year – the entire production was sold off in bulk. The bodega worked hard, however, and in 1983 the name was changed to the present one (one of the shareholders was then Marqués del Puerto, Rafael Martínez de Pisón y Gaztelu). In 1996, the bodega was bought by the Bordeaux-based Marie Brizard group, but it functions as a separate entity within the group.

Marqués del Puerto Blanco Joven (*) is a pleasant, fresh, good-value Viura. Blanco Fermentado en Barrica (**>***) is rather richer, with pronounced oaky notes that don't overwhelm and a delicious finish; Rosado (**>***) is a 50/50 Tempranillo and Garnacha mix with eight hours' maceration: very crisp and light, with a pleasant hint of richness; Crianza (**>***) has ten per cent Mazuelo and twelve months in American and French and is very much in the classic style: spicy fruit and spiky oak. Reserva (***>****) is the same formula as Crianza but from selected grapes and with twenty-two months in oak; it has maturity and complexity and a very good balance between oak and fruit. Gran Reserva (****) has six per cent Mazuelo and two per cent Graciano with thirty to thirty-six months in oak; it has the classic pot-pourri perfume and is rich, soft, and delicious. MM Reserva Especial (****>*****) has ten per cent Mazuelo with twenty-four months in oak and is a big, powerful wine with hefty structure, fruit richness, and a wonderful finish. It is so named because the first vintage (1994) was released in 2000. Román Paladino Gran Reserva (*****) is the bodega's flagship wine, and named after the "plain language" mentioned in the first verses ever written in Spanish (*see* chapter two). It's made from heavily selected grapes, and has ten per cent Graciano and five per cent Mazuelo with thirty-six months in French oak plus ninety-six months in bottle before release. It's a blockbusting wine, although not in the new-wave, high-expression style, but in the classic style: fruit, oak, maturity, and tannins all in perfect harmony.

MARQUÉS DE MURRIETA

Bodegas Marqués de Murrieta, Finca Ygay Ctra Zaragoza Km 5 Apartado 109, 26080 Logroño, La Rioja. Tel: 941 271 370. Fax: 941 251 606. Website: www.marquesdemurrieta.com. Email: rrpp@marquesdemurrieta.com. Contact: Myriam Ochoa Arróniz, PR. Chief executive: Vicente Dalmau Cebrian-Sagarriga, Conde de Creixell. Winemaker: María Vargas Montoya. Established: 1852. Type: SL. Own vineyards (ha): 300. Own production (%): 100. Number of staff: 50. Group: Pazo de Barrantes. Annual production (hl): 150,000. Group: Pazo de Barrantes. Barrels: 16,000. Type: 15,000 American, 1,000 French. Sales national: 45%; export: 55%. Top export markets: Germany, USA, UK. Visits: by appointment; groups only. Principal wines: Marqués de Murrieta Blanco Reserva; Tinto Reserva; Castillo Ygay Tinto Gran Reserva Especial; Tinto Gran Reserva

The early history of this company is the early history of "classic" Rioja (*see* chapter three). To recap briefly: Peruvian-born Luciano de Murrieta moved to Spain after Peru's independence, and enlisted in the army under General Espartero, later the Duque de la Victoria. He eventually became the general's aide-de-camp, achieving enormous influence when the general became regent. When Espartero was deposed, both he and Murrieta were forced into exile in London, and Murrieta went into banking. He lived the good life but was annoyed to see that almost every wine but Rioja was represented in the city's restaurants and banqueting halls, and vowed that he would one day do something about it.

Espartero, aka the Duque de la Victoria, was a Riojano by birth and owned a bodega there. He thought that winemaking was a good business, with profitable prospects for the future, and encouraged his younger friend to give it a try. Murrieta and the Duque returned to Logroño in 1844, once Isabella II was safely on the throne in her own right, and Murrieta duly went to Bordeaux to study winemaking in 1848, returning to Rioja to make his first vintage in the Duque's bodega, in 1852. He was the first producer in Rioja to age wines in oak casks – something considered shockingly expensive and unnecessary at the time – and started exporting to the Spanish colonies of Cuba and Mexico straight away. The business prospered and in 1860 he established his own bodega (coincidentally, the same year as the other pioneer, Riscal, *see* page 150, started his), and in 1872 bought the Ygay estate on the edge of Logroño and established the bodega that we still see today, now beautifully restored to its original magnificence. He was created the first Marqués de Murrieta that same year, and named the winery as such.

The Rioja boom years lay ahead, of course, and Murrieta prospered greatly. He was a very philanthropic man throughout his life, and at one time housed fifty poor families on the estate and put up the investment for schools and other educational institutions, and it was these charitable works, his generosity, and his loyalty to the crown which brought him the title of Marqués. Murrieta never married, and when he died in 1911 aged eighty-nine, he left generous bequests to the city of Logroño and its institutions, but the estate and title to a second nephew, José Manuel Olivares Bruguera. Olivares handed on the estate to his father Julián de Olivares, a cavalry officer, and it remained in the hands of that and another branch of the family all of whom lived in Madrid, until 1983.

The bodega gained a reputation for enormously long-lived wines of great elegance and finesse. Indeed, by the 1970s, the wines were starting to appear a little old-fashioned and in need of a new direction, but there was no clear leadership at the bodega. This arrived in 1983 with the Cebrián-Sagarriaga family, Condes de Creixell, who ran (and still runs) Pazo de Barrantes in the DO Rías Baixas. Don Vicente, the *conde*, had been looking for an opportunity to get into Rioja, and realized that there was immense untapped potential in this old estate. Massive investment was needed, of course, and the first priorities were to make the estate self-sufficient in grapes, restore the buildings, and renew the equipment. It was hard going, but, looking at the estate now, well worth the effort. Sadly, Don Vicente didn't live to see the fulfilment of his dream: he died suddenly in 1996 at the age of forty-eight. He had, however, begun a process of renewal that is bring carried on by the present *conde*, his son Vicente Dalmau Cebrián Sagarriaga, who took over in his early twenties.

The first major departure from the old ways was that wines were released much younger than previously, although still a lot older than most other bodegas in Rioja. Castillo Ygay is now released at seven to ten years old rather than the fifteen to twenty before, and the "young count", as he is known colloquially in the trade, has also brought in winemaker María Vargas, who is very widely respected in Rioja, and has also done considerable research into the individual plots that make up the 300 hectares of vineyards, and made experimental wines from several of them. The first evidence of this work was Capellanía, the name of one of the individual vineyards, which is a white made from eighty-five per cent forty-year-old Viura, ten per cent Garnacha Blanca, and five per cent Malvasía Riojana with thirty-six months in oak. This was seen at the time as an astonishing vote of confidence in traditional-style white Rioja when almost everyone else was moving away from it. The second manifestation was Dalmau Reserva, made from the oldest single vineyard on the estate: eighty-five per cent Tempranillo, ten per cent Cabernet Sauvignon, and five per cent Graciano with twenty months in oak – another classic style, but made in the modern way.

The late Don Vicente was quoted as saying that he wanted to "maintain the quality of the Rioja wines of yesteryear but without the faults". Out have gone the ancient barrels, humidity, and damp in the cellars, but the avowed intention is to stick to the spirit of what Luciano de Murrieta began. In 2002, the bodega celebrated its 150th anniversary with another single-vineyard wine. Especial Aniversario Mazuelo was harvested in 2001 from the Lucas single vineyard (planted in 1977) and bottled in January 2003. I suspect we shall see more of these individual wines in the future.

Capellanía (****) is not as oaky as you'd expect after all that time in wood. A kind of post-modern take on classic white Rioja, it is quite delicious. Marqués de Murrieta Blanco Reserva (****) is very much in the older style, with plenty of toasty oak. Reserva Tinto (****) is also very traditional with that hint of cigar-box on the nose and strawberry-and-vanilla on the palate. Dalmau (*****), in spite of being much younger, is already shaping up as a classic, with richer fruit but no less classic Rioja style. Castillo Ygay (*****) is still the flagship wine, made as a *gran reserva* only in the best vintages, with forty-eight months in cask, and rightly one of the classics of Rioja.

MARQUÉS DE RISCAL

Vinos de los Herederos de Marqués de Riscal Torrea 1, 01340 Elciego, Álava. Tel: 945 606 000. Fax: 945 606 023. Website: www.marquesderiscal.com. Email: marquesderiscal@marquesderiscal.com. Contact: Ruth Sutton. Chief executive: Alejandro Aznar. Winemaker: Francisco Hurtado de Amézaga. Established: 1860. Type: SA. Own vineyards (ha): 220. Contract (ha): 1,250. Own production: 100%; Buy in: No. Number of staff: 72. Group: Vinos Blancos de Castilla. Barrels: 37,000. Type: American. Annual production (hl): 33,750. Sales national: 45%; export: 55%. Top export markets: USA, Switzerland, UK. Visits: by appointment; email: relacionespublicas@marquesderiscal.com. Principal wines: Marqués de Riscal Rosado Joven; Reserva; Gran Reserva; Barón de Chirél

This is the other big name among the pioneers of classic Rioja, along with Murrieta (*see* page 147), mentioned in chapter three. To recap on the historical material: Camilo Hurtado de Amézaga, Marqués de Riscal de Alegre (and also Barón del Castillo de Chirél, Conde de Castronuevo), was a liberal writer in the mid-nineteenth century and had gone to Bordeaux to avoid the political turmoil that was gripping Spain at that time. There he was able to observe the Bordelais methods of winemaking and became convinced that he could do the same at home in Rioja. He was particularly close to the owner of Château Lanessan in the Haut-Médoc, and also knew the winemaker there, Jean Cadiche Pineau, who would later come to Rioja himself and end up working at Riscal.

Once Isabella II was established on the throne in 1844, it was safe for him to come home, and he started building a winery in the Bordeaux style in 1850. Such was his thoroughness that he had hired the prominent contemporary architect Ricardo Bellsola and paid for him to go to Bordeaux to study the design and construction of a Bordeaux *chai*; the task took ten years. He made his first vintage in 1860 and discovered that the local grapes were suited for cask-ageing; there are still a few bottles of that vintage in the "cathedral", a look at which is one of the most popular parts of a bodega visit. In those days the wines were sold as "Médoc Alavesa" on the basis that few, if any, customers would have known what "Rioja" was (or be able to pronounce it correctly).

The story of Jean Pineau is told in chapter three, but the end result was that he ended up working for Riscal when his contract with the local authority expired in 1868. One of Pineau's earliest recommendations was to experiment with French varieties alongside the locals, and in that same year Riscal imported vine cuttings and planted them. Once complete, the plantation had reached thirty-nine hectares and consisted of sevnty-five per cent local varieties (Tempranillo, Graciano, and Viura) and twenty-five per cent French varieties (Cabernet Sauvignon, Merlot, Malbec, and Pinot Noir). In due course the Pinot Noir, Malbec, and Merlot disappeared, but the Cabernet Sauvignon remains and is still there today, although under the CRDOCa regulations it can only appear on the back label as "other varieties" (but *see* chapter seven for possible developments). As expansion continued, more and more expertise was required in the bodega and vineyard, and a good deal of it came from France, as the skills needed were scarce or non-existent in Rioja at the time; certainly many of the senior staff at the bodega were largely French until the beginning of World War II.

The wines became well known, and won medals at international competitions. It was unusual to see a Spanish wine of any kind at such events, so the publicity was enormous – so much so that people started to fake them. Labels were forged to look like the real thing, and empty bottles were refilled, and it began to look as if Riscal would go the latter-day way of Mr Biro's ballpoint pen and Mr Macintosh's raincoat and become a generic term. Don Camilo came up with an ingenious solution that is with us still: the *malla*, a wire-mesh net around the bottle, skilfully woven to ensure that you can't get the cork out without cutting the net. Not only did it work, but it became part of the Riscal brand identity, and other companies started using it to imply that their wines were of a similar standard.

Jean Pineau oversaw some of the most important early developments at the bodega, including a big expansion in 1883, which included new presses and fermentation vats, the expanding market, and the international expositions. Riscal won first prize at the Brussels Exhibition in 1910, at which King Alfonso XII was present. This resulted in the king placing a regular order for the palace cellar, which was another promotional coup for the bodega. When the market for Rioja started to open up after World War II, Riscal was one of only a handful of names in Spanish wine from any region that had any kind of profile. I remember from my early days in the wine trade that, in 1972, we had Riscal, Murrieta, Glorioso from Bodegas Palacio, and Vega Sicilia, which was then a *vino de mesa* known only to the cognoscenti – and we were considered to be a radical Spanish specialist wine merchant.

Meanwhile, Riscal had never made a white wine. Francisco Hurtado de Amézaga, known to his confidantes as "Paco", was the rising generation of the family, and he'd been scouring northern Spain for somewhere to make a white worthy of the family name. He didn't like oaky white Rioja, and neither did he like the new "squeaky-clean" style of Viura, so he'd been looking at Chardonnay from Catalonia, Albariño from Galicia, and at Rueda, where he eventually decided to build a new bodega to make wine from the local Verdejo grape. This is a story in its own right, but will have to wait for a future book on the wines of Castile-León.

In the meantime a problem had been, quite literally, growing back in Rioja. The wine writer and Champagne specialist Tom Stevenson had visited Elciego on a number of occasions and detected something "not quite clean" about successive vintages of the wines in the mid-1980s. It sometimes happens that fungal or bacterial infections can creep up on a bodega so gently that those standing close to the wines don't notice that it's happening. But outsiders do. Stevenson eventually contacted the bodega in 1988 and asked them to do an analysis; they found, indeed, that there was some kind of infection in the system which called for a radical clean-out.

Many bodegas in Spain have a shareholding by a local or national bank (presumably on the basis that land and buildings never go down in price), and at that time a shareholding in Riscal was in the hands of the Banco de Urquijo. They sent in Luís Miguel Beneyto, an agronomist from their industrial division, and he realized there was need for radical work. He asked Paco to come back from Rueda, and Paco decided to take this opportunity to do a massive clean-up and reinvestment totalling 300 million pesetas (Euro 1.8 million at 1987 prices). This took three years to accomplish and involved almost total replacement of the casks in the bodega.

The next task was waiting, however. The pressing and fermentation halls were no longer big enough to accommodate the company's business, and Riscal decided to build a brand-new, stainless-steel fermenting hall with full computer control (thereby giving the winemaker the option of old- or new-style wines for the final selection, and new presses), but, as with a number of the more avant-garde bodegas, they chose small, modern, hydraulic basket-presses against anything else. The first vintage from the new bodegas was the 2000. Today, Paco is the technical director, and oversees all aspects of winemaking along with oenologist Javier Salamero.

Once that task was completed, the next project beckoned. Elciego is a small town with little in the way of tourist attractions, but requests for visits to Riscal were becoming more numerous. The board decided to embark on an ambitious project to provide a new corporate headquarters, with a shop, visitor centre, restaurant, and hotel included. Following the example of the company's founder, it was decided that the complex should be designed by a prestigious, contemporary architect. They chose Frank Gehry, the Canadian-born, California-based creator of, among other things, the Guggenheim Museum in Bilbao. The project is scheduled for completion in early 2005 and promises to be the biggest tourist attraction in Elciego.

The wines are all very reliable and, apart from the unfortunate glitch in the mid-1980s, always have been. Marqués de Riscal Rosado (***) is the only *joven*, made from Tempranillo and Viura: delicious, meaty, and fresh (one of the best Rioja pinks). Reserva (****) has five per cent Graciano and five per cent Mazuelo with twenty-two months in cask: crisp fruit, good weight, complex, and structured. Gran Reserva (****>*****)

in great years is magnificent, with full fruit: rich, powerful, and long. Barón de Chirél Reserva (*****) has forty-six per cent "other varieties" (*i.e.* Cabernet Sauvignon) and twenty-six months in oak. The Cabernet lifts the nose but the American oak gives it a real Riojano style, backed up by the strawberry fruit of the Tempranillo. They said they could do it (*see* chapter seven) and they have.

MARQUÉS DE VARGAS

Bodegas y Viñedos del Marqués de Vargas, Hacienda Pradolagar, Ctra Zaragoza Km 6, 26006 Logroño, La Rioja. Tel: 941 261 401. Fax: 941 238 696. Email: bvargas@jet.es. Contact/Chief executive: José Bezares Osaba. Winemaker: Javier Pérez Ruíz de Vergara. Established: 1991. Type: SA. Own vineyards (ha): 65. Own production: 100%. Number of staff: 15. Group: Bodegas y Viñedos del Conde de San Cristóbal, Pazo de San Mauro. Barrels: 2,500. Type: American, French, and Russian. Annual production (hl): 2,500. Sales national: 50%; export: 50%. Top export markets: USA, UK, Switzerland. Visits: by appointment; groups and individuals. Open weekdays: 9am–2pm; 4pm–7pm. Principal wines: Marqués de Vargas Reserva; Marqués de Vargas Reserva Privada; Hacienda Pradolagar Reserva Especial

This is a very smart, modern bodega with an immaculate, weed-free vineyard, manicured gardens, and every modern contrivance in the bodega, including a very elegant tasting room. It's situated in an area east of Logroño known as Los Tres Marqueses, because the land in these parts belongs to the Marqués de Murrieta (well, the Conde de Creixell; *see* page 147), the Marqués del Romeral, and the Marqués de Vargas, who owns twenty per cent of the company and provides much of the Pradolagar vineyard area, which is reckoned among the best in this part of Rioja. This is where Mediterranean and Atlantic influences more or less balance out, with 400 metres (1,312 feet) of altitude providing the right kind of hot day/cool night influences during the ripening season, sufficient rainfall courtesy of the Atlantic and the Cantabrian Mountains, and Mediterranean levels of sunshine. The soil is chalky clay, and the bodega uses no artificial fertilizers or pesticides. Green harvesting is routinely carried out each summer, sometimes with a further green harvest a few weeks before the vintage.

It's a single estate using only its own grapes, and has built a reputation for meticulous use of oak: small-pored (hence the Russian contingent)

and with varying levels of toast. The pursuit of quality at lower yields (average 4,500 kilograms per hectare against a legal maximum of 6,500) with longer ageing than the minimum provides wines of considerable character and longevity; indeed, these are wine which do need to be kept, and only really start to perform well from about five years old.

Marqués de Vargas Reserva Privada (****) has ten per cent each of Ganacha and Mazuelo, and twenty per cent "other varieties'" for which read Cabernet Sauvignon, with twenty-two to twenty-four months in new Russian oak, and has great structure with big fruit locked inside big tannins. Hacienda Pradolagar Reserva (*****) was first made in 2000 from selected grapes from a single vineyard on the estate and has forty per cent Cabernet Sauvignon. It has twenty-two months in new French and Russian oak and offers a subtle, complex structure with powerful fruit and endless length.

MARQUÉS DE VITORIA

Bodegas Marqués de Vitoria, Camino de Santa Lucía s/n, 01320 Oyón, Álava.
Tel: 945 622 134. Fax: 945 601 496. Website: www.bodegasmarquesdevitoria.es.
Email: info@bodegasmarquesdevitoria.es. Winemaker: Luís Zabala. Established:
1988. Type: SA. Group: Faustino. Barrels: 16,500. Visits: see Faustino (page 120)
Principal wines: Marqués de Vitoria Blanco Joven; Rosado Joven; Crianza;
Ecológico; Reserva; Gran Reserva; Original

This bodega started life as a cooperative but was eventually bought out by its main customer, Bodegas Faustino (see page 120), which is just across the road and up (or down) a bit. Today the bodega is tasked with making the group's modern wines while Faustino makes the traditional wines. All the red wines are 100 per cent Tempranillo and there is some organic production; for more details see Faustino entry.

Marqués de Vitoria Ecológico (***) has twelve months in American oak, silky fruit aromas, and a big structure, with prominent oak. Reserva (***>****) has oaky vanilla and sweet fruit, but with a structured, tannic finish. Gran Reserva (****>*****) has a surprisingly youthful perfume with rich, classic fruit and oak on the palate. Original (****) is a project begun with the 2003 vintage to make an expressive wine with selected grapes from the oldest vineyards, with minimal oak-ageing. It has three to four months in new French oak, a bite of toasty oak with structure, and dark fruit: delicious.

MARTÍNEZ LACUESTA

Bodegas Martínez Lacuesta, La Ventilla 71, Haro, La Rioja. Tel: 941 310 050. Fax: 941 303 748. Website: www.martinezlacuesta.com. Email: bodega@martinezlacuesta.com. Contact/Chief executive: Luís Martínez-Lacuesta Verde. Winemaker: Álvaro Martínez del Castillo. Established: 1895. Type: SA. Own vineyards (ha): 12. Contract (ha): 30. Own production: 10%. Buy in: Yes. Number of staff: 27. Group: No. Barrels: 8,000. Type: American. Annual production (hl): 7,000. Sales national: 90%; export: 10%. Top export markets: Mexico, USA, UK. Visits: by appointment; groups and individuals. Open weekdays: 8am–1pm; 4pm–7pm. Principal wines: Martínez Lacuesta Blanco Fermentado en Barrica; Rosado; Crianza 2000; Crianza Selección; Reserva; Gran Reserva 1996; Campeador Reserva

Félix Martínez Lacuesta was a Haro man who was big in local politics and philanthropic works, one of the leaders in the fight back against phylloxera, and a member of many important vine and wine committees and commissions. In addition, he established a bodega with his five brothers in 1895, just outside what were then the town walls but what is now almost the town centre. The brothers started exporting in 1902, mainly to the former Spanish colonies of Cuba and Mexico, as well as markets across Europe. Félix died in 1928, and the remaining brothers carried on the business, eventually passing it on to Luís Martinez-Lacuesta Almarza, the son of Emiliano, and thence to the present generation.

Wines Martínez Lacuesta (*>**) is a *corta-crianza* with some Mazuelo and Graciano and five to six months in oak, tending towards the tannic when young but softening with age. Crianza Selección (***>****) has Garnacha and eighteen months in French and American oak, still heavy on the tannins but with rich, locked-in fruit that bodes well for the future. Campeador Reserva (***>****) has that pot-pourri fragrance with clean, fresh fruit but, again, quite a lot of tannin when young.

MIGUEL MERINO

Bodegas Miguel Merino, Ctra de Logroño 16, 26330 Briones, La Rioja. Tel: 941 322 263. Fax: 941 322 294. Website: www.miguelmerino.com. Email: info@miguelmerino.com. Contact/Chief executive: Miguel Merino Navajas. Winemaker: Miguel Merino/Manuel Ruiz. Established: 1993. Type: SL. Own vineyards (ha): 9. Contract (ha): "two friends" (*see* below). Barrels: 365.

Visits: by appointment. Mon–Sat 10am–2pm. Principal wines: Miguel Merino
Reserva; Vitola Reserva; Gran Reserva; Cantiga (contract)

The fabulously historic village of Briones (pop. 875) inhabits its own little gastronomic continuum (*see* Allende, page 79) in terms of produce, food specialities, and wine. The soils, the microclimates, and the relationship with the river Ebro are all just slightly different from the rest of the Rioja Alta, which probably explains why rich Riojanos built so many magnificent red-stone mansions here in the days when even the grandest (or their servants) had to grow their own food. Until Miguel Merino established his small bodega, however, there was no commercial bodega in the town, even though its wine had been talked about for generations. Miguel worked as an export manager/consultant/salesman for many years throughout Europe and the world before achieving his dream of his own bodega, in a handsome stone house next to the N-232 Haro-Logroño road. He did, and still does, consultancy for export customers in the region and beyond (most notably Bodegas Ochoa in Navarra, whose boss, Javier Ochoa, gave Miguel enormous help and guidance in the early years), but his first love is now the bodega and its small output of high-quality wines.

From an investment point of view, Miguel started out with very little money, and so everything has been done on a hand-to-mouth basis; the first vintage (1994) wasn't even released until 2000. His nine hectares – all from within the village itself – have been assembled over a decade, and he also buys grapes from two neighbours, Jesús Samaniego and Carlos Ibaibarriaga, to make up the total. In addition, because he does have what passes for a large-scale bodega in Briones (*i.e.* bigger than the average double garage), he makes a wine called Cantiga for another neighbour, Daniel Puras, for a modest commission, because Miguel doesn't make *joven* or *crianza* wines and Daniel's grapes are picked and fermented earlier than his own red wine grapes.

Because of cost constraints, Miguel Merino has yet to afford a heat-exchanger and double-skinned tanks, so at vintage time he cloaks the stainless steel with wet towels soaked in cold water, and hoses them down as necessary to keep the temperature where he wants it. If the nights are hot after the vintage, that means staying awake all night, and if the nights are cold during malolactic fermentation, it means cloaking the tanks with hot towels and hosing them down with hot water until the secondary fermentation is complete, which may mean staying up all night again. Indeed, he almost won the "bodega anorak" trophy for this book, but that was before I went to Remírez de la Ganuza (*see* page 182).

It is impossible not to like this man; his self-effacing charm ("my job is just to let the wine make itself"), devotion to his bodega, and slight vagueness – he has half a dozen rows of experimental vines in front of the bodega, and has planted a rose bush of a different colour in front of each, but can't remember which is which – seem to ensure that one day he will be a superstar of Rioja. And when it happens, he'll probably say it's nothing to do with him; it's the soil, his neighbours, his friends, Señora de Moreno (who prefers to live in their house in Logroño as there aren't any shops in Briones), his guru Javier Ochoa, or somebody else. Well, that's when you know you are in the presence of a real achiever.

Cantiga (***) is Miguel's neighbour Daniel Puras's wine, which he makes while his tanks are idle before his own *reserva*-only vintage. It's all Tempranillo with four months in American oak and good, fresh, fruity, glugging stuff with a hint of oak at a bargain price. Miguel Moreno Reserva (***>****) has three per cent Graciano and twenty-five months in American and French oak, and delicious complexity, structure, savoury fruit, and a cigar-box finish. Vitola Reserva (****) was first made in the difficult 1997 vintage and is a selection of the best grapes from the year; big fruit, crisp tannins, good structure. Gran Reserva (*****) is only made when Miguel thinks it's worth it: vanilla and cigar-box on the nose, rich, spicy, mature fruit on the palate, and a long, gentle finish.

MONTECILLO

Bodegas Montecillo, Ctra Navarrete Km3, 26360 Fuenmayor, La Rioja.
Tel: 941 440 125. Fax: 941 440 663. Website: www.Osborne.es. Email: comunicaciones@osborne.es. Contact/Winemaker: María Martínez Sierra. Chief executive: Gonzalo Causapé Almarza. Established: 1874. Type: SA. Buy in: Yes, but only Rioja Alta grape from vines at least 35 years old. Number of staff: 30. Group: Bodegas Osborne. Barrels: 29,700. Annual production (hl): 35,000. Sales national: 50%; export: 50%. Top export markets: USA, Norway, Switzerland. Visits: by appointment; groups and individuals. Open weekdays: 7am–2.30pm. Principal wines: Montecillo Blanco; Crianza; Reserva; Gran Reserva

This bodega was founded by Celestino Navajas Matute at the time of the first Rioja boom. His sons, Alejandro and Gregorio, set up the first formal business under the name "Hijos de Celestino Najavas" a short time later. Alejandro had worked in Bordeaux and joined in with the general trend of importing that region's technology to make Rioja wine. His son José-Luís trained in Beaune, bringing a different aspect of French winemaking to the business, and was also responsible for renaming the company after El Montecillo, a hill on the outskirts of Fuenmayor, in 1947. Montecillo was one of the first bodegas to equip itself with a tasting room for visitors, as well as cooling equipment for the fermenting vats, long before the advent of stainless steel. Certainly, its reputation was one of producing quality wines over many decades when it came to the attention of sherry giant Osborne.

In the 1970s, the sherry business was heading for a bleak period, and the more forward-looking bodegas decided to invest in parallel businesses while the going was good. Osborne is a family-owned company dating back to 1772, and they snapped up Montecillo in 1973, selling off the company's eighty-hectare estate (which subsequently became Finca Valpiedra, see page 126) and invested the cash in a brand-new bodega incorporating gravity-feed technology, just outside Fuenmayor by the N-232, which was ready for the vintage of 1975. Even now, the building still looks smart and modern, and the labyrinthine cellars have stocks of vintages going back to 1928. Meanwhile, the old cellar is being renovated for future use.

The bodega owns no vineyards but buys in grapes from selected suppliers, paid for according to their quality. In some years, indeed, it buys in none at all if the quality isn't there (1983, 1992, 1993, and 1999 were difficult years, in spite of all being classified as *Buena* by the CRDOCa), but by a judicious management of stocks it maintains sales even in years when the quantity is very low or non-existent. Responsible for this is winemaker María Martínez, who joined the company in 1976 and is a no-nonsense, two-fisted veteran of the vats with outspoken views on her wines, Rioja generally, regulation, and the regional and national governments' attitude to wine. The first impression you get is that she is a conservative when it comes to Rioja wine styles, but this is not the case. On the question of a *vino de la tierra de* Alto Ebro (*see* chapter seven), for example, she's in favour: "to take away all the substandard wine which gets classified as Rioja". In the matter of Cabernet Sauvignon, she believes that it offers more dry extract than the fabulously scarce Graciano and should be permitted as a minority variety. She is passionate about lowering yields and, while not insisting on going organic, will not buy grapes whose vines have been treated with artificial sprays, insecticides, and fertilizers which, she believes, are progressively poisoning the soil. She is not alone in this view among winemakers in Rioja and beyond.

Certainly, her wines speak for themselves, and there's an interesting progression from ancient to modern in the style. It's no longer commercially available, but I was able to taste the 1978 Gran Reserva (*****) which is benchmark *gran reserva* in the classic style: lovely, ripe, mature, fragrant, delicious, irresistible – rather like the lady herself.

All red wines are 100 per cent Tempranillo. Montecillo Crianza (**>***) has fourteen to eighteen months in French oak with good, soft fruit and a decent balance. Reserva (***>****) has a minimum eighteen months in oak, good aromatics, firm tannins, and a good fruit structure. Gran Reserva (****>*****) has a minimum thirty months in French oak and ages with consummate grace. I tasted three vintages and the evolution of the wine was an education. There is still some 1982 Gran Reserva (*****) in the market and it's alive, vibrant, full of dark, tight fruit: simply superb.

MUGA

Bodegas Muga, Barrio de la Estación s/n, 26200 Haro, La Rioja.
Tel: 941 311 825. Fax: 941 312 867. Website: www.bodegasmuga.com. Email: información@bodegasmuga.com. Contact/Chief executive/Winemaker: Jorge Muga Palacín. Established: 1932. Type: SL. Own vineyards (ha): 170. Contract (ha): 180. Own production: 50%. Buy in: Yes. Number of staff: 60. Group: No. Barrels: 14,000. Type: American and French. Annual production (hl): 13,000. Sales national: 70%; export: 30%. Top export markets: USA, UK, Scandinavia. Visits: by appointment; groups (maximum 15) and individuals. Principal wines: Muga Blanco; Rosado; Crianza; Reserva Selección Especial; Prado Enea; Torre Muga; Aro

This is another "between-the-booms" bodega, founded in 1932 when the smart money was on waiting for the next upturn. This didn't deter Isaac Muga Martínez, who had decided, like so may others before and since, to stop selling grapes from the family vineyard to the big players and make his own wine. This was in part informed by the fact that Rioja was in a bit of a downturn and grapes were not fetching the kind of price they had in the past. By all accounts the business prospered, and Isaac realized that he needed bigger premises, ideally near the railway station, which was then the main despatch point for wine from the Haro region. He drew up plans for the move but, sadly, died before he could achieve them. This was in 1969, but his three children made the move in 1971 into a building which had seen many uses since it had been constructed. They extended the cellars and also built the famous tower that is visible almost from Elciego. All this took a great deal of capital, and in order to achieve it the Muga brothers, Manuel and Isaac (junior), sold a forty-nine per cent stake to a venture capital bank.

The bodega's installations are historic: everything is done in oak, and there are no stainless steel, fibreglass, or even concrete tanks in which to store the wine. Muga employs four full-time coopers whose job is to repair and rebuild the 18,000-litre *tinas* in which the wine is fermented and stored, as well as looking after the bodega's casks, so we may rightly describe this as an "old-technology bodega": fermentation in oak, fining with white of egg, ageing in cask.

The present generation of the family is led by Jorge and Manuel (known as Manu) Muga, the grandsons of the founder, and they work hard to preserve the legacy of quality they have inherited. Maintaining the *tinas* is expensive and time-consuming, but Manu Muga believes that oak vats provide better micro-oxygenation during alcoholic fermentation. His one remaining ambition is to become self-sufficient in grapes; the family vineyard holding has increased to 170 hectares but this is still not enough for the production. He keeps offering to buy vineyards from the firm's contract growers but they are unenthusiastic. "Why should they?" says Manu. "We pay top prices for quality grapes, and the *cosechero* doesn't have the expense of a bodega, all-year-round staff, and costs."

Indeed, as an aside, it could be said that many of Rioja's greatest names are very anxious to buy up plots of vines to insure themselves against the see-sawing market exemplified by the débâcle of 1999/2000, when prices in some places rose to 450 pesetas (Euro 2.75) per kilo in 1999, effectively pricing most Rioja out of the mainstream market, leaving unsold wine still in the tanks the following harvest time. It then collapsed to 160 pesetas (Euro 0.95) per kilo in 2000 in a dilute, overproduced vintage. However, even at the current (2004) rate of Euro 1.00 to Euro 1.25 a kilo for basic grapes, and a good deal more for real quality from old vines, the *cosecheros* are doing well. I was driving in the Rioja Alta countryside in the spring of 2004 with the export director of one of the most respected houses, when we were overtaken by a spanking-new but low-key, silver-grey Mercedes. "That'll be a *cosechero*, then," he muttered through gritted teeth.

If I've given the impression of low-tech, old-fashioned technology here, that doesn't come through in the wines. Quite surprisingly, although the equipment is almost unchanged from a century ago, and the classic ethos is the keynote for Muga, the wines are modern, fresh, forward-looking, and beautifully made, and the bodega and its shop wonderfully restored.

Muga Blanco Fermentado en Barrica (***) has ten per cent Malvasía fermented in Alliers oak: lovely, fresh, clean fruit. Rosado (***) is sixty per cent Garnacha, thirty per cent Tempranillo, and ten per cent Viura with ten to twelve hours' maceration and a very pleasant bite of fruit over a clean, fresh palate. In the reds, Muga Reserva (***>****) typically has twenty per cent Garnacha and ten per cent Mazuelo and Graciano with six months in *tina*, thirty months in cask, and thirty-six months in bottle. This is amazingly fresh with plenty of fruit, spiky oak notes when young, and a long, soft finish. Reserva Especial (****) is only made in better years, from grapes from higher-altitude vineyards. It's a long-lived, powerful wine with full fruit and powerful tannins, but an elegant, lingering structure. Prado Enea (****>*****) is the *gran reserva* of the bodega with at least thirty-six months in cask and thirty-six in bottle, with massive fruit, subtlety, maturity, complexity, and elegance. Torre Muga (****>*****) used to be the flagship wine before Aro (*see* below) and is always made with a rigorous selection of grapes with eighteen months in new French oak: it's spicy and spiky with dark, concentrated fruit, very crisp tannins, and a lingering warmth. Aro (*****) is a venture dating from the 2001 vintage, using grapes from three old vineyards harvesting at 3,000 kilograms per hectare (the legal maximum is 6,500) in the Haro area. It has thirty per cent Graciano with malolactic fermentation in the cask rather than the *tina*, then sixteen months in new French oak. This has powerful fruit, extraction, concentration, and complexity: a new-wave wine from a traditional bodega, just to prove that it really can be done.

MURÚA

Murúa, Ctra de Laguardia s/n, 01340 Elciego, Álava. Tel: 945 606 260. Fax: 945 606 326. Website: www.bodegasmurua.com. Email: info@bodegasmurua.com. Contact: Luís Ametzoy. Winemaker: Jesús Bauza.

Established: 1974. Type: SA. Own vineyards (ha): 110. Own production: 100%.
Buy in: No. Number of staff: 19. Group: unrelated except for Fillaboa, Villavieja.
Barrels: 2,300. Type: American and French. Annual production (hl): 2,500.
Sales national: 80%; export: 20%. Top export markets: UK, Switzerland, Germany.
Visits: by appointment; groups and individuals. Open weekdays: 10am–4pm.
Principal wines: Murúa Blanco fermentado en barrica; Reserva; Gran Reserva:
Veguín de Murúa; "M"

Let's just sort out the confusion that often arises over the name of this bodega. Murúa was the name of a bodega just down the road which was founded in 1926 and achieved something of a reputation for quality wines. In 1974, there was a hiatus in the Murúa family; no one was available to take over the bodega on the retirement of the boss, and the bodega went into mothballs. That same year, a bodega called Casa Masaveu was being established a few hundred metres up the road, and the founders, the Masaveu industrial group, with interests in everything from construction to banking, made an offer to the Murúa family for the rights to the name and other residual assets, which was accepted.

The new bodega then renamed itself Murúa, although the bodega building is still known as Casa Masaveu. Five years later, another branch of the Murúa family – Murúa Entreña – decided to resurrect the family bodega and tried to call it by the family name. There was some considerable debate about this but the legal papers showed that the name had been sold and re-registered by Masaveu, and the Murúa family duly changed the name of their company to Bodegas Muriel, which is how it remains. Interestingly, the winemaker, Jesús Bauzá, is a member of the family that owns Bodegas Bauzá, another producer a few hundred metres in the other direction, so the people on the ground really known their Elciego. Day-to-day running of the business is overseen by administration and sales manager Pedro Ribacova. The company makes only *reserva* and *gran reserva* wines from its own vineyards, and if Jesús is not happy with the quality of the grapes, the wine will be sold off to other bodegas. This happened, for example, in 1993.

Murúa Blanco Fermentado en Barrica (****) has some Garnacha Blanca and Malvasía, the ripest selection of grapes, fermented in new American oak with six months on the lees. It is, quite frankly, one of the best examples in Rioja: soft, silky, mature, and delicious, with some real character (given, I suspect, by the Garnacha Blanca). It is encouraging to find that there are one or two bodegas trying to do something original with white Rioja when so many are giving up on it, as red commands a higher price. Reserva (***>****) has Mazuelo and Graciano to about twenty-five per cent with eighteen months in mostly American oak, and this has a lovely, classic Tempranillo fruit and vanilla oak balance: fresh, clean, and with a delicate structure. Gran Reserva (****>*****) is only made in the best years (1994, 1995, 1996, 2001 were candidates). The style is amazingly fresh, even in wines ten years old, with a lot of fruit, working tannins, complexity, and structure. Veguín de Murúa Reserva (*****) is an old-vines version of the Reserva but with lots of dark, ripe, delicious fruit and excellent length. New from the 2001 vintage is "M" (*****), a high-expression wine with ten per cent Graciano, twenty-five days' maceration, and six months in a variety of oak, including American, French, and small-pore East-European casks. It has big, powerful, tight fruit and cigar-box spice, elegance and finish. That first vintage was released in September, 2004.

NAVARSOTILLO

Bodegas Navarrsotillo, Santa Cruz s/n, 31261 Andosilla, Navarra. Tel: 948 690 523. Fax: 948 690 523. Ctra N-232 Km, 354. 26500 Calahorra, La Rioja. Tel: 941 146 951. Fax: 948 690 523. Website: www.navarrsotillo.com. Email: info@navarrsotillo.com. Contact/Chief executive: Andrés Serrano. Winemakers: Ramón Serrano, Patxi Moriones. Established: 1995. Type: SC. Own vineyards (ha): 50. Contract (ha): 20. Own production: 100%. Buy in: No. Number of staff: 12. Group: No. Barrels: 400. Type: American and French. Annual production (hl): 2,500. Sales national: 20%; export: 80%. Top export markets: Germany, Holland, Poland. Visits: by appointment; groups and individuals. Principal wines: Noemus Joven; Comisatio; Magíster Bíbendi Crianza; Reserva; varietals

This is a traditional, old-fashioned family company which works with organic fruit and vegetables prepacked for the supermarket trade as well as organic vines. It had a classic reason to go into winemaking: generations of farmers selling their produce (including grapes) into the market and then deciding that they could do the wine thing for themselves. The family has been farming in Andosilla for a century, but the wine company as a separate entity was set up in 1995 by brothers Andrés and Ramón Serrano, along with their cousin, Luís Ruiz. The winery is a modern (1998) tin shed, and unpretentious on the outside, but with every modern contrivance within, including air conditioning. The tasting room is a portable building with plastic patio furniture in the car park, and it would seem that investment here is in the vineyards and the winemaking rather than the decor. My own opinion is that it's good to see a young team getting the quality of the wine right before building the signature winery. I'm sure that they will do so, eventually. There are four ranges, all organic. Noemus for *joven*, Comisatio for semi-*crianza* and *maceración carbónica* wines, Magíster Bibendi for *crianza* and *reserva* wines, and varietal wines.

Noemus Blanco (**) is a clean, crisp, simple, pleasant Viura with a pleasant freshness. Rosado (***) is made from Garnacha with six to eight hours' maceration and has a hint of that Garnacha chewy fruit, some richness, and a delicious, lip-smacking finish. Tinto (***) is a delicious Tempranillo wine with full fruit and freshness. Comisatio Joven Maceración Carbonica (***) teases out the high-end fruit of the Tempranillo in a simply delicious, if simple glugger. Magíster Bibendi is the flagship range, with grapes selected from the best vineyards with the oldest vines. Magíster Bibendi Crianza (***) has ten per cent Garnacha with twelve months in American and French oak, and has lovely fresh, crisp fruit and spice. Reserva (****) is a similar formula but made from grapes hand-selected in the vineyard, giving magnificent strawberry fruit but delicacy, complexity, and excellent length. The varietals are also hand-selected from old plots, and all have malolactic fermentation in oak casks and six to seven further months in oak. Magíster Bibendi Graciano (****>*****) has great, big fruit, sharp, oaky notes, and a long, golden finish. Mazuelo (****) is softer, with big, savoury fruit and a complex, tannic structure. Garnacha (*****) is probably the best, made as it is from grapes of vines from two ancient vineyards: one single hectare with vines planted in 1888 and the other a two-hectare vineyard planted in 1929. The grapes are fermented on top of the pulp left behind after the Noemus Rosado has undergone its maceration, and the result is an enormously subtle, musky, aromatic nose with great depth, structure, and flavour on the palate. This should live for ever.

OLABARRI

Viña Olabarri, Ctra de Anguciana s/n, 26200 Haro, La Rioja.
Tel: 941 310 937. Fax: 941 311 602. Website: www.bodegasrubi.es.
Email: info@bodegasolabarri.com. Contact: Rocío López. Chief executive: Luís

Olabarri. Winemaker: Fernando Salgado. Established: 1989. Type: SA. Own vineyards (ha): 10. Contract (ha): 20. Own production: 20%. Buy in: Yes. Number of staff: 10. Group: No. Barrels: 2,800. Type: American and French. Annual production (hl): 3,500. Sales national: 90%; export: 10%. Top export markets: Norway, Switzerland, Germany. Visits: by appointment; groups and individuals. Open weekdays: 8am–2pm. Principal wines: Viña Olabarri Crianza; Reserva; Gran Reserva; Bikandi Vendimia Seleccionada

There are two bodegas here: the smart, modern one on the Haro-Anguciana road which dates from the present company's establishment, and the old nineteenth-century cellar, built on three floors up a steep hillside (even in those days they knew about gravity feed) and now used for barrel-ageing, with a very pleasant, traditional-style dining and tasting room on the top floor (which is also the ground floor, if you see what I mean). The origins of the old cellar go back to the beginning of the nineteenth century, with the most recent additions dated at 1898, although the top-floor hospitality area has every modern convenience, including a fully equipped kitchen. The present business was founded in 1989 by Pablo Olabarri, originally under the name Bodegas Rubí (after the colour of the wine), but, as with so many others, the name of the wine became better known and the bodega changed its name to match in 2001.

Viña Olabarri Crianza (**>***) is all Tempranillo with eighteen months in American oak and six in bottle; it has a good, spicy style with some spiky, oaky notes, crisp acidity, and a good finish. Reserva (***>****) has ten per cent Garnacha and Mazuelo with fourteen months in American and French oak and twelve in bottle, and comes with considerable weight, fruit structure, and complexity. Gran Reserva (****) has twenty per cent Garnacha and Mazuelo with twenty-four months in American and French oak and thirty-six in bottle; it has dark chocolate fruit, warmth, ripeness, and staying power, with a long, golden finish. Interestingly, the Reserva is available in magnums, double-magnums, and, er, five-litre bottles (quignums?).

OLARRA

Bodegas Olarra, 26006, Polígono Cantabria I s/n, 26006 Logroño, La Rioja. Tel: 941 253 703. Fax: 941 253 703. Website: www.bodegasolarra.es. Email: bodegasolarra@bodegasolarra.es. Contact: Cándido Latorre. Chief executive: Leopoldo Limousin Laborde. Winemaker: Javier Martínez de Salinas. Established:

1973. Type: SA. Own vineyards (ha): 10. Contract (ha): 1,200. Buy in: Yes. Number of staff: 40. Group: Ondarre, Casa del Valle. Barrels: 2,500. Type: American and French. Annual production (hl): 95,000. Sales national: 50%; export: 50%. Top export markets: UK, Germany, Holland. Visits: by appointment; groups and individuals. Principal wines: Otoñal Joven; Reciente Joven Blanco; Añares Crianza; Reserva; Cerro Añon Crianza; Reserva; Summa Añares Reserva

The prime mover in this bodega was Luís Olarra, an iron and steel magnate from Bilbao who put up a third of the capital needed to build a new bodega for a company which was then called Bodegas Guiloche, and in which he had a minority shareholding. The unsual design was partly metaphoric and partly practical; the building is in the shape of a giant letter "Y" with each "transept" responsible for a different aspect of the business: reception and fermentation, *crianza*, and expedition (bottling, packing, palletizing, etc.). The metaphor is that it represents the three sub-regions of Rioja, but there is a practical element as well: the reticulate construction of the pantiled roofs was designed to maximize insulation and take advantage of prevailing temperatures on different sides of the building. It was designed by Juan Antonio Ridruejo, a noted architect of the period, who sent his assistants to California, France, and Germany to study aspects of modern winery design before coming up with the final plan. Input was provided by José-Manuel Aizpurua, later to become the technical director of the bodega, who brought in winemaker Ezequiel García, a very well-respected oenologist at the time, who'd worked for CVNE (*see* page 109) for eighteen years, to make the wines. García retired some years ago to be replaced by the current winemaker, Javier Martínez de Salinas.

The original idea (as always) was to make the greatest wines of Rioja regardless of cost, but the company has built a considerable reputation for quality wines over the years. In 1984, Luís Olarra divested himself of most of his holdings in both steel and wine, and sold his share of Olarra to the Guibert-Ucin family, also involved in the Basque steel industry, who owned one of the other thirds, thereby giving them control, and they remain the major shareholder.

Otoñal (**) is a decent, reliable, fresh, all-Tempranillo *joven*. Añares Crianza (***) has fifteen per cent Mazuelo and five per cent Graciano and shows remarkable structure and complexity at its price level. Summa Añares Reserva (****>*****) has twenty-five per cent Mazuelo and fifteen per cent Graciano from forty-year-old vines, with malolactic and then fourteen months in the cask providing a lovely classic, warm, ripe, Tempranillo fruit/oak balance with a gentle finish.

ONDARRE

Bodegas Ondarre, Ctra de Aras s/n, 31230 Viana, Navarra.
Tel: 948 645 300. Fax: 941 253 703. Website: www.bodegasolarra.es. Email:
bodegasolarra@bodegasolarra.es. Established: 1986. Type: SA. Barrels: 12,000.
Sales national: 55%; export: 45%. Visits: contact bodega. Principal wines:
Ondarre Blanco Fermentado en Barrica; Reserva; Mayor de Ondarre Reserva

This is an offshoot of Bodegas Olarra (*see* above) in the Rioja Baja which was created to concentrate on *reserva* and *gran reserva* wines, as well as sparkling wines made under the cava *denominación*, and takes its name from an ancient estate that was owned by one of the founding families.

Wines Ondarre Blanco Fermentado en Barrica (***) has ten per cent Malvasía and Garnacha Blanca from vines of more than thirty years old, fermented in new barrels with two to three months on the lees: light, fresh, but with crisp, oaky notes. Reserva (***>****) has fifteen per cent Mazuelo and ten per cent Garnacha, with a good structure and, in particularly good years, wonderful complexity. Mayor de Ondarre (****>*****) takes this a step further with eighteen months in cask and a magnificent structure and fruit-and-tannin balance in good years.

ONTAÑÓN

Bodegas Ontañón, Avda de Aragón 3, 26006 Logroño, La Rioja. Tel: 941 234
200. Fax: 941 270 482. Website: www.ontanon.es. Email: ontanon@ontanon.es.
Contact: Raquel Pérez Cuevas, technical director. Chief executive: Gabriel Pérez
Cuevas. Winemaker: Rubén Pérez Cuevas. Established: 1984. Type: SA. Own
vineyards (ha): 180. Own production: 90%. Buy in: Yes. Number of staff: 21.
Group: No. Barrels: 4,500. Type: American and French. Annual production (hl):
17,000. Sales national: 80%; export: 20%. Top export markets: Germany, UK,
Brazil. Visits: by appointment; groups and individuals. Open weekdays: 10am–12
noon; 4pm–6pm. Principal wines: Lindje de Vetiver Blanco Crianza; Ontañón
Crianza; Reserva; Gran Reserva; Arteso Tinto Semicrianza; Vino Dulce Moscatel
Riberos de M Fabio (VdlT Valles de Sadacia)

Visiting this bodega is a surreal experience. Is it a bodega with modern art or a modern-art gallery with wine? Well, it's a bit of both. Imagine coming out of a pitch-dark cellar tunnel to find a larger-than-life-size sculpture of Persephone, with breasts big enough to feed the entire population of Hades (assuming that such a luxury were available to the condemned), surrounded by unlabelled bottles undergoing their final stages of *crianza*. Imagine a barrel-ageing cellar dominated by a man astride a centaur, the two of them carrying a pole with two amphorae of wine suspended from it, amid casks of wine doing their time in oak before bottling. Imagine stained-glass windows, avant-garde paintings – oh, and gleaming stainless-steel tanks, post-modern hydraulic presses, and new French oak. Well, that's Ontañón. The bodega is a sponsor of Riojano artist and sculptor Miguel-Ángel Sainz, and if you've driven past the roundabout outside Bodegas Muga (*see* page 160) you'll have seen some of his work cast in bronze in the middle of the road. Here at Ontañón you can see his preliminary casts, as well as finished sculptures, paintings, and other work.

On a practical level, there are three bodegas at Ontañón: one in Quel in the Rioja Baja, one a fermentation cellar near the company's vineyards, and the third this showpiece in Logroño where the final ageing is done. The founder was Gabriel Pérez Mazo, son of *cosecheros* in Quel and, like so many of the new generation, determined to make his own wine rather than sell his grapes to the big bodegas. His first independent winery was in Quel itself, but he then bought a former sweet factory in Logroño: Viuda de Solano, famous in its day for coffee caramels.

Today the company's day-to-day business is in the hands of Gabriel's children, a brother-and-sister team: daughter Raquel Pérez Cuevas is the commercial director and her brother Rubén is the winemaker, and between the two of them, they carry on the tradition started by their father. They're both quite young, and the beautiful and rather shy Raquel is the one who shows visitors round this most individual of Rioja bodegas, which is unequivocally a monument to good taste; if you're in the vicinity you must visit. They also make on contract the *vino dulce* Moscatel Riberos de M Fabio under the VdlT Valles de Sadacia.

Arteso (****) is the *vino joven*, made from fifty-year-old Tempranillo, Graciano, and Garnacha, with four months in new oak, fined with egg-whites: a classic, fruit-upfront, spiky oak style but interesting that Rubén uses platinum-price Graciano in his *joven*. Ontañón Gran Reserva (****>*****) has five per cent Graciano with twenty-four months in French and American oak, with rich, classic aromas: clean, fresh, balanced, and very long.

PALACIO

Bodegas Palacio, San Lazaro 1, 01300 Laguardia, Álava. Tel: 945 600 151.
Fax: 945 600 297. Website: www.bodegaspalacio.com.
Email: cosme@bodegaspalacio.com. Contact: Natalia Lanea. Chief executive:
Jesús de Miguel. Winemaker: Roberto Rodriguez. Established: 1894. Type: SA.
Own vineyards (ha): 155. Group: Bodegas Viña Mayor, Bodegas Peñascal. Barrels:
12,000. Type: French. Annual production (hl): 11,250. Sales national: 75%;
export: 25%. Top export markets: Central Europe, UK, USA. Visits: by
appointment; groups and individuals. Principal wines: Milflores; Glorioso Crianza;
Reserva; Gran Reserva; Cosme Palacio Tinto Crianza; Blanco Crianza; Bodegas
Palacio Reserva Especial

This is one of the most pivotal bodegas in the Rioja Alta, partly because it was conceived at a time when the Rioja business was having a really difficult time and partly because, although it went through a period of heavyweight corporate ownership, it never lost its commitment to quality and individuality in its wines. The whole thing began in 1894, with Cosme Palacio y Bermejillo. He was a successful businessman and politician in Bilbao who had studied at the wine school in Montpellier, and he was one of the "second wave" of pioneers to build a bodega in Rioja. Cosme's father, Ángel, had had interests in the Rioja wine business since 1863, just after Marqués de Riscal (*see* page 150) had completed the first purpose-built bodega in the region, and before Marques de Murrieta (*see* page 147) had bought his estate at Ygay. Cosme had owned vineyards in the area since 1890. The original bodega was started by Ángel and completed by his sons Cosme and Manuel in time for then 1894 vintage.

This was not a good time in Rioja: no sooner had Cosme established his business than the phylloxera louse appeared and proceeded to decimate the vineyards. Some bodegas laid down and died, others fought the plague with every new idea at their disposal. Cosme's reaction was atypical: he simply moved his operation to Valladolid in Castile-León (where phylloxera would not strike for several years more), rented a bodega, and hired a promising young winemaker by the name of Txomin Garramiola to make a wine in the Rioja style, until he could return to Rioja. Txomin went on to make a wine called Vega Sicilia in 1915, and the region beame the DO Ribera del Duero in 1982 – but that, too, is a story which must wait for a future book on the wines of Castile-León.

The Palacio family continued to build a reputation for quality wines and, indeed, for concentrated grape juice that was a boom product after World War II in the war-torn parts of north and central Europe, where food was scarce and nutrition an urgent need. In 1972, the family sold the business to a joint venture between the sherry giant Domecq (*see* page 117) and Canadian group Seagram, building a new winery beside the old one. This, however, proved to be something of a miscegenation, and Domecq decided to build its own winery in Elciego and sold out to Seagram very shortly afterwards. Over a period of time, Seagram sold off much of the bodega's vineyards, leasing back the supply of grapes from them; then in a period of consolidation of its brands, it decided to divest itself of Palacio, offering it to the management as a buy-out. This was accomplished in 1987, headed by Jean Gervais, former manager of Barton & Guestier in Bordeaux and Seagram's European vice-president. The management of the company remained intact, and Gervais engaged Michel Rolland as a consultant to restore the wines to their former prominence. The result was the *corta-crianza* Cosme Palacio y Hermanos, named after the original founders, and still the mainstay of the company's wines.

This success was such that Palacio attracted the attention of a group from Ribera del Duero, Hijos de Antonio Barceló, which was on the acquisition trail, and in 1998 they bought the bodega. Most, but not all (*see* Valenciso, page 201) of the management stayed on. Palacio has maintained its quality profile ever since, as the Barceló Group has continued to invest, including restoring the old bodega, which had only been used for storage since the 1970s, now splendidly converted into a beautiful thirteen-bedroom hotel and restaurant (Hotel Antigua Bodega de Don Cosme Palacio – two towers in the Michelin guide). The loos are, rather beguilingly, in old storage vats, still with their taps on the walls.

A bit more author-archaeology: in 1972, when I first entered the UK wine trade, as mentioned elsewhere in this book, we had, perhaps half a dozen Spanish wines that weren't called "Spanish Burgundy" or "Spanish Chablis" and other spurious names, and one them was the Rioja of Bodegas Palacio, Glorioso Gran Reserva 1959, which was on sale at 10/11d, later 59p (perhaps £5.99 at today's prices – a bargain indeed), but it didn't sell. Stock-take after stock-take the quantity remained at eleven dozen and seven, even though we kept the price the same (and this was in the days of twenty per cent-plus inflation). Then one day, the

English comedian and writer Michael Bentine (1922–96, a founder member of the Goons) came in looking for claret. He was appearing at the local theatre, and always investigated local wine merchants wherever he was appearing in the world. After tasting a few rather modest *petits-châteaux* my boss inveigled him down to the cellar and produced a bottle of the Glorioso '59. It was, of course, much richer and more mature that the young, tough clarets he'd been tasting at twice the price. He bought the lot on the spot and immediately sent for a car to pick them up and take them to his hotel room. On a recent visit to the bodega I noticed that there's still a bin part-full of the '59, gathering dust in the silence. I did drop a few hints, but to no avail.

Red wines are all Tempranillo. Cosme Palacio y Hermanos Blanco (***) is all Viura, part barrel-fermented with five to six months on the lees in French oak and showing lovely herby notes; this is the way to bring out the freshness and individuality of the Viura. Cosme Tinto (***>****) has ten months in French oak (*i.e.* not enough for *crianza*), a great big bite of fruit and oak, and lovely balance; should run and run. El Pórtico Crianza (***) has twelve months in American oak for a more traditional style: warmer spice but less complexity than the Cosme, but big, delicious, spicy oak and fruit. El Pórtico Reserva (****) has sixteen months in American oak and a big, soft, warm style, released when it's mature and drinking well. Glorioso Crianza (****) has fourteen months in French oak and a wonderful structure, with a "layered" roll-out of flavours, delicious warmth, and ripeness. Glorioso Reserva (****) has twenty-two months in French oak, subtle, dark-fruit aromas, and crisp tannins over locked-in fruit. Bodegas Palacio Especial Reserva (****>*****) is made from the oldest vines in the best vintages and aged for as long as the winemaker decides in new French oak: spicy, rich, complex aromas, a silky mouth-feel, spice, and fruit. The first three vintages were the 1996, 2000, and 2003.

PALACIOS REMONDO

Bodegas Palacios Remondo, Avda Zaragoza 8, 26540 Alfaro, La Rioja. Tel: 941 180 207. Fax: 941 181 628. Website: www.vinosherenciaremondo.com. Email: hremondo@vinosherenciaremondo.com. Contact: Chelo Palacios Muro. Chief executive: Carmen Muro de Palacios. Winemaker: Álvaro Palacios Muro. Established: 1945–8. Type: SA. Own vineyards (ha): 100. Own production 100%. Buy in: Yes. Barrels: 2,000. Type: French and American. Sales national: 70%; export: 30%.

Top export markets: USA, Switzerland, Germany. Principal wines: Plácet; 2 Viñedos; Herencia Remondo Reserva; Gran Reserva; La Montesa; La Vendimia; Propriedad Herencia Remondo

This bodega has an impossibly long history. Hubrecht Duijker records that, during alterations to the Palacios family house, six bottles were discovered wrapped in parchment in a wall cavity, each with a medallion around its neck dated 1651. The parchment detailed a legacy of vineyards and, from this we may deduce that the family was making wine more than 350 years ago. Its roots are in Alfaro, in the Rioja Baja, and Palacios has enthusiastically joined the unofficial "Rioja Baja strikes back" movement.

The origins of the present company date back to 1945, when José Palacios Remondo set up a formal business that went through various mutations before surfacing as Bodegas José Palacios in 1948. José and his wife, Carmen, had nine children – three daughters and six sons – of whom four went on to work in the family business. Sons Antonio, Álvaro, and Rafael went to various wine schools and producers in France, America, and Australia to be up to date with the latest techniques. As the eldest son, Antonio followed his father as winemaker, while Álvaro and Rafael went off to make their own way in the wine world. Antonio qualified in 1970 and went to work in the bodega, making several changes to the firm's wines, including cutting out *crianza* for white and *rosado* wines (well before most other companies in Rioja), and experimented with temperature-controlled fermentation in the early 1970s.

At about the same time, the company moved to a bigger bodega by the main road for logistical reasons, and José built a hotel (Hotel Palacios; two towers in the Mich) next door to take advantage of the passing trade: eighty-six rooms, restaurant, swimming pool, and a museum. In 1974, José decided to do a joint-venture deal with growers in the Logroño area and built a bodega on an industrial site on the outskirts of the town, ready for the 1978 vintage. Sadly, the venture didn't last, but Palacios bought grapes and made wine in Logroño until 1999, when it was sold to a new company, Bodegas XXI, which changed its name in 2004 to Bodegas Darien (*see* page 112). José died in 2000, and in due course, the family came together to consider the future.

During the period Antonio was making wine at the bodega in Alfaro, the company was a well-respected player in Rioja, with wines of quality, reliability, and commercial success. Meanwhile, seventh child and fifth son Álvaro had been making something of a name for himself elsewhere in the wine world. His work in Gratallops (DOQ Priorato: Finca Dofi, L'Ermita) and latterly the DO Bierzo (Corullon) with his nephew Ricardo had made him a guru winemaker in Spain with a worldwide reputation. He refuses to be drawn on the precise course of events (and, indeed, family business is the business of no one else), but it would seem that questions were asked along the lines of "We have one of the world's leading winemakers in the family; why isn't he making wine for the family business?" It is reported (and this is all hearsay) that Álvaro was happy to take over as winemaker, but could not work with his brother Antonio, and an "If I come, he goes" situation developed. In the event, Álvaro came and Antonio is now "working in another bodega in Rioja". José's widow, Carmen, is the company president, and Álvaro's sister Chelo (Consuela) looks after the general management and administration of the business.

As a winemaker, Álvaro is very much a vineyard man (although mainstream vineyard work is in the hands of Santiago Munilla and José-María Marcilla), and the company owns 100 hectares of immaculately husbanded vines in the Serra de Yerga, just outside Alfaro at an altitude of 550 metres (1,804 feet; remember this is the Rioja Baja), with Tempranillo at a much lower proprtion than in the rest of Rioja. Grapes are handled with reverence, even to the extent of harvesting the Viura grapes for Plácet ("blessing") from the west side of the vines first, with a second passing to harvest those on the east later on, as they will have received less sunlight.

Álvaro made his first vintage in 2000, the year of his father's death, and made some radical changes. He dumped all but two of the bodega's grape suppliers for overproduction and bought in 2,300 new oak casks, eighty per cent French and twenty per cent American. The casks were seasoned with the Vendímia *joven* wine, then used again the same vintage for other wines. In the vineyards, he reduced yields, cut the bodega's production in the following year from more than a million bottles to around 500,000, and set a target production of no more than 5,000 kilograms per hectare (the legal maximum is 6,500) by (almost) cutting out irrigation, tougher pruning, and losing the second-rate grapes from former suppliers. In the bodega itself he reorganized everything from the fermenting hall to the barrel cellars, reception area, and tasting rooms. "Root and branch" would seem to be an appropriate adjectival phrase here.

The wines are discussed in detail below, but it might be useful to list the four ranges and describe what Álvaro is aiming at. 1) La Vendímia is a *joven* red for early drinking from younger vines by *maceración carbónica* and includes bought-in grapes (and it also seasons the new casks). 2) Plácet is the white wine, fermented in oak *tinas* under temperature control. 3) Herencia Remondo are the classic wines, *reserva* and, in great years, *gran reserva* in homage to the family's winemaking history. Herencia Remondo La Montesa is made from the grapes which were not selected for the *reserva* and the wine is aged in older oak to make a good, reliable mainstream wine in the lighter Rioja tradition. 4) Propriedad H Remondo is the flagship wine of the bodega, selected from the oldest vines on the finest sites, fermented in oak *tinas* with malolactic fermentation in new French *barricas*, and bottled when Álvaro says so. If he can be said to have three priorities for what he wants in his finished wine, I'd say they are probably structure, structure, and structure.

Wines La Vendímia (****) is all Tempranillo with four months in new French oak: big-bite oak and fruit, remarkably structured, austere finish, delicious. Plácet (***>****) is all Viura with a small percentage barrel-fermented: full, herby, mouth-filling fruit, spicy finish. HR La Montesa Crianza (****) is 35-40-15 Garnacha-Tempranillo-Mazuelo, with twelve months in mainly French oak: rich, spicy, powerful fruit and a big finish without any fruit-sweetness ("a bit Syrah-ish", I put in my notes, bizarrely). Propriedad HR (*****) is 40-35-15-10 Garnacha-Tempranillo-Mazuelo-Graciano, and has big fruit, big structure, complexity, power, and depth. These are stonking wines.

PATERNINA

Federico Paternina, Avda Santo Domingo 11, 26200 Haro, La Rioja.
Tel: 941 310 550. Fax: 941 312 778. Website: www.paternina.com.
Email: paternina@paternina.com. Winemaker: Carlos Estecha. Established: 1896.
Type: SA. Own vineyards (ha): 150. Group: Paternina Jerez, Marqués de Valparaíso Ribera del Duero. Barrels: 40,000. Sales national: 50%; export: 50%. Top export markets: EU, Scandinavia, USA. Visits: contact bodega. Principal wines: Graciela Blanco Crianza; Banda Dorada Blanco; Banda Rosa Rosado; Banda Azul Crianza; Banda Oro Crianza; Banda Oro Reserva; Banda Roja Reserva; Paternina Reserva Blanco/Tinto; Paternina Gran Reserva; Clos Paternina Reserva; Conde de los Andes Reserva; Conde de los Andes Gran Reserva

This bodega was founded by Federico de Paternina Josué, pulling together three bodegas from friends and family in Ollauri. He was one of the younger sons (too far down the line to inherit any of the titles) of the Marqués de Terán, who had started one of the three bodegas. They were good, old-fashioned cellars tunnelled into the subterranean rock, but he didn't stick at it, selling out in 1919 to a banker from Logroño called Joaquín Herrero de la Riva (acting for a group of families in the region), although Federico was retained as a consultant until his death in the 1930s. Herrero brought in a French wine-maker, Etienne Labatut, from Calvet in Bordeaux in 1921 to raise the standard of the wines, who was to remain with the firm until 1942. In 1922, the consortium bought the bodegas of the Cooperativa de Sindicatos Católicos in Haro, and the bodega moved to their premises at that time.

Another group of shareholders came into the business in 1940, with significant further investment, and their chosen chief executive was the dynamic María-Luísa Olano, who ran a very tight ship with continually increasing share prices until 1949. The next big change came in 1972 when the RuMaSA group took over the company, along with everything else which wasn't nailed down in the Spanish wine business at the time (*see* Bordón, page 97, for some non-libellous background). This was to end in tears with the state takeover in 1983 and the divesting of the company's assets.

Cometh the hour, cometh the man, and the man was Marcos Eguizábal Ramírez who had made a fortune in the construction business and bought the joint bodegas of Paternina in Haro and Franco-Españolas (Bordón) in Logroño. He is quoted as saying that they were: "In the most deplorable condition. They were in such a state that I had to restore them from scratch, and had to invest a large sum of money in order to restore them." But restore them he did. Today's Paternina winery is very modern, and there is a barrel-ageing facility and tasting room at the old Conde de los Andes bodega in Ollauri.

The wines, unashamedly traditional and old-fashioned, are particularly adored in Germany, according to export sales manager Carlos Latas. Paternina Blanco Reserva (***) is a classic Viura made only in the best years with eight to ten months' oak, not cool-fermented but made in the old-fashioned way, with some oxidation but a fresh, herby mid-palate. Banda Azul Crianza (**>***) has thirty per cent Garnacha and twelve to eighteen months in oak: decent soft fruit and nicely balanced. Banda Roja Reserva (**) has twenty-four months in oak and is in the lightly oxidized, old-fashioned style. Gran Reserva (**) at ten years old displays the same old-rose-petal fruit, rather drying out. Conde de los Andes Gran Reserva (**>***) with a minimum of ten years' ageing also has an oxidative nose, but some wild spice and fruit on the palate, yet seems to be fading fast. Clos Paternina Reserva (***) has some Cabernet Sauvignon to freshen the rose-petal nose and it delivers some decent, mature fruit. I may not be the right person to assess this very old-fashioned style of wine; I suspect that people who enjoy that sort of thing will find this to their liking. Latas has flogged truckloads of it at Anuga in Cologne, so there you go.

PÉREZ IRAZU

Bodegas Pérez Irazu, Camino del Soto 1, 01309 Elvillar de Álava, Álava.
Tel: 945 604 038. Contact: Samuel Rodolfo. Type: SC. Principal wines: Perez Irazu Joven; Crianza; Reserva

I know nothing about this bodega except that I tasted its *joven* in a café in Logroño and immediately made contact with the real, historic, headbangingly fresh young Tempranillo of the Basque Country: absolutely delicious, fresh, crisp, and absurdly cheap. My only beef was that the wine was sealed using "top-and-tail" corks with agglomerate in between, which are a breeding-ground for cork-taint – not that there was any in the wine. I was in the area of Elvillar some weeks later and called in, to discover a bodega about the size of a double garage run by two brothers (one of them Rodolfo) and a son/nephew, with a bottling line capable of taking, well, perhaps as many as twelve bottles at a time. In the five minutes I had to spare, Samuel let me taste the new wine he was bottling, and gave me a bottle of the *joven* and the *crianza*. I shall return.

Perez Irazi Joven (****) is *maceración carbónica* with fifteen per cent Viura for freshness and is just delicious (*see* above). Crianza (***) is all Tempranillo with six months in French and American oak, and is very pleasant, with a hint of oak, but lacks the lovely, uncomplicated freshness of the *joven*.

PRIMICIA

Bodegas Primicia, Ctra de Elvillar s/n, 01300 Laguardia, Álava. Tel: 945 600 296. Fax: 945 621 252. Website: www.bodegasprimicia.com. Email: bodegasprimicia@bodegasprimicia.com. Contact: Alberto Herrero. Winemaker: Manuel Ruíz Hernández, Fernando Domingo Romero. Established: 1985. Type: SA. Own vineyards (ha): 44. Contract: (ha) 125. Own production: 45%. Buy in: Yes. Barrels: 5,500. Type: American and French. Sales national: 40%; export:

60%. Top export markets: Switzerland, UK, Germany. Visits: by appointment. Open weekdays: 9am–2pm; 4pm–7pm. Principal wines: Gran Diezmo Mazuelo; Julián Madrid Reserva de La Familia, Primicia Semicrianza/Joven, Viña Carravalseca Reserva, Viña Diezmo Crianza/ Reserva; Flor de Primicia; Curium

A family company in a beautifully restored old building which was once a medieval collection point for the *diezmos* (tithes) and *primicias* (first fruits) paid by the local people to the church and the town, hence the names of the wines. The bodega was an ambition of Julián Madrid, who wanted to make wine from his own vineyards, and was founded by his two sons, who named heir best *reserva* in honour of their father. Early success saw the need for expansion, and the bodega is now fully modernized and succeeding in export markets. A characteristic of the wines has always been oaking to the legal minimum for each individual classification, and in older wood where necessary to minimize oak extract. Carravalseca is a wine from a single vineyard of that name. Flor de Primicia is *maceración carbónica*, and Curium is a high-expression wine made from hand-selected grapes from the oldest vines. I named Primicia as one of the top twenty bodegas for quality in Rioja in an edition of *Decanter* magazine in 2002.

Viña Diezmo Crianza (***) is aged in American oak and has good, big, spicy fruit and working tannins; Reserva (****) has more oak, structure, and power, and needs more time in bottle, but both of these are absolutely reliable in terms of quality and class – bigger on Tempranillo fruit and smaller on wood. Gran Diezmo Mazuelo (****) has deep, dark, locked-in fruit, crisp acidity, and an elegant balance. Julián Madrid Reserva de la Familia (****>*****) is the best-selected *reserva* of each year and often outstanding.

RAMÓN BILBAO

Bodegas Ramón Bilbao, Avda de Santo Domingo 34, 26200 Haro, La Rioja. Tel: 941 310 295. Fax: 941 310 832. Website: www.bodegasramonbilbao.es. Email: info@bodegasramonbilbao.es. Contact: Penelope López. Chief executive/Winemaker: Rodolfo Bastida. Established: 1924. Type: SA. Own vineyards (ha): 50. Contract (ha): 500. Own production: 10%. Buy in: Yes. Number of staff: 25. Group: Diego Zamora. Barrels: 7,000. Type: 70% American, 30% French. Annual production (hl): 30,000. Sales national: 70%; export: 30%. Top export markets: EU, Sweden, Germany. Visits: groups and individuals.

Principal wines: Ramón Bilbao Blanco Fermentado en Barrica; Crianza; Crianza Edición Limitada; Reserva; Gran Reserva; Viña Turzaballa; Mirto de Ramón Bilbao

Ramón Bilbao had been a wine merchant since 1896, and founded his own bodega in 1924 in the Calle Las Cuevas, where so many bodegas (*e.g.* Berceo, Carlos Serres, *see* pages 93 and 102) made their start. The Bilbao family ran it until the death of Ramón Bilbao Pozo in 1966, but the company continued under the existing management until 1972, when it became a public limited company (SA) with residual members of the family holding some of the shares. The capital raised by the flotation was sufficient to build a brand-new, purpose-built bodega at the present address. In 1999, the Diego Zamora Group (most famous, perhaps, for the orange liqueur Licor 43, although they also bought Mar de Frades in the DO Rías Baixas in 2003, where they make an Albariño barrel-fermented wine that undergoes its malolactic fermentation in a tank, with scallop shells; just thought I'd mention that) bought the company and invested heavily in new plant, refurbishment, and equipment (new oak *tinas* as well as stainless-steel tanks), as well as taking on a new winemaker to bring the range up to standard, and up to date.

The results have been spectacular, and the bodega has trodden the middle way: continuing to make *crianza* and *reserva* wines in the classic style in American oak while also turning out the high-expression Turzaballa and Mirto in French oak, which rank with the region's best.

Wines Ramón Bilbao Blanco Fermentado en Barrica (***) is all Viura, fermented in new oak and then returned to the "cleaned" barrel once fermentation is complete, for a further three to four months. The barrel, having given up its main essential oils to the white wine, is then used for *crianza* for red wine. It's big, soft, and oaky with a delicious vanilla finish. Crianza (***) has fourteen months in new American oak and has a good, lively, fresh, spiky-oak/spicy-fruit style. Reserva (***) has ten per cent Mazuelo/Garnacha/Graciano and twenty-six months in American oak and quite a bit off tannin: probably needs time in the bottle to develop. Gran Reserva (****) has five per cent each of Graciano and Garnacha, with thirty-two months in American oak, and has the classic rich, dark fruit that fills all the corners: delicious. Edición Limitada (****>*****) is all Tempranillo from old-vines plantations, fermented (including malolactic) in *tinas* for better micro-oxygenation, and then put to *crianza* for fourteen months in the barrels originally used to ferment the white wine (above).

It's not made every year, and each barrel is assessed individually; it showed spicy, sparky fruit on the nose, was savoury, concentrated, and rich, with dark fruit on the palate and excellent length. Viña Turzaballa Gran Reserva (****>*****) is all Tempranillo, and they describe it as being in the "modern classic style, made to last twenty years". It has real depth and rich, rich fruit, enormous structure, complexity, powerful tannins, and length; perhaps twenty years is not an exaggeration. Mirto (*****) is the unashamed new-wave wine, made from Tempranillo from vines more than seventy years old, hand-selected in the vineyard, picked late. It's fermented in *tinas* with malolactic fermentation in cask, and then twenty-four months in new Alliers oak with a medium to high toast and no racking, only *batonaje* (stirring) so the wine stays in contact with the yeast cells for the full period, and then is bottled without fining or filtering. This is blockbusting, mouth-filling, savoury-fruit, big-structure stuff which gives the impression that it'll live for ever.

RAMÍREZ DE LA PISCINA

Bodegas Ramírez de la Piscina, Ctra Vitoria-Laguardia s/n, 26338 San Vicente de la Sonsierra, La Rioja. Tel: 941 334 505. Fax: 941 334 506. Website: www.welcome.to/bodegas-ramirez. Email: rampiscina@knet.es. Contact/Chief executive: Cecilio Ramírez de la Piscina. Established: 1980 Type: SL. Own vineyards (ha): 9. Contract (ha): 40. Own production: 20%. Buy in: Yes. Number of staff: 4. Group: No. Barrels: 1,100. Type: American and French. Annual production (hl): 4,000. Sales national: 85%; export: 15%. Top export markets: USA, UK, Switzerland. Visits: by appointment; groups and individuals. Open weekdays: 9am–1pm; 3pm–5.30pm. Principal wines: Ramírez de la Piscina Joven; Crianza; Reserva; Selección; Santa María de la Piscina Tinto Gran Reserva

The swimming pool (*piscina*) foxes many people. It's a long story. St Joaquim and St Anne were the parents of the Virgin Mary (yes, that far back) and there is a church (built 1142) dedicated to St Anne in Jerusalem, which is, according to tradition, on the site of the house where she and Joaquim lived, and also the birthplace of the Virgin Mary. Next to this are the ruins of the holy water pool of Bethesda where, according to the scriptures, Jesus cured the man "sick of the palsy" and bade him "take up thy bed and walk", which he duly did. One pilgrim at that site during the crusades was Don Sancho Ramírez, who took the epithet *de la Piscina* ("of the pool") as did others who visited. He returned to his home in

Nájera (then in the Kingdom of Navarre, now in La Rioja) and was inducted into the Cofradía de la Vera Cruz (Brotherhood of the True Cross), a penitent order still manifest today in the annual tradition of Los Picaos, who wear white cassocks and hoods that completely cover the head and face, with a "trap-door" revealing their naked backs, and whip themselves with a cotton cat-o'-nine-tails until they bleed (often with the help of shards of broken glass in a bar of soap rubbed over the skin in advance). This used to happen in a number of places in Rioja on Maundy Thursday and Good Friday, but now only takes place in San Vicente de la Sonsierra. The practice was banned by King Carlos III in 1777 but, this being Spain, nobody took any notice. Don Sancho built a church in Nájera in the twelfth century and the family has been commemorated in La Rioja ever since. Hope you got all that.

The bodega was founded rather more recently, in 1980 by the descendants of Don Sancho and is a very smart, modern affair with elegant, vaulted barrel cellars and a very modern approach to winemaking. Head of the family is the ebullient, feisty, and flame-haired Pilar Ramírez de la Piscina who knows not only the family history going back to the time of King Sancho the Strong of Navarre, but also every aspect of what the winery is, does, and aspires to do. They made only *jóvenes* until 1986, which was the first *crianza* year, and 1989, when they made their first *gran reserva*. The wines tend to be in the classic mould, with some excellent examples in great years.

Entari Joven (**) is a pleasant, if rather simple, fresh Tempranillo. Crianza (***) has rather more structure and lovely, delicious, soft fruit; Ramírez de la Piscina Joven (**) has ten per cent Viura and is made by *maceración carbónica*: very fresh, crisp, and easy to drink. Crianza (**>***) has more character, with twelve to fourteen months in new oak, fighting fruit, and a decent length. Selección (***) is made from selected grapes with malolactic fermentation in cask and a startling bite of oak on the foretaste, but good structure and a lingering finish. Reserva (***>****) has fourteen to fifteen months in cask: a nice, spicy warm fruit and a decent finish. Santa María de la Piscina Tinto Gran Reserva (****) has twenty-four months in oak and a surprisingly youthful fruit, even when mature, although having tasted several vintages, I'd say that it's at its best at about nine to ten years old; beyond twelve it does start to dry out.

REMÍREZ DE GANUZA

Bodegas Fernando Remírez de Ganuza, La Constitución s/n, 01307
Samaniego, Álava. Tel: 945 609 022. Fax: 945 623 335. Website:
www.remirezdeganuza.com. Email: fernando@remirezdeganuza.com. Chief
executive/Winemaker: Fernando Remírez de Ganuza. Established: 1988. Type: SA.
Own vineyards (ha): 54. Buy in: No. Barrels: 950. Type: American and French.
Sales national: 50%; export: 50%. Visits: contact bodega. Principal wines: Erre
Punto (R); Remírez de Ganuza Reserva; Gran Reserva; Trasnocho; Finca de Ganuza

This is one of the most astonishing bodegas in Rioja, for its winemaking
techniques as much as the quality of its wines. It's beguilingly housed in
a beautiful old building next to the church in the mellow sandstone village
of Samaniego. Inside, everything has been restored and is spotlessly
clean, with a combination of oak *tinas* and stainless-steel tanks as well as
carefully thought-out logistics, from the tanks in the floor of the upstairs
sorting room to the helter-skelter for the grape boxes. This was
all designed by Fernando Remírez de Ganuza, who bought and sold
vineyard land and kept thinking "I'd rather like one of these for myself..."
This materialized in 1988, but it was 1991 before the first vintage, and a
few years later before his wines started to make an impact on the market.
To explain why, perhaps we should go through the production process.

There are fifty-four hectares of vines with an average age of sixty
years – ninety per cent Tempranillo and ten per cent Graciano – and they
are hand-selected in the vineyard, into plastic boxes on the *Auslese*
principle; in other words, only the ripest bunches are selected, and the
pickers return as often as is necessary until the harvest is done. The full
boxes come to the winery and are put in a lift, which takes them to the
top floor where sorting tables are erected and teams of sorters go through
them. The boxes are then shoved through a hole in the wall where they
skitter down the helter-skelter and through an automatic washer before
stacking up to be used again. On the sorting table a second hand-
selection takes place, with sub-standard bunches put into plastic boxes
under the tables; these will go to make the press-wine.

Now, so far this probably seems fairly typical of Rioja production in
the twenty-first century, but there is more. Fernando has established that,
because bunches of grapes are roughly shaped like a three-dimensional
map of Africa, the pointy bit at the bottom does not get as much sun as
the hunchy bit at the top, and there is, therefore, a difference in ripeness

in the individual grapes in the bunch (stay with this; it's good). So, at the end of the moving belt there's a divider, and somebody with a pair of secateurs cuts the bunch in half, and the pointy bit goes on one side and the hunchy part goes on the other side. The pointy bits are then dropped directly through the hole in the floor, which is the lid of the tank on the floor below: these will make the *maceración carbónica* wine (R or Erre Punto: "R" stands for Remírez, of course). The hunchy part goes to the de-stalker and will make the mainstream wines. The free-run wine in each set of tanks is run off once alcoholic fermentation is complete and the wine goes into oak *tinas* or casks to complete the malolactic fermentation. But there's more. What's left in the steel fermentation vessels is the pulp, of course, and this is where we enter the world of post-modern winemaking.

A bit more history: as you'll no doubt remember, crushing grapes to make wine comes in three phases, originally called *lágrima* ("tears": wine made by the natural pressure of the grapes one upon another), *aguapié* (literally "foot-water": the juice produced by treading the grapes under-foot), and *prensa* (literally "press": the final coarse juice squeezed out of the remaining pulp by men, horses, or oxen turning a screw press on the leftovers, usually wrapped in sacking to stop the pulp falling all over the place). Fernando has reinvented an element of this for the modern age, and it's called *trasnocho*, which means "through the night". Once the free-run (*lágrima*) wine has been run off into oak there's still a lot of goodness left in the pulp. It is at this point that most bodegas put the pulp in the press and give it a gentle, medium, and hard pressing to extract what's left, but this is too simple for Fernando. He has designed and had made balloons made out of "bouncy-castle" grade plastic which are put into the tanks and filled with warm water to provide a gentle, constant pressing of the remaining pulp, overnight (geddit?). Any stalks and pips that remain will not be crushed by the gentle pressure (just as with the human foot), and thus no bitter, woody tannins will be released into the wine. What's left in the tank in the morning goes (following on from the sub-standard bunches which were weeded out on the sorting table) into the press to extract anything that remains, and the resultant wine is sold off to other bodegas.

Some seventy per cent of the bodega's oak is American, the rest French and east European, and not just in barricas of 225 litres; there are also wines in *botas* (butts) of 500 litres and, of course, huge bins of bottles undergoing their final maturation before labelling. Fernando's policy is "not too much oak" (just enough to throw the fruit into perspective), old vines, no filtration, but both classic and new-wave styles of wine, using the traditional epithets. There are those who don't like or can't understand these wines and don't think they're "proper Rioja". I respect their right to have that opinion and understand it – but I don't share it. In terms of the work it's doing, I'd put this bodega in the front rank of what Rioja, could, can, and should be achieving in the twenty-first century, and if there were a "bodega anorak" trophy in this book, Fernando Ramírez de Ganuza would win it.

Ramírez de Ganuza Reserva (****>*****) is a needs-ten-years wine, with enormous fruit, structure, extraction, and length. "R" (Erre Punto ****) is the blockbusting *joven* with explosive fruit and big ketones: a glugging, head-banging, thirst-quencher of a wine, like Beaujolais Nouveau on speed ("drink before next autumn" is the advice); Trasnocho (*****) is vast: big fruit, big tannins, warm, ripe. My notes contain the comment "needs a hundred years", although I suspect that this may prove to be an exaggeration. Fincas de Ganuza (****) is the "second wine" of the bodega: grapes too good for the press but just not quite good enough for the mainstream, and made more in the classic Rioja style: full fruit, oaky aromatics, balance, youthful, delicious.

REMELLURI

Granja Nuestra Señora de Remelluri, Finca Remelluri, Ctra de Rivas s/n, 01330 Labastida, Álava. Tel: 945 331 801. Fax: 945 331 802. Website: www.remelluri.com. Email: info@remelluri.com. Contact: María-José Sagarzazu. Chief executive: Jaime Rodríguez Salís. Winemaker: Ana Barrón López. Established: 1967. Type: SA. Own vineyards (ha): 105. Own production: 100%. Buy in: No. Number of staff: 35. Group: No. Barrels: 4,000. Type: 85% French, 15% American. Annual production (hl): 4,500. Sales national: 80%; export: 20%. Top export markets: USA, Switzerland, Germany. Visits: by appointment; groups and individuals. Principal wines: Remelluri Reserva; Blanco; Colección Jaime Rodríguez; La Granja Remelluri Gran Reserva

This is one of the most beautiful bodegas in the most serene setting in the whole of Rioja. The vineyards are at three levels, just a few metres apart in altitude, providing perfect harvesting conditions as the grapes conveniently ripen about a week apart at each level. The uppermost vineyard is tucked right into the foot of the mountains, which brings cooling mists in the hottest part of the season as well as a spectacular view of the ruins of the craggy heights where the old monastery of Nuestra Señora de Toloño, which once farmed this site, stood. There's a small museum in the old house, and the winery is beguilingly old-fashioned, with a mixture of stainless steel and oak *tinas* for fermentation, and French and American oak barrels for different stages of production.

The estate had, however, been badly neglected for decades when it was bought by Jaime Rodríguez Salís in the 1960s. He bought surrounding lands and replanted the vineyards, selling the grapes to other producers while he renovated old farm buildings and built new ones to serve as a bodega. Interestingly, they were so well-designed that you can't tell which is which. The first vintage with the bodega's name on it was the 1971, since when it has gone from strength to strength, especially under the hands of Jaime's son Telmo Rodríguez, who is now a winemaking guru in many different areas of Spain. Originally the bodega made all its wine in oak *tinas*, but in 1984 they switched to stainless steel. Interestingly, they returned to partial fermentation in *tinas* in the 1990s, feeling that there was a need for the characteristics attributable to both methods. The wines throughout have been excellent, and visitors can now taste a range of them as well as having lunch in the splendid dining room over-looking the vineyards. Until recently, Remelluri only made *reservas*, with the occasional *gran reserva* in particularly good years, but recently there has been a white *crianza* made from Garnacha Blanca, Rousanne, Viognier, and Moscatel (note: no Viura), and a top-of-the-range Colección Jaime Rodríguez, which is mainly old-vines Tempranillo from the best plots.

Remelluri Blanco (***>****) has fourteen months in cask and a lovely crisp, oaky style but with quite a lot of aromatics unusual for white Rioja, due to the unique grape mix (*see* above). Reserva (****) is classic in style, with plenty of warm fruit, good balance with oak and tannins, and golden length. Gran Reserva (***>*****) is more of the same but with extra ripeness, warmth, colour, and character.

RIOJANAS

Bodegas Riojanas, Ctra Estación 1-21, 26350 Cenicero, La Rioja.
Tel: 941 454 050. Fax: 941 454 529. Website; Riojanas.com. Email:
bodega@bodegasriojanas.com. Chief executive: Felipe Frías Echevarría.

Winemaker: Felipe Nalda Frías. Established: 1890. Type: SA. Own vineyards (ha): 200; Group: Bodegas Torreduero. Barrels: 25,000. Sales national: 70%; export: 30%. Top export markets: Germany, Sweden, Switzerland. Visits: by appointment, Mon–Fri 11am. Principal wines: Canchales Joven Blanco/Tinto/Rosado; Monte Real Crianza/ Reserva/Gran Reserva/Reserva Especial; Viña Albina Blanco Joven/Blanco Fermentado en Barrica; Blanco Reserva; Tinto Reserva/Gran Reserva/Reserva Especial; Gran Albina Reserva/Vino Especial/Semidulce Blanco; Puerta Vieja Joven Blanco/Rosado; Crianza

This is a prominent and quite elegant bodega on the main street in Cenicero, if a little old-fashioned (but none the worse for that) with its Victorian Gothic architecture and medieval-style banqueting hall. It's a labyrinthine structure built on a hillside to take advantage of gravity, with a creaking lift to take you back to the top when you've got to the bottom.

It all began in 1890 as a venture by the Catalan Rafael Carreras Picó. After his death, the business was sold to the Artacho brothers, Román and Fortunato. The distaff branch of the Artacho family (the Frias) own it still, although there have been eight extensions to the bodega since the family took over. There is a bewildering array of ranges of wine, and most of them are very traditional in style; I tasted them with the winemaker, Felipe Nalda Frías, great-nephew of the founder.

Wines Viña Albina Blanco Fermentado en Barrica (**) is all Viura, fresh, clean, delicious, and uncomplicated. Canchales Joven Tinto (**) is Tempranillo 50/50 *maceración carbónica* with light, fresh, chewy fruit: another delicious, uncomplicated, everyday wine. Puerta Vieja Crianza (**) has fifteen per cent Mazuelo and five per cent Graciano with eighteen months in American oak and is a decent, everyday *crianza* in the classic style. Viña Albina Reserva (***) has a similar grape mix, but twenty-four to thirty months in American oak and is the bodega's best-seller, as well it might be at the price: nice traditional mix of fruit and oak. I seem to have written "good slurping stuff"; it must have been late in the day. Monte Real Reserva (***>****) has the same grapes and ageing but selected only from vineyards in Cenicero and San Vicente de la Sonsierra: it has richer, softer oak, and is ripe, with a better structure. Monte Real Gran Reserva (***) has an oxidative element, rather old-fashioned, soft, and gentle on the palate, but the sample I was tasting, at ten years old, was drying out, though still drinkable. Gran Albina Vino Especial (****) is selected only from the best plots in Cenicero itself, with twenty per cent Graciano and ten per cent Mazuelo and twenty-four months in new American oak: big, spicy fruit and plenty of it, good length. Monte Real Crianza (***) has eighteen months in new American oak, very nice, fresh, and clean on the palate with spicy/spiky overtones; Gran Albina Reserva (****) has fifteen per cent Mazuelo and five per cent Graciano, with twenty-four months in new oak: a big, figgy, spicy nose but lovely, crisp, tight fruit and lip-smacking acidity. Viña Albina Blanco Semidulce has five per cent Malvasía and is a late-harvest, botrytized wine at a yield of 800 kilograms per hectare (against the legal maximum for white wines of 8,000; the equivalent of about five hectolitres per hectare): lovely, spicy, and delicious on the nose, with a delicate, fragile sweetness on the palate. Best of the bunch, though, was Felipe's very first vintage: the Monte Real 1964 (*****), generally regarded as the best year of the twentieth century, and with nine years in oak. It had the colour of dried blood, a fabulous, faded pot-pourri nose, with a hint of oxidation, though not excessive, and lovely soft fruit on the palate, gently fading into the distance. And they still have some available, if you can afford a bottle.

RIOJA SANTIAGO

Bodegas Rioja Santiago, Barrio Estación s/n, 26200 Haro, La Rioja.
Tel: 941 310 200. Fax: 941 312 679. Website: www.bodegasriojasantiago.com.
Email: riojasantiago@fer.es. Contact/Winemaker: Carlos Soto López. Established: 1870. Type: SA. Own vineyards (ha): No. Contract (ha): No. Own production: No. Buy in: Yes. Number of staff: 25. Group: No. Barrels: 2,700. Type: American. Annual production (hl): 30,000. Sales national: 20%; export: 80%. Top export markets: Germany, Holland, UK. Visits: by appointment; groups only, minimum 10 people. Open weekdays: 8.30am–2.50pm; 3.30pm–7pm. Principal wines: Vizconde de Ayala/Rioja Santiago Crianza; Reserva; Gran Reserva

The company was founded in 1870 in Labastida by Ángel Santiago Munilla, but early success, particularly in export markets, brought him to Haro and the origins of the present bodega in 1904. He was succeeded by his two sons, Jesús and Ángel, who went on to take over Bodegas Vizconde de Ayala, which remains as a brand within the product range. A turning point in its fortunes came with the discovery of a way to bottle sangría and keep it stable; the American agent for the product was a subsidiary of the Pepsi Cola company, and Pepsi bought a fifty per cent stake in Rioja Santiago in 1970, buying up the rest of the shares in 1975. This brought with it a great deal of investment, and much of the modern equipment in the bodega today is as a result of the Pepsi years. Pepsi divested itself of the company in the 1980s to the Barrios family, who sold it to the present owners – Aurelio González Villarejo and José Fermín Hernandez – in 1998, who now own fifty per cent each. In spite of the changes in ownership, the bodega has hung on to most of its key staff (which is always a good sign).

The style is classic but not, as Carlos Soto puts it "in the style of Tondonia" (*see* page 196). All the grapes are bought in from all over the region and, yes, he says that competition for quality grapes is pushing the price up, but it is, of course, the same for everyone. The bodega stands just beside the bridge over the river Tirón, which gives it a pleasant aspect, but was a disadvantage when they tried to dig a tunnel between two underground cellars; incoming water forced them to abandon the project.

Wines These are all Tempranillo. Rioja Santiago Joven (***) has four months in third-vintage oak (typically November to February) and bright, Tempranillo fruit with a good structure and freshness. Vizconde de Ayala Crianza (****) has twelve months in oak and a classic strawberries-and-cream aroma, with lovely crisp, lip-smacking fruit and just a touch of toasty oak on the palate. Reserva (****) is made only with grapes from Rioja Alta and Alavesa, has twenty-four months in oak, and a mature, slightly gamey, and almost balsamic nose, but good savoury fruit, maturity, and structure.

RODA

Bodegas Roda, Avda Vizcaya 5, 26200 Haro, La Rioja. Tel: 941 303 001. Fax: 941 312 703. Website: www.roda.es. Email: rodarioja@roda.es. Contact: Ibone Candina. Chief executive/Winemaker: Agustín Santolaya. Winemaker: Carlos Díez de la Concpeción. Established: 1987. Type: SA. Own vineyards (ha): 70. Contract (ha): 100. Buy in: Yes. Number of staff: 20. Group: No. Barrels: 1,800. Type: French. Annual production (hl): 3,300. Sales national: 50%; export: 50%. Top export markets: Switzerland, Germany, Belgium. Visits: by appointment. Open weekdays: winter 8am–2pm, 3pm–5pm; summer 8am–3pm. Principal wines: Cirsión; Roda I; Roda II

This bodega has a reputation for being one of the *enfants terribles* of Rioja: reinventing the style of the wine while using only traditional grapes and ageing methods. The name comes from the first two letters of each of the surnames of the founding Catalan family, Mario Rottllán and his wife, Carmen Daurella. Mario is actually a chemist by training, but worked in wine importing in his native Barcelona; when he saw what the rest of the world was drinking he spied a gap in the market for something individual and unique. He chose Haro because of the surrounding vineyard land, and hired viticulturist Agustín Santolaya to head the new company. Santolaya, it was rumoured, knew every centimetre of vineyard and terroir in the Rioja Alta, and he was tasked with finding the best of them for the new bodega. The end result was a comprehensive survey of most of the Rioja Alta, during which he identified seventeen sites in the sub-region which had the soils, vines, and microclimate for which he was looking. Rotllán then went in and either bought the vineyards or signed lucrative long-term deals with their owners. Most of the grapes are Tempranillo, although there is one plot of Garnacha, and the average age of the vines is fifty-five years; no grape is used from vines under thirty years old. In the process, Santolaya identified 550 clones of Tempranillo but discovered that only six were actually being grown in the region, so he planted an experimental vineyard with twelve vines of each of these clones to see how they develop. There is some small amount of Graciano and Mazuelo, but these are new plantations and so currently play no part in the wines. Vineyards are not organic, but there are no artificial sprays or treatments, or chemical fertilizers.

Agustín Santolaya oversees all aspects of the winemaking, but Carlos Díez is the man at the vat on a day-to-day basis. I remember my first visit to the bodega, back in 2001; he was passing round cask samples of Roda I and Cirsión to a party of international journalists, with the words: "This is my $100 wine... And this is my $300 wine..." In euros they have turned out to be rather cheaper than that.

Winemaking is pin-sharp here, and tannin management is something of a bee in the bodega's bonnet. Ripeness levels, skin maceration, higher-than-normal fermentation temperatures (up to 30°C/86°F), and slow malolactic fermentation also form part of the matrix. Indeed, Carlos and Agustín regularly suck the pips to make sure that polymerization is taking place or will take place when the fermentation temperature reaches the right level. The fermented wines from the seventeen different sites are vinified and aged separately for twelve months in French oak, and then classified. Those that are more advanced and approachable go into Roda II; more structured and austere wines go into Roda. Anything sub-standard (by Roda standards, that is) is sold off; there is a waiting list for this bodega's cast-offs, according to legend. Indeed, there was no income at all until 1996, eight years after the company's foundation, and the first wine badged as Roda was released in 1992.

And then there's Cirsión, and the rise of a new winemaking theory. I'm not an oenologist or viticulturist so I can't comment on the biochemical aspects of this, but I'll tell you what the man said. It is an historical fact, though, that in the days before the hand refractometer and other modern items of vineyard equipment, the great winemakers would judge the readiness of the grapes for harvesting simply by picking one and tasting it. Fruit ripeness, sugar levels, phenolic ripeness, and everything else were revealed to the experienced palate of the *viñero/enologo*. Many of the greatest winemakers still do this (though, I suspect, with the backup of a battery of modern, computerized equipment) and, indeed, Santolaya and Díez do it as well. In a small area of vineyards, mainly between Haro and Villabuena, there were certain individual vines whose grapes had a more "winey" taste than the others – as if the polymerization of the tannins had already started even before the grapes were picked. They decided to pull out these particular bunches and vinify them separately to see what kind of wine they made. The trouble was that it wasn't the same vines, or even the same vineyards, every year, so grape-sucking was to become part of the pre-harvest experience.

Anyway, the first appearance (of the 1995 vintage, in 1999) of Cirsión was occasioned by an earthquake in Haro, with blood-red skies, UFO sightings, an eclipse of the moon, miraculous showers of live frogs, and the moving of mountains into the sea... Oh, well, all right: it wasn't quite like that, but it did make headlines in the national wine press, anyway, and I have to say, on the three occasions upon which I have tasted various vintages of this wine, I have given it never less than eighteen (a young vintage) and as much as 19.5 out of twenty (a mature vintage), so if all the above is bullshit, then it's quality bullshit. And, indeed, if this is the new face of Rioja bullshit, then I'm up for a bucketful.

Wines Roda II (****) has some Garnacha and Graciano, sixteen months in oak, ripe structure, soft, warm tannins, complexity, and good length. Roda I (****>*****) tends to be all Tempranillo with sixteen months in oak, huge fruit, spice, power, tannins, and ripeness. Cirsión (*****) is 100 per cent Tempranillo and the time in oak differs from vintage to vintage, depending on the winemakers' tastings.

SÁENZ DE SANTAMARÍA

Bodegas Sáenz de Santamaría, Ctra de Haro Km 1, 26350 Cenicero, La Rioja. Tel: 941 454 008. Fax: 941 454 688. Email: bsantamaria@jet.es. Contact: Manuel Tato Lozano. Silvia Zabalo Díaz, export manager. Chief executive: José Santamaría González. Winemaker: Alfredo Bernáldez Fernández. Established: 1993. Type: SL. Own vineyards (ha): 60. Own production: 100%. Buy in: No. Number of staff: 7. Group: No. Barrels: 1,800. Type: American and French. Annual production (hl): 12,000. Sales national: 80%; export: 20%. Top export markets: Canada, Germany, UK. Visits: by appointment; groups and individuals. Open weekdays: 8am–7pm. Principal wines: Rondan Crianza; Reserva; Blanco Crianza; Rosado; Tinto Joven; Señorío de Rondan Gran Reserva

Although the family's been going for very much longer as *cosecheros*, the present company dates from 1993, when they decided to start making their own wines, and the bodega is a smart, modern affair on the main road which bypasses Cenicero. The vineyards are spread out behind and above the bodega, and José Santamaría oversees all aspects of viticulture and winemaking. The brand name "Rondan" is the name of one of the company's vineyards, and Señorío de Rondan comes exclusively from that vineyard. One aspect of unusual practice here is that wines are bottled under vacuum; when tasting at the bodega I had to ask twice for a replacement bottle, only to discover that the wines were perfectly all right, but that they needed a good ten or fifteen minutes after opening to stabilize in the presence of air.

Rondan Blanco Crianza Fermentado en Barrica (**) is all Viura, fermented in American oak with a further six months in cask – rather an old-fashioned style with that classic hint of oxidation in older vintages, but pleasant freshness and toasty oak in more recent vintages. Rosado (*) is seventy per cent Garnacha and thirty per cent Viura with twenty-four to forty-eight hours' maceration, and is light, fresh, and delicately perfumed but unexciting. Aliboca Joven (**) has thirty per cent Garnacha and is named after another vineyard; this was the first one I tasted that seemed to be high on volatile acidity, which proved to be a result of the vacuum in the ullage. Once the wine had breathed, it proved to be a very nice, fresh affair; I wrote "swigging fruit and not much else, but who cares?" Rondan Crianza (**>***) was another one that needed to breathe. It has five per cent each of Garnacha and Mazuelo, twelve months in oak, a decent structure, and pleasant fruit; this wine represents forty per cent of the bodega's production. Reserva (***) has ten per cent Mazuelo with twenty-four months in oak, a good, rich structure and style, with a nice balance of fruit and oak. Señorío de Rondan Gran Reserva (***>****) is made with grapes from eighty-year-old Tempranillo vines, and the bodega made its first vintage in 1994. The wine has great depth and complexity, with beautifully balanced fruit and oak.

SIERRA CANTABRIA

Bodegas Sierra Cantabria, Amorebieta 3, 26338 San Vicente de la Sonsierra, La Rioja. Email: sierra-cantabria@fer.es

SEÑORÍO DE SAN VICENTE

Señorío de San Vicente, Los Remedios 27, 26338 San Vicente de la Sonsierra, La Rioja. Tel: 941 308 040. Fax: 941 334 371. Website: www.eguren.com. Email: sanvicen@fer.es. Contact: José-Manuel Azofra. Chief Executive/ Winemaker: Marcos Eguren. Established: 1957 (Sierra Cantabria); 1991 (Señorío de San Vicente). Type: SA. Own vineyards (ha): 70 (Sierra Cantabria); 18 (Señorío de San Vicente). Group: Numathia Terma, Finca El Bosque, Dominio de Eguren. Barrels: 2,200 (Sierra Cantabria); 450 (Señorío de San Vicente). Type: French and American. Sales national: 50%; export: 50%. Top export markets: EU, USA, Switzerland. Visits: by appointment. Principal wines: Sierra Cantabria Organza Blanco; Rosado Joven; Tinto Joven; Crianza; Reserva; Gran Reserva; Cuvée Especial; Colección Privada; Finca El Bosque; Murmurón; El Puntido; Aancio; Señorío de San Vicente

A primary word about the company relationships. These two bodegas are within walking distance of each other in San Vicente, and Señorío de San Vicente was set up in 1991 as a separate company to exploit the single vineyard of the same name, which had formerly provided grapes for Sierra Cantabria. The same thing is happening in the nearby village of Páganos, where a new bodega was built (first vintage El Puntido 2001), which in 2004 became a bodega in its own right under the name Viñedos de Páganos SL. El Bosque is also a separate estate but, for the moment, still part of Sierra Cantabria's core business operation.

The Eguren family's grape-growing credentials go back to the 1870s, but the first formal company, Sierra Cantabria, was founded in 1958 and the old building is still in use. The prime movers in this were brothers Guillermo and Victorino Eguren, plus their viticulturist brother-in-law Martín Cendoya. Victorino and Martín were later to set up Heredad Ugarte (*see* page 129). The bodega started bottling in 1974 and expanded into bigger premises, working up an increasing reputation for quality. The next generation, headed by Marcos Eguren, took over in 1989 and Marcos proved to be, if anything, more enthusiastic than his father and uncle when it came to expansion. He it was who hived off Señorío de San Vicente as a separate operation to exploit the eighteen-hectare single vineyard, and the bodega is immaculately and beautifully restored. He was also an enthusiast when it came to the new-wave, "high-expression" wines, and now produces some of the best examples in Rioja.

The latest project is the (2001) bodega in Páganos making wines from the surrounding vineyard; indeed, what we're seeing under the stewardship of Marcos Eguren is a gradual move away from centralized processing of grapes trucked in from around the region to individual bodegas making wine from grapes grown in their own backyard which is, of course, what the concept of terroir is all about. Oak *tinas* for fermentation form a part of the winemaking process in all three bodegas and the quality is simply exemplary.

The Sierra Cantabria Organza (****) is another recent project: an attempt to make something really special and individual in a white Rioja, using thirty per cent Malvasía and twenty-two per cent Garnacha Blanca, barrel-fermented with three months on the less and six months *crianza*. The result is a big, minerally style, but surprisingly not heavily oaky, with a dry, crisp acidity, and impressive structure and complexity. Indeed, I tasted this after a long flight of red wines and it stood up very well. Reds: Sierra Cantabria Crianza (***) has five per cent Graciano and fourteen months in oak: good, fresh, with soft fruit – delicious, gentle hints of oak. Reserva (****) has some Graciano from thirty-year-old vines with eighteen months in forty per cent new oak: perfumed, with soft-fruit on a tender, silky palate – delicious. Gran Reserva (****) is all Tempranillo with twenty-four months in American oak; this is a more traditional style with lovely soft fruit, a hint of spice, and a long, complex finish. Cuvée Especial (****) is all Tempranillo from thirty-year-old vines with malolactic fermentation in barrel and four months in new French oak followed by ten months in American. This gives the wine a slightly harder edge; "bolder, more exciting" I wrote in my notes, with a crisp, modern style of fresh fruit and fresh tannins – perhaps a halfway house between the classic and high-expression styles. (I used to wonder why Spanish wine companies use the French word *cuvée* to mean a selection or blend, when there is a perfectly good Spanish word – *cubo* – that translates directly from the French. Then I realized that *cubo* also translates as "bucket", which is not suitably romantic…) Colección Privada (*****) is all Tempranillo from fifty-year-old vines harvested at twenty-six hectolitres per hectare (the legal maximum is forty-six), with fifty per cent *maceración carbónica* and eighteen months in oak. This is very much in the new-wave style, with an explosive burst of flavour, rather like dark chocolate with the fruit locked inside it, developing in the mouth into a blockbusting finish: I wrote "fab" in my notes. Señorío de San Vicente (*****) is made from the shy-bearing Tempranillo Peludo from the single vineyard Finca la Canoca, hand-selected on the vine for the ripest bunches and again on the sorting table at the bodega. It has twenty months in new oak (eighty per cent French) and this is high-expression wine of the first water: big, rich structure on the nose; massive, powerful heat; ripeness, tannins, and locked-in fruit on the palate; needs time in the bottle to quieten it down but another "fab" wine. El Puntido (*****) is the wine from Viñedos del Páganos (first vintage 2001), all Tempranillo with eighteen months in new French oak, including malolactic fermentation and the first four months on the lees; this has a subtle, perfumed but mineral nose which hides a big, tannic punch on the palate but with massive locked-in fruit: breathtaking in more ways than one. Finca El Bosque (*****) uses Tempranillo for this tiny (1.5-hectare) vineyard, planted in 1973, harvested typically in November after everything else has been gathered, hand-selected in the vineyard, and then selected again in the bodega and fermented in small, French oak *tinas* of 8,000 kilograms' capacity. The wine then spends twenty-one months in French and East-European oak. The result is a wine of enormous power, fruit, and tannins, but a very rich, complex, and perfumed nose, and some unexpected delicacy on the length – another one to keep. Amancio (*****) is the ultimate high-expression wine, using Tempranillo from a single vineyard in La Veguilla, double hand-selected and fermented in small, French oak *tinas* of 500 litres' capacity, followed by twenty-four months in new French oak. The wine has the power and blockbusting fruit of the other wines but in a more subtle, controlled style with deep, dark fruit and a subtle richness. I gave it nineteen out of twenty.

SOLAGÜEN

Bodegas Solagüen, Unión de Cosecheros de Cosecheros de Labastida, 01330 Labastida, Álava. Tel: 945 331 161. Fax: 945 331 118. Website: www.solaguen.com. Email: bodegas@solaguen.com. Contact/Chief executive: José Linaza. Winemaker: Manuel Ruiz. Established: 1964. Type: S Co-op. Members: 200. Own vineyards (ha): 500. Group: No. Barrels: 6,000. Type: American. Annual production (hl): 26,000. Sales national: 60%; export: 40%. Top export markets: UK, Germany, USA. Visits: by appointment; groups and individuals. Open weekdays: 8am–1pm; 3pm–6.30pm. Principal wines: Montebuena Joven Tinto, Blanco, Rosado; Solagüen Crianza, Reserva, Gran Reserva; Manuel Quintano Reserva Especial; Castillo Labastida

This is another bodega better known by its brand name than its full title, and more than happy to live with that. It's a relatively modern co-op whose purpose in coming together was rather different from that of the pre-Franco co-ops, which simply wanted to raise the cash to buy and equip a bodega. The 108 Solagüen founders realized (with remarkable foresight) that Rioja was going to grow to become a major force in the wine world, and wanted to exploit it for themselves, rather than for the big bodegas to whom they were then selling their grapes.

Today, they process four million kilograms (8.8 million pounds) of grapes from the members' vineyards and sell in twenty-six countries in addition to Spain. In the UK, they supply the house Rioja to The Wine Society, which speaks volumes for the quality of the wines. The bodega is still mainly original but smart, spotless, and an unpretentious and demonstrably working environment. This was one of the first bodegas to establish a "cask club", where private or corporate customers could reserve a whole cask of wine to be bottled at their convenience and then either delivered or kept in the bodega for consumption at celebratory events in the Manuel Quintano dining room. This now accounts for a large percentage of the bodega's business, which means that they are getting early cash flow and a bit more than wholesale price for the wine, while the customer is paying less than retail with no worries about inflation.

And, of course, "Manuel Quintano" is the name of the bodega's flagship wine, because it was from the village that the clerical pioneer (*see* chapter three) travelled to Bordeaux and first experimented with that region's methods in Rioja.

Wines Solagüen Joven Tinto (**) is a simple, fresh, delicious glugger with plenty of fruit and no oak. Castillo Labastida (**) is a *corta-crianza* with three to four months in American oak, effectively the same wine as the Tinto Joven but with the oak, which adds a little more complexity and crispness. Solagüen Crianza (***) has a variable sixteen to twenty months in oak and could technically be called *reserva*, but winemaker Manuel Ruíz prefers to make a top-end *crianza* rather than a borderline *reserva*: lovely aromatic fruit and oak, good harmony, delicious. Reserva (***) has twenty-eight to thirty months in oak, more tannins, good weight and fruit. The Wine Society (***) own-label is a non-vintage blend, typically with about fourteen months in oak, specified by the society to reflect the classic Rioja (*crianza*) style, which it does impeccably: soft, classic Tempranillo nose; crisp, fresh fruit; hints of toasty oak; delicious, warm, long: benchmark Rioja. Manuel Quintano (****) is made from grapes from fifty-year-old vines with thirty-six to forty months in oak: lovely, structured fruit and subtle aromatics with big, clean, modern, bright fruit.

TONDONIA

R López de Heredia-Viña Tondonia. Avda Vizcaya 3, 26200 Haro, La Rioja.
Tel: 941 310 244. Fax: 941 310 788. Website: www.lopezdeheredia.com.
Email: bodega@lopezdeheredia.com. Contact/Chief executive: María-José López de Heredia. Winemaker: Mercedes López de Heredia. Established: 1877. Type: SA.
Own vineyards (ha): 170. Barrels: 15,000. Visits: by appointment, Mon–Fri.
Principal wines: Viña Bosconia Reserva, Gran Reserva; Viña Cubillo Crianza; Viña Gravonia Blanco Crianza; Viña Tondonia Rosado Crianza, Blanco Reserva; Blanco Gran Reserva; Tinto Crianza; Tinto Reserva; Tinto Gran Reserva

I hope that you will forgive if I quote my (very brief) profile from *The New Spain* (2004 edition): "Little has changed here in a century, with grape selection and winemaking done by hand, and the wines fined with egg-whites and aged with a fine disregard for the vagaries of fashion or popular taste." This is the shrine at which the traditionalists of Rioja worship.

There's a wonderful photograph hanging in one of the bodega halls of the founder, Rafael López de Heredia Landeta, swathed in overcoat and tartan gabardine, wearing a bowler hat, waiting for a train in the snow at Haro station, with the towers of the bodega in the background. It was taken in 1910, but snow has been an increasingly rare visitor to Haro since that time. Rafael was born in Chile to parents of Alavesa origin in 1857, and came to Spain in 1869, at a time when Rioja was getting ready for its first boom period. He was sent to complete his schooling in France and, as with many people at the that time, came back to Spain with an ambition to make wine, with France the target export market. After a brief period working in the chocolate business (in 1877 at the age of twenty), he transferred to wine, buying and selling, although not growing grapes or making wine.

In 1881, the business had expanded sufficiently for him to buy into the business and cellars of a French company, Armande Heff y Rousille, and the joint venture did good export business, particularly in Cuba and England. As the business expanded, the company excavated underground galleries through the hill beside the bodega, and Rafael made an important decision which has stood the company in good stead ever since. He calculated that there would need to be more buildings and more storage in the long-term future, and used the stone excavated from these underground caverns to build foundations for future buildings, and filled them with the rubble. In later years, the rubble was dug out, fashioned into building stones, and the new buildings constructed with them, thereby saving a fortune in infrastructure costs. This continued until as recently as the 1970s.

Once the phylloxera problem had been solved, Heff went back to France and Rafael bought out his share of the business with the help of outside investors. But troubled times were ahead. With the "bust" of the 1890s in Rioja, the company was liquidated in 1899. But Rafael persuaded the Banco de España to come up with the cash to restart the business, and managed to click with the next upturn in Rioja. He invested heavily in vineyards, and started the trend for naming his wines after them: Gravonia, Cubillo, Bosconia, Zaconia, and, most famously, Tondonia (planted 1914) are all vineyards that still belong to the company today.

In 1924, Rafael turned the company into an SA under its present-day name and also brought in his two sons, Rafael Junior and Julio César. They built the business up after his retirement (he died in 1937), and

Rafael Junior lived to a ripe old age, in an apartment at the top of the bodega; the famous "Swiss-style" tower marked the head of the lift-shaft that carried him from his home to the fermentation hall, even in the days when he could only get around in a wheelchair; he lived until 1985. The next generation was represented by Pedro López de Heredia, and it is his three children, the fourth generation, the great-grandchildren of the founder, who now run things: Maria-José runs the bodega, her brother, Julio-César, is the viticulturist, and sister, Mercedes, is the winemaker.

Today, the bodega looks as it did when Rafael Junior died and, indeed, much as it did when his father died: huge underground caverns, thick with cobwebs, with uncounted millions of bottles stashed away from floor to ceiling; the offices rich with old wooden counters and engraved glass; the winemaking still following the ancient rituals laid down by the founder, with anything up to sixty months in oak (although it has to be said that the bodega has always had a policy of using old oak, with subsequent minimal effect on the wine; the barrel adds a very slow, gentle burnish to the wine rather than injecting vanillin and other oaky notes) and countless years in the bottle. A visit is an instance of time travel, with the opportunity to taste wines dating back to the turn of the twentieth century. I once asked the delightful, elfin-featured chief executive María-José López Heredia how often they open the old bottles. She told me that for important family celebrations – weddings, baptisms, etc. – they usually open something centenarian, and even the oldest vintages can still come through, although they usually have to open three bottles before they find one that's still alive. However, this does means that the wines are built to last, as witness a major tasting I undertook before writing this book. Only one white Rioja made it through to the final top ten, and it was the 1987 (still on sale) Viña Tondonia Blanco Reserva. If you want to see the living history of classic Rioja, you must visit this bodega. A word of warning (to men): please don't fall in love with María-José. There's a queue.

Viña Gravonia Blanco Crianza (***) is all Viura, with thirty-six months in oak and lovely, gently oaky notes. Viña Bosconia Tinto Crianza (***) has Graciano and Mazuelo with thirty-six months in oak, and is a little softer and gentler than Tondonia. Tinto Gran Reserva (****) has a similar mix with seventy-two months in oak: mature, oaky, and delicious.

Viña Tondonia is the flagship range. Blanco Reserva (****) has fifteen per cent Malvasía and forty-eight months in oak. Blanco Gran Reserva

(*****) has smoky hints and dairy ice-cream fruit. Crianza Rosado (***) is probably the only oak-aged *rosado* left in Rioja, made from seventy per cent Garnacha, twenty-five per cent Tempranillo, and five per cent Viura, with thirty-six months in oak; that bit of oak really does make a difference to the savouriness of the fruit. Tinto Reserva (*****) has fifteen per cent Garnacha and five per cent each of Garnacha and Mazuelo, with forty-eight months in oak: a sublime blend of fruit, oak, and maturity. Tinto Gran Reserva (*****) is a similar blend but seventy-two months in oak – very old fashioned, very sublime, wonderful.

TORRE DE OÑA

Torre de Oña SA, Término San Martín, 01330 Laguardia, Álava. Tel: 945 621 154. Fax: 945 621 171. Website: www.riojalta.com/baron. Email: baron@riojalta.com. Contact: Gabriela Rezola, PR. Chief executive: Guillermo de Aranzábal. Winemaker: José Gallego. Established: 1987. Type: SA. Own vineyards (ha): 50. Group: La Rioja Alta (*see* page 137), Lagar de Cervera, Áster. Barrels: 4,000. Type: French. Sales national: 75%; export: 25%. Visits: contact bodega.
Principal wine: Barón de Oña Reserva

This is another manifestation of the "château obsession" that refuses to leave Rioja: the concept of a winery on a private estate sitting among its own vineyards. It's understandable, of course, as Bordeaux set the agenda for the establishment of "classic" Rioja, but just slightly odd when you consider that it was Rioja's ability to select from cool highland, hot lowland, and quirky microclimatic vineyards that won the wine its early reputation for consistency.

However, this is a beautiful bodega sitting serenely within its own vineyards. It was actually created by Jaime Rodríguez of Remelluri (*see* page 184) as part of a joint venture with a Cuban businessman called Leandro Vázquez, which foundered not long afterwards, and was sold as a going concern to La Rioja Alta (*see* page 137), which had been looking for a venture to make a more modern style of wine than that made at the main bodega in Haro. Torre de Oña was completely different: French oak, younger vines, a different winemaking tradition. And only one wine, year in and year out. Barón de Oña Reserva (****) has some Mazuelo and spends twenty-four months in oak: a wine of great structure, style, and perfume, high tannins and excellent keeping qualities. Current vintages are about ten years old.

VALDEMAR

Bodegas Valdemar, Camino Viejo de Logroño s/n, 01320 Oyón, Álava.
Tel: 945 622 188. Fax: 945 622 111. Website: www.bujanda.com. Email:
bujanda@bujanda.com. Contact: Ana Martínez Bujanda. Chief executive: Jesús
Martínez Bujanda. Winemaker: Gonzalo Ortiz. Established: 1889. Type: SA.
Own vineyards (ha): 400. Own production: 100%. Buy in: No. Group: Finca
Valpiedra (see page 126), Finca Antigua. Barrels: 14,000. Sales national: 50%;
export: 50%. Top export markets: Canada, EU, UK. Visits: contact bodega.
Principal wines: Valdemar Joven Tinto, Blanco, Rosado; Conde de Valdemar
Blanco Fermentado en Barrica, Crianza, Reserva, Gran Reserva, Garnacha Reserva;
Vendimia Seleccionada Gran Reserva

This is yet another bodega that changed its name from Martínez Bujanda
to the name of its main wine brand, Valdemar – in this case in 2003. It's
a classic but modern bodega whose wines have continued to improve,
year on year. It was founded by Joaquín Martínez Bujanda in 1889 in
Oyón, where he had been a *cosechero* with a modest ten hectares of vines.
He made his own wine but continued to sell it to larger bodegas and,
indeed, the family name didn't appear on a label until 1966. The business
had expanded, however, and Joaquín's son Marcelino took over the company
in 1927, expanding the bodega and buying new vineyards as well as the
bodega's first oak casks. In 1945, he handed it on to his son, Jesús
Martínez Bujanda, by which time the concern owned 200 hectares of
vineyards, and he continued in his father's footsteps, buying vineyards
and investing in the bodega. By the late 1970s, however, Jesús was
approaching retirement age, and the bodega was bursting at the seams.
He handed the business on to his three children, Carlos, Pilar, and Jesús
Junior; the last set about designing a new bodega from scratch. He had
already designed a new complex for El Coto (see page 119) and had something of a reputation for knowing what he was about in these matters. The
foundation stone was laid in 1981 and the new bodega made its first vintage
in 1984. At that time, it was certainly the most modern bodega in Rioja,
and quite possibly in Europe; even today the winking computer screens,
spotless walls and floors, and shining steel tanks have that "state-of-the-
art" look. Jesús Senior, it is said, had three priorities when it came to
making wine: "cleanliness, cleanliness, and cleanliness". That philosophy
is also still apparent today. The old bodega in the town has been lovingly
restored as a small wine museum. Currently, Jesús Junior (Jesús Senior

may have retired but still drops in on a regular basis to make sure that everything's all right) acts as chief executive, Carlos looks after exports, and Pilar runs the office and administration side of things. The company launched one of Rioja's first varietal Garnacha *reserva* reds in the late 1990s (the 1994 vintage) and has continued to innovate, most spectacularly, perhaps, at Finca Valpiedra (*see* page 126).

Valdemar Tinto Joven (****) is a real stab at making historic Tempranillo wine: young, bags of fruit, fresh, and delicious. Conde de Valdemar Blanco Fermentado en Barrica (***) is all Viura, with five months on the lees and the right balance of crisp oak and fresh fruit. Crianza (***>****) has twelve to fifteen per cent Mazuelo and sixteen to eighteen months in oak: good, classic *crianza* with fruit and oak in balance. Reserva (****) has a similar grape mix and twenty-four to twenty-six months in oak: real heavyweight, classic quality. Gran Reserva (****) has a similar grape mix but thirty months in oak and a grand, elegant structure. Garnacha Reserva (****>*****) has twenty months in oak and is notable for its warmth, ripeness, and yet somehow freshness: delicious.

VALENCISO

Compañía Bodeguera de Valenciso, Apartado 227, 26200 Haro, La Rioja.
Tel: 941 304 724. Fax: 941 304 728. Website: www.valenciso.com. Email: valenciso@valenciso.com. Contact: Luís Valentín. Chief executive: Luís Valentín/Carmen Enciso. Winemaker: Alicia Eyaralar. Established: 1998. Type: SA. Own vineyards (ha): 3. Contract (ha): 15. Own production: 100%. Buy in: No. Number of staff: 5. Group: No. Barrels: 367. Type: French. Annual production (hl): 100. Sales national: 85%; export: 15%. Top export markets: USA, UK, Switzerland. Visits: No. Principal wine: Valenciso Reserva

This is a tale of wish-fulfilment and niche-market success that might be dreamed about by senior executives of the mega Rioja bodegas, who spend their lives on long-haul flights, attending board meetings, making presentations, and taking potential clients out to expensive dinners in far-flung cities. Luís Valentín and Carmen Enciso (Valenciso: geddit?) have both been there and done that; they worked together for fifteen years at Bodegas Palacio (*see* page 170), where Luís worked in financial management (and as managing director from 1992–8) and Carmen was responsible for the bodega's marketing (and the hotel) when it belonged to the management-buyout team that had bought it from Canadian group Seagram. When it was sold to the Barceló group in 1998, Luís was forty and had a small shareholding, as well as severance pay, as did Carmen. They had both nurtured the dream of owning their own bodega and making their own wine, but neither had the money (even with the generous settlement from Barceló) to start up on their own; even by pooling their investments they couldn't think of financing a new bodega.

However, after fifteen years with a high-powered bodega like Palacio, they did have contacts, and they decided to team up and visit investor-land. It worked. Their individual reputations from Palacio stood them in good stead, and investors came: one is a *cosechero* in Elciego with 150 hectares of vines (who used to supply Palacio); another is Jean Gervais, the original major shareholder of the management buyout of Palacio in 1987, now really retired but always prepared to taste and advise; a third is a French cooperage; a fourth is a distribution company in Barcelona (see what I mean about contacts?), and there are about 150 small investors with one to two thousand euros apiece in shares. "If it fails," says Luís, "only Carmen and I stand to lose everything; for everyone else we hope it would be only as disappointing as their favourite football team losing at the weekend."

So how do you make wine without a bodega? Well, the *cosechero* in Elciego allows them to use his bodega to make the wine with selected Tempranillo from his vineyards (they own three hectares and rent fifteen of his). They called in consultant winemaker Alicia Eyaralar to oversee the production, they rent space to store the barrels where they can find it (Laguardia for most), and they bottle under contract, where they can. Andrés Proensa in his 2004 guide put it in a nutshell: "They have no vineyard [actually they have bought the three hectares since he wrote that], they work with the fifteen hectares they control; they make the wine in Elciego and age it in Laguardia in rented cellars... Nevertheless they have given one of the best wines to Rioja in the last few years." There is a new bodega under construction in Ollauri, and this is scheduled to make the 2005 vintage. Luís spent a year at Pétrus in Bordeaux learning winemaking – not so that he could make the wine but so that he could make informed decisions about the equipment the new bodega would need. It will have concrete tanks with cooling *placas* rather than stainless steel, to reduce the reductive element of stainless steel. Well, this is the new Rioja, folks: *tot homines, quot sententiae* (Publius Terentius Afer c. 185–159 BC).

The first vintage was in 1998, when they experimented with American oak, although they have subsequently decided to use only French, and only one wine, a *reserva*, will be made. They buy "flor-quality" Catalan corks for fifty-five centimos each from Palafrugell (cooler, tighter cells) and don't believe in the trend for high-expression wines. They just want to make good Rioja.

As it happened, I visited their temporary offices in Haro shortly after the takeover of the CRDOCa by the OIPVR and I asked Luís what he thought about the change. He smiled. "When I was at Palacio," he said, "I used to do all that stuff: committee meetings, study groups, financial projections. Now, we're so small that the CRDOCa hardly notices we're here at all." He professes himself a very happy man, and who wouldn't be, working alongside the elegant and enigmatically beautiful Carmen Enciso?

Valenciso Reserva (****>*****) has fourteen to sixteen months in French oak: aromatic, with soft, delicious fruit, soft tannins, gentle, elegant length. This should age with consummate grace.

VALSACRO

Bodegas Valsacro, Ctra N-232 Km, 364. 26510 Pradejón, La Rioja.
Tel: 941 398 008. Fax: 941 398 070. Website: www.valsacro.com. Email: escudero@prorioja.es. Contact: José-María Escudero. Chief executive/Winemaker: Amador Escudero. Established: 1997. Type: SA. Own vineyards (ha): 120. Own production: 100%. Number of staff: 12. Group: Escudero. Barrels: 1,850. Type: French and American. Annual production (hl): 6,000. Sales national: 50%; export: 50%. Top export markets: USA, Switzerland, Germany. Visits: weekdays only; contact Ángeles Escudero at the bodega. Principal wines: Valsacro; Valsacro Dioro

This is the magnificent new winery created by the Escudero brothers (*see* page 215) to be another château-style bodega nestling among (or, at least, near) its own vineyards – and also a member of the "Rioja Baja Strikes Back" tendency. The style is epic, with gigantic steel fermentation tanks and casks in the same cathedral-like hall, with experimental fermentation and ageing in different oak to assess the relative qualities. All wine movements are done by gravity, and everything has been designed from the ground up to be the most modern available. The wines are largely at an experimental stage, with different *cuvées* aged in different oaks towards a final determination of the eventual style, but quality is at the forefront. Cabernet Sauvignon and Chardonnay are unashamedly a part of the vineyard mix, but as befits a Rioja Baja bodega, Garnacha tends to dominate the reds. However, Amador Escudero makes the wines the way he wants them, with a fine disregard for convention.

Valsacro (****) is made with a minority of Garnacha and might also contain Mazuelo, Bobal, and Monastrell, as well as Cabernet Sauvignon, depending on the vintage. The bodega has experimented with ageing in Alliers, American, and Romanian oak and will no doubt continue to do so, but a typical period in cask for this wine is sixteen to eighteen months: big, deep, dark fruit; clean, crisp tannins; ripe. Vasacro Dioro (*****) is made from vines of more than seventy years old, typically sixty-five per cent Garnacha, twenty-five per cent Tempranillo, and ten per cent an assortment of others, with as long as Amador thinks it needs in French and American oak: it has a big, smoky, austere nose with dark-chocolate hints on the palate; austere, weighty, and "fab". I gave it nineteen out of twenty.

VALSERRANO

Viñedos y Bodegas de La Marquesa, Herrería 76, 01307 Villabuena, Álava. Tel: 945 609 085. Fax: 945 623 304. Website: www.araex.com. Email: lamarquesa@worldonline.es. Contact/Chief executive: Juan-Pablo de Simón. Winemaker: Jaime de Simón. Established: 1880. Type: SL. Own vineyards (ha): 70. Contract (ha). Own production: 90%. Buy in: 10%. Number of staff: 8. Group: No. Barrels: 2,700. Type: 60% American, 40% French. Annual production (hl): 40. Sales national: 40%; export: 60%. Top export markets: UK, Switzerland, USA. Visits: by appointment; groups and individuals. Open weekdays: 9am–1pm; 4pm–6pm. Principal wines: Valserrano Blanco Fermentado en Barrica; Tinto Crianza; Reserva; Reserva Selección Limitada; Gran Reserva; Finca Monteviejo; Mazuelo; Graciano

This bodega started out in 1880 as bodegas Marqués de Solano, and changed its name in 1942 to Bodegas SMS after the three shareholding families: Samaniego, Milans del Bosch, and Solano. Later ownership passed in its entirety to the Milans del Bosch family, and in 1998 the business became a limited company with the name Bodegas de la Marquesa, under the directorship of Juan-Pablo de Simón Milans de Bosch. Indeed, as you read this, there are suggestions that the name should change again, this time to Bodegas Valserrano – which is the name of the main wine, of course.

The bodega is just down the hill from Izadi and Luís Cañas (*see* pages 130 and 140), and although Juan-Pablo is still in charge, his sons Pablo and Jaime are gradually taking over. Pablo is a lawyer, and looks after the general management and commercial development, and Jaime is a winemaker. The bodega is small and beautifully kept, and, having visited this and its two illustrious neighbours, you get the feeling that there is something in the soil in Villabuena which produces a better class of grape (they'd all tell you that, of course). They make two ranges of wine, which they describe as "traditional" and "modern". Juan-Pablo describes this latter range as having more fruit, more acidity, and more new oak: a style he describes, rather beguilingly, as *estilo australiano de Rioja*. It consists of two varietals and a single-estate wine. This bodega was, incidentally, one of the first (along with Contino, *see* page 105) to launch a varietal Graciano in 1993.

Valserrano Blanco Fermentado en Barrica (***) is all Viura fermented with Champagne yeast with six months on the lees: very spicy nose, almost ice-creamy, and a lovely palate with a hint of richness on the finish. Tinto Crianza (***) has ten per cent Mazuelo and is aged in mainly American oak: big Tempranillo fruit, good weight, and structure; Reserva (***>****) has ten per cent Graciano, which shows on the palate: a lot of spice, powerful fruit. Reserva Selección Limitada (****) has a similar grape mix but is made in a more modern style from hand-selected grapes with twenty-four months in French and American oak. Fresh, spicy, with savoury fruit; complex, structured, rich, and well-balanced, this is technically a *gran reserva*, but Jaime thinks the description would imply that's it's old-fashioned. Gran Reserva (****) has twenty-four months in American oak, and has classic sweet fruit and vanilla, fading slightly on the length. Valserrano Mazuelo (****) is made from fifteen-year-old vines and has twelve months in oak: big, extracted, and powerful, with a lot of fruit but the higher acidity compensates, delicious. Graciano (****>*****) is harvested every year and fermented in small tanks, but only bottled as a varietal wine in the better years and when it's surplus to requirements for the mainstream wine. It's a big-fruit, big-tannin, powerful wine which needs bottle-age to develop, but takes on great elegance when mature. Finca Montevieja (*****) has five per cent Graciano and

Garnacha from a single vineyard planted in 1948, and is aged for variable periods in French and American oak; it has beautiful structure with clean, tight, dark fruit and great length.

VIÑA HERMOSA

Santiago Ijalba-Viña Hermosa, Apartado 109, Avda de La Rioja s/n, 26221 Gimileo, La Rioja. Tel: 941 304 231; Fax: 941 304 326. Website: www.santiagoijalba.com. Email: santiagoijalba@fer.es. Contact/Chief executive/Winemaker: Santiago Ijalba García. Established: 1998. Type: SA. Own vineyards (ha): 10. Contract (ha): 130. Own production: 8%. Buy in: Yes. Number of staff: 8. Group: No. Barrels: 1,500. Type: American and French. Annual production (hl): 4,500. Sales national: 73%; export: 27%. Top export markets: France, Mexico, Ireland. Visits: by appointment; groups and individuals. Open weekdays: 9am–12 noon. Principal wines: Viña Hermosa Joven; Crianza; Reserva; Gran Reserva; Jarrero; Abando Crianza; Mutuo; Tinto de Autor; Blanco Fermentado en Barrica; Ogga, Reserva, Tinto de Autor

This is another bodega whose company name is hardly known; indeed, on my first visit I drove past the bodega half a dozen times before I realized that I had, in fact, arrived. Santiago Ijalba García actually wanted to work in a bank and passed all the entrance exams at the age of sixteen in 1964, but his family wanted him to learn the business side of things first. They had good contacts at Bodegas Ramón Bilbao (*see* page 178) in Haro and Santiago went to work for them, in spite of the fact that he'd never shown much interest in the wine industry. Once in, however, he was hooked, and rose very rapidly through the business, eventually to become general manager while still in his teens. He worked for Ramón Bilbao for thirty-four years, and began to dream of owning his own bodega and making his own wine. When the Diego Zamora group showed an interest in buying Ramón Bilbao in 1998 (the purchase was completed the following year), Santiago took the opportunity to move on and start his own business. He bought a 4.5-hectare site on the N-232 at Gimileo, between Haro and Briones, and built a smart new bodega on it in time for the 1999 vintage. The rest of the site was planted with vines, and now extends to ten hectares, although most grapes come in from contract growers. The bodega now also incorporates a shop, wine club, and dining room. Santiago's son, Roberto Ijalba Pérez, has also joined the business, specializing in winemaking. The kit is modern, some of the wines are organic, and all are made with the natural yeast in the bloom on the grapes; bottles are closed with small-pore Catalan corks. They have experimented with screw cap closures, but Santiago believes that they send a message that the wine under them is "industrial" and he also believes that the base of the cork actually offers a "micro-*crianza*" to the wine over a period of time. The Viña Hermosa range is in the classic style; the rest are more modern and heading towards high-expression.

Wines Viña Hermosa Blanco Joven (**) is a pleasant, fresh, everyday Viura glugger. Rosado (**) is Garnacha with nice, chewy fruit and a deliciously crisp finish. Tinto (**>***) has six months in American oak, with lovely fruit/oak balance; it drinks early but gives the impression of future improvement. Crianza has fourteen to sixteen months in oak (***) and spicy, good, rich fruit. Reserva (****) has some Garnacha, Mazuelo, and Graciano, and even when mature retains fresh, bright, rich fruit with oak in proportion. Gran Reserva (****) is all Tempranillo from the Haro area with twenty-six months in oak and a big, structured style with high fruit and tannin; it ages with consummate elegance. Mutuo (****) is from a single organic vineyard, and has ten per cent each of Garnacha and Mazuelo with fourteen months in new American oak: rich, ripe, spicy-spiky fruit, complex structure, needs bottle-age. Jarrero (****>*****) is all Tempranillo from forty- to fifty-year-old vines but fermented 70/30 by the regular method and *maceración carbónica* and blended afterwards, with four to five months in French and American oak. It has the lovely lifted Tempranillo fruit of *maceración carbónica* wines, with the spicy, complex structure of the classic style: elegant yet fresh. Abando (****>*****) is made from selected Tempranillo from four individual vineyards with old vines with sixteen months in American and French oak: great big, deep-dark fruit but a softer style in spite of its intensity. Ogga (*****) is the flagship wine, made with Tempranillo from selected sixty-year-old vines, with three days' pre-fermentation maceration for maximum extraction, and twenty months in French oak. This has a "slow-burn", soft spice on the nose, building to a rich, powerful, heavy but balanced follow-through – excellent. I gave it nineteen out of twenty.

VIÑA IJALBA

Viña Ijalba, Ctra de Pamplona Km 1, 26006 Logroño, La Rioja. Tel: 941 261 100. Fax: 941 261 128. Website: www.ijalba.com. Email: vinaijalba@ijalba.com.

Contact/Chief executive: Marisol Ruíz Perez. Chief executive: Juan Carlos Sancha. Winemaker: César Simón. Established: 1991. Type: SA. Own vineyards (ha): 80. Contract (ha): 30. Own production: 75%. Buy in: Yes. Number of staff: 18. Group: No. Barrels: 3,000. Type: American 70%, French 30%. Annual production (hl): 10,000. Sales national: 46%; export: 54%. Top export markets: Switzerland, UK, Germany. Visits: by appointment; groups and individuals. Open weekdays: 9am–2pm; 4pm–8pm. Principal wines: Genolí Blanco Joven; Ijalba Blanco Fermentado en Barrica; Aloque Rosado Joven; Livor Tinto Joven; Solferino Tinto Joven Maceración Carbónica; Ijalba Crianza; Graciano; Reserva; Reserva Selección Especial; Dionisio Ruíz Ijalba; Múrice Crianza

This is one of the most visually stunning bodegas in Rioja, with a magnificent tower-top tasting room with splendid views over the city of Logroño. The founder was Dionisio Ruíz Ijalba, who made his fortune in gravel extraction and found himself with seventy-five hectares of worked-out gravel pits. Useless for any other crop, in 1975 he decided to plant vines on them, in spite of never having had experience of the wine business, although he "was able to recognize what a vine was". For the next fifteen years he grew grapes and sold them to other bodegas, but always wanted to build his own bodega. This was realized in 1991 with a first vintage in 1992, and he also made the decision to go completely organic, with low-yielding vines and no artificial sprays or fertilizers; the first organic vintage was the 1998. With astonishing foresight he had planted sixteen hectares of Graciano, representing twenty per cent of the bodega's own vineyards, compared with a regional average for the variety of just 0.4 per cent.

In charge of day-to-day running of the bodega is Juan Carlos Sancha González, who is a brilliant viticulturist and an associate professor of viticulture at the University of Rioja. His work with long-forgotten varieties of Rioja (especially the Maturana) is detailed in chapter five. Fermentation is in stainless steel and French oak *tinas*, and the *maceración carbonica* wines are still pressed by foot, albeit inside a large tank rather than a stone trough. All the wines go into a distinctive wide-lipped bottle with a very modern label design.

Wines Ijalba Maturana Blanco (***) is barrel-fermented in new French oak: very clean and aromatic fruit on the nose and a bright gooseberry palate – crisp, with lip-smacking acidity; delicious. Solferino (***) is the *maceración carbónica* Tempranillo, foot-trodden in the tank: very bright, yeasty fruit and lovely, simple, fresh, delicious fruit; lovers of Beaujolais

Nouveau (if there are any left) would immediately recognize the style. Ijalba Graciano (****>*****) has three months in new Alliers oak, spicy, brambly fruit on the nose ("like the smell of blackberry bushes after the rain" I wrote), huge structure, tannins, fruit – a long way to go. Dionisio Ruíz (*****) is made from Maturana Tinta with malolactic fermentation in the barrel and twelve months in Alliers oak: even spicier than the Graciano but with similar power, fruit, and structure, and very, very long. Ijalba Reserva (*****) has twenty per cent Graciano fermented 50/50 in oak *tinas* and stainless steel, with twenty-four months in new Alliers oak; a ten-year-old example showed amazing youthfulness, aromatics, big fruit and structure with plenty of working tannins and a long way to go – excellent.

VIÑA REAL

Viña Real, Ctra Logroño–Laguardia Km 4.8, 01300 Laguardia, Álava. Tel: 945 625 210. Fax: 945 625 209. Website: www.cvne.com. Email: laguardia@cvne.com. Contact: María Urrutia. Chief executive: Víctor Urrutia. Winemaker: José-María Ryan Murúa. Established: 1879. Type: SA. Own vineyards (ha): 150. Contract (ha): 450. Own production: 50%. Buy in: Yes, but only in Álava. Number of staff: 156. Group: CVNE/Contino. Barrels: 14,000. Type: American and French. Annual production (hl): 20,000. Sales national: 80%; export: 20%. Top export markets: UK, Switzerland, Mexico. Visits: by appointment; groups and individuals. Open weekdays: 10am–2pm; 4pm–7pm. Principal wines: Viña Real Crianza; Reserva; Gran Reserva; Blanco Fermentado en Barrica

This is an astonishing venture by CVNE (*see* page 109). They used to make both the Imperial (Alta grapes) and Viña Real (Alavesa grapes) in the main bodega in Haro but decided that they needed extra capacity, and took the decision to created a purpose-built winery, designed by French architect Philippe Mazières on a stunning hillside site beside the Logroño-Laguardia road, just north of the river in Álava. From the outside, the aspect is of a long, rectangular building with a gigantic oak *tina* at the end, and this is the intended view. The "*tina*" is the most ingenious part of the building, and is fifty-six metres (184 feet) wide and sixteen metres (fifty-three feet) high. When CVNE built its new bodega in 1989, they installed the famous "flying saucer" technology, in which individual tanks are filled with grapes on a carousel, and the tanks are then lifted and emptied into static tanks.

Viña Real takes this a step further: inside the circular *tina* building, the static fermentation tanks are ranged around the circumference of the building with barrel storage arranged in inner circles. Right in the centre is a rotating arm that swings to an opening high in the roof. Tanks of grapes come through from the reception area (at the highest level, up the hill) and the arm can be swung to empty into any one of the static tanks, according to the wishes of the winemaker. In this way José-María Ryan has absolute batch control. Once fermentation is complete, the wine can then be run off into tanks at the lower level for assessment. The whole exercise cost in the region of twenty-four million euros and is breathtaking in its scope and compass. The first vintage was made there in 2002, but the official inauguration of the building, with much ceremony and merrymaking, took place in July 2004. Although the wines were regularly regarded as among Rioja's best, the move to the new bodega has occasioned an upward shift in quality, particularly noticeable in cask-wines which are ageing towards *reserva* status. If star ratings have a > (in the form ***>) at the end, that means the wines which will be released in the future are likely to be better than the given mark.

Wines Viña Real Blanco Fermentado en Barrica (***) is all Viura, with six months on the lees (so it could be called *crianza* but they don't because of the image of oaked white Rioja); it has full, savoury fruit, and ripe, delicious oaky hints. Crianza (***>) has fifteen per cent Garnacha and Mazuelo with eighteen months in oak: fresh, clear, good, basic fruit and a nice style. Reserva (****>) has ten per cent Graciano and Garnacha with twenty-four months in oak: very classy, lovely structure and balance, still fresh with crisp fruit after five years, will improve. Gran Reserva (****>*****) has five per cent Graciano and typically thirty months in cask; this has always been a classic with amazing freshness in the fruit even after seven or eight years, although it will likely be 2009–10 before we see the first *gran reservas* from the new bodega. They should be spectacular.

VIÑA SALCEDA

Viña Salceda, Ctra Cenicero Km 3, 01340 Elciego, Álava. Tel: 945 606 125. Fax: 945 606 069. Website: www.vinasalceda.com. Email : info@vinasalceda.com. Contact: Nuria Lagunilla. Chief executive: Julián Chivite López. Winemaker: Víctor Manzanos. Established: 1969. Type: SL. Own vineyards (ha): 40. Group: Bodegas Chivite. Barrels: 8,000. Type: American and French. Annual production (hl): 23,670. Sales national: 85%; export: 15%. Visits: by appointment; groups and individuals. Principal wines: Viña Salceda Crianza; Reserva; Conde de la Salceda Reserva

My first visit to this bodega was on November 10, 1989, and I know because I have on my desk a glazed earthenware jug inscribed *Recuerdo de la visita a Viña Salceda – John Radford, 10-11-89* which is currently full of pens, pencils, and a wine thermometer (very useful). A great deal has changed however, since that first visit. The postal address is Elciego but the bodega itself is immediately north of the river Ebro, on the road from Cenicero to Elciego, the river, of course being the border between La Rioja and Álava.

The original company was founded in 1969 under the name Cepas de Elciego, making wine from grapes grown on land belonging to the Conde de Salceda; the first vintage was the 1970, but there was no bodega here at that time. The company changed its name to Larrea y Rabanera, after two of the main shareholders, and it was this entity that started the bodega we see today in 1973, completed in time for the 1974 vintage. From 1976, the company changed its name to Viña Salceda, reflecting that its origins lay in the lands of the Conde de Salceda, and indeed, that he was one of the company's main board directors at that time. By this time, there were some 200 shareholders in the business, many of them *cosecheros*, and the company made good, middle-of-the-road wines. Indeed, very little had changed when I visited, thirteen years later; the wines were workmanlike, decent, and well-made, and that was about the top and bottom of it.

The big change came in 1998, when the family firm of Chivite bought the bodega. They had been looking for a base in Rioja for some considerable time, and Salceda's pedigree, good reputation, and, above all, potential for development, made it an attractive acquisition. Fernando Chivite kept on the existing winemaker, Víctor Manzanos, who had been doing the best he could with the grapes and equipment available, but invested heavily in new kit and vineyard improvements. Given the lead-time needed for the greatest wines, it was 2003 before the first Conde de la Salceda from the new regime (1998) came on the market, but the increase in quality and a slight shift to a more modern style is apparent. Fernando's primary ambition is to produce wines that are "a substitute for big-name Rioja" that are affordable, and that people can buy with confidence.

Viña Salceda Crianza (***) has ten to fifteen per cent Graciano and

Mazuelo and fifteen months in American oak: good, solid *crianza* quality in the classic style. Reserva (***>****) has a similar grape-mix to the Crianza, but the individual bunches are double-selected for individual site and age of vines to pick out the best for Reserva, which gets fifteen to eighteen months in oak: good, soft, nice, ripe fruit and maturing gently. Conde de la Salceda (****>*****) Reserva has five per cent Graciano and the grapes come from three particularly old vineyards, hand-selected with twelve to eighteen months in new Alliers oak: very deep, dark fruit, with a subtle perfume, elegant fruit balance, richness, and a structure that borders on the austere, implying that this wine is in it for the long haul.

YSIOS

Ysios, Camino de la Hoya, 01300 Laguardia, Álava. Tel: 945 600 640.
Fax: 945 600 641. Website: www.byb.es. Email: ysios@byb.es.
Contact: Isabel Adrián, communications director; email: iadrianl@byb.es.
Winemakers: Diego Pinilla, Hervé Romat. Established: 1998. Own vineyards (ha): 50. Group: Allied Domecq. Barrels: 2,000. Visits: contact bodega.
Principal wines: Ysios Reserva; Vendimia Seleccionada

One of the most daring architectural styles of the new wave in Rioja. Set against a dramatic mountain backdrop, the aluminium roof soars and leaps, the central galley looms, cyclops-like, with a view to the city of Laguardia on its fortified hill, and the whole effect is breathtaking. The architect was Santiago Calatrava, famous for his airborne shapes and outrageous curlicues – architecture in Rioja has never been so flambuoyant. The central salon has the view up towards the city, and is used as a diningroom, for presentations, and all that sort of thing.

Ysios is, metaphorically, the little Russian doll, the one that comes out last, in the great structure that is Allied Domecq. Ysios is inside the Iverus group of bodegas, within the Bodegas y Bebidas Group in Spain, which is inside the great babushka that is Allied Domecq. The wines are pretty good, too. Hervé Romat, originally from Bordeaux, is the group consultant winemaker and his plan is to resurrect the terroir of the Rioja Alavesa (he is not, of course, alone in this ambition). Day-to-day control in the winery, however, is the hands of Diego Pinilla, who studied at the universities of Pamplona and Bordeauz, and has made wine at Château Canon La Gaffelière in St-Émilion; Brown Brothers in Milawa, Australia; Clos du Val in the Napa Valley, and Concha y Toro in Chile.

The bodega makes wines only from its own fifty hectares of Tempranillo and the exact amount of time spent in oak varies according to the vintage, but the ageing criteria are never less than those for *reserva*. Some of the vineyard is still rather young, so we may expect to see some spectacular wines in the second decade of the twenty-first century.

Wines Ysios Reserva (***>****) has very tender fruit, in rather a contrast to some of the blockbusting styles being made elsewhere in Rioja, but is subtle and complex. Vendimia Seleccionada (****) is, as its name implies, selected from the best grapes, and also has a delicate, herby-spicy fruit on the nose but more warmth, concentration, and spice on the palate: delicious.

OTHER BODEGAS

These are bodegas which have yet to hit the headlines. They may be large co-ops starting to get their quality act together or smaller, perhaps family-run bodegas with little or no toe-hold in the marketplace outside their home region. It should be emphasized that I have not been able to visit any of these, and all the information (where there is any and excepting the tasting notes) has been supplied by the bodegas themselves.

BACOVINO

Grupo Bacovino, Laguardia 3, 01307 Baños de Ebro, Álava. Tel: 945 609 124. Fax: 945 609 124. Website: www.bacovino.com. Email : info@bacovino.com. Contact/Chief executive: Julio Carro Frías. Winemaker: AM García. Established: 2003. Type: SC. Own vineyards (ha): 150. Own production: 100%. Number of staff: 2. Group: Bodegas Santos Sodupe, Bodegas Perez Maestresala, Heredad García de Olano, Bodegas y Viñedos Zuazo Gastón, Viña el Recio, Bodegas José Basoko. Barrels: 1,000. Annual production (hl): 10,000. Sales national: 99%; Export: 1%. Top export markets: Germany, UK. Visits: by appointment; groups and individuals. Open weekdays: 9am–1pm; 4pm–6pm. Principal wines: Santos Sodupe Crianza; Blanco Barrica; Rosado; García de Olano Crianza; Finca Barronte Crianza Especial; Zuazo Gaston Corta-Crianza; Viña el Recio Maceración; Maestresala

A grouping of small artisanal producers in the area around Villabuena and Baños de Ebro, including Pérez Maestrasala and José Basoco.

CINCEL

Bodegas Virgen del Valle SA, Bodegas Ctra a Villabuena 3, 01307 Samaniego,

Álava. Tel: 941 609 033. Fax: 945 609 106. Email: bodegavirvalle@sea.es. Chief executive: Javier Fauste Romano. Established: 1987.

Principal wines: Cincel Reserva, Gran Reserva; Cosecha Familiar

A small family company making very good wines in this small Basque village. The present company dates from 1987, when it was taken over by Javier Fauste. Since then, it has been extended and re-equipped by him, and the wines, all called Cincel, are much improved, especially the *gran reservas*. Cincel Reserva (***) has some Graciano and Mazuelo with eighteen months in oak: ripe, spicy fruit in the classic style, good structure, some tannin still working away. Gran Reserva (****) is a similar grape mix but with up to thirty-six months in oak: lovely and rich, with perfumed fruit, and dreaming oak – very classic, delicious.

CYRANO

Viña Bajoz, Avenida de los Comuneros 90, 49810 Morales de Toro, Zamora. Tel: 980 698 023. Fax: 980 698 020. Website: www.vinabajoz.com. Email: info@vinabajoz.com. Contact name: Meg Clubley; email: meg@vinabajoz.com. Chief executive: Maximo Pérez. Winemaker; Eloy Jalón. Established: 1962. Type: S Co-op. Own vineyards (ha): No. Contract (ha): 8 ha. Own production: 100%. Buy in: No. Number of staff: 40. Group: Bajoz. Barrels: American, French. Annual production (hl): 360. Sales national: 70%; export: 30%. Top export markets: China, Mexico, USA. Principal wine: Cyrano Crianza

This is a new venture in Rioja by Viña Bajoz, which belies its cooperative status by being one of the most dynamic producers in its native DO Toro. The wine is made by the winery team from Toro in rented bodega space from grapes grown in contract vineyards (with twenty-five-year-old vines) in the Rioja Alavesa: mostly Tempranillo with a very small amount of Graciano and Mazuelo. So far, only a *crianza* has been made, but they have ambitions to broaden the range as time goes by. The wine is "modern traditional", aged only in American oak, and fined with egg-whites. Cyrano Crianza (***>****) has fourteen months in new American with a little French oak and has that sweet-fruit, toasty-oak style on the mid-palate, with excellent length. They've obviously found some good plots of vines here, and future vintages should be well worth waiting for.

EL PATROCINIO

Bodega Cooperativa El Patrocinio, Ctra de Cenicero, 26313 Uruñuela, La Rioja. Tel: 941 371 319. Fax: 941 371 435. Website: www.bodegaspatrocinio.com.

Email: info@bodegaspatrocinio.es. Established: 1986. Type: Cooperative/SL. Members: 170. Own vineyards (ha): 525. Own production: 100%. Principal wines: Sancho Garcés, Señorío de Uruñuela, Zinio

A modern co-op with members as shareholders in an SL, this company appears to be working hard to improve its wines and vineyards, as well as investing in the bodega and laboratory. Zinio Vendímia Seleccionada (***>****) is all Tempranillo from fifty-year-old vines with, typically, eighteen months in oak. It has warmth and ripeness, some austere but working tannins, and the promise of a great future.

ESCUDERO

Bodegas Escudero, Ctra de Arnedo s/n, 26587 Grávalos, La Rioja. Tel: 941 398 008 Fax: 941 398 070. Website: www.bodegasescudero.com. Email: info@bodegasescudero.com. Contact/Chief executive/Winemaker: Amador Escudero. Established: 1852. Type: SA. Group: Valsacro. Own vineyards (ha): 110. Barrels: 1,000. Visits: by appointment; contact Ángeles Escudero. Open: Jan–Sep, Mon–Sat, 11am–12 noon and 5pm–6pm. Principal wines: Bécquer; Bécquer Primicia; Solar de Bécquer Blanco, Crianza, Reserva

This ancient bodega belongs to the Escudero family, and was heavily modernized by Benito Escudero in the twentieth century. His sons Amador (winemaker) and Jesús (viticulturist) are now running the show, but found in the late 1990s that the bodega was simply not big enough to accommodate the expanding business, and started an ambitious project to create an entirely new, château-style bodega with the extra capacity. This is Valsacro (*see* page 203), which made its first vintage in 2001, and where (for still wines) the story continues. In the meantime, Escudero now specializes in sparkling wines made under the cava DO. The wines are named, incidentally, after the writer and poet Gustavo Adolfo Bécquer (1836–70) who had a summer home in the area. For details of the wines *see* Valsacro.

GARRIDO

Bodegas Eduardo Garrido, Plaza de la Constitución, 26339 Ábalos, La Rioja. Tel: 941 334 187. Fax: 941 334 010. Contact/Chief executive/Winemaker: Eduardo Garrido García. Established: 1922. Type: SL. Own vineyards (ha): 2. Barrels: 140. Visits: contact bodega. Principal wines Eduardo Garrido García Joven; Crianza; Reserva; Gran Reserva

This is a family-owned bodega which also has a small museum devoted to wine- and farming-related ancient skills of La Rioja. The Eduardo Garrido García Gran Reserva (***>****) is made from eighty per cent Tempranillo with ten per cent each of Garnacha and Mazuelo from vines of more than thirty years old. The style is classic with big fruit, a hint of liquorice, and a crisp, dry finish

HEREDAD DE BAROJA

Bodegas Heredad de Baroja, Cercas Altas, 6, 01309 Elvillar de Álava, Álava. Tel: 945 604 068. Fax: 945 604 105. Website: www.heredadbaroja.com. Email: info@heredadbaroja.com. Established: 1964. Type: SA. Contact/ Winemaker: Fernando Meruelo. Sales national: 50%; export: 50%. Visits: contact bodega. Principal wines: Viña Baroja Joven; Heredad de Baroja Crianza, Reserva Gran Reserva; Gran Baroja; Cautivo Banco, Tempranillo, Crianza, Reserva, Gran Reserva; Lar de Paula

Fernando Meruelo was a winemaker at Faustino Martínez (*see* page 120) for eleven years, where he helped to develop the Faustino VII range. He started out on his own in 1964 and has built the bodega into something very attractive and successful. His latest venture is the wine Lar de Paula, which will eventually become a separate, stand-alone bodega. The Lar de Paula (****) is hot, spicy, local Tempranillo which opens up into a big, warm structure with lovely fruit. Cautivo Crianza (***) is typical fresh, high-fruit Basque Tempranillo: clean, with a spicy finish. Reserva (****) is a bigger version of the Crianza: delicious. Gran Reserva (****) is more classic, a little faded pot-pourri on the nose but good, soft fruit and gentle, mellow length.

HONORIO RUBIO

Honorio Rubio Villar, Ctra Badarán 36, 26311 Cordovín, La Rioja. Tel: 941 367 343. Fax: 941 367 343. Email: bodegashonoriorubio@hotmail.com. Contact/Chief executive: Honorio Rubio Villar. Established: 1985. Type: private company. Own vineyards (ha): 114. Barrels: 160. Visits: by appointment.

Principal wines: Pasus; Senda de Haro; Tremendus; Rivagrande; Honorio Rubio

The bodega is over 100 years old – much older than the present company – with cellars which were excavated into the rock. It has passed from grandfathers to grandchildren for several generations, and today has very modern installations. In addition, the average age of the vineyard is forty-five years. The Tremendus (*) is a Tempranillo from fifteen-year-old vines with decent fruit but with quite a bit of tannin for a *joven*: pleasant enough. Honorio Rubio (***) has ten per cent Garnacha and five per cent Mazuelo from fifteen-year-old vines, made by *maceración carbónica* with five months in oak: a rather classic style in spite of its modern production method, with good, clean fruit and prominent tannins – "needs food" was one of my notes. Pasus (***) has ten per cent Mazuelo from twenty-five-year-old vines with fourteen months in American and French oak: clean, savoury fruit with a bite of oak on the finish; might have scored higher with less oak.

MARQUÉS DE REINOSA

Marqués de Reinosa, S Co-op, Ctra Rincón de Soto s/n, 26560 Autol, La Rioja. Tel: 941 742 015. Fax: 941 742 015. Website: www.marquesdereinosa.com. Email: bodegas@marquesdereinosa.com. Winemakers: Ana Isabel Rubio. Established: 1956. Type: Cooperative. Own vineyards (ha): 1,075. Own production: 100%. Barrels: 900. Sales national: 100%. Visits: contact bodega. Principal wines: Viñestral Blanco/Rosado/Tinto Joven; Crianza; Reserva; Cecios Rosado/Tinto Joven/Crianza/Reserva; Marqués de Reinosa Tinto Joven; Ecológico; Crianza; Reserva

The bodega was originally the property of the Marqués de Reinosa, one of the pioneering *bodegueros* of the late nineteenth century, and was reconstituted as a co-op, named in his honour, in 1956. Marqués de Reinosa Tinto Joven (***) is all Tempranillo, a lovely fresh, clean, rich-fruit glugger with more than a hint of style, and amazing value for money. Tinto Joven Ecológico (**) is organic but has forty per cent Garnacha and lacks the bright fruit of the Tempranillo, yet is still very pleasant. Crianza (***) is all Tempranillo from fifty-year-old vines and has good structure and fruit for a very modest price.

MARTÍNEZ LAORDEN

Bodegas Heredad Martínez Laorden, Ctra Huércanos s/n, 26350 Cenicero, La Rioja. Tel: 941 454 446. Fax: 941 454 766. Email: bmlrioja@eniac.es. Chief executive: José-María Martínez Armendáriz. Winemaker: David León Olarte. Established: 1994. Type: SL. Own vineyards (ha): 40. Barrels: 243. Visits: by appointment; contact bodega. Principal wines: La Orbe; Lanzado

This is a very smart bodega, a family-owned enterprise conceived from the start as an environmentally friendly business, with construction using materials from renewable sources and production methods designed to minimize waste – for example in recycling and repurifying water used in cooling the fermentation tanks. La Orbe (****) is all Tempranillo from thirty-year-old vines, with six months in American and French oak. It has good, tight fruit, is well-knit, and in need of several years in the bottle to show its best.

NAVA-RIOJA

Bodegas Nava-Rioja, Carretera Eje del Ebro s/n, 31261 Andosilla, Navarra. Tel: 948 690 454; Fax: 948 674 491. Email: nava-rioja@telefonica.net. Contact: Gorka Troya Oterino, technical director. Chief executive: José María Pardo Ordóñez. Winemaker: Gorka Troya Oterino. Established: 1999. Type: SAT. Own vineyards (ha): 50. Contract (ha): 38. Own production: 57%. Buy in: Yes. Number of staff: 4. Group: No. Barrels: 176. Type: French. Annual production (hl): 4,000. Sales national: 95%; export: 5%. Top export markets: Italy, France. Visits: by appointment; groups and individuals. Open weekdays: by arrangement. Principal wines: Pardoño Joven; Crianza

Pardoño Joven (**>***) has decent fruit and some spicy aromatics; very pleasant. Crianza (***) has a good basic fruit and a decent balance.

OLARTIA

Vinícola de Rodezno, Plaza de la Asunción 8, 26222 Rodezno, La Rioja. Tel: 941 338 296. Fax: 941 338 360. Email: avillaluenga@teleline.es. Chief executive: Alfonso López Villaluenga. Winemaker: Fernando Vadillo Lacuesta. Established: 1997. Type: SL. Own vineyards (ha): 1.2. Buy in: Yes. Barrels: 800. Visits: by appointment; Open: Mon–Sat 10am–1pm, 4pm–7pm, Sun mornings. Principal wines: Olartia Joven; Viña Olartia Crianza; Señorío de Olartia Reserva/Gran Reserva

This is a small company in a beautiful nineteenth-century family house on its own 1.7-hectare estate, in the middle of the village, making small quantities of high-quality wine from mainly Tempranillo grapes. There is a shop and a banqueting room. The Señorío de Olartia Gran Reserva (****) has twenty per cent Graciano and ten per cent Mazuelo, all from fifty-year-old vines, with up to thirty months in oak: considerable maturity, but still quite strong tannins. It's warm, ripe, surprisingly youthful, and very long.

OSTATU

Bodegas Ostatu SC, Bodegas Ctra de Vitoria-Laguardia 1, 01307 Samaniego, Álava. Tel: 945 609 133. Fax: 945 623 338. Website: www.ostatu.com. Email: bod.ostatu@euskalnet.net. Chief executive: Doroteo Sáenz de Samaniego.

Winemaker: Iñigo Sáenz de Samaniego. Established: 1970. Type: SC. Own vineyards (ha): 31. Barrels: 375. Sales national: 805; export: 20%. Top export Markets: USA, France, Switzerland. Visits: contact bodega. Principal wines: Ostatu Blanco Fermentado en Barrica; Blanco Joven; Tinto Maceración Carbonica; Selección Crianza; Mazarredo Crianza; Gloria de Ostatu

This is a third-generation bodega farming small plots of old vines planted by their grandfather in the days before the family made wine. The Ostatu Fermentado en Barrica (***) has some Malvasía and was fermented in new American oak with a total of two months on the lees: good, crisp, fresh, and delicious. Selección (***>****) has five per cent Graciano with some *maceración carbónica* and fourteen months in oak: in good years, this has excellent fruit and structure. Gloria de Ostatu (****>*****) has ten per cent Graciano from the oldest vines in the family vineyard and eighteen months in new French oak: a big wine with great complexity, tight fruit, and a long finish.

PECIÑA

Bodegas Hermanos Peciña, Ctra Vitoria Km 47, 26338 San Vicente de la Sonsierra, La Rioja. Tel: 941 334 366. Fax: 941 334 180. Website: www.bodegashermanospecina.com. Email: hermanospecina@arsystel.com. Contact: Mikel Martinez. Chief executive/winemaker: Pedro Peciña. Established: 1992. Type: SL. Own vineyards (ha): 50. Own production: 100%. Buy in: No. Number of staff: 11. Group: No. Barrels: 3,500. Annual production (hl): 3,000. Sales national: 75, export: 25. Top export markets: USA, UK, Mexico. Visits: by appointment; groups and individuals. Open weekdays: 9am–1.30pm; 3pm–6.30pm. Principal wines: Señorío de P Peciña Joven; Crianza; Reserva; Gran Reserva; Reserva Vendimia Seleccionada

This is another *cosechero* family which decided to make its own wine in a smart, new bodega, well-equipped with modern installations but with an ambition to produce traditional, quality wines. On the face of it, they're succeeding. The Señorío de P Peciña Joven (***>****) has three per cent Graciano and two per cent Garnacha and is an excellent example of fresh Tempranillo fruit: delicious, gluggable, and amazing value for money. Crianza (***) has the same grape mix as the Joven, with twenty-four months in oak, and is well-made with a decent structure, but doesn't quite have the same bright fruit. Gran Reserva (****>*****) is from the same grape mix, but from vines of more than forty years old with thirty months in oak;

this has serious potential for quality: spice and fruit, no hint of oxidation, and great length.

PUELLES

Bodegas Puelles, Camino de los Molinos s/n, 26339 Ábalos, La Rioja.
Tel: 941 334 415. Fax: 941 334 132. Website: www.bodegaspuelles.com. Email: informacion@bodegaspuelles.com. Contact/Chief Executive: Jesús Puelles Fernández. Winemaker: Fernando Salgado. Established: not known. Type: Private family company. Own vineyards (ha): 19. Contract (ha): 70. Own Production: 70%. Buy in: No. Number of staff: 4–5. Group: No. Barrels: 800. Type: American and French. Annual production (hl): 2,100. Sales national: 80%; export: 20%. Top export markets: Switzerland, Germany, Denmark. Visits: open weekdays 9am–2pm; 4pm–8pm. Principal wines: Puelles Blanco; Joven; Crianza; Reserva; Gran Reserva; Zenus; El Molino de Puelles

Apparently nobody does know precisely when the Puelles family started making wine, but they say it has been "for many generations" and that they've been in Ábalos as long as anyone can remember. The present generation is led by brothers Jesús and Félix, and they have been instrumental in restoring the El Molino estate, named after an old watermill the family bought in 1844 (hence "El Molino de Puelles"). After the change in the *reglamento* in 1989 which permitted smaller bodegas to make *crianza* wines, the family decided to expand, and created the Club del Molino, in which the bodega's customers can buy a cask of wine, as it were, *en primeur* (¿*en primero?*) which gave the company "pump-priming" capital to modernize and increase its capacity. It worked. El Molino de Puelles (****>*****) is the single-estate wine from around the old mill. It is organic and all Tempranillo, with ten months in oak: big fruit, big, big tannins, and excellent structure with great length. This will run and run.

PUJANZA

Bodegas y Viñedos Pujanza, Ctra El Villar s/n, 01300 Laguardia, Álava. Tel: 945 600 548. Fax: 945 600 522. Email: bvpujanza@jet.es. Established: 1998. Type: SL. Own vineyards (ha): 40. Principal wines: Pujanza; Pujanza Norte; Qertos

The Basque Country regional government instituted a subsidy scheme to encourage *cosecheros* (of which the region has many) to convert themselves into bodegas, and this is an example: a family business now making and bottling its own wines, from its own very substantial vineyard holdings. The style is typically Basque – fresh Tempranillo fruit – but with a tannic extraction giving more than average weight and structure to the wines. Pujanza (***) has a very nice elegance, fruit, and structure. Pujanza Norte (****) is a much bigger, more powerful wine with considerable staying power. This is a bodega to watch.

RIOJA VEGA

Rioja Vega, Ctra Mendavia-Logroño, Km 32, 31230 Viana, Navarra.
Tel: 948 646 263 Fax: 948 645 612. Website: www.riojavega.com.
Email: info@riojavega.com. Chief executive: Antonio Barrero. Winemaker: Javier Marquínez. Established: 1882. Type: SA. Own vineyards (ha): 75. Group: Príncipe de Viana. Barrels: 4,500. Sales national: 60%; export: 40%. Top export markets: USA, Canada, Germany. Visits: contact bodega. Principal wines: Rioja Vega Blanco, Blanco Fermentado en Barrica, Rosado, Tinto, Crianza, Reserva; Muerza Vendimia Seleccionada

The bodega was founded in Haro in 1882 by Felipe Ugalde, and painstakingly built up as a small family business for its first fifty years of existence. In the 1940s, intermarriage with the Muerza family brought in more investment. This was consolidated in 1983, when the company was taken over by the Navarra bodega Príncipe de Viana and subsequently, in 2002, moved to a very smart, state-of-the-art purpose-built bodega in Viana in the Rioja Baja, although the 2001 was the first vintage made there. The consultant winemaker is Joseba Altuna, former winemaker at Príncipe de Viana and now semi-retired. All wines have about thirty per cent Garnacha. Rioja Vega Tinto Joven (***) is an excellent glugger with delicious fruit. Crianza (****) is astonishingly good for the price: packed with fruit and spice – delicious. Reserva (****) has a vibrant "alive" kind of fruit on the mid-palate but an excellent fruit/oak balance.

SEÑORÍO DE LÍBANO

Señorío de Líbano, Río s/n, 26212 Sajazarra, La Rioja. Tel: 941 320 066;
Fax: 941 320 251. Website: www.castillo-de-sajazarra.com. Email:
bodega@castillo-de-sajazarra.com. Contact/Chief executive: Álvaro Ruanes.
Winemaker: Rubén Jiménez. Established: 1983. Type: SA. Own vineyards (ha):
48; Own production: 100%. Buy in: No. Number of staff: 15. Group: No. Barrels:
2,600. Type: American and French. Annual production (hl): 2,200. Sales national:
95%; export: 5%. Top export markets: Switzerland, Sweden, USA. Visits: by appointment; groups and individuals. Open weekdays: 9am–1pm. Principal wines:
Castillo de Sajazarra Reserva; Solar de Líbano Reserva; Líbano La Roma Reserva

The main wine is called Sajazarra Castle, and, for once, the bodega really is situated in a small (as castles go) sixteenth-century castle in the small village of Sajzarra (pop. 240), very pretty and beautifully restored, with thoroughly modern winery equipment, including 20,0000-litre oak *tinas* for the malolactic fermentation. The company makes only *reservas* and *gran reservas* and the standard is high. Líbano la Roma Reserva (****) has five per cent Mazuelo and Graciano with variable amounts of time in oak, according to the vintage, but never less than eighteen months. The wine is in the grand style, with big tannins, plenty of locked-in fruit, and consummate elegance of structure.

TOBÍA

Bodegas Tobía, (offices) General Yagüe 26, 26006 Logroño, La Rioja. Bodega: Crtra N-232 Km 438, 26340 San Asensio, La Rioja. Tel: 941 457 425. Fax: 941 457 401. Website: www.bodegastobia.com. Email: tobia@bodegastobia.com. Contact/Chief executive/Winemaker: Óscar Tobía López. Established: 1994. Type: Private company. Own vineyards (ha): 17. Contract (ha): 60. Own production: 20%. Buy in: Yes. Number of staff: 5. Group: No. Barrels: 950. Type: American, French and Hungarian. Annual production (hl): 5,000. Sales national: 70%; export: 30%. Visits: by appointment. Principal wines: Viña Tobía Tinto Joven; Rosado Joven; Blanco Joven; Tinto Crianza; Blanco Crianza; Tinto Reserva; Alma de Tobía Tinto de Autor; Blanco Fermentado en Barrica; Rosado Fermentado en Barrica

This bodega offers an encouraging picture of the future of Rioja. Óscar Tobía is a young winemaker in a small winery who seems to be working hard to achieve quality wines, particularly with Alma de Tobía, a range which includes a red *vino de autor* and a barrel-fermeneted *rosado*, the like of which we have not seen since Marqués de Riscal changed its *rosado* from *crianza* to *joven*. This is a bodega to watch. Alma de Tobía Tinto Singular (****) has ten per cent Garnacha and five per cent Mazuelo with fourteen months in French oak and offers a very subtle, deep (I used the word "brooding") fruit, rather austere but very well-structured and a similarly austere finish: "should do well".

TORRES LIBRADA

Bodegas Torres Librada, Ctra Corella s/n, Finca Estarijo, 26540 Alfaro, La Rioja. Tel: 941 741 003. Fax: 941 741 003. Email: dang@fer.es. Chief executive: Amadeo Torres Librada. Winemaker: Alicia Torres. Established: 1987. Type: Private company. Own vineyards (ha): 30; Barrels: 350. Visits: contact bodega. Open weekdays: Mon–Fri 9am–1.30pm; 3pm–7pm; Sat 10.30am–1.30pm. Principal wines: Estarijo Joven, Crianza; Torrescudo Crianza, Reserva

A small bodega making wines only from its own small estate: the site of an historic pre-war aerodrome. A very modern winery and generally a reputation for very good wines. The Torrescudo Crianza (***) has ten per cent Graciano and thus a bright, tannic fruit structure; needs bottle-ageing to give of its best.

TORRIQUE

Torrique SL Bodegas, Avda del Ebro s/n, Pol. Ind. El Sequero, 26509 Agoncillo, La Rioja. Website: www.bodegastorrique.com. Email: info@bodegastorrique.com. Chief executive: Beatríz Marquez Algaba. Winemaker: Pilar García del Pino. Established: 2000. Type: SL. Barrels: 100. Principal wines: Campo Alto; Cacharel Viñedos; Castillo de Madroñiz; Castillo de Vineldón; Valdelamillo Joven; Crianza

This is a new (2000) venture by a group with bodegas in Ribera del Duero, La Mancha, and Rueda. The Valdelamillo Crianza (***>****) is classic in style: warmth and spice; very clean, crisp fruit; good length; excellent value. Cacharel Viñedos (***>****) has more concentration and a lot of tannin, but still shows excellent spicy fruit. Castillo de Madroñiz Reserva (***) is in a more old-fashioned style with a whiff of oxidation, but decent power and length.

URBINA

Pedro Benito Urbina, Campillo 33-35, 26214 Cuzcurrita de Río Tirón, La Rioja. Tel: 941 224 272 Fax: 941 224 272. Website: www.urbinavinos.com. Email: urbina@fer.es. Chief executive: Jesús Ángel Benito Urbina. Winemaker: Santiago Benito Sáez. Own vineyards (ha): 70. Barrels: 2,000. Visits: by appointment. Principal wines: Urbina Blanco Joven, Rosado Joven, Tinto Joven, Selección; Crianza, Reserva, Reserva Especial, Gran Reserva

This is a fourth-generation family operation turning out wine in the classic style with one or two surprises at the upper end. They farm using traditional methods, and while not organic, use as little in the way of pesticides and fungicides as possible. The Urbina Crianza (****) is all Tempranillo from twenty-year-old vines with fifteen months in American oak; I wrote "Yes!": real, old-style, strawberries-and-cream Rioja, mature, rich, fulsome, delicious. Gran Reserva (****) has five per cent each of Graciano and Mazuelo and twenty-four months in oak: lovely, aromatic, perfumed nose, spot-on balance of fruit and tannins, delicious length. These wines should be better known.

VINÍCOLA REAL

Bodegas Vinícola Real, Ctra de Nalda Km 9, 26120 Albelda de Iregua, La Rioja. Tel: 941 444 233. Fax: 941 444 233. Website: www.vinicolareal.com. Email: info@vinicolareal.com. Chief executive: Rubén Rodríguez Ruiz. Winemaker: Miguel Ángel Rodriguez. Established: 1990. Type: SL. Own vineyards (ha): 10. Barrels: 900. Sales national: 80%; export: 20%. Top export markets: Switzerland, Puerto Rico, Germany. Visits: by appointment. Open: Mon–Fri 4pm–6pm. Principal wines: Viña los Valles; Cueva del Monge Blanco; 200 Monges; Liturgia

The monkish connection is with the ninth-century Monastery of San Martín, from which illuminated manuscripts have survived. One of them, the Vigilan Codex, reveals that at one point 200 monks (*monges*; the modern Castellano spelling is *monjes*) lived there and, no doubt, grew grapes and made wine. The bodega is very smart and modern and was founded on the principle of low-quantity, high-quality production; the vineyards are partly organic, grapes are manually selected, fermentation is painstaking, and ageing is much longer than the minimum. The bodega complex also has a diningroom, shop, and hotel. The Cueva del Monge Blanco Fermentado en Barrica (****) has twenty per cent Malvasía and five per cent each of Garnacha Blanca and Moscatel, with eighty per cent fermented in new oak, with five months on the lees – something of a departure in terms of complexity and fruit for a white Rioja. Viña los Valles (***>****) is a fully organic red with fifteen per cent each Garnacha and Graciano and fermented in oak *tinas* with nine months in 50/50 French and American oak: lots of soft tannins, good balance, and length; should improve. 200 Monges Reserva (****) has ten per cent Graciano and four per cent Mazuelo from twenty-five-year-old vines in a single ten-hectare vineyard, and twenty-four months in new oak: good, solid fruit and plenty of working tannins, the oak shows through but in balance with the fruit; long on the finish.

Appendix I – Bodegas in Rioja

Any list of bodegas in Rioja is something of a movable feast, as new ones join, some leave, close, amalgamate or change their names. This has been compiled from three sources (some of which disagreed with each other) and is presented as an accurate a "snapshot" of the membership, in the spring of 2004, as is practicable. A very good resource for checking on bodegas' contact details is the Spanish website **http://elmundovino.elmundo.es** – it is not infallible, but is often very useful if a contact does prove to be out of date. Some bodegas named after people list themselves by the first name, other by the surname, so if in doubt please check for both.

TYPES OF BODEGA

Alamacenistas are companies that generally make little or no wine of their own but typically buy new wines after the vintage, and store them. They may subsequently blend their own *cuvées* and put them on the market, or sell the mature wine back into the trade.

Cosecheros are mainly in the business of growing grapes, but many will also make wine of their own, for family use or to sell – "*cosechero*" Rioja is a popular and very cheap option in wine shops and bars in Rioja. There are some 20,000 individual growers in Rioja. Those listed here are registered members of the CRDOCa, but the vast majority are registered with local co-ops or other bodegas, who in turn are members of the CRDOCa.

Crianza bodegas are those that make wine, age it, and put it on to the market. They might or might not own vineyards, and, even if they do, most will also buy grapes or wines from contract suppliers. Most of the famous names in Rioja come into this category.

BUSINESS DESCRIPTIONS

Spanish business are described in a number of ways, and for guidance this is the general nature of each:

C.B. (Comunidad de Bienes) Literally "Community of Goods", this is a partnership business in which the partners (likely to be greater in number than an Empresa and wider than a single family) provide work and/or assets that are jointly used, and the property and profits shared.

Empresas Independent growers are simply listed by the name of the person in charge, typically the head of the family, and will be registered with one or more private bodega(s) or a co-op for the sale of grapes. The next step for this type of business is often to become an S.A.T. (*see* below).

S.A. (Sociedad Anónima) Describes a public limited company (*i.e.* one that is quoted on the stock exchange).

S.A.L. (Sociedad Anónima Laboral) This is a legal status widely used in the food and wine industry in which fifty-one per cent of the shares belong to an unlimited number of employees, otherwise similar to an S.A.

S.A.T. (Sociedad Agricultural de Transformación) Describes a private company, usually family owned, but a formally registered and constituted partnership business.

S.C. (Sociedad Civil) A business based on a private contract between the partners. Where the partners share ownership of property this changes to become a C.B. (*see* above).

S.Co-op (Sociedad Cooperativa) Co-ops have *socios* (members) who jointly own the business that takes all of their grapes. There has been a strong trend in recent years to convert co-ops into limited companies (*see* below) to speed decision-making and centralize marketing and export promotion.

S.L. (Sociedad Limitada) describes a limited company with private shareholders.

BODEGAS

Abadía, S.C., Bodegas
Santiago, 2, 01307 Villabuena, Álava
Tel: 945 609 009
Almacenista

Ábalos Ortega, Julián y Uno
Cerrillo Vervalle, s/n, 26340 San
Asensio, La Rioja
Tel: 941 457 035
Cosechero

Abecia Hornillos, Patrocinio
La Yeca, 01307 Villabuena, Álava
Tel: 945 623 371
Cosechero

Abeica, Bodegas, S.L.
Paraje El Calvario, s/n. 26339 Ábalos,
La Rioja
Tel: 941 308 009 Fax: 941 334 392
Email: abeica@sp-editores.es
Crianza

Abel Mendoza Monge, S.L., Bodegas
Ctra. Peñacerrada, 7, 26338 San
Vicente de la Sonsierra, La Rioja
Tel: 941 308 010 Fax: 941 308 010
Email: jarrarte@datalogia.es
Cosechero

Afersa, S.A., Bodegas
Ctra. Logroño, s/n. 26340 San
Asensio, La Rioja
Tel: 941 457 394 Fax: 941 457 394
Email: afersa@eniac.es
Crianza

AGE, S.A., Bodegas
Barrio de la Estación, s/n, 26360
Fuenmayor, La Rioja
Tel: 941 293 500 Fax: 941 293 501
Email: bodegasage@byb.es
Crianza

Agrícola de Labastida, S.L.
El Olmo, 8, 01330 Labastida, Álava
Tel: 941 331 230 Fax: 941 331 259
Crianza

Aguirre Gómez-Segura, Emérito
Ollanco, s/n, 01308 Lanciego, Álava
Tel: 945 608 006
Cosechero

Aguirre Viteri, Jaime Higinio
Camino del Soto, s/n, 01306 Lapuebla
de Labarca, Álava
Tel: 945 607 148
Cosechero

Ajuarte, S.A., Bodegas
Calvo Sotel:o, 7, 26230 Casalarreina,
La Rioja
Tel: 941 324 638
Crianza

Akutain, Bodegas
La Manzanera, s/n. 26200 Haro,
La Rioja
Tel: 941 302 651 Fax: 943 271 140
Email: bodega_akutain@hotmail.com
Crianza

Alavesas, S.A., Bodegas
Ctra. Elciego, s/n, 01300 Laguardia,
Álava
Tel: 945 600100 Fax: 945 600 031
Crianza
Email: bodega@cofradiasamaniego.com

Albaida, Bodegas
Ctra. De Albarite, Km. 826120 Albelda
de Iregua. La Rioja
Tel: 941 443 048 Fax: 941 443 048
Crianza

Alberto Gutiérrez Andrés, S.L.
Cuevas, 28, 26200 Haro, La Rioja
Tel: 941 310 023 Fax: 941 310 393
Crianza

Alcalde López, S.C.
Mayor, 35, 01306 Lapuebla de
Labarca, Álava
Tel: 945 607 016
Cosechero

Alcalde Muro, Francisco
Ctra. Elciego, s/n, 01306 Lapuebla de
Labarca, Álava
Tel: 945607 057
Cosechero

Aldazábal Echeita, Hnos.
El Tesoro, s/n, 01307 Navaridas, Álava
Tel: 945606-197
Cosechero

Alejandro Grijalba, S.C.
Bodegas, 83, 01306 Lapuebla de
Labarca, Álava
Tel: 945 607 034
Cosechero

Alejos, S.A., Bodegas
Pol. El Sequero - Parcela 27, 26509
Agoncillo, La Rioja
Tel: 941 437 051 Fax: 941 437 077
Email: b.a.alabanza@tel:eline.es
Crianza

Alfredo Lezana, C.B.
Laguardia, 8, 01307 Baños de Ebro,
Álava
Tel: 945 609 224
Cosechero

Alicia Rojas, S.A., Bodegas
Ctra. Nacional 232, km. 376-377.
26513 Ausejo, La Rioja
Tel: 941 430 010 Fax: 941 430 286
Email: info@bodegasaliciarojas.com
Crianza

Allona Dueñas, Daniel
Abajo, s/n, 26224 Torrecilla sobre
Alesanco, La Rioja
Tel: 941 379 213
Cosechero

Alonso González, Carlos
Hospital, 9. 26339 Ábalos, La Rioja
Tel: 941 334 164 Fax: 941 334 164
Crianza

Altanza, S.A., Bodegas
Ctra. N-232, km. 419,5, 26360
Fuenmayor, La Rioja
Tel: 941 450 860 Fax: 941 450 804
Email: altanza@bodegasaltanza.com
Crianza

Amestoy Crespo, Elena y otra
Calvo Sotelo, 30, 01308 Lanciego, Álava
Tel: 945 608 033
Cosechero

Amestoy, S.C., Bodegas
Barrio El Campillar, 01300 Laguardia,
Álava
Tel: 945 621 296
Cosechero

Amézola de la Mora, S.A., Bodegas
Paraje Viña Vieja, s/n. 26359
Toremontalbo, La Rioja
Tel: 941 454 532 Fax: 941 454 537
Email: bodegasamezola@fer.es
Crianza

Amutio Olave, Tomás
Ctra. de Badarán, s/n, 26320 Baños
de Río Tobía, La Rioja
Tel: 941 374 147
Almacenista

Antigua Usanza, S.A., Bodegas
Camino Garugele, 26338 San Vicente
de la Sonsierra, La Rioja
Tel: 941 334 156 Fax: 941 334 156
Email: usanza@prorioja.es
Crianza

Antón Sáenz, Mariano
Ctra. Vitoria, s/n, 01300 Laguardia,
Álava
Tel: 945 600 189
Cosechero

Antoñana Lagos, Hnos.
Las Cuevas, s/n, 01307 Samaniego,
Álava
Cosechero

Apilánez Ruiz y Dos Más, Vicente
Las Vistillas, s/n, 26338 San Vicente
de la Sonsierra, La Rioja
Tel: 941 334 411 Fax: 941 334 411
Crianza

Arabarte, S.L.
Ctra. de Samaniego, s/n, 01307
Villabuena, Álava
Tel: 945 290 002 Fax: 945 290 026
Email: gobea@infonegocio.com
Crianza

Araco, S.A.T.
Ctra. Lapuebla, s/n, 01300 Laguardia,
Álava
Tel: 945 600 209 Fax: 945 600 067
Email: araco@bodegasaraco.com
Crianza

Araico, S.C.
San Torcuato, 4, 01307 Villabuena,
Álava
Tel: 945 623 366
Almacenista

Arnáez Gonzalo, Segundo y B.
Acosta, 17, 26223 Hormilla, La Rioja
Tel: 941 417 734 / 600 489 892
Cosechero

Artoje, S.L., Bodegas
Trav. Magdalena, 5, 26324 Alesanco,
La Rioja
Tel: 941 379 283 Fax: 941 379 283
Crianza

Atucha, Miguel, Bodegas
Barrio de Cantarranas, s/n, 26200
Haro, La Rioja
Tel: 941 312 162 Fax: 944 238 816
Crianza

Ayala Lete e Hijos, Ramón, Bodegas
Real, 2. 26290 Briñas, La Rioja
Tel: 941 312 212 Fax: 941 312 212
Email: rayala@conlared.com
Crianza

Ayesa, S.C.
Ctra. Vitoria, s/n, 01300 Laguardia,
Álava
Tel: 945 600 008
Crianza

Azpillaga Urarte, S.C., Bodegas
Camino Elvillar, s/n, 01308 Lanciego,
Álava
Tel: 945 608 045
Cosechero

Bagordi, S.L., Bodegas
Ctra. Estel:la, km., 33, 31261
Andosilla, Navarra
Tel: 948 674 860 Fax: 948 674 238
Email: info@bagordi.com
Crianza

Baigorri Juarrero, María Dolores
Mayor, 17, 01307 Villabuena, Álava
Tel: 945 609 053 Fax: 945 271 212
Almacenista

Baigorri, S.A., Bodegas
Camino de Baños, 13, 01307
Villabuena, Álava
Tel: 945 141 116
Email: amalur@amalurviajes.com
Crianza

Baños Bezares, S.L., Bodegas
Solana, 20. 26290 Briñas, La Rioja
Tel: 941 312 423 Fax: 945 247 178
Crianza

Bargondía y otro, Ángel
Ctra. Ollauri, 35. 26223 Hormilla,
La Rioja
Tel: 941 417 814
Almacenista

Barón de Ley, S.A., Bodegas
Ctra. De Mendavia-Lodosa, km. 5,
31587 Mendavía, Navarra
Tel: 948 694 303 Fax: 948 694 304
Email: info@barondeley.com
Crianza

Basoco Basoco, José
Mayor, 25, 01330 Labastida, Álava
Tel: 941 331 619
Email: j.basoco@euskalnet.net
Cosechero

Basoco Ramírez de la Piscina, G.
Herrerías, 47, 01307 Villabuena, Álava
Tel: 945 609 092
Cosechero

Bauza, S.C., Bodegas
Tendedero, s/n, 01340 Elciego, Álava
Tel: 945 606 216
Email: bodegasbauza@vodafone.es
Crianza

Bello Berganzo, S.C., Herederos
Matadero Arriba, s/n, 01307
Samaniego, Álava
Tel: 945 623 327
Cosechero

Bello Sáez, Marino
Matarredo, 27, 01307 Samaniego,
Álava
Tel: 945 609 257
Cosechero

Benés Manzanares y otro, Ángel
Valdecañas, 22, 26311 Cordovín,
La Rioja
Tel: 941 367 024 Fax: 941 367 024
Cosechero

Benetakoa, S.C.
Carretera Samaniego, 01307
Villabuena, Álava
Tel: 945 609 098
Email: contacta@benetakoa.com
Crianza

Benigno Basoco, S.C., Bodegas
Herrerías, 31, 01307 Villabuena, Álava
Tel: 945 609 142
Almacenista

Benito Urbina, Pedro
Campillo, 33 35, 26214 Cuzcurrita de
Río Tirón, La Rioja
Tel: 941 224 272 Fax: 941 224 272
Email: urbina@fer.es
Crianza

Berberana, S.A., Bodegas
Ctra. Elciego, s/n, 26350 Cenicero,
La Rioja
Tel: 941 453 100 Fax: 941 453 114
Email: info@berberana.com
Crianza

Berceo, S.A., Bodegas
Cuevas, 32, 26200 Haro, La Rioja
Tel: 941 310 744 Fax: 941 304 313
Email: administracion@gurpegui.com
Crianza

Beronia, Bodegas
Ctra. Ollauri-Nájera, Km 1.8, 26220
Ollauri, La Rioja
Tel: 941 338 000 Fax: 941 338 266
Email: beronia@beronia.es
Crianza

Berrueco Pérez, J.A. y E.
Herrería Travesía, 2, 01307
Villabuena, Álava
Tel: 945 609 034
Crianza

Berzal Fernández, Luis María
y 4 más, S.C.
Las Bodegas, s/n, 01307 Baños de
Ebro, Álava
Tel: 945 609 135
Cosechero

Berzal Fernández, Luis María y Luciano
Avda. del Puente, 31, 01307 Baños
de Ebro, Álava
Tel: 945 609 051
Cosechero

Berzal Martínez, Antonio
Ctra. Villabuena, 40, 01307 Baños de
Ebro, Álava
Tel: 945 609 211
Cosechero

Berzal Muñoz, S.C.
Avda. del Río Ebro, 30, 01307 Baños
de Ebro, Álava
Tel: 945 609 310
Cosechero

Berzal Otero, S.C., Bodegas
Avda. Puente Río Ebro, 29, 01307
Baños de Ebro, Álava
Tel: 945 609 037
Cosechero

Besa Iradier, S.C., Bodegas
San Torcuato, 6, 01307 Villabuena,
Álava
Tel: 945 609 125
Cosechero

Besa Maestresala, S.C., Bodegas
La Colina, 7, 01307 Villabuena,
Álava
Tel: 945 609 009
Almacenista

Besa Ruiz, Javier
Ctra. de Baños, s/n, 01307 Villabuena,
Álava
Tel: 945 609 093/123 324
Crianza

Bezares Angulo, Hnos.
Suso, 16. 26290 Briñas, La Rioja
Tel: 941 312 251 Fax: 941 312 251
Cosechero

Bilbaínas, S.A., Bodegas
Estación, 3, 26200 Haro, La Rioja
Tel: 941 310 147 Fax: 941 310 706
Email: boharo@codorniu.es
Crianza

Biurko Gorri, S.A.L.
Las Cruces, s/n, 31229 Bargota,
Navarra
Tel: 948 648 370 Fax: 948 648 370
Crianza

Blanco Martínez de Osaba, Jesús
Calvo Sotel:o, s/n, 01308 Lanciego,
Álava
Tel: 945 608 132
Almacenista

Blanco Pascual, Roberto
Las Cuevas, 13 15, 01307 Baños
de Ebro, Álava
Tel: 945 609 287
Cosechero

Bodegas y Bebidas Grandes Vinos, S.L.U.
Apartado 131, 26080 Logroño, La
Rioja
Tel: 941 279 900 Fax: 941 279 901
Email: campoviejo@byb.es
Crianza

Bretón Criadores, S.L., Bodegas
Ctra. de Fuenmayor Km 1,5, 26370
Navarrete, La Rioja
Tel: 941 440 840 Fax: 941 440 812
Email: info@bodegasbreton.com
Crianza

Burgo Viejo, Bodegas
Concordia, 8, 26540 Alfaro, La Rioja
Tel: 941 183 405 Fax: 941 181 603
Email: bodegas@burgoviejo.com
Crianza

Cadarso Ciordia, S.L., Bodegas
Mayor, s/n, 31239 Aras, Navarra
Tel: 948 644 040
Crianza

Calleja Guzmán, Guillermo
Extramuros Norte, 10, 01340 Elciego,
Álava
Tel: 945 606 190
Cosechero

Calleja Heredia, S.C., David y E.
El Pago, 1, 01308 Lanciego, Álava
Tel: 945 128 224
Cosechero

Campanile, S.L.
Barrihuelo, 73, 01340 Elciego, Álava
Tel: 944 630 938 Fax: 944 630 938
Email: diez-caballero@terra.es
Crianza

Campillo, S.L., Bodegas
Finca Villa Lucía, 01300 Laguardia,
Álava
Tel: 945 600 826 Fax: 945 600 837
Email:miguelangel@
        bodegascampillo.es
Crianza

Campinun Calleja, Juan Antonio
Avda. de Navarra, 2 2° B, 01322
Yécora, Álava
Tel: 941 259 627
Cosechero

Cañas Estebas, Lorenzo
Camino Redajales, s/n. 26311
Cordovín, La Rioja
Tel: 941 367 237
Cosechero

Cándido Besa, S.C., Bodegas
Herrerías, 27, 01307 Villabuena, Álava
Tel: 945 609 149/609 089
Almacenista

Cantera Corcuera, Javier
San Felipe Abad, 7. 26223 Azofra,
La Rioja
Tel: 941 379 019 Fax: 941 231 515
Almacenista

Capellán, Bodegas
Ctra. De Haro, 20. 26223 Hormilla,
La Rioja
Tel: 941 417 709
Almacenista

Cardema, S.L., Bodegas
Las Huertas, 7. 26360 Fuenmayor,
La Rioja
Tel: 941 451 083 Fax: 941 451 083
Email: cardema@arsys.net
Cosechero

Carlos Serres, S.A., Bodegas
Avda. Sto. Domingo, 40, 26200 Haro,
La Rioja
Tel: 941 310 279 Fax: 941 310 418
Email: info@carlosserres.com
Crianza

Casa Juan, S.A., Bodegas
Sancho Abarca, 22, 01300 Laguardia,
Álava
Tel: 945 606 525 Fax: 945 606 526
Email: info@bodegas-casajuan.com
Crianza

Casado Manzanos, Luis A.
Ctra. Elciego, s/n, 01306 Lapuebla de
Labarca, Álava
Tel: 945 607 133 Fax: 945 627 256
Email: lacasado@dieznet.com
Crianza

Casado Morales, S.C., Bodegas
Avda. de la Póveda, 12 14, 01306
Lapuebla de Labarca, Álava
Tel: 945 607 017 Fax: 945 607 017
Email: bcasado@euskalnet.net
Crianza

Castillo Alonso, Bodegas
Bajada del Valle, 29. 26330 Briones,
La Rioja
Tel: 941 322 018 Fax: 941 322 018
Email: orizabal@wanadoo.es
Crianza

Castillo de Cuzcurrita, S.A.
Del Puente, 26214 Cuzcurrita de Río
Tirón, La Rioja
Tel: 941 301 620   Fax: 944 151 071
Crianza

Castillo de Fuenmayor, S.A., Bodegas
Ctra. N-232, km. 13, 26360
Fuenmayor, La Rioja
Tel: 941 450 387   Fax: 941 451 005
Email: administracion@
          castillodefuenmayor.com
Crianza

Castillo de Mendoza, S.L.
Juan XXIII, 20, 26338 San Vicente de
la Sonsierra, La Rioja
Tel: 941 334 496   Fax: 941 334 496
Crianza

Castillo Pérez, Domingo
Horno, 13, 26330 Briones, La Rioja
Tel: 941 322 018
Cosechero

Castresana, S.L., Bodegas
Cmno. el Calvario, s/n. 26211 Tirgo,
La Rioja
Tel: 941 301 684   Fax: 941 301 588
Email: bodegascastresana@
          bodegascastresana.com
Crianza

Cialu, Bodegas
Avda. La Rioja, 50. 26321 Bobadilla,
La Rioja
Tel: 941 374 224   Fax:941 374 224
Crianza

Cicerón, Bodegas
Avda. Juan Carlos I, 8. 26559
Aldeanueva de Ebro. La Rioja
Tel: 679 963 474   Fax: 941 163 159
Crianza

Ciego del Rey S.L, Bodegas
Mayor 5. 26540 Alfaro, La Rioja
Tel: 941 180 988   Fax: 941 180 988
Crianza

Cidacos, S.L., Bodegas El
Ctra. Carbonera, s/n, 26512 Tudelilla,
La Rioja
Tel: 941 152 058   Fax: 941 152 303
Email: bodegaselcidacos@tel:efonica.net
Crianza

Coca Amelibia, Monserrat
Páganos, 18, 01300 Laguardia, Álava
Tel: 945 600 197
Cosechero

Comercializadora La Rioja Alta, S.L.U.
Ctra. de Haro, km. 2.6, 01330
Labastida, Álava
Tel: 941 310 346   Fax: 941 312 854
Email: riojalta@jet.es
Crianza

Comunidad Autónoma de La Rioja - "La Grajera"
Av. de Burgos, km. 6, 26071 Logroño,
LA RIOJA
Tel: 941 291 364
Fax: 941 291 723
Email: gestion.medios@larioja.org
Crianza

Consejo de La Alta, S.A.
Avda. de Fuenmayor, s/n, 26350
Cenicero, La Rioja
Tel: 941 455 005   Fax: 941 455 010
Email: comercial@consejodelaalta.com
Crianza

Córdoba Grijalba, Pedro
Ctra. Elciego, 36, 01306 Lapuebla de
Labarca, Álava
Tel: 945 607 065
Cosechero

Córdoba Medrano, S.C.
Plaza el Plano, 51º, 01306 Lapuebla
de Labarca, Álava
Tel: 945 627 212 Fax: 945 606 325
Cosechero

Córdoba Velilla, Ernesto
Bodegas, 39, 01306 Lapuebla de
Labarca, Álava
Tel: 945 607 097
Cosechero

Corral, S.A., Bodegas
Ctra. N-120, km. 10, 26370
Navarrete, La Rioja
Tel: 941 440 193 Fax: 941 440 195
Email: info@donjacobo.es
Crianza

Corres Orive, Santiago
Pecho las Cuevas, s/n, 26340 San
Asensio, La Rioja
Tel: 941 457 226
Cosechero

Cosecheros Alaveses, S.A.
Ctra. de Logroño, s/n, 01300
Laguardia, Álava
Tel: 945 600 119 Fax: 945 600 850
Email: info@artadi.com
Crianza

Cosecheros de Tudelilla, S.A.T.
Camino del Prado, s/n. 26512
Tudelilla, La Rioja
Tel: 941 152 131 Fax: 941 152 047
Cosechero

Coto de Rioja, S.A., El
Camino Viejo de Logroño, 01320
Oyón, Álava
Tel: 945 622 216 Fax: 945 622 315
Email: cotorioja@elcoto.com
Crianza

Criadores de Rioja, S.A.U
Ctra. De Clavijo, s/n. 26141 Alberite,
La Rioja
Tel: 941 436 702 Fax: 941 436 430
Email: info@criadoresderioja.com
Crianza

C.O.V.I.A.L.
Santa Engracia, 25, 01300 Laguardia,
Álava
Tel: 945 600 263/600 225
Almacenista

Covilda, S.C.L., Bodegas
Ctra. Logroño, s/n. 26340 San
Asensio. La Rioja
Tel: 941 457 133 Fax: 941 457 133
Email: covilda@tel:eline.es
Crianza

Cuna de Reyes
Ctra. Uruñuela, s/n. 26300 Nájera.
La Rioja
Tel: 941 228 608 Fax: 941 206-287
Email: gruasgarte@fer.es
Crianza

C.V.N.E.
Barrio de la Estación, s/n, 26200
Haro, La Rioja
Tel: 941 304 800 Fax: 941 304 815
Email: haro@cvne.com
Crianza

C.V.N.E. Viña Real
Ctra. Logroño Laguardia km 4.8,
01300 Laguardia
Tel: 945 625 210
Crianza

Darien, S.L., Bodegas y Viñedos
Avda. Mendavia, 29, 26006 Logroño,
La Rioja
Tel: 941 258 130 Fax: 941 270 352
Email: info@darien.es
Crianza

Davalillo, S. Coop. Ltda., Vinícola
Ctra. N-232, 26340 San Asensio,
La Rioja
Tel: 941 457 133 Fax: 941 457 133
Crianza

Dehesa de Zeledas, Bodegas
Ctra. Piqueras, 34. 26130 Ribafrecha.
La Rioja
Tel: 941 434 114 / 615 248 217
Email: dehesadezaladas@terra.es
Cosechero

Dinastía Vivanco, S.A., Bodegas
Ctra. Nacional, 232, km. 197,3.
26330 Briones, La Rioja
Tel: 941 322 332 Fax: 941 322 316
Email: infobodega@dinastiavivanco.es
Crianza

Domecq, S.A., Bodegas
Ctra. Villabuena, 01340 Elciego, Álava
Tel: 945 606 001 Fax: 945 606 235
Email: rioja@domecq.es
Crianza

Domínguez Fernández, Eduardo C.
San Marcelo, 8, 26290 Briñas,
La Rioja
Tel: 941 312 226 Fax: 941 312 226
Crianza

Dominio de Nobleza, S.L.
Bodegas San Cristóbal, 79. 26360
Fuenmayor. La Rioja
Tel: 941 450 507 Fax: 941 450 187
Email: bodegas@dominiodenobleza.com
Crianza

Dunviro, S. Coop., Bodegas
Ctra. de Logroño, km. 362,8. 26500
Calahorra, La Rioja
Tel: 941 148 161 Fax: 941 130 626
Email: bodegasdunviro@hotmail.com
Crianza

D. Mateos, S.L., Bodegas
Camino los Agudos, s/n. 26559
Aldeanueva de Ebro, La Rioja
Tel: 941 163 174 Fax: 941 163 174
Email: bodegasdmateos@hotmail.com
Crianza

Echave Román, S.C.
La Horca, 01330 Labastida, Álava
Tel: 945 144 884 Fax: 945 145 073
Cosechero

Eduardo Garrido, S.L., Bodegas
Plaza de la Constitución, 26339
Ábalos, La Rioja
Tel: 941 334 187 Fax: 941 334 010
Crianza

El Arca de Noe, Bodega Cooperativa
Víctor Cardenal s/n, 26340 San
Asensio, La Rioja
Tel: 941 457 231 Fax: 941 457 000
Email: arcadenoe@eresmas.com
Crianza

El Fabulista, S.L., Bodegas
Plaza de San Juan, s/n, 01300
Laguardia, Álava
Tel: 945 621 192
Email: bfabulista@dieznet.com
Almacenista

Ctra. de Cenicero, 26313 Uruñuela, La
Rioja
Tel: 941 371 319 Fax: 941 371 435
Email: info@bodegaspatrocinio.es
Crianza

El Robredal
Finca El Montecillo, s/n. 26360
Fuenmayor. La Rioja
Tel: 941 450 270 Fax: 941 450 270
Email: montecillo@fer.es
Crianza

El Roble, S.C., Bodegas
San Roque, 40, 01307 Villabuena,
Álava
Tel: 945 287 412
Almacenista

El Trujal
Avda. La Rioja, 28, 26340 San
Asensio, La Rioja
Tel: 941 457 536 Fax: 941 457 536
Cosechero

Escribano Pascual, Antonio
Matarredo Abajo, 6, 01307
Samaniego, Álava
Tel: 945 623 331
Crianza

Escudero, S.A., Bodegas
Ctra. de Arnedo, s/n, 26587 Grávalos,
La Rioja
Tel: 941 398 008 Fax: 941 398 070
Email: escudero@prorioja.es
Crianza

Eskuernak, S.A.T.
La Lleca, 26, 01307 Villabuena, Álava
Tel: 945 623 301/609 043
Almacenista

**Espada Grijalba, José Esteban
y 2 Más, SC.**
Bodegas, 7, 01306 Lapuebla de
Labarca, Álava
Tel: 945 607 059/607 122
Almacenista

Espada Ojeda, S.C.
Tejerías, s/n, 01306 Lapuebla de
Labarca, Álava
Tel: 945 627 349
Cosechero

Estebas Cañas, Abel
Ctra. Badarán, 38, 26311 Cordovín,
La Rioja
Tel: 941 347 064
Cosechero

Estebas Manzanares, Rodolfo
La Ermita, 31, 26311 Cordovín,
La Rioja
Tel: 941 367 386
Cosechero

Estraunza, S.A., Bodegas
Avda. la Póveda, s/n, 01306 Lapuebla
de Labarca, Álava
Tel: 945 627 245 Fax: 945 627 293
Crianza

Explotaciones Agrovinícolas Riojanas, S.L
Zumalacárregui, 48, 26338 San
Vicente de la Sonsierra, La Rioja
Tel: 941 334 331
Crianza

Explotaciones Vitivinícolas, S.L.
F. Río Hondillo Ctra. De Logroño, s/nº,
01300 Laguardia, Álava
Tel: 945 606 525 Fax: 945 606 526
Crianza

Exportaciones Heredad de Aduna, S.L.
del Medio, 35, 01307 Samaniego,
Álava
Tel: 945 623 343
Almacenista

Ezquerra Ocio, Alicia
La Lombilla, 01307 Leza, Álava
Tel: 945 605 008
Cosechero

Faustino, S.L., Bodegas
Ctra. Logroño, 01320 Oyón, Álava
Tel: 945 622 500
Fax: 945 622 106/601 489
Email: info@bodegasfaustino.es
Crianza

Faustino Rivero Ulecia, S.L.
Pol. Raposal, parcela 23, 26580
Arnedo, La Rioja
Tel: 941 385 072 Fax: 941 382 255
Email: rosa@faustinorivero.net
Crianza

Federico Paternina, S.A.
Avda. Santo Domingo, 11, 26200
Haro, La Rioja
Tel: 941 310 550 Fax: 941 312 778
Email: paternina@paternina.com
Crianza

Fernández Calleja, S.C.
Avda. Diputación, 30, 01309
Navaridas, Álava
Tel: 945 605 056
Cosechero

Fernández de Manzanos, S.L., Bodegas y Viñedos
Ctra. San Adrián-Azagra Km 47,
31560 Azagra, Navarra
Tel: 948 692 500 Fax: 948 692 500
Email: info@bodegasfernandez
        demanzanos.com
Crianza

Fernández de Piérola, S.L., Bodegas
Ctra. de Logroño, s/n. Finca El Somo,
01314 Moreda, Álava
Tel: 945 622 480 Fax: 945 622 489
Email: bodegas@pierola.com
Crianza

Fernández Eguiluz, S.L., Bodegas
Los Morales, 7 bajo, 26339 Ábalos,
La Rioja
Tel: 941 334 166 Fax: 941 308 055
Email: p.larosa@terra.es
Cosechero

Fernández Fernández, Federico Luís
Ctra. Ollauri, 26223 Hormilla, La Rioja
Tel: 941 417 722
Cosechero

Fernández Gasco, Florentino
Camino Sto. Domingo, 27, 26340 San
Asensio, La Rioja
Tel: 941 457 173 Fax: 941 457 172
Crianza

Fernández Manero, Gerardo
Camino de Valdeloshilos, s/n. 26223
Hormilla, La Rioja
Tel: 941 417 871
Cosechero

Fernández Medrano, Balbino
La Póveda, 01306 Lapuebla de
Labarca, Álava
Tel: 945 607 018 Fax: 945 607 018
Crianza

Fernández Muñoz, Ignacio
Mayor, 26, 01307 Baños de Ebro,
Álava
Tel: 945 623 383
Cosechero

Fernández Rivera, S.C.
Mayor, 44, 01307 Villabuena, Álava
Tel: 945 609 171
Cosechero

Fernando Remírez de Ganuza, S.A., Bodegas
La Constitución, s/n, 01307
Samaniego, Álava
Tel: 945 609 022 Fax: 945 623 335
Crianza

Fernández Sobrón
Pol. Industrial Buicio - Parcela 18.
26360 Fuenmayor. La Rioja
Tel: 941 435 231 Fax: 941 435 231
Email: enriquerioja@vodafone.es
Crianza

Fin de Siglo, S.L., Bodegas
Camino de Arenzana de Arriba, 16.
26311 Arenzana de Abajo, La Rioja
Tel: 941 410 042 Fax: 941 440 043
Email: bfs@bodegasfindesiglo.com
Crianza

Finca Allende, S.L.
Plaza Ibarra, 1, 26330 Briones,
La Rioja
Tel: 941 322 301 Fax: 941 322 302
Email: sales@finca-allende.com
Crianza

Finca Valpiedra, S.L.
Termino Montecillo, s/n. 26360
Fuenmayor, La Rioja
Tel: 941 450 876 Fax: 941 450 875
Email: info@fincavalpiedra.com
Crianza

Florentino de Lecanda, S.A.
Las Cuevas, 36 Apartado 68, 26200
Haro, La Rioja
Tel: 941 303 477 Fax: 941 312 707
Email: florentinodelecanda@fer.es
Crianza

Fortuño Gil, Francisco
La Lleca, 3, 01307 Villabuena, Álava
Tel: 945 609 150
Cosechero

Francés Moreno, José Luis
Ctra. Zaragoza, 6, 26513 Ausejo, La
Rioja
Tel: 941 430 039
Cosechero

Franco Españolas, S.A., Bodegas
Cabo Noval, 2, 26006 Logroño, La
Rioja
Tel: 941 251 300 Fax: 941 262 948
Email: comercial@
    francoespanolas.com
Crianza

**Francisco García Ramírez e Hijos, S.L.,
Bodega**
Ctra. Ventas, s/n. 26143 Murillo de
Río Leza. La Rioja
Tel: 941 432 372 Fax: 941 432 156
Crianza

Fuenmayor, S.A., Bodegas
Pol. Industrial Buicio - Parcela 56.
26360 Fuenmayor, La Rioja
Tel: 941 450 935 Fax: 941 450 936
Email: bodegasfuenmayor@
    bodegasfuenmayor.com
Crianza

Fuente Rubia S.L., Bodegas y Viñedos
Pol. El Roturo, s/n. 26511 El Villar de
Arnedo. La Rioja
Tel: 618 712 267 Fax: 941 159 107
Cosechero

Gailur, S.L., Bodegas
Avda. Puente del Río Ebro, 76, 01307
Baños de Ebro, Álava
Tel: 943 830 386 Fax: 943 835 952
Email: bodegasgailur@euskalnet.net
Crianza

Galar Rubio, S.C.
San Juan, 36, 01308 Cripán, Álava
Tel: 945 608 109
Cosechero

Galarza, S.C.
Las Bodegas, s/n, 01307 Leza, Álava
Tel: 945 605 004
Almacenista

Gallurralde Córdoba/Martion, S.C.
El Soto, s/n, 01306 Lapuebla de
Labarca, Álava
Tel: 945 607 167
Cosechero

García Berrueco, Juan José
La Lleca, 37, 01307 Villabuena, Álava
Tel: 945 609 119
Cosechero

García Chavarri, Amador
Ctra. De Villabuena, s/n, 01307
Baños de Ebro, Álava
Tel: 945 623 322/945 290 385
Almacenista

García Crespo, S.C., Bodegas
Calvo Sotel:o, 17 A, 01308 Lanciego,
Álava
Tel: 945 608 127
Email: direccion.lan@fer.es
Cosechero

García de Olano, S.C., Bodegas
Ctra. Laguardia-Vitoria, 01300
Laguardia, Álava
Tel: 945 621 146 Fax: 945 621 146
Crianza

García Hernando, Alfonso, Bodegas
Víctor Cardenal, 63, 26340 San
Asensio, La Rioja
Tel: 941 457 488 Fax: 941 457 488
Cosechero

García Martel:o, Rodolfo
Cmno. Los Olivares, Pol. 2 Parc. 183,
01309 Navaridas, Álava
Tel: 945 605 036 Fax: 945 605 036
Crianza

García-Olano Ruiz-Ocenda, César
Santa Engracia, 36, 01300 Laguardia,
Álava
Tel: 945 600 232
Cosechero

**García Ramírez de la Piscina,
Socorro y Hnos.**
Barco, 2, 01340 Elciego, Álava
Tel: 945 606 070
Cosechero

García y dos más, Ricardo
Camino de Haro, s/n, 26223 Hormilla,
La Rioja
Tel: 639 322 934
Almacenista

Garrido Alcalde, Pablo
Bodegas, 101, 01306 Lapuebla de
Labarca, Álava
Tel: 945 607 069
Cosechero

Garrido Medrano, S.C.
Travesía. de Assa, 2, 01306 Lapuebla
de Labarca, Álava
Tel: 945 607 138
Almacenista

Gartedamar, S.A.
Ctra. de Assa, s/n, 01309 Elvillar de
Álava, Álava
Tel: 945 604 093
Cosechero

Gil Cue, José Antonio
San Roque, 01307 Villabuena, Álava
Tel: 945 609 021
Cosechero

Gil Varela, José A. y Dos Más
Buenavista, 95, 26338 San Vicente de
la Sonsierra, La Rioja
Tel: 941 334 471
Cosechero

Gómez Cruzado, S.A., Bodegas y Viñedos
Avda. de Vizcaya, 6, 26200 Haro,
La Rioja
Tel: 941 312 502 Fax: 941 303 567
Email: gcruzado@infonegocio.com
Crianza

Gómez de Segura Ibáñez, S.L., Bodegas
Barrio El Campillar, 7, 01300
Laguardia, Álava
Tel: 945 600 227 Fax: 945 600 227
Crianza

Gómez Montoya, Delicias
Polígono 2 - Parcela 299, 01306
Lapuebla de Labarca, Álava
Tel: 945 134 554
Cosechero

Esteban González, Bodegas
Los Carros, 34, 26340 San Asensio,
La Rioja
Tel: 687 936 272 Fax: 947 336 272
Email: gonzalezpuras@terra.es
Almacenista

González Fernández, Juan María
Plaza Don Ramón, 51, 01307
Navaridas, Álava
Tel: 941 457 513
Cosechero

González Mendieta, Jorge
Curillos, s/n, 01308 Lanciego, Álava
Tel: 945 608 037
Cosechero

Gorra, S.L.
Barranco San Roque, s/n, 01307
Villabuena, Álava
Tel: 946 824 108   Fax: 946 824 108
Crianza

Granja Ntra. Sra. Remelluri, S.A.
Ctra. Rivas de Tereso, s/n, 01330
Labastida, Álava
Tel: 945 331 801   Fax: 945 331 802
Email: remellur@sea.es
Crianza

Gregorio Martínez, S.L., Bodegas
La Dehesa Polígono 1 - Parcela 12,
26190 Nalda, La Rioja
Tel: 941 220 226   Fax: 941 203 849
Email: cc112682@cconline.es
Crianza

Grijalba Medrano, S.C.
Avda. de la Póveda, 37, 01306
Lapuebla de Labarca, Álava
Tel: 945 607 120
Cosechero

Guía Real, S.A., Bodegas
Ctra. N-232, Km. 13. 26360
Fuenmayor. La Rioja
Tel: 941 450 387   Fax: 941 451 005
Crianza

Guridi Galarraga, José Ignacio
Ctra. Navaridas, s/n, 01300 Laguardia,
Álava
Tel: 943 815 608
Almacenista

Gutiérrez Ezquerra, José Ramón
El Horno, 1, 01307 Leza, Álava
Tel: 945 605 152
Cosechero

Guzmán Aldazábal, Javier
Madrid, s/n, 01307 Navaridas, Álava
Tel: 945 605 172   Fax: 945 600 255
Crianza

Hacienda Grimón, S.L.
Gallera, 6, 26131 Lagunilla de Jubera,
La Rioja
Tel: 629 787 525   Fax: 941 482 184
Crianza

Heras Cordón, S.L., Bodegas y Viñedos
Ctra. Lapuelba, Km. 2 - Apdo. 29.
26360 Fuenmayor, La Rioja
Tel: 941 451 413   Fax: 941 450 265
Email: bodegas@herascordon.com
Crianza

Heredad de Aduna, S.L., Bodegas
Matarredo, 39, 01307 Samaniego,
Álava
Tel: 945 623 343   Fax: 945 623 343
Crianza

Heredad de Baroja, S.A., Bodegas
Cercas Altas, 6, 01309 Elvillar de
Álava, Álava
Tel: 945 604 068   Fax: 945 604 105
Crianza

Heredad de Don Tomás, S.L.
Calvo Sotel:o, 21, 01308 Lanciego,
Álava
Tel: 945 608 150
Crianza

Heredad Linares, S.L.
Camino Escobosa, s/n. 26360 El
Cortijo (Logroño), La Rioja
Tel: 941 450 042   Fax: 941 450 042
Email: heredadlinares@terra.es
Cosechero

Heredad Martínez Laorden, S.L., Bodegas
Ctra. Huércanos, s/n. 26350 Cenicero,
La Rioja
Tel: 941 454 446 Fax: 941 454 766
Email: bmlrioja@eniac.es
Almacenista

Heredad Pangua Sodupe, S.C.
Camino Santo Domingo, s/n. 26340
San Asensio, La Rioja
Tel: 941 457 609 Fax: 941 457 609
Email: heredadpanguasodupe@
wanadoo.es
Crianza

Heredad Ugarte, S.A.
Crtra. Logroño-Vitoria km 69, 01300
Laguardia, Álava
Tel: 945 282 844 Fax: 945 271 319
Email: info@heredadugarte.com
Crianza

Herencia Fontemayore, S.L.
Ctra. La Estación, Km. 1,5. 26360
Fuenmayor, La Rioja
Tel: 629 108 806
Almacenista

Hermanos Alonso Pangua
Prado, s/n, 26338 San Vicente de la
Sonsierra, La Rioja
Tel: 945 260 413
Almacenista

Hermanos Antón García, S.C.
Rua Mayor de Peralta, 4, 01300
Laguardia, Álava
Tel: 945 600 026
Cosechero

Hermanos Berzal Troncoso, S.L.
Avda. Puente del Ebro, 34, 01307
Baños de Ebro, Álava
Tel: 945 609 039
Email: dominioberzal@euskalnet.net
Crianza

Hermanos Blanco Gasco, S.L., Bodegas
Cerrillo Verballe, s/n, 26340 San
Asensio, La Rioja
Tel: 941 249 792
Cosechero

Hermanos Calahorra Medrano, C.B.
García Brieva, 23, 26529 Cabreton de
Cervera, La Rioja
Tel: 941 198 574
Cosechero

Hermanos Fernández, S.C.
Plaza Nueva, 3, 01309 Laserna-
Laguardia, Álava
Tel: 945 621 103
Cosechero

Hermanos Frías del Val, S.L.
Herrerías, 13, 01307 Villabuena, Álava
Tel: 945 609 172
Cosechero

Hermanos Laredo Villanueva, C.B., Bodegas
Mayor, 18, 01307 Leza, Álava
Tel: 945 605 178 Fax: 945 605 178
Crianza

Hermanos Marín Palacios, S.C., Bodegas
San Torcuato, 5, 01307 Villabuena,
Álava
Tel: 945 609 045
Almacenista

Hermanos Otero Muñoz, S.C., Bodegas
Plaza de la Constitución, 16, 01307
Baños de Ebro, Álava
Tel: 945 609 134 Fax: 945 609 134
Crianza

Hermanos Pascual Miguel, S.C.
Las Cuevas, 3, 01307 Baños de Ebro,
Álava
Tel: 945 609 195
Cosechero

Hermanos Peciña, S.L., Bodegas
General Mola, 5. 26338 San Vicente
de la Sonsierra, La Rioja
Tel: 941 334 366 Fax: 941 334 180
Email: hermanospecina@wanadoo.es
Crianza

Hermanos Pérez Baigorri, S.C., y M.Pz. S
Camino de Baños, s/n, 01307
Villabuena, Álava
Tel: 945 609 256
Cosechero

Hermedaña, S. Coop., Bodega
Ctra. Navarrete, s/n. 26375 Entrena.
La Rioja
Tel: 941 446 512 Fax: 941 446 513
Email: bhermedana@terra.es
Crianza

Hermosilla, S.L., Bodegas
Las Piscinas, s/n, 01307 Baños de
Ebro, Álava
Tel: 945 609 162
Crianza

Herrera Besa, María Dolores
La Lleca, 17, 01307 Villabuena, Álava
Tel: 945 609 069
Cosechero

Hostaler I, S.L.
Ctra. Garray, km. 73, 26580 Arnedo,
La Rioja
Tel: 941 380 057 Fax: 941 380 156
Crianza

Hrdros. de Ramón Pardo Simón
La Yeca, s/n, 01307 Villabuena, Álava
Tel: 945 609 005
Cosechero

Huergo, S.L., Bodegas
Ctra. Burgos, Km. 10, 26370
Navarrete, La Rioja
Tel: 941 441 065 Fax: 941 441 065
Almacenista

Ibaiondo, S.A., Bodegas
Avda. Costa del Vino, 7 y 9, 26200
Haro, La Rioja
Tel: 941 312 162 Fax: 944 238 816
Crianza

Ibáñez Bujanda, S.C., Félix
Mayor, 17, 01306 Lapuebla de
Labarca, Álava
Tel: 945 627 342
Almacenista

Salomón, Bodegas
Camino Real, 17. 26338 San Vicente
de la Sonsierra, La Rioja
Tel: 941 334 342
Cosechero

Ibáñez del Río, Salvador
Camino de las Cuevas, 1. 26311
Cordovín, La Rioja
Tel: 941 418 637
Cosechero

Ibáñez Vázquez, S.C.
San Juan, 10, 01322 Yécora, Álava
Tel: 945 601 028
Cosechero

Idiáquez, S.C., Bodegas
San Vicente, 31, 01307 Baños de
Ebro, Álava
Tel: 941 123 395
Cosechero

Ilurce, S.A.T., Bodegas y Viñedos
Avda. de Logroño, 7, 26540 Alfaro,
La Rioja
Tel: 941 180 829 Fax: 941 183 897
Email: ilurce@fer.es
Almacenista

Interlocal Virgen de la Vega, B.C.
Avda. de Santo Domingo, 42, 26200
Haro, La Rioja
Tel: 941 310 729 Fax: 941 310 729
Email: virgendelavega@fer.es
Crianza

Iñiguez, S.C.
Calvo Sotel:o, 17, 01307 Lanciego,
Álava
Tel: 945 608 013
Cosechero

Interlocal del Najerilla, Sociedad Cooperativa, B.
Ctra. Anguiano, s/n, 26311 Arenaza de
Abajo, La Rioja
Tel: 941 362 783 Fax: 941 410 369
Crianza

Ironda, S.L., Bodegas
Ctra. De Burgos, km. 53, 26370
Navarrete, La Rioja
Tel: 941 440 736 Fax: 941 440 548
Email: bodegas-ironda@terra.es
Crianza

Isidro Milagro, S.L., Bodegas
Ctra. de Corella, s/n, 26540, Alfaro,
La Rioja
Tel: 941 183 044
Almacenista

Jalón Ayala, S.C.
La Plaza, 6, 01311 Yécora, Álava
Tel: 945 601 130
Cosechero

Jelen Rioja, S.A.
Camino de Ventosa, s/n, 26371
Ventosa, La Rioja
Tel: 629 793 861
Email: info@jelenrioja.com
Crianza

J.E.R., S.L., Bodegas
La Planigüela, Pol. 10, Parcela 426,
26314 Huércanos, La Rioja
Tel: 617 328 629 Fax: 941 231 515
Email: info@bodegasjer.es
Crianza

Jon Zamalloa, S.C., Bodega
Camino Los Linares, 7, 01330
Labastida, Álava
Tel: 639 382 671 Fax: 944 575135
Email: jagoba@jet.es
Crianza

José Ma. Sáenz Cosecheros y Criadores, Bodegas
Ctra. LR-123, Km. 61. 26511 El Villar
de Arnedo, La Rioja
Tel: 941 159 034 Fax: 941 159 034
Crianza

Juan Alcorta
Camino de la Puebla, 50. 26006
Logroño, La Rioja
Tel: 941 279 900 Fax: 941 279 901
Email: info@byb.es
Crianza

La Emperatriz, Bodegas
Finca Viña La Emperatriz. 26241
Baños de Rioja, La Rioja
Tel: 941 300 105 Fax: 941 300 231
Email: correo@bodegaslaemperatriz.com
Crianza

La Encina, Bodegas y Viñedos, S.L.
Carretera N-124, km. 45, 26290
Brinas, La Rioja
Tel: 941 305 630 Fax: 941 313 028
Email: reinoso.laencina@eniac.es
Crianza

Laespada Sola, Miguel
Ctra. Vitoria, s/n, 01300 Laguardia,
Álava
Almacenista

Bodegas Lagunilla-Berberana
Ctra. de Vitoria Km 182.5, 26360
Fuenmayor (La Rioja)
Tel: 941 450 100 Fax: 941 453 114
Email: info@lagunilla.com
Crianza

Landaluce, S.C.
Ctra. Vitoria, s/n, 01300 Laguardia,
Álava
Tel: 945 600 774
Cosechero

Lan, S.A., Bodegas
Paraje de Buicio, s/n, 26360
Fuenmayor, La Rioja
Tel: 941 450 950 Fax: 941 450 567
Email: bodegaslan@fer.es
Crianza

**Lapuebla de Labarca, L.T.D., S.Coop.
Vitivinícola**
del Soto, s/n, 01306 Lapuebla de
Labarca, Álava
Tel: 945627 232 Fax: 945627 295
Email: covila@eniac.es
Crianza

Lar de Viñas
Mayor Alta, 9. 26360 Fuenmayor,
La Rioja
Tel: 941 450 177 Fax: 941 287 167
Email: lardevinas@fghispania.com
Crianza

La Reja Dorada, C.B., Bodegas
Rua Vieja, 19. 26001 Logroño.
La Rioja
Tel: 941 236 980 Fax: 941 236 980
Almacenista

Larchago, S.A., Bodegas
Excma. Diputación, s/n, 01306
Lapuebla de Labarca, Álava
Tel: 945231 974 Fax: 945135512
Crianza

Larrea Merino, Miguel Ángel
El Prado, 1, 26310 Badarán, La Rioja
Tel: 941 367 393
Cosechero

Larreina Rodríguez, Eusebio
Trav. Del Castillo, 5, 01306 Lapuebla
de Labarca, Álava
Tel: 945 607 152 Fax: 945 500 541
Email: pontezuela@eresmas.com
Crianza

Las Heras Sánchez, María. V. Blanca
Los Palacios, s/n, 01307 Villabuena,
Álava
Tel: 945 131 503
Cosechero

Las Orcas, S.L., Bodegas
Sancho Abarca, 4, 01300 Laguardia, Álava
Tel: 945 621 124 Fax: 945 621 124
Crianza

Lavalle, S.L., Bodegas
Plazuela San Román, 51, 01307
Navaridas, Álava
Tel: 945 605 032
Cosechero

Lecea, Luis Alberto
Cerillo de Vervalle. 26340 San
Asensio, La Rioja
Tel: 941 457 444 Fax: 941 457 444
Crianza

Leza García, C.B., Bodegas
San Ignacio, 26. 26313 Uruñuela, La
Rioja
Tel: 941 371 142 Fax: 941 371 035
Email: bodegaslezagarcia@wanadoo.es
Crianza

Lheg, S.L., Bodegas
Eras San Cristobal, 50, 26360
Fuenmayor, La Rioja
Tel: 941 450 507 Fax: 941 450 507
Crianza

López Corral, C.B., Bodegas
Barrio Bodegas, 141. 26375 Entrena,
La Rioja
Tel: 941 446 088
Cosechero

López Garcia, Antonio
Polígono 22, Parcela 410, 01300
Laguardia, Álava
Tel: 945 621 178
Cosechero

López de Heredia-Viña Tondonia, S.A., R.
Avda. Vizcaya, 3, 26200 Haro, La
Rioja
Tel: 941 310 244 Fax: 941 310 788
Email: bodega@lopezdeheredia.com
Crianza

López Maestu, Santiago
Pecho de Saturnino 1, 26340 San
Asensio, La Rioja
Tel: 941 457 504/457 057
Cosechero

López Peciña, Fernando
Alto de San Antón, s/n, 26315 Alesón,
La Rioja
Tel: 941 342 419
Almacenista

Los Arlos, S.L., Bodegas
Avda. de la Póveda, 16, 01306
Lapuebla de Labarca, Álava
Tel: 945 607 003
Almacenista

Lozano Martínez, C.B., Hnos.
Ctra. Alescano, s/n. 26311 Cordovín,
La Rioja
Tel: 941 367 283 Fax: 941 367 283
Email: info@bodegaslozano.com
Cosechero

Luberri, S.C., Bodegas
Ctra. Villabuena, 66, 01307 Baños de
Ebro, Álava
Tel: 945 606 034 Fax: 945 606 034
Crianza

Luis Alegre, S.A., Bodegas
Ctra. De Navaridas, s/n, 01300
Laguardia, Álava
Tel: 945 600 089 Fax: 945 600 729
Email: luisalegre@arrakis.es
Crianza

Luis Cañas, S.A., Bodegas
Ctra. De Samaniego, s/n, 01307
Villabuena, Álava
Tel: 945 623 373 Fax: 945609 289
Email: bodegas@luiscanas.com
Crianza

Luis Gurpegui Muga, S.A., Bodegas
Avda. Celso Muerza, 8, 31570 San
Adrián, Navarra
Tel: 948 670 050 Fax: 948 670 259
Email: administracion@gurpegui.com
Crianza

San Pedro, 14, 01309 Elvillar de
Álava, Álava
Tel: 945 604 064 Fax: 945 604 064
Crianza

Luis R., S.C., Bodegas de
Mayor, 2, 01308 Lanciego, Álava
Tel: 945 608 022
Crianza

L. Casado, S.L., Bodegas
Mayor, 22, 01306 Lapuebla de
Labarca, Álava
Tel: 945 607 001 Fax: 945 607 001
Crianza

Madrid Castañeda, Juan Ramón
Páganos, 74, 01300 Laguardia, Álava
Tel: 945 600 296 Fax: 945 621 252
Crianza

Manuel Pérez Artacho, S.L., Bodegas
Ctra. Logroño-Haro, 26350 Cenicero,
La Rioja
Tel: 941 454 693/454 204
Almacenista

Manzanos, S.C., Hermanos
Fernando Salazar, 35. 26222
Rodezno, La Rioja
Tel: 941 338 059
Cosecher

Marañon Medrano, Luis María y Carlos
Ctra. Logroño, km. 8 Par.3 Manz.6 Pl
109, 01300 Laguardia, Álava
Tel: 945 600 028
Almacenista

María-Theresa Eguiluz
San Roque s/n. 26290 Briñas. La
Rioja
Tel: 941 310 952
Crianza

Marín Díez, Luis
Finca La Asomante. 26370 Navarrete,
La Rioja
Tel: 944 630 024 Fax: 944 644 105
Email: matiasmarin@tel:efonica.net
Crianza

Marqués de Campo Nuble, S.L.
Avda. del Ebro, s/n, 26540 Alfaro,
La Rioja
Tel: 941 183 502 Fax: 941 183 157
Email: camponuble@camponuble.com
Crianza

Marqués de Carrión, S.A., Bodegas
Camino de la Estación, s/n, 26330
Briones, La Rioja
Tel: 941 322 246 Fax: 941 301 010
Email: mtejada@jge.es
Crianza

Marqués de Griñón, S.A.
Hacienda de Susar
Avda. del Ebro, s/n, 26540 Alfaro, La
Rioja
Tel: 941 453 100   Fax: 941 453 114
Email: adelgado@haciendas-espana.com
Crianza

Marqués de Mataflorida, Bodegas
Camino de los Vinateros, s/n. 26141
Alberite, La Rioja
Tel: 941 436 729 Fax: 941 436 958
Email: bodegas_marques_mataflorida@
terra.com
Crianza

Marqués de Murrieta, S.A., Bodegas
Finca Ygay Ctra. Zaragoza, km.5
Apartado 109. 26080 Logroño, La Rioja
Tel: 941 271 370 Fax: 941 251 606
Email: rrpp@marquesdemurrieta.com
Crianza

Marqués de Reinosa, S. Coop
Ctra. Rincón de Soto, s/n, 26560
Autol, La Rioja
Tel: 941 742 015 Fax: 941 742 015
Email: bodegas@marquesdereinosa.com
Crianza

**Marqués de Riscal, S.A., Vinos de los
Herederos de**
Torrea, 1, 01340 Elciego, Álava
Tel: 945 606 000 Fax: 945 606 023
Email: riscal@sea.es
Crianza

Marqués de Roansan, S.L., Bod.
Calahorra, 8 B Polígono La Portalada,
26006 Logroño, La Rioja
Tel: 941 233 904
Almacenista

**Marqués de Vargas, S.A., Bodegas y
Viñedos**
Ctra. Zaragoza, km. 6 Pradolagar.
26006 Logroño, La Rioja
Tel: 941 261 401 Fax: 941 238 696
Email: bvargas@jet.es
Crianza

Marqués de Vitoria, S.A., Bodegas
Camino de Santa Lucía, 01320 Oyón
Tel: 945622 134 Fax: 945601 496
Email:info@bodegasmarquesdevitoria.es
Crianza

Marqués del Puerto, S.A., Bodegas
Ctra. Logroño s/n. 26360 Fuenmayor,
La Rioja
Tel: 941 450 001 Fax: 941 450 051
Email: bmp@mbrizard.com
Crianza

Marquesa, S.L., Viñedos y Bodegas de la
Herrería, 76, 01307 Villabuena, Álava
Tel: 945 609 085 Fax: 945 123 304
Email: lamarque@worldonline.es
Crianza

Marquiegui Ayastuy, José Manuel
Ctra. Samaniego, 19 1° dcha., 01307
Villabuena, Álava
Almacenista

Martínez-Cañas Ruiz-Oña, Tomás
La Lleca, s/n, 01307 Villabuena, Álava
Tel: 945 609 186
Cosechero

Martínez Álvarez, Herencia
Victor Romans, 21. 26360 Fuenmayor,
La Rioja
Tel: 941 450 320
Cosechero

Martínez Benito, María Teodora
Dolores S. De Tapia, 90, 01300
Laguardia, Álava
Tel: 945 600 191
Cosechero

Martínez Bobadilla, Bonifacio
Mayor, 20. 26311 Cárdenas, La Rioja
Tel: 941 367 219 Fax: 941 500 005
Email: castillantico@yahoo.es
Cosechero

Martínez Cañas, A./ Berrueco Pérez, L.
San Torcuato, 7, 01307 Villabuena,
Álava
Tel: 945 609 073
Cosechero

Martínez de Ayala, Francisco
José L. Oriol, 46, 01330 Labastida,
Álava
Tel: 941 331 058
Almacenista

Martínez García, S.C.
La Lleca, s/n, 01307 Villabuena, Álava
Tel: 945 609 013
Cosechero

Martínez Guzmán, S.C.
El Puente, 1, 01307 Navaridas, Álava
Tel: 945 605 037
Cosechero

Martínez Lacuesta, S.A., Bodegas
La Ventilla, 71, 26200 Haro, La Rioja
Tel: 941 310 050 Fax: 941 310 748
Email: bodega@martinezlacuesta.com
Crianza

Mendoza Lardy, S.L.U.
El Bullon, s/n. 26338 San Vicente de
la Sonsierra, La Rioja
Tel: 941 334 040 Fax: 941 334 040
Cosechero

Martínez López, Adolfo
El Barranco, s/n, 26509 Alcanadre, La
Rioja
Tel: 941 165 304
Cosechero

Martínez Palacios, S.L., Bodegas
Real, 22, 26220 Ollauri, La Rioja
Tel: 626 782 009 Fax: 941 338 023
Email: bodegasmtzpalacios@yahoo.es
Crianza

Martínez Rubio, C.B., Florentino
La Ermita, 33. 26311 Cordovín, La
Rioja
Tel: 941 418 614 Fax: 941 418 614
Crianza

Martínez Ruiz, José María
Bodegas, s/n, 01307 Villabuena, Álava
Tel: 608 144 597
Almacenista

Martínez San Vicente, J.J., S.C.
Calvo Sotel:o, 17, 01308 Lanciego,
Álava
Tel: 945 608 208
Cosechero

Martínez San Vicente, M. y A./T. Ibáñez
Calvo Sotel:o, s/n, 01308 Lanciego,
Álava
Tel: 945 628 222
Cosechero

Mayor de Migueloa, S.L., Bodegas
Mayor, 20, 01300 Laguardia, Álava
Tel: 945 621 175 Fax: 941 231 022
Crianza

Mayorazgo J. Zacarías de Bivián, S.A.
Plazuela Campillo, 1, 26214
Cuzcurrita de Río Tirón, La Rioja
Tel: 941 301 625 Fax: 941 301 627
Crianza

Medievo S.L., Bodegas del
Circunvalación San Roque, s/n, 26559
Aldeanueva de Ebro, La Rioja
Tel: 941 163 141 Fax: 941 144 204
Email: bmedevio@terra.es
Crianza

Medrano Grijalba, Carmelo
Avda. Vitoria, s/n, 01306 Lapuebla de
Labarca, Álava
Tel: 941 286 020
Almacenista

Medrano Grijalba, Francisco Javier
Avenida Diputación, 27, 01306
Lapuebla de Labarca, Álava
Tel: 945 607 023
Crianza

Melón , José
Avda. de Logroño, 2. 26006 El Cortijo,
La Rioja
Tel: 941 227 716
Cosechero

Méndez, Ricardo
Calvo Sotel:o, 1. 26313 Uruñuela,
La Rioja
Tel: 941 371 033 Fax: 941 371 033
Cosechero

Mendieta García, Juan José
Curillos, s/n, 01308 Lanciego, Álava
Tel: 945 608 134 Fax: 945 608 140
Email: bodegamendieta@hotmail.com
Cosechero

Miguel Blanco, Roberto
La Serna, s/n, 01307 Baños de Ebro,
Álava
Tel: 945 623 323
Cosechero

Miguel Merino, S.L., Bodegas
Ctra. de Logroño, 16, 26330 Briones,
La Rioja
Tel: 941 322 263 Fax: 941 322 294
Email: info@miguelmerino.com
Crianza

Miguel Muñoz, S.C.
Avda. del Puente, 8, 01307 Baños de
Ebro, Álava
Tel: 945 609 191
Cosechero

Mitarte, S.L.
El Cortijo, s/n, 01330 Labastida, Álava
Tel: 607 343 289
Crianza

Mojón Alto, S.L., Bodegas
Las Bodegas, 108 110. 26210
Anguciana, La Rioja
Tel: 619 271 694
Email: bodegasmojonalto@knet.es
Crianza

Monge Ruiz, José María
La Fortel:eza, 11. 26338 San Vicente
de la Sonsierra, La Rioja
Tel: 941 334 451
Cosechero

Monje Amestoy, S.C.
Camino de Rehoyos, s/n, 01340
Elciego, Álava
Tel: 945 606 010
Email: luberri@infonegocio.com
Crianza

Monteblán, S.L., Bodegas
Ctra. Santa Ana, 11. 26374 Medrano,
La Rioja
Tel: 941 444 912/636 431 915
Cosechero

Montecillo, S.A., Bodegas
Ctra. de Navarrete, Km. 3. 26360
Fuenmayor, La Rioja
Tel: 941 440 125 Fax: 941 440 663
Email: maria.martinez@osborne.es
Crianza

Montirake, S.L.U.
Mayor, 13, 01307 Leza, Álava
Tel: 945 605 034
Cosechero

Moraza, S.L., Bodegas
Ctra. Peñacerrada, s/n, 26338 San
Vicente de la Sonsierra, La Rioja
Tel: 941 334 473 Fax: 941 334 473
Crianza

Moreno Peña, David
Ctra. de Villar de Torre, s/n, 26310
Badarán, La Rioja
Tel: 941 367 338 Fax: 941 418 685
Email: davidmoreno@davidmoreno.es
Crianza

Muga Echeita, Máximo
El Tesoro, s/n, 01307 Navaridas, Álava
Tel: 945 605 106
Cosechero

Muga Foncea, César Oscar
Cantarranas, 6, 26200 Haro, La Rioja
Tel: 941 310 160 Fax: 941 310 160
Almacenista

Muga, Bodegas
Barrio Estación, s/n, 26200 Haro,
La Rioja
Tel: 941 311 825 Fax: 941 312 867
Email: info@bodegasmuga.com
Crianza

Muguruza Ruíz, Alberto
Mayor, 15, 01309 Leza (Álava)
Tel: 945 605 189
Almacenista

Muñoz Troncoso, S.C., Bodegas
San Cristóbal, 13, 01307 Baños de
Ebro, Álava
Tel: 945 609 192
Cosechero

Muriel, S.L., Bodegas
Ctra. Laguardia-Cenicero, 01340
Elciego, Álava
Tel: 945 606 268 Fax: 945 606 371
Crianza

Murillo Hernández, Francisco
Avda. Azcárraga, 27 29, 26350
Cenicero, La Rioja
Tel: 944 495 839 Fax: 944 263 725
Crianza

Murillo Viteri, Bodegas
Avda. Azcárraga, 27 29. 26250
Cenicero, La Rioja
Tel: 944 495 839 Fax: 944 263 725
Email: imurillo@euskalnet.net
Crianza

Muro Bujanda y Otros, S.C., M.A.
Ctra. de Laguardia, s/n, 01306
Lapuebla de Labarca, Álava
Tel: 945 607 081
Crianza

Muro Garrido, S.C.
Mayor, 29, 01306 Lapuebla de
Labarca, Álava
Tel: 945 607 115
Cosechero

Muro Nájera, Jesús Francisco
Ctra. Elciego, s/n, 01306 Lapuebla de
Labarca, Álava
Tel: 945 607 165
Cosechero

Murua, S.A., Bodegas
Ctra. Laguardia, s/n, 01340 Elciego,
Álava
Tel: 945 606 260 Fax: 945 606 326
Email: info@bodegasmurua.com
Crianza

Narro Marín, Aída
Escuelas, 14, 26224 Alesanco,
La Rioja
Tel: 941 379 151
Cosechero

Navajas, S.L., Bodegas
Camino Belgarauz 2. 26370 Navarrete,
La Rioja
Tel: 941 440 140 Fax: 941 440 657
Email: bodegasnavajas@terra.es
Crianza

Nava-Rioja, Bodegas
Ctra Eje del Ebro s/n, 31261
Andosilla, Navarra
Tel: 948 690 454; Fax: 948 674 491
Email: nava-rioja@tel:efonica.net
Crianza

Navarrete, S. Coop. Ltda. Comarcal de
Ctra. Entrena, s/n. 26370 Navarrete,
La Rioja
Tel: 941 440 626 Fax: 941 440 835
Email: comarcal@fer.es
Crianza

Navarrsotillo, S.C.
Santa Cruz s/n, 31261 Andosilla, Navarra
Tel: 948 690 523; Fax: 948 690 523
Ctra. N- 232, km. 354. 26500
Calahorra, La Rioja
Tel: 941 146 951 Fax: 948 690 523
Email: info@navarrsotillo.com
Crianza

Nestares Eguizabal, S.L., Bodegas
Alberto Villabuena, 82, 26144 Galilea,
La Rioja
Tel: 619 777 669
Crianza

Nieto Cerezo, María Victoria
Norte, 26, 01340 Elciego, Álava
Tel: 945 606 001
Cosechero

Novoa Alonso, Pilar
Ctra. de Laguardia, 01306 Lapuebla
de Labarca, Álava
Tel: 945 607 075
Cosechero

Nuestra Sra. Del Campo, Bodega
Cooperativa
Ctra. De Viñaspre, 01308 Lanciego,
Álava
Tel: 945 608 047
Crianza

Nuestra Sra. de Vico, Bodega
Cooperativa
Pol. Raposal, parcela 77. 26580
Arnedo, La Rioja
Tel: 941 380 257 Fax: 941 380 257
Crianza

Ochagavía Díez, Juan Pedro
Estación, 31, 26509 Alcanadre, La
Rioja
Tel: 941 165 010 Fax: 941 165 010
Almacenista

Olarra, S.A., Bodegas
Polígono Cantabria I, s/n. 26006
Logroño, La Rioja
Tel: 941 253 703 Fax: 941 253 703
Email: bodegasolarra@bodegasolarra.es
Crianza

Ondalan, S.A.
Ctra. De Logroño, 22, 01320 Oyón,
Álava
Tel: 945 622 537 Fax: 945 622 538
Email: bodegasondalan@terra.es
Crianza

Ondarre, S.A., Bodegas
Ctra. de Aras, s/n, 31230 Viana,
Navarra
Tel: 948 645 300 Fax: 941 253 703
Email: bodegasolarra@bodegasolarra.es
Crianza

Onraita Mendiola, Isabel
Barrihuelo Menor, 34, 01340 Elciego,
Álava
Tel: 945 131 637
Cosechero

Ontañón, S.A., Bodegas
Avda. de Aragón, 3. Pol. La Portalada.
26006 Logroño, La Rioja
Tel: 941 234 200 Fax: 941 270 482
Email: ontanon@ontanon.es
Crianza

Ortega Ezquerro, S.L., Bodegas y Viñedos
Plaza del Frontón, 3, 26512 Tudelilla,
La Rioja
Tel: 941 152 046
Crianza

Ortiz de Viñaspre, C.B., Bodegas
Marqués de Estel:la, 13, 01307
Navaridas, Álava
Tel: 945 605 100/945 605 162
Cosechero

Osoti Viñedos Ecológicos, S.L.
Julián Gallarre, 1, 31261 Andosilla,
Navarra
Tel: 948 674 010 Fax: 948 674 832
Email: sgurucharri@
      bodegasansebastian.com
Crianza

Ostatu, S.C., Bodegas
Ctra. de Vitoria-Laguardia, 1, 01307
Samaniego, Álava
Tel: 945 609 133 Fax: 945 623 338
Crianza

Palacio, S.A., Bodegas
San Lázaro, 1, 01300 Laguardia, Álava
Tel: 945 600 151 Fax: 945 600 297
Email: nlanea@bodegaspalacio.com
Crianza

Palacios Remondo, S.A., Bodegas
Avda. Zaragoza, 8, 26540 Alfaro,
La Rioja
Tel: 941 180 207 Fax: 941 181 628
Email: hremondo@
      vinosherenciaremondo.com
Crianza

Palacios Sáez, Luis María
San Andrés, 16, 01340 Elciego, Álava
Tel: 945 606 305 Fax: 945 606 348
Crianza

Pardo García, Raúl José
Santa María, 6, 01307 Villabuena,
Álava
Tel: 639 013 796
Cosechero

Pascual Berganzo, S.C.
Abajo, 10, 01307 Samaniego, Álava
Tel: 945 623 337
Cosechero

Pascual Larrieta, Miguel Ángel
Camino Santa Lucía, s/n, 01307
Samaniego, Álava
Tel: 945 609 059 Fax: 945 609 059
Crianza

Pascual Weigand, Valentín
Dr. Azcárraga, 23, 26350 Cenicero,
La Rioja
Tel: 941 454 006
Almacenista

Pastor Domeco, S.A.T.
Avda. Gonzalo de Berceo, 91, 26559
Aldeanueva de Ebro, La Rioja
Tel: 941 142 390 Fax: 941 142 391
Email: pastordomeco@infonegocio.com
Crianza

Pastor Fernández, Pedro José
Del Hedro, 2, 26371 Ventosa. La Rioja
Tel: 941 441 811
Cosechero

Pedro Martínez Alesanco, S.L., Bodegas
José García, 20, 26310 Badarán, La
Rioja
Tel: 941 367 075 Fax: 941 367 075
Email: bodegamartinezalesanco@
        tel:efonica.net
Crianza

Pérez Azpillaga, R./Bermúdez, P.A., S.C.
Calvo Sotel:o, 17, 01308 Lanciego,
Álava
Tel: 945 608 016
Cosechero

Pérez Basoco, S.C.
Palacios, s/n, 01307 Villabuena, Álava
Tel: 945 623 370
Cosechero

Pérez de Loza e Hijos, S.L., F.
Las Cuevas, s/n, 01307 Leza, Álava
Tel: 945 605 009
Almacenista

Pérez Fernández, José María
Segunda Travesía San Roque, 13,
26338 San Vicente de la Sonsierra,
La Rioja
Tel: 941 333 430
Almacenista

Pérez Irazu, S.C.
Camino del Soto, 1, 01309 Elvillar de
Álava, Álava
Tel: 945 604 038/604 123
Crianza

Pérez Maestresala, S.C., Bodegas
San Torcuato, 3, 01307 Villabuena,
Álava
Tel: 945 609 076
Cosechero

Pérez Ubago, Santiago, Bodegas
Santa Eulalia, s/n, 26371 Ventosa,
La Rioja
Tel: 941 441 804
Cosechero

Pérez Virgala, Miguel Ángel
Cañerías, 3 A, 01309 Elvillar de Álava,
Álava
Tel: 945604 003
Cosechero

Perica, S.L., Bodegas
Av. de la Rioja, 59. 26340 San
Asensio, La Rioja
Tel: 941 457 152 Fax: 941 457 240
Email: correo@bodegasperica.com
Crianza

Petralanda Uría, Ignacio
Avda. Estación, 44. 26360
Fuenmayor, La Rioja
Tel: 941 450 462 Fax: 941 450 620
Email: petralanda@knet.es
Crianza

Primicia, S.A., Bodegas
Ctra. De Elvillar, s/n, 01300 Laguardia, Álava
Tel: 945 600 296 Fax: 945 621 252
Crianza

Propiedad Grial, S.L.
Avda. Estación, 28. 26360
Fuenmayor, La Rioja
Tel: 941 450 194 Fax: 941 450 194
Email: prop.grial@terra.es
Crianza

Prudencio Larrea, S.L.
La Charca, 6. 26311 Cordovín,
La Rioja
Tel: 941 367 178 Fax: 941 367 178
Cosechero

Puelles, Bodegas
Camino Los Molinos, s/n, 26339
Ábalos, La Rioja
Tel: 941 334 415 Fax: 941 334 132
Email: informacion@bodegaspuelles.com
Crianza

Puente del Ea, S.L., Bodegas y Viñedos
La Fuente, 8. 26212 Sajazarra.
La Rioja
Tel: 941 320 210 Fax: 941 320 405
Email: puentedea@terra.es
Crianza

Pujanza, S.L.U., Bodegas y Viñedos
Ctra. El Villar, s/n, 01300 Laguardia,
Álava
Tel: 945 600 548 Fax: 945 600 522
Email: bvpujanza@jet.es
Crianza

Quintana Quintana, S.C., P.
Larrazuria, 46, 01330 Labastida,
Álava
Tel: 945 331 022 Fax: 945 312 125
Crianza

Ramírez Aguirre, Jesús, Bodegas
El Moral, 8 10, 14 16. 26338 San
Vicente de la Sonsierra, La Rioja
Tel: 941 334 216 Fax: 941 322 038
Crianza

Ramírez Peciña Pérez, Antonio
Santa María, s/n, 01307 Villabuena,
Álava
Tel: 945 609 088
Cosechero

Ramírez de la Piscina, S.L., Bodegas
Ctra. Vitoria-Laguardia, s/n. 26338
San Vicente de la Sonsierra, La Rioja
Tel: 941 334 505 Fax: 941 334 506
Email: rampiscina@knet.es
Crianza

Ramón Bilbao, S.A., Bodegas
Av. Santo Domingo, 34. 26200 Haro,
La Rioja
Tel: 941 310 295 Fax: 941 310 832
Email: info@bodegasramonbilbao.es
Crianza

Real Compañía de Vinos, S.A.
Calle del Monte, 26350 Cenicero, La
Rioja
Tel: 941 454 007 Fax: 941 454 530
Crianza

Real de Nájera, S. Coop., Bodega
Ctra. de Burgos, s/n. 26300 Nájera.
La Rioja
Tel: 941 360 245 Fax: 941 410 385
Email: realdenajera@jet.es
Crianza

Real Divisa, S.A., Bodegas de la
Montalvo, s/n, 26339 Ábalos, La Rioja
Tel: 941 258 133 Fax: 941 258 155
Email: realdivisa@fer.es
Crianza

Real Junta, S.A.
San Cristóbal, 20 21, 26360
Fuenmayor, La Rioja
Tel: 941 450 141   Fax: 941 450 141
Email: bodegas@realjunta.com
Crianza

Reina Calleja, José Ramón
San Cristóbal, 68, 26360 Fuenmayor,
La Rioja
Tel: 941 450 105   Fax: 941 210 287
Email: daytor@riojatel:.com
Cosechero

Resa Monje, María Nieves
General Varela, 37. 26338 San
Vicente de la Sonsierra, La Rioja
Tel: 941 334 107
Cosechero

Rey de Viñas, S.A., Bodegas
Cmno. Viejo de Fuenmayor, s/n. 26080
Logroño, La Rioja
Tel: 941 203 944   Fax: 941 214 802
Email: reydevinas@hisa.com
Crianza

Ribera Salazar, José Luis
01307 Baños de Ebro, Álava
Tel: 945 609 223
Cosechero

Rincón del Prado, S.L., El
Las Bodegas, s/n, 26310 Badarán,
La Rioja
Tel: 941 367 213
Crianza

Río Estebas, César del
San Martín, 57, 26311 Cordovín, La
Rioja
Tel: 941 367 061   Fax: 941 367 061
Almacenista

Rioja Alta, S.A., La
Avda. de Vizcaya, s/n, 26200 Haro, La
Rioja
Tel: 941 310 346   Fax: 941 312 854
Email: riojalta@riojalta.com
Crianza

Rioja Santiago, S.A., Bodegas
Barrio de la Estación, 26200 Haro,
La Rioja
Tel: 941 310 200   Fax: 941 312 679
Email: riojasantiago@
          bodegasriojasantiago.com
Crianza

Rioja Vega, S.A.
Ctra, Mendavia-Logroño. km. 32,
31230 Viana, Navarra
Tel: 948 646 263   Fax: 948 645 612
Email: info@riojavega.com
Crianza

Riojanas, S.A., Bodegas
Ctra. Estación, 1 21. 26350 Cenicero,
La Rioja
Tel: 941 454 050   Fax: 941 454 529
Email: bodega@bodegasriojanas.com
Crianza

Roda, S.A., Bodegas
Avda. Vizcaya, 5, 26200 Haro, La
Rioja
Tel: 941 303 001   Fax: 941 312 703
Email: rodarioja@roda.es
Crianza

Rodríguez Muro y Uno Más, S.C., E.
Avda. Diputación, s/n, 01306
Lapuebla de Labarca, Álava
Tel: 945 607 166
Cosechero

Rubio del Río, Cecilio
Camino de Torrecilla, 6, 26225
Canillas de Río Tuerto, La Rioja
Tel: 941 379 077
Cosechero

Rubio Villar, Honorio
Ctra. Badarán, 36. 26311 Cordovín,
La Rioja
Tel: 941 367 343 Fax: 941 367 343
Email: bodegashonoriorubio@hotmail.com
Crianza

Ruconia, S.L., Bodegas
Ctra. de San Asensio, s/n (junto N-
120), 26300 Nájero, La Rioja
Tel: 941 362 059 Fax: 941 362 467
Email: bodegasruconia@tel:efonica.net
Almacenista

Ruiz del Portal
Los Morales, 12, 26339 Ábalos,
La Rioja
Tel: 941 334 474
Cosechero

Ruiz de Oña Calvete, S.C.
Santa María, 3, 01307 Villabuena,
Álava
Tel: 945 609 120
Cosechero

Ruiz de Ubago Grijalba, S.C.
Real, 3, 01306 Lapuebla de Labarca,
Álava
Tel: 945 607 032
Cosechero

Ruiz de Ubago Muro, Galo
Bodegas, 10, 01306 Lapuebla de
Labarca, Álava
Tel: 945 607 032
Cosechero

Ruiz de Viñaspre, S.C., Viñedos
Herrerías, 47, 01309 Elvillar de Álava
Tel: 945 604 052
Cosechero

Ruiz de Viñaspre, S.L., Bodegas
Plaza de Oriente, 8, 01309 Elvillar de
Álava, Álava
Tel: 941 207 438
Crianza

Ruiz Gómez, S.L., Bodegas
Las Cuevas, s/n, 26340 San Asensio,
La Rioja
Tel: 941 457 129
Crianza

Ruiz Monge, Teodoro
2a. Travesía San Roque, 9. 26338
San Vicente de la Sonsierra, La Rioja
Tel: 941 334 221 Fax: 941 334 221
Almacenista

Ruiz Zapatero, Víctor
01309 Elvillar de Álava, Álava
Tel: 941 221 281
Cosechero

Ruyavi, S.L., Bodegas y Viñedos
Avda. La Póveda, s/n, 01306 Lapuebla
de Labarca, Álava
Tel: 945 607 156
Cosechero

R.M. Rioja, S.L.
Polígono Ind. Casablanca, Nave 36,
01300 Laguardia, Álava
Tel: 945 625 055
Almacenista

Sáenz Alcalde, S.C.
Las Bodegas, s/n, 01306 Lapuebla de
Labarca, Álava
Tel: 945 607 163
Cosechero

Sáenz Blanco, Ramón
Mayor, s/n, 01307 Baños de Ebro,
Álava
Tel: 945 609 212
Almacenista

Sáenz de Cabezón San Martín, S.L.
Ctra. Navarrete, s/n, 26360
Fuenmayor, La Rioja
Tel: 941 450 046
Almacenista

Sáenz de Samaniego Zuñeda, S.C.
Muriarte, 23, 01307 Samaniego, Álava
Tel: 945 609 112
Cosechero

Sáenz de Santamaría, S.L., Bodegas
Ctra. De Haro, Km. 1. 26350
Cenicero, La Rioja
Tel: 941 454 008 Fax: 941 454 063
Email: bsantamaria@jet.es
Crianza

Sáenz Espinosa, Francisco Javier
El Sol, 15, 26511 El Villar de Arnedo,
La Rioja
Tel: 619 179 490
Crianza

Sáenz Garrido, S.L.
Las Tres Cuestas, 4 6, 26512
Tudelilla, La Rioja
Tel: 609 581 343 Fax: 941 208 899
Email: crissaenz@eresmas.com
Crianza

Sáenz Garrido, Vicente, Bodegas
Velilla, 2527. 26375 Entrena,
La Rioja
Tel: 941 446 418 Fax: 941 446 418
Almacenista

Salazar Fernández, Jorge
Buena Vista, 1, 01307 Villabuena,
Álava
Tel: 945 609 421
Cosechero

Sampedro Pérez-Viñaspre, Carlos
Páganos, 38, 01300 Laguardia, Álava
Tel: 945 600 146 Fax: 945 600 146
Crianza

San Cebrín, S. Coop. Ag.
Ctra. Circunvalación, s/n, 26340 San
Asensio, La Rioja
Tel: 941 457 640 Fax: 941 457 641
Email: bodega@sancebrin.com
Crianza

San Esteban Protomártir, B.C.
Ctra. de Agoncillo, s/n, 26143 Murillo
de Río Leza, La Rioja
Tel: 941 432 031 Fax: 941 432 031
Crianza

San Gregorio, S. Coop. Bodegas
San Gregorio, 1, 31560 Azagra,
Navarra
Tel: 948 692 137 Fax: 948 692 137
Crianza

San Justo y San Isidro, S. Cooperativa
Estación, s/n. 26570 Quel. La Rioja
Tel: 941 392 030 Fax: 941 392 030
Crianza

San Martín de Ábalos, S.L., Bodegas
Camino del Prado, s/n, 26211
Fonzaleche, La Rioja
Tel: 944 492 391 Fax: 944 263 299
Crianza

San Miguel, Bodega Cooperativa
Ctra. Zaragoza, km. 7. 26513 Ausejo,
La Rioja
Tel: 941 430 005 Fax: 941 430 209
Email: cep@bodsanmiguel.jazztel.es
Crianza

San Pedro, S.C., Bodegas
Camino de los Molinos, s/n, 01300
Laguardia, Álava
Tel: 945621 204 Fax: 945600 040
Crianza

San Roque, Bodega Cooperativa
Ctra. Assa, 01309 Elvillar de Álava,
Álava
Tel: 945 604 005
Crianza

San Sixto, S. Coop., Bodegas
Ctra. De Vitoria, 01311 Yécora, Álava
Tel: 941 258 581/110 230
Crianza

San Tirso, Bodega Cooperativa
Ctra. Lanciego, s/n, 01308 Cripán,
Álava
Tel: 945608 095
Crianza

Santa Daría, Bodega Cooperativa
Ctra. Logroño, s/n, 26350 Cenicero,
La Rioja
Tel: 941 454 110 Fax: 941 454 618
Email: santa.daria@fer.es
Crianza

Santamaría López, S.L.
Camino de la Hoya, 3, 01300
Laguardia, Álava
Tel: 945621 212 Fax: 945621 222
Email: santamaria@
    santamarialopez.com
Crianza

Santiago Aragón Palacios, C.B.
Mayor, 46. 26225. Canillas de Río
Tuerto, La Rioja
Tel: 941 379 071
Cosechero

Santiago Ijalba, S.A.
Apartado 109, Avda. de La Rioja, s/n,
26221 Gimileo, La Rioja
Tel: 941 304 231 Fax: 941 304 436
Email: santiagoijalba@fer.es
Crianza

Santiago, S.C., Bodegas de
San Vicente, s/n, 01307 Baños de
Ebro, Álava
Tel: 945 609 201 Fax: 945 609 201
Crianza

Santuario Vinícola Riojano, S.A.
Ctra. Arnedo, Km. 14, 26589
Arnedillo, La Rioja
Tel: 941 394 063 Fax: 941 394 200
Email: ritual@pegarrido.com
Crianza

Seisas Ruiz, Ángel
Del Campo, 11. 26290 Briñas, La
Rioja
Tel: 941 311 400/312 126
Fax: 941 303 725
Cosechero

Senda Galiana, S.A.U., Bodegas y Viñas
Cerro San Cristóbal, s/n, 26142
Villamedian de Iregua, La Rioja
Tel: 941 435375 Fax: 941 435003
Email: info@sendagaliana.com
Crianza

Sendero Royal
Carretera LR-384 de la 232 a
Aldeanueva. 26559 Aldeanueva de
Ebro, La Rioja
Tel: 941 163 031 Fax: 941 163 031
Crianza

Señorío de Arana, S.A.
Ctra. San Vicente, s/n, 01330
Labastida, Álava
Tel: 941 331 150
Email: senoriodearana@infonegocio.com
Crianza

Señorío de las Viñas, S.L.
Mayor, s/n, 01309 Laserna -
Laguardia, Álava
Tel: 945 621 110 Fax: 945 621 110
Crianza

Señorío de Líbano, S.A.
Del Río, s/n, 26212 Sajazarra,
La Rioja
Tel: 941 320 066 Fax: 941 320 251
Email: bodega@castillo-de-sajazarra.com
Crianza

Señorío de San Vicente, S.A.
Los Remedios, 27, 26338 San Vicente
de la Sonsierra, La Rioja
Tel: 941 308 040 Fax: 941 334 371
Email: sanvicen@fer.es
Crianza

Señorío de Somalo, S.L.
Ctra. Baños, 62. 26321 Bobadilla, La
Rioja
Tel: 941 202 351 Fax: 941 202 351
Email: exclusivasomalo@tel:efonica.net
Crianza

Señorío de Urarte, S.L., Bodegas
Calvo Sotel:o, 16 B, 01308 Lanciego,
Álava
Tel: 945608 043
Crianza

Señorío de Villarrica, S.L.
Cmno. Santo Domingo, 27. 26340
San Asensio. La Rioja
Tel: 941 457 171 Fax: 941 457 172
Email: villarrica@fer.es
Crianza

Señorío de Yerga, S.A., Bodegas
Barrio de las Bodegas, 8. 26142
Villamediana de Iregua, La Rioja
Tel: 941 435 003/436 072
Fax: 941 435 003
Email: info@senoriodeyerga.com
Crianza

Sierra Cantabria, Bodegas
Amorebieta, 3. 26338 San Vicente de
la Sonsierra. La Rioja
Tel: 941 334 080 Fax: 941 334 371
Email: sierra-cantabria@fer.es
Crianza

Sodupe Orive, Santos
La Barrera, 3. 26340 San Asensio,
La Rioja
Tel: 941 457 484 Fax: 941 457 484
Crianza

Solabal, S.A.T., Bodegas y Viñedos
Trav. Camino San Bartolomé, 6, 26339
Ábalos, La Rioja
Tel: 941 334 492 Fax: 941 334 492
Email: solabal@terra.es
Crianza

Solana de Ramírez Ruiz, S.A.T., Bodegas
Arana, 24, 26339 Ábalos, La Rioja
Tel: 941 308 049 Fax: 941 308 049
Email: solramirez@infonegocio.com
Crianza

Solar de Ayala, S.L.
San Juan, 4, 01300 Laguardia, Álava
Tel: 945 600 044 Fax: 945 621 139
Crianza

Sonsierra, S. Coop., Bodegas
El Remedio, s/n, 26338 San Vicente
de la Sonsierra, La Rioja
Tel: 941 334 031 Fax: 941 334 245
Email: sonsierra@sonsierra.com
Crianza

T. y M. Etxeita, S.C.
Madrid, 8, 01307 Navaridas, Álava
Tel: 945 605 042
Cosechero

Tejada Arangüena, S. C.
Herrerías, 36, 01309 Elvillar de Álava,
Álava
Tel: 945 604 009
Cosechero

Tobía, Bodegas
Crtra. N-232 Km. 438, 26340 San
Asensio, La Rioja; General Yague 26,
26006 Logroño, La Rioja
Tel: 941 457 425 Fax: 941 457 401
Email: tobia@bodegastobia.com
Crianza

Tobías Azofra, Ciriaco
Ctra. Baños, 48, 26321 Bobadilla,
La Rioja
Tel: 941 374 224
Cosechero

Torre de Oña, S.A.
Término San Martín, 01330 Laguardia,
Álava
Tel: 945 621 154 Fax: 945 621 171
Crianza

Torre Foncea, S.L., Bodegas
Avda. de Cenicero, 28 bajo. 26360
Fuenmayor, La Rioja
Almacenista

Torre Rioja, S.A.
Sancho Abarca, 4, 01300 Laguardia,
Álava
Tel: 945 600 142
Crianza

Torre San Millán, S.L., Bodega
Ctra. Vitoria, km. 2, 01312
Barriobusto, Álava
Tel: 945 601 440/601 430
Email: info@bodega-torresanmillan.com
Crianza

Torres Librada, Bodegas
Ctra. Corella, s/n. Finca Estarijo.
26540 Alfaro, La Rioja
Tel: 941 741 003 Fax: 941 741 003
Crianza

Torrique, S.L., Bodegas
Avda. del Ebro,s/n. Pol. Ind. El
Sequero. 26509 Agoncillo, La Rioja
Email: info@bodegastorrique.com
Almacenista

Treviño Ruiz de las Heras, C.B., Bodegas
Avda. Escobosa, 1, 26380 El Cortijo,
La Rioja
Tel: 941 227 991 Fax: 941 214 625
Crianza

Ubide, S.A., Bodegas
Camino de Rio Hondillo, s/n, 01300
Laguardia, Álava
Tel: 944 367 010 Fax: 944 367 131
Email: ubide@tel:eline.es
Crianza

Ugarte Fernández, S.C., Antonio
Ctra. Navaridas, 3, 01300 Laguardia,
Álava Tel: 945 600 180
Cosechero

Unión de Cosecheros de Labastida, S.C.
01330 Labastida, Álava
Tel: 945 331 161 Fax: 945 331 161
Email: bodegas@solaguen.com
Crianza

Unión de Viticultores Riojanos, S.L.
Ctra. De Cenicero, s/n, Apdo. 3.
26360 Fuenmayor, La Rioja
Tel: 941 451 129 Fax: 941 450 297
Email: uvrioja@apdo.com
Crianza

Unión Viti-Vinícola, S.A.
Ctra. Logroño, 26350 Cenicero,
La Rioja
Tel: 941 454 000 Fax: 941 454 400
Email: marquesdecaceres@fer.es
Crianza

Urarte Espinosa, Juan José
El Redondo, s/n, 01309 Assa, Álava
Tel: 945 600 102 Fax: 945 600 102
Crianza

Urquidi Olave, Santos
Paraje Kanogal, s/n, 01330 Labastida,
Álava
Tel: 941 331 050
Cosechero

Valdegamarra, S.C.
Lepanto, 18, 01309 Elvillar de Álava,
Álava
Tel: 945 604 081
Cosechero

Valdelacierva, S.A., Bodegas
Ctra. Burgos, km. 13, 26370
Navarrete, La Rioja
Tel: 941 440 620 Fax: 941 440 787
Email: manuel.zaldivar@tel:eline.es
Crianza

Valdelana, S.L., Bodegas
Puente Barricuelo, 67, 01340 Elciego,
Álava
Tel: 945 606 055 Fax: 945 606 055
Crianza

Valdemar, S.A., Bodegas
Camino Viejo de Logroño, s/n, 01320
Oyón, Álava
Tel: 945 622 188 Fax: 945 622 111
Email: bujanda@bujanda.com
Crianza

Valenciso, Compañía Bodeguera
Apartado 227, 26200 Haro, La Rioja
Tel: 941 304 724; Fax: 941 304 728
Email: valenciso@valenciso.com
Crianza

Valgrande, S.A., Bodegas
El Remedio, 33, 26338 San Vicente
de la Sonsierra, La Rioja
Tel: 941 334 089 Fax: 947 545609
Crianza

Valle del Zamaca, S.C., Vinícola
Zamudio, 2. 26221 Gimileo, La Rioja
Tel: 941 311 947 Fax: 941 311 947
Email: bodegas.zamaca@
        tel:efonica.net
Crianza

Vallemayor, S.L., Bodegas
Ctra. Logroño-Vitoria, 38, 26360
Fuenmayor, La Rioja
Tel: 941 450 142 Fax: 941 450 376
Email: vallemayor@fer.es
Crianza

Valsacro, S.A., Bodegas
Ctra. N-232, km. 364. 26510
Pradejón. La Rioja
Tel: 941 398 008 Fax: 941 398 070
Email: escudero@prorioja.es
Crianza

Varal, S.A.T., Bodegas
San Vicente, s/n, 01307 Baños de
Ebro, Álava
Tel: 945 623 321
Almacenista

Velasco Barrios, Ángel
Cuevas Altas, 10, 26371 Sotes,
La Rioja
Tel: 941 441 785 Fax: 941 441 785
Crianza

Velilla Garrido, Aitor
Bodegas, 111, 01306 Lapuebla de
Labarca, Álava
Tel: 945 607 140
Cosechero

Vicente Eguilaz, Manuel Tomás
Finca San Rafael, s/n, 01300
Laguardia, Álava
Tel: 945 621 102
Cosechero

Viguera Gómez, José María
Ruavieja, 19, 26001 Logroño, La Rioja
Tel: 941 236 980
Almacenista

Villar Ruiz, Ángel Emilio
San Andrés, 11, 01300 Laguardia,
Álava
Tel: 945 600 892
Cosechero

Villarnedo, S.L., Bodegas
Prolongación El Cortijo, 25. 26511
El Villar de Arnedo, La Rioja
Tel: 941 159 036 Fax: 941 159 210
Crianza

Villoslada-Solar y Uno Más, S.C., J.
Ctra. Elciego, 36, 01306 Lapuebla de
Labarca, Álava
Tel: 945 607 010
Cosechero

Viña Berneda, S.L., Bodegas
Ctra. Somalo, 59, 26313 Uruñuela,
La Rioja
Tel: 941 371 304   Fax: 941 371 304
Crianza

Viña Cerzana
Ctra. Ollauri, s/n. 26223 Hormilla,
La Rioja
Tel: 639 322 934   Fax: 941 362 968
Crianza

Viña Eguíluz, S.L.
Camino de San Bartoomé, s/n. 26339
Ábalos, La Rioja
Tel: 941 334 064   Fax: 941 334 064
Email: eguiluz@basico.reterioja.es
Crianza

Viña El Fustal, S.L., Bodegas
Camino del Cristo, 2, 01308
Samaniego, Álava
Tel: 945 140 450   Fax: 945 143 810
Crianza

Viña Herminia, S.L., Bodegas
Camino de los Agudos, 1. 26559
Aldeanueva de Ebro, La Rioja
Tel: 941 142 305   Fax: 941 142 303
Email: vherminia@vherminia.es
Crianza

Viña Ijalba, S.A.
Ctra. Pamplona, km. 1, 26006
Logroño, La Rioja
Tel: 941 261 100   Fax: 941 261 128
Email: vinaijalba@ijalba.com
Crianza

Viña Olabarri, S.A.
Ctra. Haro-Anguciana, s/n, 26200
Haro, La Rioja
Tel: 941 310 937   Fax: 941 311 602
Email: info@bodegasolabarri.com
Crianza

Viña Olmaza
Calvo Sotel:o, 7, 26338 San Vicente
de la Sonsierra, La Rioja
Tel: 941 334 472
Cosechero

Viña Paterna, S.A.
Camino de la Puebla, 77, 01340
Elciego, Álava
Tel: 945 606 277   Fax: 945 606 277
Crianza

Viña Ribera Palacios, S.C.
Barrihuelo, s/n, 01340 Elciego, Álava
Tel: 945 606 036
Cosechero

Viña Salceda, S.L.
Ctra. Cenicero, km. 3, 01340 Elciego,
Álava
Tel: 945 606 125   Fax: 945 606 069
Email: info@vinasalceda.com
Crianza

Viña Valoria, S.A.
Ctra. De Burgos, km. 5, 26006
Logroño, La Rioja
Tel: 941 204 059   Fax: 941 204 155
Email: bodega@vina-valrio.es
Crianza

Viña Villabuena, S.A.
Herrería, Travesía 2, n° 5, 01307
Villabuena, Álava
Tel: 945 609 086   Fax: 945 609 261
Email: izadi@izadi.com
Crianza

Viñadores Artesanos, S.L.
Camino Tejera, s/n, 01340 Elciego,
Álava
Tel: 945 606 042
Crianza

Viñalobera, S.L., Bodegas
Camino de Corella, 7, 26559
Aldeanueva de Ebro, La Rioja
Tel: 941 144 101 Fax: 941 144 101
Crianza

Viñas Nuevas, S.A.T.
Avda. de la Rioja, 110, 26559
Aldeanueva de Ebro, La Rioja
Tel: 941 163 028; Fax: 941 163 028
Crianza

Viñedos de Aldeanueva, S. Coop.
Avda. Juan Carlos I, 100, 26559
Aldeanueva de Ebro, La Rioja
Tel: 941 163 039 Fax: 941 163 585
Email: va@aldeanueva.com
Crianza

Viñedos de Castejones, S.L.U.
Ollanco, s/n, 01308 Lanciego, Álava
Tel: 945 609 006
Cosechero

Viñedos de Páganos
Ctra Navaridas, s/n, 01300 Páganos-
Laguardia, Álava
Tel: 941 334 080 Fax: 941 334 371
Email: info@eguren.com
Crianza

Viñedos del Contino, S.A.
Finca San Rafael, 01321 Laserna-
Laguardia, Álava
Tel: 945 600 201 Fax: 945 621 114
Email: laserna@contino-sa.com
Crianza

Viñedos Lacalle Laorden, S.A.
Santa Engracia, 9 11, 01300
Laguardia, Álava
Tel: 945 600 119
Crianza

Viñedos Montalvillo, S.L.
Ctra. N-232, km 351, 26559
Aldeanueva de Ebro, La Rioja
Tel: 941 743 035 Fax: 941 743 035
Email: montalvillo@vodafone.es
Crianza

Viñedos Ruíz Jiménez
Ctra. Comarcal, 115 Km. 43,5. 26559
Aldeanueva de Ebro, La Rioja
Tel: 610 455 596 Fax: 941 163 577
Email: vrjimenz@masbytes.com
Crianza

Viñegra Varela, S.C.
Avenida Diputación, 1, 01309
Navaridas, Álava
Tel: 945 605 043
Cosechero

Viñegra-Don Teófilo I, S.L., Bodegas
Coscojal, 42, 01309 Elvillar de Álava,
Álava
Tel: 945 231 924
Crianza

Vinícola de Ábalos, S.L.L.
Virgen de la Rosa, 17, 26339 Ábalos,
La Rioja
Tel: 941 308 193
Cosechero

Vinícola de Rodezno, S.L.
Plaza de la Asunción, 8, 26222
Rodezno, La Rioja
Tel: 941 338 296 Fax: 941 338 360
Email: avillaluenga@tel:eline.es
Crianza

Vinícola Real, S.L., Bodegas
Cttra. De Nalda, Km 9. 26120 Abelda
de Iregua, La Rioja
Tel: 941 444 233 Fax: 941 444 233
Email: info@vinicolareal.com
Crianza

Vinícola Riojana de Alcanadre, S.C.
San Isidro, 46 48. 26599 Alcanadre,
La Rioja
Tel: 941 165 036 Fax: 941 165 289
Email: vinicola@
riojanadealcanadre.com
Crianza

Vinos de Benjamín Romeo, S.L.
Amorebieta, 6 Baja, 26338 San
Vicente de la Sonsierra, La Rioja
Tel: 941 334 228
Crianza

Vinos Iradier
Avda. La Rioja, 17, 26339 Ábalos,
La Rioja
Tel: 941 334 251 Fax: 941 334 251
Email: vinosiradier@
vinosiradier.euskalnet.net
Almacenista

Vinos Merino, S.L.
Camino de la Lucera, 11, 26512
Tudelilla, La Rioja
Tel: 945 384 098 Fax: 945 384 098
Almacenista

Virgen del Valle, S.A., Bodegas
Ctra. a Villabuena, 3, 01307
Samaniego, Álava
Tel: 941 609 033 Fax: 945 609 106
Email: bodegavirvalle@sea.es
Crianza

Viteri Iriarte, Ignacio
Avda. Vitoria, 13, 01306 Lapuebla de
Labarca, Álava
Tel: 945 607 100
Cosechero

Viteri Vicente, Gerardo
Norte, 9 2º izda., 26001 Logroño,
La Rioja
Tel: 941 277 019 Fax: 941 227 337
Cosechero

Vitivinícola Viña Almudena, S.L.
Paraje El Romeral, s/n, 01340 Elciego,
Álava
Tel: 945 606 525 Fax: 945 606 526
Crianza

Vitoriano Gómez, Raquel
Sancho Abarca, 01300 Laguardia,
Álava
Tel: 945 600 069
Almacenista

Yolanda Aransay Peña
Mayor, 93. 26311 Cárdenas. La Rioja
Tel: 941 367 073
Cosechero

Ysios, S.L.
Camino de la Hoya, 01300 Laguardia,
Álava
Tel: 945 600 640 Fax: 945 600 641
Email: ysios@byb.es
Crianza

Zaldívar Ortiz de Latierro, J.I.
Otero, 29, 01330 Labastida, Álava
Tel: 945 148 182
Cosechero

Zautua Espiga, Jesús
Barrio Bodegas, 35. 26224 Alesanco,
La Rioja
Tel: 941 379 078
Cosechero

Zuazo Gastón, S.C., Bodegas y Viñedos
Tejerías, s/n, 01306 Lapuebla de
Labarca, Álava
Tel: 945 627 228
Email: zuazogaston@airtel:.net
Crianza

Zugober, S.A.
Tejerías, s/n, 01306 Lapuebla de
Labarca, Álava
Tel: 945 627 228 Fax: 945 627 281
Email: zugober@zugober.com
Crianza

Appendix II – The Reglamento

With the establishment of the new Organización Interprofesional del Vino de Rioja (OIPVR) there will, inevitably, be changes to the rules over the forthcoming years. New techniques, additional grape varieties, a shift in the "emphasis" of style are all likely to evolve as the new body gets into its stride. The CRDOCa will still "police" the Reglamento but will no longer make policy on its own.

The most recent change has, of course, been the creation of the OIPVR, but below is an edited and annotated [italics] translation of the Reglamento as it stood after last major change, which was put into place on the November 28, 2001.

PRODUCTION
Grapes for Rioja wine may only be grown in delimited vineyards which are listed in the official registry of vineyards in the following towns and villages:

Rioja Alta (province of La Rioja):
Ábalos, Alesanco, Alesón, Anguciana, Arenzana de Abajo, Arenzana de Arriba, Azofra,Badarán, Bañares, Baños de Río Tobia, Baños de Rioja, Berceo, Bezares, Bobadilla, Briñas, Briones, Camprovín, Canillas, Cañas, Cárdenas, Casalarreina, Castañares de Rioja., Cellórigo, Cenicero, Cidamón, Cihuri, Cirueña, Cordovín, Cuzcurrita de Río Tirón, Daroca de Rioja, Entrena, Estollo, Foncea, Fonzaleche, Fuenmayor, Galbárruli, Gimileo, Haro, Hervías, Herramélluri, Hormilla, Hormilleja, Hornos de Moncalvillo, Huércanos, Lardero, Leiva, Logrofño, Manjarrés, Matute, Medrano, Nájera, Navarrete, Ochánduri, Ollauri, Rodezno, Sajazarra, San

Asensio, San Millan de Yecora, San Torcuato, San Vicente de la Sonsierra, Santa Colombia, Sojuela, Sorzano, Sotés, Tirgo, Tormantos, Torrecilla sobre Alesanco, Torremontalbo, Treviana, Tricio, Uruñuela, Ventosa, Villalba de Rioja, Villar de Torre, Villarejo, Zarratón.

Rioja Alta (province of Burgos):
El Ternero (Miranda de Ebro – there is no bodega in Miranda, there are only vineyards).

Rioja Baja (province of La Rioja):
Agoncillo, Aguilar del Río Alhama, Albelda, Alberite, Alcanadre, Aldeanueva de Ebro, Alfaro, Arnedillo, Arnedo, Arrúbal, Ausejo, Autol, Bergasa, Bergasilla, Calahorra, Cervera del Río Alhama, Clavijo, Corera, Cornago, El Redal, El Villar de Arnedo, Galilea, Grávalos, Herce, Igea, Lagunilla de Jubera, Leza del Río Leza, Molinos de Ocón, Murillo de Río Leza, Muro de Aguas, Nalda, Ocon (La Villa), Pradejón, Préjano, Quel, Ribafrecha, Rincón de Soto, Santa Engracia de Jubera (zona Norte), Santa Eulalia Bajera, Tudelilla, Villamediana de Iregua, Villarroya.

Rioja Baja (province of Navarra):
Andosilla, Aras, Azagra, Bargota, Mendavia, San Adrian, Sartaguda, Viana.

Rioja Alavesa:
Baños de Ebro, Barriobusto, Cripán, Elciego, Elvillar de Álava, Labastida, Labraza, Laguardia, Lanciego, Lapuebla de Labarca, Leza, Moreda de Álava, Navaridas, Oyón, Salinillas de Buradón, Samaniego, Villabuena de Álava, Yecora.

GRAPE VARIETIES
Only the following grapes may be grown for the production of Rioja wine:

For red wines:
Tempranillo (primary), Garnacha, Graciano, Mazuelo

For white wines:
Malvasía Riojana, Garnacha Blanca, Viura (primary).

(In practice, many other grape varieties, including historic Riojano stocks are grown experimentally – *see* Chapter 6 for more details. The OIPVR is already considering the addition of Sauvignon Blanc and Chardonnay to the canon for whites, and there are lobbyists for Cabernet Sauvignon, Merlot, and Syrah hard at work.)

VITICULTURE

Density of plantation for vines
Minimum 2,850 per ha, maximum 4,000 per ha.

Irrigation
Permitted in individual years in individual cases according to the environmental conditions.

Pruning and training
Vines may be trained *en vaso* with a maximum of twelve buds per vine on a maximum of six *pulgares*. Vines may also be trained *en espaldera*. If these are pruned *doble cordón* the same rules apply as for *en vaso* – twelve buds on six *pulgares*. If they are pruned *vara y pulgar* each *vara* may carry one or two *pulgares*, but with a maximum of ten buds per vine.

The exception to this rule is the Garnacha which may have fourteen buds per vine regardless of training system. In any case, the maximum number of buds per hectare is 36,000 for all varieties except Garnacha, which is permitted 42,000 per ha.

THE VINTAGE
Grapes may only be harvested with a minimum potential of 10.5 degrees of alcohol for red grapes and ten degrees of alcohol for whites (in practice potential alcohol of 12–13.5 degrees are routine levels of ripeness). These levels may be modified in exceptional vintages on a case-by-case basis. The CRDOCa fixes the start date of the harvest and might make stipulations about transporting the grapes to the bodega (in very hot years grapes can deteriorate on the journey).

YIELDS
Maximum production for red grapes is 65,000 kg/ha and for whites

90,000 kg/ha. This limit may be modified by the CRDOCa by twenty per cent in either direction on a year by year basis according to the predicted quality of the harvest (for example the limits were set at 118 per cent for the 2003 vintage).

Extraction of juice per kg ["*rendimiento*" in Spanish] is set at seventy litres per 100 kg, colloquially know as seventy per cent. This can be increased to seventy-two per cent if the CRDOCa thinks the quality is high enough. (This grosses up to 45.5–46.8 hl/ha for red grapes and 63–64.9 hl/ha for whites). It can also reduce the *rendimiento* if quality is reduced. Basket presses (a current trend) and pneumatic presses are permitted, but not continuous nor centrifugal presses.

WINEMAKING

Red and white wines must be fermented separately (they may be blended later – traditional red Rioja used to have a percentage of white wine added to lighten the colour; *rosado* wines may be a blend of red and white finished wines or made from red grapes macerated for a few hours to extract skin colour). Red wines made from split grapes [*i.e.* those which have been fermented prior to pressing – see chapter 6] must be made from at least 95% Tempranillo, Garnacha Tinta, Graciano, and Mazuela; wines from whole grapes must be at least 85% of these varieties.

White wines must be 100% permitted varieties.

Rosado wines must be at least 25% permitted red varieties.

AGEING OF WINES

All wines must be aged in a registered *bodega de crianza*. *Reserva* and *gran reserva* wines are (theoretically) only made in very good and excellent years or from particularly good plots. Wines may declare their origins in a subzone [*i.e.* Rioja Alta, Alavesa, Baja] if all the grape is sourced and the wine made in that subzone.

Crianza

Red wines must spend a minimum of two years in cask and bottle from October 1 of the vintage year before release, of which at least twelve months must be spent in (approximately) 225-litre oak *barricas*. They may not be released until October 1 after the expiration of the two years (and therefore a 2004 vintage may be released on October 1, 2006).

White and *rosado* wines must spend at least one year in cask and bottle with at least six months in *barrica*.

Reserva

Red wines must spend at least twelve months in *barrica* and a total of three years in cask and bottle (and therefore a 2004 vintage may be released on the October 1, 2007).

White and *rosado* wines must spend at least two years in cask and bottle with at least six months in *barrica*.

Gran Reserva

Red wines must spend at least 2 years in barrica followed by three years in bottle (and therefore a 2004 vintage may be released on October 1, 2009).

White and *rosado* wines must spend at least four years in cask and bottle with at least six months in barrica.

The vintage date given on the label of the wine must represent at least eighty-five per cent of the wine in the bottle.

ANALYSIS OF WINES

Wines must achieve the following minimum alcoholic strengths (chaptalization is forbidden in Spain):

11.5 degrees of alcohol for reds; 10.5 degrees for whites and *rosados*. It is not permitted to mix strong and weak wines to make up the level ("1% abv" is also known as "1 degree" below). Some wines which carry a sub-zonal name [*i.e.* Rioja Alta, Alavesa, Baja] must achieve higher alcohol - whites from Rioja Alta and Alavesa must achieve 11 degrees. Reds from Rioja Baja must achieve 12 degrees, whites 11 degrees and *rosados* 11.5 degrees. Wines from anywhere in the region at *reserva* or higher level must achieve a minimum of 12 degrees for reds and 11 degrees for whites and *rosados*.

Volatile acidity (expressed as acetic) in young wines must not exceed 0.05 g/l for each degree of alcohol. Wines of more than 1 year old must not exceed 1 g/l up to 10 degrees plus 0.06 g/l for each subsequent degree.

Exclusions

Vineyards classified for the DOCa Rioja are not permitted to produce grapes for *vino de mesa* (unless subsequently declassified by the CRDOCa).

There are also regulations governing temperature control of *crianza* cellars, other wine-based products which may be made in the bodegas with the permission of the CRDOCa, and rules covering the timing of declarations of grape harvest quantities and must obtained from them. In addition the reglamento details the penalties and sanctions which the CDOCa may levy against any bodega which breaks the rules.

Bibliography

Items marked with a * are only available in Spanish

BOOKS

Duijker, Hubrecht, *The Wines of Rioja.* London: Mitchell Beazley, 1987.
Excellent on bodega histories and anecdotes.

Jeffs, Julian, *The Wines of Spain.* London: Faber and Faber (now the
Mitchell Beazley Classic Wine Series and uniform with this volume)
1999.Voluminous knowledge and precision.

Palacios Sánchez, Juan Manuel. Historia del Vino de Rioja*. La Prensa del
Rioja, 1991 Hagiography (of the region, not individual bodegas) but
with a good deal of historical detail.

Peñín, José, *12 Great Spanish Bodegas.* Madrid: Pi & Erre Ediciones 1996.
Hagiography, but it is quality hagiography with detailed descriptions
of the bodegas, their histories and personalities.

Radford, John, *The New Spain* (new edition). London Mitchell Beazley
2004. A jolly good book. Buy it if you have not done so already.

Watson, Jeremy, *The New and Classical Wines of Spain.* Barcelona: Montagud
Editores, 2002. Probably the most detailed book ever on the vast
panoply of Spanish wine Authors, various.
Personalities of Rioja. Nueva Imagen Publicidad 2003. Hagiography,
appallingly written (or translated, or maybe both) and with dreadful
full-slap photographs, but some useful information.
Guía Completa de los Vinos de La Rioja*. Gobierno de la Rioja, 2004. The "La"
is significant, as the *gobierno* (government) does not spend its taxpayers'
money promoting Rioja wines from Navarra or Álava, so it's incomplete,
but still very useful as a listing of names, addresses, and other details.

ANNUALS

Peñín, José, *Guía Peñín de los Vinos de España**. Madrid: Pi & Erre
Ediciones.
Wines tasted and evaluated by one of the top three Spanish wine
writers.

Proensa, Andrés, *Guía Proensa de los Mejores Vinos de España**. Andrés
Proensa.
Wines tasted and evaluated by another of the top three Spanish
wine writers.

Guía de Vinos Gourmets*. Club de Gourmets.
Yearly survey based on the tastings of the Club de Gourmets in
Madrid. Excellent technical detail.

WEBSITE

http://elmundovino.elmundo.es*
Wines tasted and evaluated by a team under the supervision of
Víctor de la Serna, the other one of the top three Spanish wine
writers. The site is operated by *El Mundo*, one of Spain's leading
broadsheet newspapers.

MAGAZINE

La Prensa del Rioja
Quarterly magazine detailing everything that happens in the Rioja
wine world.

That's all, Folks!

Index